548 Treasured Recipes, Including Top Prize-Winners

THE TENTH in our best-selling cookbook series, *2003 Taste of Home Annual Recipes* is sure to hold a valued place in your collection. Every page of this beautiful full-color book is full of family-favorite recipes shared by fantastic cooks from across the country.

Here, you'll find each of the 529 recipes published during 2002 in *Taste of Home*—North America's most popular cooking magazine—plus 19 bonus recipes. That's 548 recipes in all!

Whether you're fixing dinner for your family, cooking for a holiday crowd or whipping up something for yourself, you'll have plenty of fitting, delicious recipes from which to pick. To get you started, take a peek at the winners of our six national recipe contests.

 • **Yeast Bread Bonanza.** Nothing smells more heavenly than homemade bread or rolls baking in the oven. The only thing that can top the aroma of first-place winner Almond Bear Claws (p. 98) and second-place Potato Pan Rolls (p. 98) is their fabulous taste.

 • **Catch of the Day.** If you'd like to reel in some terrific seafood recipes, cast your net into contest-winner Seafood Lasagna (p. 68) and Spicy Island Shrimp (p. 75), which finished second. Each of the runners-up will have you hooked, too.

 • **Gelatin Gems.** It's no surprise gelatin dishes are popular at all sorts of gatherings. In fact, Jell-O is so well-liked, we received over *6,300* recipes for our contest! So take a look at top prize-winning Orange Cream Cheesecake (p. 140) and second-place Strawberry Graham Dessert (p. 141)...even if you think you don't care for gelatin, you're sure to find your resistance dissolving!

 • **Garden-Fresh Beans.** Green and yellow beans crop up in summer gardens by the bushel...in a variety of fresh-tasting recipes, too. Green Bean Mushroom Pie (p. 59) got top honors for being the best of the beans, with German-Style Green Beans (p. 54) in second.

 • **Potatoes, Please.** It's a common request at dinner tables across the country. Your family will eagerly dig in to Creamy Chive Mashed Potatoes (p. 50), judged the top tater, and second-place spuds Ultimate Scalloped Potatoes (p. 57). Then they'll quickly ask for a second helping!

 • **Best Bars.** You can't beat bar cookies for quick, convenient and tasty treats, whether for a potluck dinner, picnic or at-home snacking. Grand prize Apple Pie Bars (p. 118) are especially appealing, as are Chocolate Chip Graham Bars (p. 119), which came in second.

With 548 recipes in this colorful big cookbook, you won't run out of choices anytime soon. You're sure to find something special for everyone and every occasion.

PICK OF THE CROP. Green Bean Mushroom Pie (p. 59) won the grand prize and German-Style Green Beans (p. 54) took second place in our national garden-fresh beans contest.

2003 Taste of Home Annual Recipes

Editor: Jean Steiner
Art Director: Niki Malmberg
Food Editor: Janaan Cunningham
Associate Editors: Julie Schnittka,
Susan Uphill, Heidi Reuter Lloyd
Art Associates: Jami Zewen, Kristin Bork
Production: Ellen Lloyd, Catherine Fletcher

Taste of Home®

Executive Editor: Kathy Pohl
Food Editor: Janaan Cunningham
Associate Food Editor: Diane Werner
Senior Recipe Editor: Sue A. Jurack
Test Kitchen Director: Karen Johnson
Managing Editor: Ann Kaiser
Assistant Managing Editor: Barbara Schuetz
Copy Editor: Kristine Krueger
Associate Editors: Sharon Selz, Faithann Stoner
Test Kitchen Home Economists:
Patricia Schmeling, Sue Draheim,
Peggy Fleming, Julie Herzfeldt, Joylyn Jans,
Kristin Koepnick, Mark Morgan,
Wendy Stenman, Karen Wright
Test Kitchen Assistants: Kris Lehman,
Megan Taylor
Editorial Assistants: Barb Czysz,
Mary Ann Koebernik
Design Director: Jim Sibilski
Art Director: Emma Acevedo
Food Photography: Rob Hagen, Dan Roberts
Food Photography Artists: Stephanie Marchese,
Vicky Marie Moseley
Photo Studio Manager: Anne Schimmel
Production: Ellen Lloyd, Catherine Fletcher
Chairman and Founder: Roy Reiman
President: Tom Curl

Taste of Home Books
©2002 Reiman Media Group, Inc.
5400 S. 60th St., Greendale WI 53129

International Standard Book Number:
0-89821-352-5
International Standard Serial Number:
1094-3463

PICTURED AT RIGHT. Clockwise from upper left: Pepperoni Pizza Salad, Giant Focaccia Sandwich, Lemon Cream Dessert and BLT Macaroni Salad (p. 178); Caraway Scones (p. 95) and Beef Goulash Soup (p. 35); Blue Cheese Walnut Cheesecake (p. 13); Sugared Raisin Pear Diamonds (p. 113); Ginger Beef Stir-Fry, Zesty Sugar Snap Peas and Easy Boston Cream Cake (pp. 274-275).

Taste of Home *2003* Annual Recipes

PICTURED ON FRONT COVER. From top: Dilly Bean Potato Salad (p. 29), Yankee-Doodle Sirloin Roast (p. 298) and Lemon Cream Dessert (p. 178).

PICTURED ON BACK COVER. From top: Orange Cream Cheesecake (p. 140) and Strawberry Graham Dessert (p. 141).

FOR ADDITIONAL COPIES of this book, write *Taste of Home* Books, P.O. Box 908, Greendale WI 53129.

To order by credit card, call toll-free 1-800/344-2560 or visit our Web site at www.reimanpub.com.

Snacks & Beverages

From sweet to savory...there's something for everyone in this chapter's satisfying assortment of snacks and beverages.

MADE FOR MUNCHING. Clockwise from upper left: Cucumber Shrimp Appetizers (p. 9); Olive Pinwheel Bread and Strawberry Fruit Dip (p. 9); Mexican Fiesta Dip (p. 19); Blue Cheese Walnut Cheesecake (p. 13); Melon Fruit Slush (p. 16).

Slow-Cooked Smokies

I include these little smokies smothered in barbecue sauce on all my appetizer buffets, since they're popular with both kids and adults. —Sundra Hauck
Bogalusa, Louisiana

1 package (1 pound) miniature smoked sausage links
1 bottle (28 ounces) barbecue sauce
1-1/4 cups water
3 tablespoons Worcestershire sauce
3 tablespoons steak sauce
1/2 teaspoon pepper

In a slow cooker, combine all ingredients; mix well. Cover and cook on low for 6-7 hours. Serve with a slotted spoon. **Yield:** 8 servings.

—— 🍷 🍷 🍷 ——

Crab Cheese Fondue

(Pictured below)

We used to host fondue parties regularly with our friends and try to outdo each other with the most wonderful recipes. This thick and cheesy blend with its mild crab flavor was always a hit. —Mary Houchin
Swansea, Illinois

3/4 cup milk
1/2 cup condensed cream of mushroom *or* celery soup, undiluted
2 cups (8 ounces) shredded cheddar cheese

8 ounces process cheese (Velveeta), cubed
1 can (6 ounces) crabmeat, drained, flaked and cartilage removed
2 teaspoons lemon juice
1 garlic clove, halved
Cubed French bread, cherry tomatoes, baby zucchini, cooked new potatoes *and/or* artichoke hearts for dipping

In a saucepan, combine milk and soup until blended. Add cheeses; cook and stir over low heat until melted. Stir in crab and lemon juice; remove from the heat.

Rub the interior of a fondue pot with the cut side of garlic; discard garlic. Pour cheese mixture into pot; keep at a gentle simmer over low heat. Serve with bread cubes, tomatoes, zucchini, potatoes and/or artichoke hearts. **Yield:** 3 cups.

—— 🍷 🍷 🍷 ——

Jack-o'-Lantern Jumble

(Pictured below)

Perfect for Halloween, this snack mix pairs sweet candy corn with crisp cereal. It's then tossed with a savory seasoning that has a hint of peanut butter. The bowl empties in no time. —DeEtta Rasmussen
Fort Madison, Iowa

4 cups Corn Chex
4 cups Rice Chex
1 cup salted peanuts

FOLKS are sure to fall for Jack-o'-Lantern Jumble and Crab Cheese Fondue (shown below, from top) when you serve them at your next autumn gathering.

1/4 cup butter *or* margarine
1/4 cup peanut butter
2-1/4 teaspoons Worcestershire sauce
1/2 teaspoon salt
1/4 teaspoon garlic powder
1 cup candy corn

In a large bowl, combine the cereal and peanuts. In a small saucepan over medium heat, combine the butter, peanut butter, Worcestershire sauce, salt and garlic powder; cook and stir until butter and peanut butter are melted. Pour over cereal mixture and toss to coat.

Spread into a greased 15-in. x 10-in. x 1-in. baking pan. Bake at 250° for 1 hour, stirring every 15 minutes. Cool; stir in candy corn. Store in an airtight container. **Yield:** about 2 quarts.

—— 🥄 🥄 🥄 ——

Baked Spinach Dip Loaf

A crusty round loaf of sourdough bread provides not only "dippers" but also the serving bowl for this popular spinach dip.
—Frieda Meding
Trochu, Alberta

✓ Uses less fat, sugar or salt. Includes Nutritional Analysis and Diabetic Exchanges.

2 packages (8 ounces *each*) cream cheese, softened
1 cup mayonnaise
1 package (10 ounces) frozen chopped spinach, thawed and squeezed dry
1 cup (4 ounces) shredded cheddar cheese
1 can (8 ounces) water chestnuts, drained and chopped
5 bacon strips, cooked and crumbled
1 green onion, chopped
2 teaspoons dill weed
1 garlic clove, minced
1/2 teaspoon seasoned salt
1/8 teaspoon pepper
1 unsliced round loaf (1 pound) sourdough bread
Raw vegetables

In a mixing bowl, beat cream cheese and mayonnaise. Stir in the next nine ingredients. Cut a 1-1/2-in. slice off top of bread; set aside. Carefully hollow out bottom, leaving a 1/2-in. shell. Cube removed bread and set aside. Fill the shell with spinach dip; replace top. Wrap in heavy-duty foil; place on a baking sheet.

Bake at 375° for 1-1/4 to 1-1/2 hours or until the dip is heated through. Open the foil carefully. Serve warm with bread cubes and raw vegetables. **Yield:** 4-1/2 cups dip.

Nutritional Analysis: One 1/4-cup serving (prepared with reduced-fat cream cheese, fat-free mayonnaise and reduced-fat cheddar cheese; calculated without bread or vegetables) equals 105 calories, 7 g fat (4 g saturated fat), 20 mg cholesterol, 303 mg sodium, 6 g carbohydrate, 1 g fiber, 6 g protein. **Diabetic Exchanges:** 2 vegetable, 1 fat.

—— 🥄 🥄 🥄 ——

Peachy Avocado Salsa

This bright and colorful salsa tastes so fresh, it's a welcome change from the store-bought varieties. It's wonderful served with tortilla chips. I usually make a double batch since my husband and our two children can't seem to get enough of it.
—Shelly Platten
Amherst, Wisconsin

✓ Uses less fat, sugar or salt. Includes Nutritional Analysis and Diabetic Exchanges.

1 can (15-1/4 ounces) sliced peaches, drained and diced
1 medium ripe avocado, peeled and diced
1 tablespoon lime juice
2 cups diced seeded tomatoes
1/4 cup diced onion
2 tablespoons minced fresh cilantro *or* parsley
1 tablespoon cider vinegar
1 to 2 teaspoons seeded chopped jalapeno pepper*
1 garlic clove, minced
1/4 teaspoon salt

In a bowl, combine the peaches, avocado and lime juice. Add the remaining ingredients; lightly toss just until combined. Refrigerate for at least 30 minutes. Serve with tortilla chips, fish or chicken. **Yield:** 3 cups.

Nutritional Analysis: One serving (1/4 cup) equals 51 calories, 3 g fat (trace saturated fat), 0 cholesterol, 55 mg sodium, 7 g carbohydrate, 2 g fiber, 1 g protein. **Diabetic Exchanges:** 1 vegetable, 1/2 fat.

*Editor's Note: When cutting or seeding hot peppers, use rubber or plastic gloves to protect your hands. Avoid touching your face.

🥄 Storing Salsa

Store fresh salsa, tightly covered, in the refrigerator for no more than 5 days.

Brought to room temperature, salsa is a terrific topping for fish or chicken.

Peaches 'n' Cream Cooler

(Pictured below)

Here's a delicious way to cool off on a sultry summer evening. This creamy fruit drink is not too sweet but plenty refreshing. My family and friends love it!
—*Carol Gillespie, Chambersburg, Pennsylvania*

✓ Uses less fat, sugar or salt. Includes Nutritional Analysis and Diabetic Exchanges.

     1 cup apricot nectar, chilled
 1/2 cup unsweetened pineapple juice, chilled
 1/2 cup half-and-half cream
     1 tablespoon lemon juice
     1 tablespoon honey
     1 teaspoon vanilla extract
 1/4 teaspoon almond extract
     2 cups frozen sliced peaches
     4 ice cubes
 3/4 cup sparkling water, chilled

In a blender, combine the first nine ingredients; cover and process until smooth. Add sparkling water; cover and process until blended. Pour into glasses; serve immediately. **Yield:** 4 servings.

Nutritional Analysis: One 1-cup serving (prepared with fat-free half-and-half) equals 209 calories, trace fat (trace saturated fat), 0 cholesterol, 40 mg sodium, 51 g carbohydrate, 3 g fiber, 2 g protein.

Veggie Tomato Juice

A friend gave me this recipe years ago, and I've been making it ever since. It's also wonderful in recipes that call for tomato juice. —*Marge Hodel Roanoke, Illinois*

✓ Uses less fat, sugar or salt. Includes Nutritional Analysis and Diabetic Exchanges.

   16 cups quartered ripe tomatoes (about 7 pounds)
     3 cups coarsely chopped celery
     2 large onions, sliced
     2 cups coarsely chopped cooked peeled beets
 1-1/2 cups coarsely chopped carrots
     1 cup chopped fresh spinach
 1/2 cup minced fresh parsley
     2 tablespoons sugar
     1 tablespoon salt

In a Dutch oven or large kettle, combine all ingredients; crush the tomatoes slightly. Bring to a boil. Reduce heat; cover and simmer for 1-1/2 hours or until vegetables are tender, stirring frequently. Cool. Press the mixture through a food mill or fine sieve. Refrigerate or freeze. Shake or stir well before serving. **Yield:** 4-1/2 pints.

Nutritional Analysis: One serving (6 ounces) equals 100 calories, 1 g fat (trace saturated fat), 0 cholesterol, 669 mg sodium, 23 g carbohydrate, 5 g fiber, 4 g protein. **Diabetic Exchanges:** 1 starch, 1 vegetable.

—— 🍷 🍷 🍷 ——

Bacon Tomato Spread

This creamy spread uses one of our favorite cuts of pork. It's really good with summer garden tomatoes and is a hit at picnics and other gatherings.
—*Patricia Staudt, Marble Rock, Iowa*

     1 package (8 ounces) cream cheese, softened
     2 teaspoons prepared mustard
 1/2 teaspoon celery seed
     1 medium tomato, peeled, seeded and finely chopped
 1/4 cup chopped green pepper
     8 bacon strips, diced
Crackers *or* raw vegetables

In a mixing bowl, beat cream cheese, mustard and celery seed until blended. Stir in tomato and green pepper. Cover and refrigerate for at least 1 hour. In a skillet, cook bacon until crisp; remove to paper towels to drain. Discard drippings. Stir bacon into spread just before serving. Serve with crackers. **Yield:** about 1-3/4 cups.

Cucumber Shrimp Appetizers

(Pictured on page 4)

When my friend's husband needed lower-fat snacks, she served him this shrimp spread on top of cucumber slices. —Patricia Kile, Greentown, Pennsylvania

☑ Uses less fat, sugar or salt. Includes Nutritional Analysis and Diabetic Exchanges.

 1 can (8 ounces) unsweetened crushed
     pineapple, drained
 1 can (4 ounces) tiny shrimp, rinsed and
     drained
 1/4 cup reduced-fat mayonnaise
 1 tablespoon finely chopped green onion
 2 teaspoons Dijon mustard
 1-1/2 teaspoons minced fresh dill
 1 medium cucumber (8 inches), cut into
     1/4-inch slices
Fresh dill sprigs, optional

In a bowl, combine pineapple, shrimp, mayonnaise, onion, mustard and dill. Spoon onto cucumber slices. Garnish with dill sprigs if desired. **Yield:** 32 appetizers.
Nutritional Analysis: One appetizer equals 16 calories, 1 g fat (trace saturated fat), 7 mg cholesterol, 29 mg sodium, 2 g carbohydrate, trace fiber, 1 g protein. **Diabetic Exchange:** Free food.

— 🍷 🍷 🍷 —

Olive Pinwheel Bread

(Pictured at right and on page 4)

This attractive well-seasoned loaf is perfect for parties but easy enough to prepare for every day.
—Barbara Manfra, Saugus, Massachusetts

☑ Uses less fat, sugar or salt. Includes Nutritional Analysis and Diabetic Exchanges.

 1 tube (10 ounces) refrigerated pizza crust
 1 tablespoon olive *or* canola oil
 1 tablespoon minced fresh rosemary *or* 1
     teaspoon dried rosemary, *crushed*
 1/2 cup chopped ripe olives
 1 egg yolk, lightly beaten

Unroll pizza dough and place on a lightly floured surface. Brush with oil; sprinkle with rosemary and olives. Roll up jelly-roll style, starting with a short side; pinch seam to seal and tuck ends under. Place seam side down on a greased baking sheet. Brush with egg yolk. Bake at 350° for 20-25 minutes or until golden brown. Cool. **Yield:** 1 loaf (10 slices).
Nutritional Analysis: One slice equals 100 calories, 4 g fat (trace saturated fat), 21 mg cholesterol, 248 mg sodium, 14 g carbohydrate, 1 g fiber, 3 g protein. **Diabetic Exchanges:** 1 starch, 1/2 fat.

FROM savory to sweet, Olive Pinwheel Bread and Strawberry Fruit Dip (shown above, top to bottom) will satisfy any craving.

Strawberry Fruit Dip

(Pictured above and on page 4)

Our family enjoys fruit of all kinds, so this strawberry-flavored dip is one of our favorites. It's sweet, fluffy and yummy enough to eat by itself with a spoon! But we especially like it with strawberries, bananas and blackberries. —Virginia Krites, Cridersville, Ohio

 1 carton (8 ounces) spreadable strawberry
     cream cheese
 2 tablespoons strawberry preserves
 1 carton (8 ounces) frozen whipped
     topping, thawed
 1 jar (7 ounces) marshmallow creme
Assorted fresh fruit

In a mixing bowl, beat cream cheese and strawberry preserves until blended. Fold in the whipped topping and marshmallow creme. Cover and refrigerate until serving. Serve with assorted fresh fruit. **Yield:** 4 cups.

Treats Capture Halloween Spirit

THERE IS no trick to scaring up some Halloween fun with the "spooktacular" treats featured here. They're sure to be popular with boys and "ghouls" of all ages!

— 🍷 🍷 🍷 —

Popcorn Owls
(Pictured below)

Sweet chewy popcorn balls are a "hoot" when they're formed into wide-eyed owls perfect for a Halloween party. They take a bit of crafting, but draw a lot of compliments.   *—Emma Magielda, Amsterdam, New York*

5 quarts popped popcorn
2 cups sugar
1-1/2 cups water
1/2 cup light corn syrup
1/2 teaspoon salt
3 tablespoons butter *or* margarine
1 teaspoon white vinegar
1 to 2 tablespoons marshmallow creme

PARTY GUESTS will have a ball munching on Popcorn Owls and Chocolate Caramel Apples (shown above, top to bottom).

20 candy corn candies
20 candy orange slices
10 M&M miniature baking bits
Black shoestring licorice

Place popcorn in a large bowl; keep warm in a 200° oven. In a heavy saucepan, combine the sugar, water, corn syrup and salt. Cook over medium heat until a candy thermometer reads 250° (hard-ball stage). Remove from the heat; stir in butter and vinegar until butter is melted. Immediately pour over popcorn; toss to coat.

When mixture is cool enough to handle, quickly shape into five 3-1/4-in. balls and five 4-in. balls, dipping hands in cold water to prevent sticking. Flatten bottom of popcorn balls slightly for stability. Place a small ball on top of a large ball, forming the owl's head and body.

Immediately decorate owl, using marshmallow creme to attach candies. Add candy corn for claws. Press orange slices into sides for wings. Flatten and cut additional orange slices to make triangle ears and nose and 3/4-in. circular eyes. Press M&M's into orange circles to complete the eyes. Add a 3-in. licorice strip above eyes. **Yield:** 5 owls.

Editor's Note: This recipe was prepared with popcorn popped in oil. We recommend that you test your candy thermometer before each use by bringing water to a boil; the thermometer should read 212°. Adjust your recipe temperature up or down based on your test.

— ♖ ♖ ♖ —

Chocolate Caramel Apples

(Pictured at left)

Caramel apples get dressed up for this harvesttime holiday with chocolate, nuts and toffee bits. Cut into wedges, these scrumptious apples are easy to share.
—Linda Smith, Frederick, Maryland

1 package (14 ounces) caramels
2 tablespoons water
4 wooden sticks
4 large tart apples
2 cups chopped pecans *or* peanuts
1 cup (6 ounces) semisweet chocolate chips
1 teaspoon shortening
1 cup English toffee bits *or* almond brickle chips

In a microwave-safe bowl, combine the caramels and water. Microwave, uncovered, on high for 1 minute; stir. Microwave 30-45 seconds longer or until the caramels are melted. Insert wooden sticks into apples; dip apples into the caramel mixture, turning to coat. Coat with nuts; set ap-

ples on waxed paper to cool.

Melt chocolate chips and shortening; drizzle over apples. Sprinkle with toffee bits. Set on waxed paper to cool. Cut into wedges to serve. **Yield:** 8 servings.

Editor's Note: This recipe was tested with Hershey caramels in an 850-watt microwave.

— ♖ ♖ ♖ —

Pizza Dip in a Pumpkin

I make this dip in the fall when entertaining. Everyone enjoys the pizza flavor. Kids especially like dipping with bread that's cut into the shape of bats, cats, pumpkins and ghosts. So get out your cookie cutters!
—Laurene Hunsicker, Canton, Pennsylvania

1 small pie pumpkin (about 2-1/2 pounds)
1/2 cup finely chopped onion
1/4 cup finely chopped green pepper
1 tablespoon butter *or* margarine
2-1/2 cups pizza sauce
1 cup (4 ounces) shredded mozzarella cheese
1/2 cup finely chopped pepperoni
1/2 cup grated Parmesan cheese
1 teaspoon Italian seasoning
Breadsticks

Cut top off of pumpkin; scoop out seeds and fibers. Replace top; place pumpkin on an ungreased baking sheet. Bake at 350° for 20-25 minutes or until hot.

Meanwhile, in a small saucepan, saute onion and green pepper in butter until tender. Stir in the pizza sauce, mozzarella cheese, pepperoni, Parmesan cheese and Italian seasoning. Cook and stir over medium heat until heated through and cheese is melted. Pour into hot pumpkin. Serve with breadsticks. **Yield:** 3 cups.

— ♖ ♖ ♖ —

Orange Halloween Punch

This eye-catching orange punch is a Halloween tradition at my house. It's refreshing, frothy and quick to stir up with only five ingredients. *—Edie DeSpain*
Logan, Utah

1 can (46 ounces) pineapple juice, chilled
3 cups lemon-lime soda, chilled
3 cups orange drink
2 liters ginger ale, chilled
1/2 gallon orange sherbet

In a punch bowl, combine the juice, soda and orange drink. Stir in ginger ale. Top with scoops of sherbet. Serve immediately. **Yield:** about 6 quarts.

Picnic Beans with Dip

(Pictured below)

Here's a fun way to enjoy fresh-picked beans...with a creamy well-seasoned dip. Try it with other vegetables, too, such as broccoli, celery and carrots.
—Martha Bergman, Cleveland Heights, Ohio

☑ Uses less fat, sugar or salt. Includes Nutritional Analysis and Diabetic Exchanges.

      1 **pound fresh green *and/or* wax beans**
  1/2 **cup mayonnaise**
  1/2 **cup half-and-half cream**
      6 **tablespoons vegetable oil**
      2 **tablespoons white vinegar**
      1 **tablespoon Dijon mustard**
      1 **small onion, quartered**
      1 **teaspoon salt**
  1/4 **teaspoon ground coriander**
  1/4 **teaspoon dried savory**
  1/4 **teaspoon pepper**
  1/8 **teaspoon dried thyme**

Place beans in a saucepan and cover with water; bring to a boil. Cook, uncovered, for 8-10 minutes or until crisp-tender. Drain and rinse with cold water. Refrigerate until serving.

In a blender or food processor, combine the remaining ingredients. Cover and process until smooth. Refrigerate for at least 1 hour. Serve with beans for dipping. **Yield:** 1-2/3 cups dip.

Nutritional Analysis: 2 tablespoons of dip (prepared with fat-free mayonnaise and fat-free half-and-half) equals 85 calories, 7 g fat (1 g saturated fat), 1 mg cholesterol, 293 mg sodium, 5 g carbohydrate, 2 g fiber, trace protein. **Diabetic Exchange:** 2 fat.

— 🍷 🍷 🍷 —

Cream Cheese Clam Dip

My husband and his brother operate a 400-cow dairy farm, so we enjoy many foods featuring an assortment of dairy products. This dip is my mom's recipe.
—Cathy Hanehan, Saratoga Springs, New York

☑ Uses less fat, sugar or salt. Includes Nutritional Analysis and Diabetic Exchanges.

      1 **package (8 ounces) cream cheese, cubed**
      1 **can (6-1/2 ounces) chopped clams, drained**
      1 **tablespoon lemon juice**
      2 **teaspoons Worcestershire sauce**
  1/4 **teaspoon salt**
  1/8 **teaspoon pepper**
Crackers and raw vegetables

In a blender or food processor, combine the first six ingredients; cover and process until smooth. Serve with crackers and vegetables. **Yield:** 1-1/4 cups.

Nutritional Analysis: One 2-tablespoon serving (prepared with reduced-fat cream cheese; calculated without crackers and vegetables) equals 81 calories, 4 g fat (3 g saturated fat), 25 mg cholesterol, 158 mg sodium, 3 g carbohydrate, trace fiber, 7 g protein. **Diabetic Exchanges:** 1 lean meat, 1/2 fat.

— 🍷 🍷 🍷 —

Cheese Boereg

The rich-tasting filling of this appetizer is made with mozzarella and ricotta cheese, then baked between buttery layered dough. —*Jean Ecos*
Hartland, Wisconsin

      1 **egg, lightly beaten**
      1 **egg white, lightly beaten**
      1 **cup ricotta cheese**
  1/4 **cup minced fresh parsley**
      4 **cups (16 ounces) shredded mozzarella *or* Muenster cheese**
      1 **package (8 ounces) frozen phyllo dough, thawed**
  1/2 **cup butter (no substitutes), melted**

In a bowl, combine the egg, egg white, ricotta and parsley. Stir in mozzarella; set aside. Unroll phyllo dough; cut the stack of sheets in half widthwise. Place one sheet of phyllo dough in a greased 13-in. x 9-in. x 2-in. baking pan; brush with butter. Repeat nine times (keep remaining dough

covered with plastic wrap to avoid drying out).

Spread cheese mixture evenly over top. Layer with remaining dough, brushing butter on every other sheet. Bake at 350° for 25-30 minutes or until golden brown. Cut into squares or triangles. **Yield:** 16-20 appetizer servings.

— ▼ ▼ ▼ —

Oyster Cracker Snack

This is a quick-to-fix recipe I make often. Everyone eats these crackers by the handfuls! —*Verona Koehlmoos Pilger, Nebraska*

☑ Uses less fat, sugar or salt. Includes Nutritional Analysis and Diabetic Exchanges.

    2 packages (10 ounces *each*) oyster crackers
  3/4 cup vegetable *or* canola oil
    1 envelope ranch salad dressing mix
    1 teaspoon dill weed
  1/2 teaspoon onion powder
  1/2 teaspoon garlic powder
  1/2 teaspoon lemon-pepper seasoning

Place crackers in a large bowl. In a small bowl, combine the remaining ingredients; pour over crackers and mix well. Let stand for 2 hours. Store in an airtight container. **Yield:** 12 cups.

Nutritional Analysis: One serving (1/2 cup) equals 168 calories, 10 g fat (1 g saturated fat), 0 cholesterol, 411 mg sodium, 18 g carbohydrate, 1 g fiber, 2 g protein. **Diabetic Exchanges:** 2 fat, 1 starch.

— ▼ ▼ ▼ —

Horseradish Deviled Eggs

People say, "Wow!" when they taste these flavorful tangy deviled eggs. The bold combination of ground mustard, dill and horseradish is so appealing…the plate is always emptied whenever I serve these eggs. —*Ruth Roth, Linville, North Carolina*

    6 hard-cooked eggs
  1/4 cup mayonnaise
    1 to 2 tablespoons prepared horseradish
  1/2 teaspoon dill weed
  1/4 teaspoon ground mustard
  1/8 teaspoon salt
Dash pepper
Dash paprika

Cut eggs in half lengthwise. Remove yolks; set whites aside. In a bowl, mash the yolks. Add mayonnaise, horseradish, dill, mustard, salt and pepper; mix well. Pipe or spoon into egg whites. Sprinkle with paprika. Refrigerate until serving. **Yield:** 1 dozen.

Blue Cheese Walnut Cheesecake

(Pictured above and on page 4)

This elegant party spread is smooth and creamy and has a mild blue cheese flavor. It's popular every time I serve it. Garnished with chopped walnuts, it looks like you fussed, but it's not that tricky to prepare. —*Rita Reifenstein, Evans City, Pennsylvania*

    2 packages (8 ounces *each*) cream cheese, softened
    8 ounces crumbled blue cheese
2-1/4 cups sour cream, *divided*
    3 eggs
  1/8 teaspoon pepper
  1/2 cup chopped walnuts, toasted
Red grapes, sliced star fruit and fresh herbs, optional
Assorted crackers

In a mixing bowl, beat cream cheese and blue cheese until fluffy. Add 1 cup of sour cream until blended. Add eggs; beat on low speed just until combined. Stir in pepper. Pour into a greased 9-in. springform pan. Place pan on a baking sheet.

Bake at 325° for 25-30 minutes or until center is almost set (top may crack). Let stand on a wire rack for 5 minutes; spread with remaining sour cream. Bake 5 minutes longer.

Cool on a wire rack for 10 minutes. Carefully run a knife around edge of pan to loosen; cool 1 hour longer. Refrigerate overnight. Remove sides of pan. Sprinkle with walnuts. Garnish with grapes, star fruit and herbs if desired. Serve with crackers. Refrigerate leftovers. **Yield:** 26 servings.

dough lightly with reserved marinade.

Combine the basil, oregano and thyme; sprinkle over marinade. Sprinkle with 1 cup Monterey Jack cheese, ham, artichokes, tomatoes, olives and feta cheese. Sprinkle with remaining Monterey Jack cheese. Bake at 400° for 20-25 minutes or until crust and cheese are lightly browned. **Yield:** 4-6 servings.

SWEET Fruit Smoothies, Party-Time Popcorn and Mediterranean Pizza (shown above, top to bottom) are simply super for snacking.

Sweet Fruit Smoothies

(Pictured at left)

Sipping one of these thick smoothies is a wonderful way to get fruit into your diet. —Helen Reed Amherst, Ohio

- 1 can (14 ounces) sweetened condensed milk
- 1 carton (8 ounces) strawberry yogurt
- 2 tablespoons lemon juice
- 1 can (8 ounces) crushed pineapple, undrained
- 1 medium ripe banana, sliced
- 1 cup halved fresh strawberries
- 1 cup crushed ice

In batches, process the milk, yogurt, lemon juice and fruit in a blender or food processor until smooth. Add ice; cover and process until smooth. Pour into glasses; serve immediately. **Yield:** 5-6 servings.

Mediterranean Pizza

(Pictured above)

Tangy marinated artichokes add flavor to both the crust and the topping of this delicious specialty pizza. —Pamela Brooks, South Berwick, Maine

- 2 jars (6-1/2 ounces *each*) marinated artichoke hearts
- 1 loaf (1 pound) frozen bread dough, thawed
- 1 teaspoon dried basil
- 1 teaspoon dried oregano
- 1/2 teaspoon dried thyme
- 2 cups (8 ounces) shredded Monterey Jack cheese, *divided*
- 1/4 pound thinly sliced deli ham, julienned
- 1 cup halved cherry tomatoes
- 1 cup chopped ripe olives
- 1/4 cup crumbled feta *or* blue cheese

Drain artichokes, reserving marinade. Chop artichokes; set aside. On a floured surface, roll bread dough into a 15-in. circle. Transfer to a greased 14-in. pizza pan; build up edges slightly. Brush the

Party-Time Popcorn

(Pictured above left)

This fun snack mix combines crunchy peanuts and popcorn with a perky dill flavor, plus other seasonings. —Darlene Smith, Brownsburg, Indiana

- 2 quarts popped popcorn
- 3 cups shoestring potato sticks
- 1 cup salted mixed nuts *or* peanuts
- 1/4 cup butter *or* margarine, melted
- 1 teaspoon dill weed
- 1 teaspoon Worcestershire sauce
- 1/2 teaspoon lemon-pepper seasoning
- 1/4 teaspoon garlic powder
- 1/4 teaspoon onion salt

In an ungreased roasting pan, combine the popcorn, potato sticks and nuts. Combine the remaining ingredients; pour over popcorn mixture and toss to coat. Bake, uncovered, at 325° for 8-10 minutes, stirring once. Store in an airtight container. **Yield:** 2 quarts.

Chicken Nuggets

With a crisp golden coating, these moist and tender bite-size pieces of chicken are greeted with enthusiasm whenever I serve them as a hearty snack or party appetizer. —*Cathryn White, Newark, Delaware*

      1 cup dry bread crumbs
  1/2 cup grated Parmesan cheese
      2 teaspoons dried basil
      2 teaspoons dried thyme
      2 teaspoons paprika
      1 teaspoon salt
      1 teaspoon pepper
  3/4 cup butter *or* margarine, melted
2-1/2 pounds boneless skinless chicken breasts,
      cut into 1-inch cubes

In a shallow bowl, combine the first seven ingredients. Place butter in another shallow bowl. Dip chicken in butter, then roll in bread crumb mixture. Place in a greased 15-in. x 10-in. x 1-in. baking pan. Bake, uncovered, at 400° for 15-20 minutes or until juices run clear. **Yield:** 8 servings.

Tangy Onion Flowers

These flavorful baked onions are a great accompaniment to grilled meat. They aren't crisp like the deep-fried "blooming onions" served in restaurants, but we think they are equally delicious. —*Karen Owen, Rising Sun, Indiana*

✓ Uses less fat, sugar or salt. Includes Nutritional Analysis and Diabetic Exchanges.

      4 large sweet onions, peeled
  1/4 cup red wine vinegar *or* cider vinegar
      1 tablespoon brown sugar
      1 teaspoon dried oregano
  1/2 teaspoon salt
  1/4 teaspoon pepper
  1/2 cup coarsely crushed fat-free salad
      croutons

Place the onions root end up on a microwave-safe plate. Microwave, uncovered, on high for 10-12 minutes or until crisp-tender. Invert onto a cutting board. Slice each onion into eight wedges to within 1/2 in. of bottom; fan out. Place each onion on a 12-in. square piece of foil coated with non-stick cooking spray.

In a small bowl, combine vinegar, brown sugar, oregano, salt and pepper. Brush some over onions; set remaining mixture aside. Fold foil around onions; seal tightly. Place on a baking sheet. Bake at 425° for 30-35 minutes or until tender. Open foil carefully. Place onions on a serving platter. Drizzle with remaining vinegar mixture; sprinkle with crou-tons. **Yield:** 4 onions (8 servings).

Nutritional Analysis: One serving (half of an onion) equals 48 calories, trace fat (trace saturated fat), 0 cholesterol, 203 mg sodium, 11 g carbohydrate, 1 g fiber, 1 g protein. **Diabetic Exchange:** 2 vegetable.

Editor's Note: This recipe was tested in an 850-watt microwave.

Microwave Pizza Dip

Pizza toppings such as cheese, pepperoni, mushrooms, onions and green pepper deliciously combine in this savory dip. It's a favorite at all kinds of parties. —*Katie Koziolek, Hartland, Minnesota*

      1 cup *each* chopped onion, mushrooms and
      green pepper
1-1/2 cups (6 ounces) shredded mozzarella
      cheese
  3/4 cup grated Parmesan cheese, *divided*
      2 teaspoons dried parsley flakes
  3/4 cup chopped pepperoni, hard salami *or*
      fully cooked Polish sausage
  3/4 cup pizza sauce
Crisp breadsticks *or* garlic toast

In a 1-qt. microwave-safe dish, combine the onion, mushrooms and green pepper. Cover and microwave on high for 2-3 minutes or until vegetables are crisp-tender; drain on paper towels. In a small bowl, combine the mozzarella, 1/2 cup Parmesan and parsley.

Spread vegetable mixture in an 8-in. square microwave-safe dish. Top with pepperoni, cheese mixture and pizza sauce. Microwave, uncovered, at 70% power for 5-8 minutes or until cheese is melted, rotating a half turn once. Top with remaining Parmesan. Serve warm with breadsticks or garlic toast. **Yield:** 10-12 servings.

Editor's Note: This recipe was tested in an 850-watt microwave.

Party Planning

If you're serving a dip with crackers or chips at a party, 1 cup of dip should serve eight people (each person will eat about 2 tablespoons). Four cups of dip will provide about 160 cracker-size servings.

For a pretty dip holder, use a large green, red or yellow pepper. Just remove the top and scrape the pepper clean of ribs and seeds. A scooped-out cucumber or small squash will work as well.

California Fried Walnuts

We grow walnuts for a living, so they go into just about everything at our house. Walnut halves made this way are crunchy, sweet and salty. —Alcy Thorne
Los Molinos, California

6 cups water
4 cups walnut halves
1/2 cup sugar
Oil for frying
1-1/4 teaspoons salt

In a large saucepan, bring water to a boil. Add walnuts; boil for 1 minute. Drain; rinse under hot water. In a large bowl, toss walnuts with sugar. In an electric skillet, heat 1/2 in. of oil to 350°. Fry walnuts for 5 minutes or until dark brown, stirring often. Drain in a colander over paper towels. Sprinkle with salt. Store in an airtight container. **Yield:** 4 cups.

— 🍶 🍶 🍶 —

Venison Cheese Dip

(Pictured below)

This hearty cheesy dip is so yummy that even those who don't enjoy venison will dig right in. My grandsons put it in a bowl and eat it with a spoon! —Karen Smith
Mackinaw, Illinois

1 pound ground venison
3/4 cup chopped onion, *divided*
3/4 cup chopped green pepper, *divided*
2 tablespoons vegetable oil
1 pound process cheese (Velveeta), cubed
1 can (15 ounces) chili without beans
1 bottle (12 ounces) chili sauce
1/2 teaspoon garlic salt
1/2 teaspoon salt
1/2 teaspoon pepper

1/2 cup shredded cheddar cheese
Nacho chips

In a large skillet over medium heat, cook the venison, 1/2 cup onion and 1/2 cup green pepper in oil until meat is no longer pink; drain. Stir in the next six ingredients; cook and stir until the cheese is melted. Transfer to a serving dish. Sprinkle with cheddar cheese and remaining onion and green pepper. Serve with chips. **Yield:** 6 cups.

— 🍶 🍶 🍶 —

Cilantro Bean Dip

This chunky fresh-tasting dip gets a little kick from hot pepper sauce. —Wendy Prevost, Cody, Wyoming

✓ Uses less fat, sugar or salt. Includes Nutritional Analysis and Diabetic Exchanges.

1 can (15-1/4 ounces) shoepeg corn, drained *or* 2 cups frozen shoepeg corn, thawed
1 can (15 ounces) black beans, rinsed and drained
1 large tomato, chopped
3/4 cup chopped sweet red pepper
1/2 cup chopped red onion
1/2 cup Italian salad dressing
1/4 cup minced fresh cilantro
3/4 teaspoon hot pepper sauce
1/2 teaspoon garlic powder
Tortilla chips

In a bowl, combine the corn, beans, tomato, red pepper and onion. In a small bowl, combine the salad dressing, cilantro, hot pepper sauce and garlic powder. Pour over corn mixture and gently stir to coat. Serve with tortilla chips. **Yield:** 5 cups.
Nutritional Analysis: 1/4 cup dip (prepared with frozen corn and fat-free Italian dressing) equals 46 calories, trace fat (trace saturated fat), trace cholesterol, 158 mg sodium, 9 g carbohydrate, 2 g fiber, 2 g protein. **Diabetic Exchange:** 1/2 starch.

— 🍶 🍶 🍶 —

Melon Fruit Slush

(Pictured on page 4)

This pretty pink drink features fresh honeydew and cantaloupe as well as luscious pineapple, strawberries and bananas. —Jane Walker, Dewey, Arizona

1 can (20 ounces) crushed pineapple, undrained
1 package (10 ounces) frozen sweetened sliced strawberries, thawed
4 medium ripe bananas, cut into chunks

1 cup cubed cantaloupe
1 cup cubed honeydew
2-1/2 cups water
3/4 cup orange juice concentrate
3/4 cup lemonade concentrate
6 liters lemon-lime soda, chilled

In a blender, process the fruit in batches until smooth. Pour into a 3-qt. freezer container. Stir in the water and concentrates. Cover and freeze until icy. To serve, spoon 1/2 cup into a glass; add about 1 cup soda. **Yield:** 20-25 servings.

— ▼ ▼ ▼ —

Rainbow Gelatin Cubes

These gelatin cubes are fun to serve and to eat! I vary the colors to match the occasion—pink and blue for a baby shower, school colors for a graduation party, etc. Kids of all ages snap them up. —Deanna Pietrowicz
Bridgeport, Connecticut

✓ Uses less fat, sugar or salt. Includes Nutritional Analysis and Diabetic Exchanges.

4 packages (3 ounces *each*) assorted flavored gelatin
6 envelopes unflavored gelatin, *divided*
5-3/4 cups boiling water, *divided*
1 can (14 ounces) sweetened condensed milk
1/4 cup cold water

In a bowl, combine one package flavored gelatin and one envelope unflavored gelatin. Stir in 1 cup boiling water until dissolved. Pour into a 13-in. x 9-in. x 2-in. dish coated with nonstick cooking spray; refrigerate until set but not firm, about 20 minutes.

In a bowl, combine the condensed milk and 1 cup boiling water. In another bowl, sprinkle two envelopes unflavored gelatin over cold water; let stand for 1 minute. Stir in 3/4 cup boiling water. Add to the milk mixture. Spoon 1/4 cup of the creamy gelatin mixture over the first flavored gelatin layer. Refrigerate until set but not firm, about 25 minutes.

Repeat from beginning of recipe twice, alternating flavored gelatin with creamy gelatin layers. Chill each layer until set but not firm before spooning next layer on top. Make final flavored gelatin; spoon over top. Refrigerate for at least 1 hour before cutting into 1-in. squares. **Yield:** about 9 dozen.

Nutritional Analysis: One serving (two cubes, prepared with sugar-free gelatin and fat-free sweetened condensed milk) equals 26 calories, trace fat (0 saturated fat), 0 cholesterol, 27 mg sodium, 4 g carbohydrate, 0 fiber, 2 g protein. **Diabetic Exchange:** 1/2 fruit.

Spicy Ribbon Potato Chips

(Pictured above)

You won't settle for store-bought chips again after munching these crispy deep-fried snacks. Seasoned with chili powder and cayenne pepper, the zippy paper-thin chips are surefire crowd-pleasers.
—Sue Murphy, Greenwood, Michigan

4 medium unpeeled baking potatoes
4 teaspoons salt, *divided*
4 cups ice water
1 tablespoon chili powder
1 teaspoon garlic salt
1/4 to 1/2 teaspoon cayenne pepper
Oil for deep-fat frying

Using a vegetable peeler or metal cheese slicer, cut potatoes into very thin lengthwise strips. Place in a large bowl; add 3 teaspoons salt and ice water. Soak for 30 minutes; drain. Place potatoes on paper towels and pat dry. In a bowl, combine the chili powder, garlic salt, cayenne and remaining salt; set aside.

In an electric skillet or deep-fat fryer, heat oil to 375°. Cook potatoes in oil in batches for 3-4 minutes or until deep golden brown, stirring frequently. Remove with a slotted spoon; drain on paper towels. Immediately sprinkle with seasoning mixture. Store in an airtight container. **Yield:** 6-8 servings.

2 tablespoons orange juice
1 to 2 teaspoons grated orange peel
1/4 teaspoon salt
1/8 teaspoon pepper

In a large bowl, combine all ingredients; toss to coat. Cover and refrigerate for at least 30 minutes before serving. **Yield:** 3 cups.

Nutritional Analysis: One serving (1/4 cup) equals 18 calories, trace fat (trace saturated fat), 0 cholesterol, 54 mg sodium, 4 g carbohydrate, 1 g fiber, 1 g protein. **Diabetic Exchange:** Free food.

*Editor's Note: When cutting or seeding hot peppers, use rubber or plastic gloves to protect your hands. Avoid touching your face.

— ⛴ ⛴ ⛴ —

Christmas Cheese Ball

(Pictured above)

This rich creamy spread looks so festive with flecks of green onion and red pimiento dotting the cheddar cheese. —Sundra Hauck, Bogalusa, Louisiana

1 package (8 ounces) cream cheese, softened
2 cups (8 ounces) shredded cheddar cheese
2 green onions, chopped
1 jar (2 ounces) diced pimientos, drained
2 tablespoons butter *or* margarine, melted
2 teaspoons Worcestershire sauce
Assorted crackers

In a mixing bowl, beat cream cheese until fluffy. Beat in cheddar cheese, onions, pimientos, butter and Worcestershire sauce. Press into a small bowl; smooth top. Cover and refrigerate. Remove from refrigerator 15 minutes before unmolding. Serve with crackers. **Yield:** 1 cheese ball (2-1/2 cups).

— ⛴ ⛴ ⛴ —

Cantaloupe Salsa

My husband and I host parties frequently in our backyard, and this recipe is welcome on warm summer evenings. —Debbie Smith, Tuscon, Arizona

✓ Uses less fat, sugar or salt. Includes Nutritional Analysis and Diabetic Exchanges.

2 cups coarsely chopped cantaloupe
2 cups coarsely chopped cherry tomatoes
1/4 cup chopped green onions
1/4 cup minced fresh basil *or* 4 teaspoons dried basil
2 tablespoons diced seeded jalapeno pepper*
2 tablespoons lime juice

Bacon-Wrapped Water Chestnuts

My husband and I do lots of entertaining and always start off with appetizers like these tempting morsels. —Midge Scurlock, Creston, Iowa

8 bacon strips
2 cans (8 ounces *each*) whole water chestnuts, drained
3/4 cup ketchup
1 jar (2-1/2 ounces) strained peach baby food
1/4 cup sugar
Dash salt

Cut bacon strips in half lengthwise and then in half widthwise. Wrap each bacon piece around a water chestnut; secure with a toothpick. Place in an ungreased 13-in. x 9-in. x 2-in. baking dish. Bake, uncovered, at 350° for 25 minutes, turning once; drain if necessary.

In a small bowl, combine the remaining ingredients. Drizzle over water chestnuts. Bake 25-35 minutes longer or until bacon is crisp. Serve warm. **Yield:** 32 appetizers.

— ⛴ ⛴ ⛴ —

Pesto Chicken Pizzas

These quick-fix "pizzas" make a great meal or after-school snack. —Brigitte Raven, Greenfield, Indiana

1 cup minced fresh cilantro
1 cup minced fresh parsley
1/3 cup chopped walnuts
1/3 cup grated Parmesan cheese
2 garlic cloves
1/4 cup olive *or* vegetable oil
8 flour tortillas (6 inches)
1 cup diced cooked chicken
2 cups diced tomatoes

1 can (2-1/4 ounces) sliced ripe olives,
   drained
1/2 cup shredded mozzarella cheese
1/2 cup shredded cheddar cheese

For pesto, combine first five ingredients in a blender or food processor. Cover; process until smooth. While processing, add oil in steady stream.
   Place tortillas on two ungreased baking sheets. Spread each with about 1 tablespoon pesto. Sprinkle with chicken, tomatoes, olives and cheeses. Bake at 450° for 5-8 minutes or until cheese is melted. **Yield:** 8 servings.

Horseradish Meatballs

These spicy meatballs with their thick savory sauce are a popular party food. —*Joyce Benninger*
Owen Sound, Ontario

✓ Uses less fat, sugar or salt. Includes Nutritional Analysis and Diabetic Exchanges.

2 eggs
1 tablespoon prepared horseradish
1/2 cup dry bread crumbs
1/4 cup chopped green onions
1/2 teaspoon salt
1/4 teaspoon pepper
1-1/2 pounds ground beef
1/2 pound ground pork *or* turkey
SAUCE:
1/2 cup water
1/2 cup ketchup
1/2 cup chili sauce
1 small onion, finely chopped
1/4 cup packed brown sugar
1/4 cup cider vinegar
1 tablespoon prepared horseradish
1 tablespoon Worcestershire sauce
1 garlic clove, minced
1 teaspoon ground mustard
1/4 teaspoon hot pepper sauce

In a large bowl, combine the first six ingredients. Crumble meat over mixture; mix well. Shape into 1-1/2-in. balls. Place in a greased 15-in. x 10-in. x 1-in. baking pan. Bake, uncovered, at 350° for 35-40 minutes or until no longer pink.
   Meanwhile, in a large saucepan, combine sauce ingredients. Bring to a boil, stirring often. Reduce heat; simmer, uncovered, for 10 minutes. Add meatballs; stir gently to coat. **Yield:** 3 dozen.
   Nutritional Analysis: One serving (2 meatballs, prepared with egg substitute, lean ground beef and ground turkey) equals 130 calories, 5 g fat (2 g saturated fat), 24 mg cholesterol, 454 mg sodium, 10 g carbohydrate, trace fiber, 11 g protein. **Diabetic Exchanges:** 1 lean meat, 1 fat, 1/2 starch.

Mexican Fiesta Dip

(Pictured below and on page 4)

I lost 30 pounds by using slimmed-down ingredients in my recipes, and I still get to enjoy goodies like this savory dip. —*Angela Oelschlaege*
Tonganoxie, Kansas

✓ Uses less fat, sugar or salt. Includes Nutritional Analysis and Diabetic Exchanges.

1 pound lean ground turkey
1 envelope reduced-sodium taco seasoning
2/3 cup water
1 can (16 ounces) fat-free refried beans
1-1/2 cups shredded lettuce
1 jar (16 ounces) salsa
1 cup (4 ounces) shredded reduced-fat
   cheddar cheese
4 canned jalapenos, sliced
1 cup (8 ounces) reduced-fat sour cream
1/3 cup sliced ripe olives
1 package (13-1/2 ounces) baked tortilla
   chips

In a nonstick skillet coated with nonstick cooking spray, cook turkey until no longer pink; drain if necessary. Stir in taco seasoning and water; cook and stir for 2-4 minutes or until most of the liquid has evaporated. Spread refried beans on a 12-in. serving platter. Top with the turkey, lettuce, salsa, cheese, jalapenos, sour cream and olives. Serve with chips. **Yield:** 12 servings.
   Nutritional Analysis: One serving equals 282 calories, 8 g fat (3 g saturated fat), 41 mg cholesterol, 936 mg sodium, 39 g carbohydrate, 5 g fiber, 15 g protein. **Diabetic Exchanges:** 2-1/2 starch, 1-1/2 lean meat.

Salads & Dressings

Whether they call for fresh fruits or vegetables, or tender pasta or rice, variety is the key ingredient in these refreshing salads.

TOSS ONE TOGETHER. Clockwise from upper left: Tangy Tuna Macaroni Salad (p. 30), Springtime Luncheon Salad (p. 25), Sesame Spinach Salad (p. 26), Three-Bean Tomato Cups (p. 31) and Apple Cider Gelatin Salad (p. 27).

filling into the egg; return all to the pan, stirring constantly. Bring to a gentle boil; cook and stir 2 minutes longer. Cool.

In a mixing bowl, beat cream cheese until smooth; add cooled filling. Fold in whipped cream. Spread over gelatin (dish will be full). Sprinkle with nuts and coconut. **Yield:** 12 servings.

— 🏆 🏆 🏆 —

Beet Spinach Salad

My husband and I like this salad's fresh taste and the fact that it uses beets, spinach, mint and onions, all of which we grow in our large garden.
—Margaret Shaeffer, Sewell, New Jersey

  2 large fresh beets
  2 tablespoons red wine vinegar *or* cider vinegar
  1 teaspoon Dijon mustard
  1/4 cup olive *or* vegetable oil
1-1/2 teaspoons sugar
  1/8 teaspoon salt
Dash pepper
  1/2 cup chopped green onions
  1/2 teaspoon minced fresh mint
  4 cups torn fresh spinach
  1 medium navel orange, peeled and sectioned
  1/2 cup fresh raspberries

Place beets in a large saucepan and cover with water. Bring to a boil. Reduce heat; cover and simmer for 30 minutes or until tender. Cool; peel and cut into 1/4-in. strips.

In a small bowl, whisk vinegar and mustard until blended; gradually whisk in oil. Add the sugar, salt and pepper. In a large bowl, combine the beets, onions, mint and 2 tablespoons vinaigrette. Cover and refrigerate for 30 minutes.

In a large salad bowl, combine the spinach, orange sections, beet mixture and remaining vinaigrette; toss. Top with raspberries. Serve immediately. **Yield:** 4 servings.

— 🏆 🏆 🏆 —

Frosted Orange Salad

(Pictured above)

Pineapple, bananas and marshmallows are folded into orange Jell-O in this refreshing salad. Frosted with a creamy topping, pecans and coconut, this yummy dish is a real crowd-pleaser. I have been making it for years. —Anna Jean Key, Muskogee, Oklahoma

  3 packages (3 ounces *each*) orange gelatin
  3 cups boiling water
  1 can (20 ounces) crushed pineapple
  3 cups cold water
  4 medium firm bananas, sliced
2-1/2 cups miniature marshmallows
  1/2 cup sugar
  1 tablespoon all-purpose flour
  1 egg, beaten
  1 package (8 ounces) cream cheese, softened
  1 cup whipping cream, whipped
  3/4 cup chopped pecans, toasted
  1/2 cup flaked coconut, toasted

In a bowl, dissolve gelatin in boiling water. Drain pineapple, reserving juice. Stir cold water, bananas, marshmallows and pineapple into gelatin. Pour into a 13-in. x 9-in. x 2-in. dish coated with nonstick cooking spray; refrigerate until firm.

Meanwhile, in a saucepan, combine sugar and flour. Stir in reserved pineapple juice until smooth. Bring to a boil over medium heat; cook and stir for 2 minutes or until thickened and bubbly. Reduce heat; cook and stir 2 minutes longer. Remove from the heat. Stir a small amount of hot

Grilled Salmon Caesar Salad

Flaky grilled salmon, lettuce, tomatoes and homemade croutons star in this attractive salad. A Caesar-style dressing coats the colorful concoction.
—Clara Barrett, Madison, Florida

  2 salmon fillets (1 pound *each*)
  3 cups cubed French bread
  1 tablespoon olive *or* vegetable oil
  1/4 teaspoon garlic powder

1 bunch romaine, torn
2 cups small cherry tomatoes
DRESSING:
3 tablespoons olive *or* vegetable oil
2 tablespoons lemon juice
4-1/2 teaspoons mayonnaise
2-1/4 teaspoons sugar
2 garlic cloves, minced
1/2 teaspoon salt
1/8 teaspoon pepper
1 tablespoon grated Parmesan cheese

Coat grill rack with nonstick cooking spray before starting the grill. Place salmon skin side down on grill. Grill, covered, over medium-hot heat for 15-20 minutes or until fish flakes easily with a fork. Cool.

For croutons, toss the bread cubes, oil and garlic powder in a bowl. In a nonstick skillet, saute bread cubes for 5-6 minutes or until golden brown, stirring occasionally. Remove from the heat; set aside.

Flake salmon into chunks. In a large bowl, combine romaine and tomatoes. In a small bowl, combine the oil, lemon juice, mayonnaise, sugar, garlic, salt and pepper. Pour over salad and toss to coat. Add the salmon, croutons and Parmesan cheese; toss gently. **Yield:** 6 servings.

— 🍴 🍴 🍴 —

Fruit 'n' Spinach Salad

A hint of ginger in the dressing accents this delightful salad. —Rebecca Baird, Salt Lake City, Utah

✓ Uses less fat, sugar or salt. Includes Nutritional Analysis and Diabetic Exchanges.

1 pound fresh spinach, torn
4 cups whole strawberries, sliced
1 can (11 ounces) mandarin oranges, drained
1 star fruit, sliced
GINGER SALAD DRESSING:
1/3 cup lemon juice
2 tablespoons olive *or* canola oil
2 tablespoons sugar
3/4 teaspoon ground ginger *or* 1 tablespoon minced fresh gingerroot
2 teaspoons grated lemon peel

Arrange spinach and fruit on salad plates. In a jar with a tight-fitting lid, combine the dressing ingredients; shake well. Drizzle over salads; serve immediately. **Yield:** 4 servings.

Nutritional Analysis: One serving equals 189 calories, 8 g fat (1 g saturated fat), 0 cholesterol, 96 mg sodium, 30 g carbohydrate, 5 g fiber, 5 g protein. **Diabetic Exchanges:** 2 fruit, 1 fat.

Tart Lemon Ring Mold

(Pictured below)

This gelatin mold looks as good as it tastes! With its sunny lemon color, it brightens up any table. I usually make two because it disappears so quickly. My husband raves about it. —Patricia Ryzow
Thousand Oaks, California

1 envelope unflavored gelatin
1 cup cold water
2 packages (3 ounces *each*) lemon gelatin
2 cups boiling water
1 can (12 ounces) frozen limeade concentrate, thawed
2 cups whipping cream
3 tablespoons confectioners' sugar
Fresh strawberries

In a small saucepan, sprinkle unflavored gelatin over cold water; let stand for 1 minute. Bring to a boil; cook and stir until gelatin is dissolved. In a large mixing bowl, dissolve lemon gelatin in boiling water. Stir in unflavored gelatin mixture and limeade concentrate. Refrigerate until slightly thickened.

In a small mixing bowl, beat cream until soft peaks form. Add sugar, 1 tablespoon at a time, beating until stiff peaks form. Beat the gelatin until frothy. Stir in the whipped cream. Pour into an 8-cup ring mold coated with nonstick cooking spray; refrigerate until set.

Unmold onto a serving platter. Fill the center with strawberries. **Yield:** 10-14 servings.

Roasted Green Bean Salad

(Pictured below)

This easy-to-fix recipe turns homegrown green beans into something special. A tangy dill and Dijon vinaigrette coats the crisp-tender beans without overpowering them, so the fresh-picked flavor comes through.
—Kathy Shell, San Diego, California

>   2 pounds fresh green beans
>   3 tablespoons olive *or* vegetable oil, *divided*
>   3/4 teaspoon salt, *divided*
>   2 tablespoons white wine vinegar *or* cider vinegar
> 1-1/2 teaspoons Dijon mustard
>   2 tablespoons snipped fresh dill *or* 2 teaspoons dill weed
> 1-1/2 teaspoons sugar
>   1/4 teaspoon pepper

In a bowl, toss beans with 1 tablespoon oil and 1/2 teaspoon salt. Spread in a single layer in an ungreased 15-in. x 10-in. x 1-in. baking pan. Roast, uncovered, at 400° for 30-40 minutes or until beans are tender and lightly browned, stirring twice.

Meanwhile, in a small bowl, whisk the vinegar, mustard, dill, sugar, pepper and remaining salt. Slowly whisk in remaining oil. Transfer beans to a large serving bowl. Add vinaigrette and toss to coat. **Yield:** 4-6 servings.

Mint Vinaigrette

A hint of mint in this vinaigrette makes it a refreshingly different salad topping. —Kelly Colegrove
Tonawanda, New York

☑ Uses less fat, sugar or salt. Includes Nutritional Analysis and Diabetic Exchanges.

> 1/4 cup canola oil
> 1/4 cup red wine vinegar *or* cider vinegar
>   2 tablespoons sugar
>   1 teaspoon dried oregano
>   1 teaspoon dried mint
>   1 teaspoon garlic powder
>   1 teaspoon dried parsley flakes
> 1/8 teaspoon pepper
> Salad greens

In a jar with a tight-fitting lid, combine the first eight ingredients; shake well. Drizzle over greens. **Yield:** 1/2 cup.

Nutritional Analysis: One serving (2 tablespoons dressing) equals 166 calories, 14 g fat (1 g saturated fat), 0 cholesterol, 23 mg sodium, 10 g carbohydrate, 2 g fiber, 2 g protein. **Diabetic Exchanges:** 3 fat, 1/2 fruit.

———— ☕ ☕ ☕ ————

Citrus Chiffon Salad

Crushed pineapple and orange juice, with a hint of lemon, give this creamy gelatin salad a pleasant tang.
—Kathy Newman, Cedarburg, Wisconsin

☑ Uses less fat, sugar or salt. Includes Nutritional Analysis and Diabetic Exchanges.

>   1 cup orange juice
>   1 tablespoon lemon juice
>   1 package (.3 ounce) sugar-free lemon *or* orange gelatin
>   1 package (8 ounces) fat-free cream cheese, cubed
>   1 cup reduced-fat whipped topping
>   1 can (8 ounces) unsweetened crushed pineapple, undrained
> 1/3 cup reduced-fat mayonnaise

In a small saucepan, bring orange and lemon juices to a boil; stir in gelatin until dissolved. In a blender or food processor, process the cream cheese, whipped topping, pineapple and mayonnaise until smooth. Add gelatin mixture; cover and process until blended. Pour into a 4-cup mold coated with nonstick cooking spray. Refrigerate for several hours or overnight until firm. **Yield:** 8 servings.

Nutritional Analysis: One serving equals 153 calories, 9 g fat (5 g saturated fat), 19 mg cholesterol, 193 mg sodium, 12 g carbohydrate, trace fiber, 4 g protein. **Diabetic Exchanges:** 2 fat, 1 fruit.

Honeydew Shrimp Salad

(Pictured above)

A creamy pickle relish dressing deliciously complements this shrimp and fruit medley.
—Lynda Mohan, Scottsdale, Arizona

   1 **pound cooked medium shrimp, peeled and deveined**
1/4 **cup chopped celery**
   1 **hard-cooked egg, chopped**
   2 **tablespoons sunflower kernels**
1/3 **cup mayonnaise**
4-1/2 **teaspoons Thousand Island salad dressing**
   1 **tablespoon sweet pickle relish**
1/4 **teaspoon salt**
1/8 **teaspoon pepper**
   1 **large honeydew, quartered and seeded**

In a large bowl, combine the shrimp, celery, egg and sunflower kernels. In a small bowl, combine the mayonnaise, salad dressing, pickle relish, salt and pepper. Pour over shrimp mixture and toss to coat. Spoon onto honeydew quarters. **Yield:** 4 servings.

— 🍵 🍵 🍵 —

Confetti Beet Salad

Because most of the ingredients are ones I have on hand, this salad is a great choice when I need a quick dish to round out a meal. —Elaina Pacella
Sewaren, New Jersey

   1 **can (15 ounces) diced beets, rinsed and well drained**
   1 **can (15 ounces) black beans, rinsed and drained**
   1 **can (11 ounces) yellow, white *or* shoepeg corn, drained**
2/3 **cup diced red onion**
1/2 **cup diced sweet red pepper**

   3 **to 4 tablespoons minced fresh cilantro *or* parsley**
   3 **tablespoons olive *or* vegetable oil**
   3 **tablespoons red wine vinegar *or* cider vinegar**
1/2 **teaspoon salt**
1/4 **teaspoon pepper**

In a large bowl, combine all of the ingredients. Cover and refrigerate for at least 2 hours before serving. **Yield:** 6 servings.

— 🍵 🍵 🍵 —

Springtime Luncheon Salad

(Pictured on page 21)

Chicken salad nestled in a molded gelatin ring makes this a perfect light luncheon. —Julie Dillion
Boise, Idaho

   2 **envelopes unflavored gelatin**
2-1/2 **cups orange juice, *divided***
   2 **cups sugar**
Dash salt
   4 **egg yolks, beaten**
   3 **medium navel oranges, peeled and sectioned**
   3 **tablespoons lemon juice**
   1 **teaspoon grated orange peel**
   1 **teaspoon grated lemon peel**
   2 **cups whipping cream, whipped**
CHICKEN SALAD:
   6 **cups cubed cooked chicken**
   1 **cup chopped celery**
   1 **cup mayonnaise**
1/8 **teaspoon white vinegar**
Salt and pepper to taste
1/2 **cup whipping cream, whipped**
1/2 **cup sliced almonds, toasted**

In a saucepan, sprinkle gelatin over 1 cup orange juice; let stand for 1 minute. Stir in sugar and salt. Cook and stir over low heat until gelatin and sugar are completely dissolved. Remove from the heat. Stir a small amount of hot mixture into egg yolks; return all to the pan, stirring constantly. Bring to a gentle boil; cook and stir 2 minutes longer. Remove from the heat.

Stir in orange sections, lemon juice, grated peel and remaining orange juice. Cool. Fold in whipped cream. Pour into a 9-cup ring mold coated with nonstick cooking spray. Chill until set.

In a large bowl, combine chicken and celery. In a small bowl, combine mayonnaise, vinegar, salt and pepper; fold in whipped cream. Fold into chicken mixture. Unmold gelatin onto a serving platter. Fill center with chicken salad. **Yield:** 8-10 servings.

Sesame Spinach Salad

(Pictured above and on page 21)

Toasted sesame seeds are a nice contrast to the hearty ingredients and thick creamy dressing in this spinach salad. I make this dish at least once a month.
—Sue Collins, Shawnee, Kansas

>   2 packages (10 ounces *each*) fresh spinach, torn
>   1 pint cherry tomatoes, halved
>   2 ripe avocados, peeled and sliced
>   1 package (5 ounces) frozen cooked salad shrimp, thawed
>   3/4 pound fresh mushrooms, sliced
>   3 hard-cooked eggs, chopped
>   1/2 cup sesame seeds, toasted
>   1/4 cup shredded Parmesan cheese
> **CREAMY DRESSING:**
>   2 cups (16 ounces) sour cream
>   1 cup mayonnaise
>   1/4 cup finely chopped onion
>   2 tablespoons sugar
>   2 tablespoons white vinegar
>   1 teaspoon salt
>   1/2 teaspoon garlic powder

In a large salad bowl, toss the spinach, tomatoes, avocados, shrimp, mushrooms, eggs and sesame seeds. Sprinkle with Parmesan cheese. In a small bowl, combine the dressing ingredients; mix well. Serve with salad. Refrigerate leftovers. **Yield:** 20 servings.

Black Bean Fiesta Salad

This salad has a colorful blend of black beans and veggies drizzled with a tangy dressing. It's as good as it is good for you!
—Bob Wedemeyer
Lynnwood, Washington

✓ Uses less fat, sugar or salt. Includes Nutritional Analysis and Diabetic Exchanges.

>   1 can (15 ounces) black beans, rinsed and drained
>   1 cup frozen corn, thawed
>   1 green pepper, diced
>   1 sweet red pepper, diced
>   1 cup diced red onion
>   2 celery ribs, chopped
> 3/4 cup cubed Monterey Jack cheese
>   3 tablespoons lemon juice
>   3 tablespoons red wine vinegar *or* cider vinegar
>   2 tablespoons olive *or* canola oil
>   2 garlic cloves, minced
>   1 tablespoon Italian seasoning
>   1 teaspoon pepper
>   1/2 teaspoon ground cumin

In a large bowl, combine beans, corn, peppers, onion, celery and cheese. In a jar with a tight-fitting lid, combine the remaining ingredients; shake well. Pour over vegetable mixture and toss gently. Cover and chill for 2 hours or overnight. **Yield:** 6 servings.

Nutritional Analysis: One 3/4-cup serving (prepared with reduced-fat cheese) equals 192 calories, 8 g fat (3 g saturated fat), 10 mg cholesterol, 354 mg sodium, 22 g carbohydrate, 6 g fiber, 9 g protein. **Diabetic Exchanges:** 1 very lean meat, 1 vegetable, 1 starch, 1 fat.

Southwestern Layered Salad

I made this eye-catching salad for my parents' 50th anniversary party and everyone enjoyed it. The dressing adds pizzazz to layers of egg, avocado and veggies.
—Mary VanLangendon, Green Bay, Wisconsin

>   8 cups shredded romaine
>   8 hard-cooked eggs, sliced
> 3-1/2 cups cherry tomatoes, quartered
>   2 cans (11 ounces *each*) whole kernel corn, drained
>   1 can (16 ounces) black beans, rinsed and drained
>   1/2 cup thinly sliced green onions
>   2 medium ripe avocados, peeled and diced
>   1 tablespoon lime juice

CILANTRO DRESSING:
1-1/2 cups mayonnaise
  2/3 cup salsa
    2 tablespoons lime juice
  1/2 teaspoon ground cumin
  1/2 teaspoon ground chili powder
1-1/4 cups minced fresh cilantro
**Sliced ripe olives, cherry tomatoes and shredded
  cheddar cheese, optional**

Place the romaine in a large salad bowl. Arrange some egg slices around edge of bowl; place remaining eggs over romaine. Top with tomatoes. Combine the corn, beans and onions; spoon over tomatoes. Toss avocados with lime juice; spoon over bean and corn layer.

For dressing, in a bowl, combine the mayonnaise, salsa, lime juice, cumin and chili powder. Stir in cilantro. Spoon over avocados, spreading to sides of bowl. Garnish with olives, cherry tomatoes and cheese if desired. **Yield:** 16 servings.

— 🝙 🝙 🝙 —

Apple Cider Gelatin Salad

(Pictured on page 20)

Apple cider and crisp apples lend a hint of fall to this refreshing salad that's perfect for autumn parties.
—*Cyndi Brinkhaus, South Coast Metro, California*

    2 envelopes unflavored gelatin
  1/2 cup cold water
    2 cups apple cider *or* juice
  1/2 cup sugar
  1/3 cup lemon juice
  1/4 teaspoon ground cloves
Dash salt
    1 cup diced unpeeled apples
  1/2 cup chopped walnuts
  1/2 cup chopped celery
TOPPING:
  3/4 cup sour cream
  1/4 cup mayonnaise
    1 tablespoon sugar
Ground cinnamon
Cinnamon sticks, optional

In a small bowl, sprinkle gelatin over cold water; let stand for 1 minute. In a saucepan, bring cider to a boil; stir in the gelatin mixture and sugar until dissolved. Stir in lemon juice, cloves and salt. Pour into a large bowl. Refrigerate until slightly thickened, about 1 hour.

Fold in apples, walnuts and celery. Pour into a 1-qt. dish or individual dishes. Refrigerate until firm, about 2 hours.

For topping, combine the sour cream, mayonnaise and sugar in a bowl until blended. Dollop over salad; sprinkle with cinnamon. Garnish with cinnamon sticks if desired. **Yield:** 6 servings.

— 🝙 🝙 🝙 —

'I Wish I Had That Recipe...'

"MY WIFE and I had a very good seafood dinner at Anthony's Fish Grotto in San Diego, California. It included a delicious coleslaw made with creamy pineapple dressing," writes Gary Montgomery of Swink, Colorado.

"We'd like very much to have the recipe for this outstanding coleslaw and hope *Taste of Home* can help."

We contacted Beverly Weber Mascari—who owns Anthony's with her cousins Craig and Rick Ghio—and she was glad to share the popular recipe.

"The special dressing makes our coleslaw unique," she agrees. "It is one of our most requested menu items by visitors from all over the United States.

"Craig created the recipe in the early 1970s. We mix red and green cabbage when making it."

Started in 1946 by Catherine "Mama" Ghio, Anthony's Fish Grotto also has locations in Chula Vista, La Mesa and Rancho Bernardo, California.

In San Diego, the restaurant is located at 1360 N. Harbor Dr. (at Ash St.) and offers casual family sit-down dining daily from 11 a.m. to 10 p.m. For more information, call 1-619/232-5103 or visit *www.gofishanthonys.com.*

Anthony's Pineapple Coleslaw

    1 cup mayonnaise
  1/3 cup crushed pineapple
    1 tablespoon milk
    1 tablespoon ketchup
    1 teaspoon sugar
    1 teaspoon poppy seeds, optional
    1 teaspoon Worcestershire sauce
    8 to 10 cups coleslaw mix

In a small bowl, combine the mayonnaise, pineapple, milk, ketchup, sugar, poppy seeds if desired and Worcestershire sauce. Place the coleslaw mix in a large bowl; add dressing and toss to coat. Cover and refrigerate for 2 hours. **Yield:** 4-6 servings.

— 🝙 🝙 🝙 —

Spinach Floret Salad

(Pictured above)

A light sweet dressing gives this colorful salad a "can't resist" flavor. Everyone in my family enjoys it—even those who say they aren't usually fans of spinach.
—Helen Lamb, Seymour, Missouri

    4 cups torn spinach
    2 cups torn iceberg lettuce
1-1/2 cups broccoli florets
1-1/4 cups cauliflowerets
    1 cup chow mein noodles
    8 bacon strips, cooked and crumbled, optional
    2 hard-cooked eggs, sliced
    2 green onions, finely chopped
    3 fresh mushrooms, thinly sliced
    3 radishes, sliced
DRESSING:
    1 cup vegetable oil
3/4 cup sugar
1/3 cup cider vinegar
1/4 cup chopped onion
    1 teaspoon salt
    1 teaspoon Worcestershire sauce

In a large salad bowl, toss the first 10 ingredients. Place all of the dressing ingredients in a blender; cover and process until combined. Serve with the salad. Refrigerate any leftover dressing. **Yield:** 8-10 servings.

Hawaiian Chicken Salad

My mom signed me up for cooking classes when I was in seventh grade. I've been hooked ever since! I only use fresh ingredients in this salad, which combines a number of tropical flavors. —Bob Wedemeyer
Lynnwood, Washington

    5 cups cubed cooked chicken
    1 can (16 ounces) pineapple chunks, drained
    1 can (8 ounces) sliced water chestnuts, drained
    1 cup julienned green pepper
    1 cup seedless green grapes
    1 cup seedless red grapes
    1 cup (4 ounces) shredded cheddar cheese
3/4 cup salted cashews
1/2 cup chopped celery
1/2 cup chopped green onions
DRESSING:
1/3 cup mayonnaise
1/3 cup plain yogurt
    4 teaspoons apple juice
1/4 to 1/2 teaspoon salt

In a large salad bowl, combine the first 10 ingredients. Combine all of the dressing ingredients; pour over salad and toss to coat. Cover and refrigerate for at least 4 hours or until ready to serve. **Yield:** 10 servings.

Cranberry Fluff

(Pictured at right)

This fluffy fruit salad gets its luscious sweet-tart flavor from cranberries and unsweetened whipped cream. We like it because it's not as sweet as many other "fluffs". I'm often asked for the secret to this fun salad.
—Lavonne Hartel, Williston, North Dakota

    4 cups fresh *or* frozen cranberries
    3 cups miniature marshmallows
3/4 cup sugar
    2 cups diced unpeeled tart apples
1/2 cup halved green grapes
1/2 cup chopped nuts
1/4 teaspoon salt
    1 cup whipping cream, whipped

Place cranberries in a food processor or blender; cover and process until finely chopped. Transfer to a bowl; add the marshmallows and sugar. Cover and refrigerate for 4 hours or overnight. Just before serving, stir in the apples, grapes, nuts and salt. Fold in whipped cream. **Yield:** 10-12 servings.

Dilly Bean Potato Salad

(Pictured at right and on front cover)

Green beans and dill pickles perk up this pretty potato salad, and the Italian-style dressing adds a refreshing tang. My Irish grandmother made it for family gatherings, and even though I've changed it a bit, Nanny always comes to mind when I dish it up.
— *Marguerite Novicke, Vineland, New Jersey*

- 1 pound fresh green beans
- 4 pounds red potatoes
- 1 medium red onion, thinly sliced and separated into rings
- 1 medium Vidalia *or* sweet onion, thinly sliced and separated into rings
- 1 cup chopped celery
- 8 dill pickles, sliced
- 2 tablespoons snipped fresh dill *or* 2 teaspoons dill weed
- 2 tablespoons minced fresh parsley
- 4 garlic cloves, minced

VINAIGRETTE:
- 3/4 cup olive *or* vegetable oil
- 1/3 to 1/2 cup tarragon vinegar *or* cider vinegar
- 1/3 to 1/2 cup white wine vinegar *or* cider vinegar
- 1 envelope Italian salad dressing mix
- 2 tablespoons sugar
- 1 teaspoon salt
- 1 teaspoon pepper

Celery salt and seasoned salt to taste

Place 1 in. of water and beans in a skillet; bring to a boil. Reduce heat. Cover and simmer for 8-10 minutes or until beans are crisp-tender; drain and set aside.

Place potatoes in a large saucepan or Dutch oven and cover with water. Bring to a boil. Reduce heat. Cover and cook for 15-20 minutes or until tender; drain and cool. Cut into 1/4-in. slices; place in a large bowl. Add the onions, celery, pickles, dill, parsley and garlic.

In a jar with a tight-fitting lid, combine the vinaigrette ingredients; shake well. Drizzle over potato mixture. Add beans; gently toss. **Yield:** 14-16 servings.

Hot Potato Pointers

Use just-bought potatoes in dishes such as potato salad—they absorb less water when boiled and less mayonnaise when prepared. Plus, they're less likely to break when you mix the salad.

Older potatoes are better for baking and making french fries. They are drier, meatier and starchier, so they have a lighter texture when baked. Their lower water content means the oil will spatter less when you fry them.

Cooking a potato in its skin will retain most of its nutrients. This is true whether you bake or boil the spud.

lar dish at a restaurant, I came home and worked up my own version. My family declared it a winner.
—Marjorie Zalewski, Toledo, Ohio

> 3 **large ripe pears, cut into 1/4-inch slices**
> 6 **cups torn mixed salad greens**
> 6 **slices red onion, separated into rings**
> 2 **ounces crumbled blue cheese**
> 1/4 **cup sunflower kernels**

RASPBERRY VINAIGRETTE:
> 1/2 **cup olive *or* vegetable oil**
> 1/2 **cup honey**
> 1/3 **cup white wine vinegar *or* cider vinegar**
> 1 **tablespoon Dijon mustard**

1-1/2 **teaspoons lemon juice**
> 1 **cup fresh *or* frozen raspberries, thawed**
> 1/4 **teaspoon salt**

Pepper to taste

In a nonstick skillet, saute pears for 2-3 minutes on each side or until tender. On salad plates, arrange greens, pears, onion, blue cheese and sunflower kernels. In a blender, combine vinaigrette ingredients; cover and process until smooth. Drizzle over salads; serve immediately. **Yield:** 8-10 servings.

———— 🍴 🍴 🍴 ————

Cran-Raspberry Sherbet Mold

(Pictured above)

Folks who love the flavor of raspberries and cranberries rave about this tart molded gelatin salad. It's easy to make and pretty enough for company and festive occasions. —Judith Outlaw, Washougal, Washington

> 2 **packages (3 ounces *each*) raspberry gelatin**

1-1/2 **cups boiling water**
> 1 **can (16 ounces) jellied cranberry sauce**
> 2 **cups raspberry sherbet, softened**
> 1 **tablespoon lemon juice**

Cranberries, raspberries, orange segments and fresh mint, optional

In a large bowl, dissolve gelatin in boiling water. Stir in cranberry sauce until smooth. Refrigerate for 30 minutes or until slightly thickened. Fold in sherbet and lemon juice. Transfer to a 6-cup ring mold coated with nonstick cooking spray. Refrigerate until firm.

Unmold onto a serving platter. If desired, fill center with cranberries and raspberries, and garnish with oranges and mint. **Yield:** 10-12 servings.

———— 🍴 🍴 🍴 ————

Warm Pear Salad

Pear slices tossed with salad greens, red onion and blue cheese are drizzled with tangy raspberry vinaigrette in this refreshing salad. After enjoying a simi-

———— 🍴 🍴 🍴 ————

Tangy Tuna Macaroni Salad

(Pictured on page 20)

A well-seasoned vinegar, mayonnaise and yogurt dressing perks up this chilled tuna and macaroni salad. Green peas, parsley and olives add color to the medley. —Ruth Peterson, Jenison, Michigan

✓ Uses less fat, sugar or salt. Includes Nutritional Analysis and Diabetic Exchanges.

> 1 **cup uncooked elbow macaroni**
> 1 **cup chopped celery**
> 1 **can (6 ounces) light water-packed tuna, drained and flaked**
> 3/4 **cup frozen peas, thawed**
> 3 **tablespoons minced fresh parsley**
> 2 **tablespoons sliced stuffed olives**
> 1/2 **cup reduced-fat mayonnaise**
> 1/2 **cup fat-free plain yogurt**
> 1 **tablespoon red wine vinegar *or* cider vinegar**
> 1/2 **teaspoon paprika**
> 1/4 **teaspoon salt**
> 1/4 **teaspoon garlic salt**
> 1/4 **teaspoon ground mustard**

Cook macaroni according to package directions; drain and rinse in cold water. In a serving bowl, combine the macaroni, celery, tuna, peas, parsley and olives. In a small bowl, combine the remaining ingredients; add to tuna mixture and toss to coat. Cover and refrigerate for at least 4 hours or overnight. **Yield:** 6 servings.

Nutritional Analysis: One serving (3/4 cup) equals 163 calories, 3 g fat (trace saturated fat), 12 mg cholesterol, 540 mg sodium, 23 g carbohydrate, 2 g fiber, 11 g protein. **Diabetic Exchanges:** 1-1/2 starch, 1 lean meat.

— 🍺 🍺 🍺 —

Asparagus in Vinaigrette

This chilled asparagus salad is light and tangy. It's quick to fix, too, which makes it ideal for a summer barbecue or picnic. It goes great with any main entree.
—*Sonja Blow, Reeds Spring, Missouri*

2 **pounds fresh asparagus, trimmed and cut into 2-inch pieces**
2 **green onions, chopped**
2 **tablespoons diced green pepper**
2 **tablespoons sweet pickle relish**
1 **garlic clove, minced**
1/3 **cup olive *or* vegetable oil**
2 **tablespoons lemon juice**
1 **tablespoon diced onion**
1 **tablespoon minced fresh parsley**
3/4 **teaspoon salt**
1/4 **teaspoon pepper**

Place asparagus in a steamer basket. Place in a saucepan over 1 in. of water; bring to a boil. Cover and steam for 6-8 minutes or until crisp-tender. Rinse with cold water; drain well. Place in a bowl; add the green onions, green pepper, pickle relish and garlic.

In a small bowl, whisk the oil, lemon juice, onion, parsley, salt and pepper. Pour over asparagus mixture and toss to coat. Cover and refrigerate until chilled. Serve with a slotted spoon. **Yield:** 8 servings.

— 🍺 🍺 🍺 —

Three-Bean Tomato Cups

(Pictured at right and on page 20)

Cilantro and cumin give this delightful salad a Mexican flair. Served in hollowed-out tomatoes, the tasty bean blend makes a pretty addition to a ladies' luncheon or special-occasion meal. Garlic lovers might want to add a second clove. —*Audrey Green Ballon Kentwood, Louisiana*

3/4 **pound fresh green beans, cut into 2-inch pieces**
1/2 **pound fresh wax beans, cut into 2-inch pieces**
1 **can (15 ounces) black beans, rinsed and drained**
1 **medium sweet red pepper, cut into 1-1/2-inch strips**
3 **green onions, sliced**
1/4 **cup minced fresh cilantro *or* parsley**
1/4 **cup olive *or* vegetable oil**
3 **tablespoons red wine vinegar *or* cider vinegar**
1 **teaspoon ground cumin**
1 **garlic clove, minced**
1/2 **teaspoon salt**
1/4 **teaspoon pepper**
6 **large firm tomatoes**

Place the green and wax beans in a saucepan and cover with water; bring to a boil. Cook, uncovered, for 8-10 minutes or until crisp-tender. Drain and place in a large bowl. Add the black beans, red pepper, onions and cilantro.

In a jar with a tight-fitting lid, combine the oil, vinegar, cumin, garlic, salt and pepper; shake well. Pour over bean mixture and toss to coat. Cover and refrigerate for 30 minutes.

Cut a 1/4-in. slice off the top of each tomato; scoop out and discard pulp. Using a slotted spoon, fill tomato cups with the bean mixture. **Yield:** 6 servings.

Tomato Tip

For stuffed tomatoes, turn the hollowed-out tomatoes upside down on paper towels to drain for about 15 minutes before stuffing.

Soups & Sandwiches

Pair any of these heartwarming soups and piled-high sandwiches for a family-pleasing lunch or light supper.

—— 🍲 🍲 🍲 ——

WINNING TWOSOME. Clockwise from upper left: Venison on Caraway Rolls (p. 34), Vegetarian Black Bean Soup (p. 34), Sourdough Veggie Sandwiches (p. 38) and Country Potato Chowder (p. 37).

Vegetarian Black Bean Soup

(Pictured on page 33)

This chunky soup is chock-full of hearty ingredients like potatoes and black beans. The tasty vegetable broth is a nice change from chicken or beef.
—*Heather Baldry, Knoxville, Tennessee*

☑ Uses less fat, sugar or salt. Includes Nutritional Analysis and Diabetic Exchanges.

- 1 cup chopped onion
- 2 garlic cloves, minced
- 1 can (14-1/2 ounces) vegetable broth, *divided*
- 2 cans (15 ounces *each*) black beans, rinsed and drained
- 1 cup diced peeled potato
- 1/2 teaspoon dried thyme
- 1/2 teaspoon ground cumin
- 1 can (14-1/2 ounces) diced tomatoes, undrained
- 1/4 to 1/2 teaspoon hot pepper sauce
- 2 green onions, sliced

In a saucepan, bring the onion, garlic and 1/4 cup broth to a boil. Reduce heat; cover and simmer for 6-8 minutes or until onion is tender. Stir in the beans, potato, thyme, cumin and remaining broth; return to a boil. Reduce heat; cover and simmer for 20-25 minutes or until potatoes are tender.

Stir in tomatoes and hot pepper sauce; heat through. Sprinkle with green onions. **Yield:** 6 servings.

Nutritional Analysis: One serving (1 cup) equals 173 calories, 2 g fat (trace saturated fat), 0 cholesterol, 818 mg sodium, 30 g carbohydrate, 10 g fiber, 10 g protein. **Diabetic Exchanges:** 1-1/2 starch, 1 lean meat.

Rosemary Corn Soup

When our granddaughter Kim hosted the family Thanksgiving dinner at her home for the first time, she served a five-course meal, much to our surprise! For the first course, she ladled up steaming bowls of this rich creamy soup. It was absolutely delicious.
—*Thelma Reid, Guthrie, Oklahoma*

- 2 cups chopped onions
- 1/2 cup diced carrots
- 1/2 cup diced celery
- 3 tablespoons butter *or* margarine, *divided*
- 7-1/2 cups fresh *or* frozen corn, *divided*
- 6 cups chicken broth
- 1 tablespoon minced fresh rosemary *or* 1 teaspoon dried rosemary, crushed

- 2 garlic cloves, minced
- 1/4 teaspoon cayenne pepper
- 1 medium sweet red pepper, chopped
- 1 cup half-and-half cream

Salt and pepper to taste

In a large saucepan, saute onions, carrots and celery in 2 tablespoons butter until tender. Add 3-1/2 cups corn, broth, rosemary, garlic and cayenne. Bring to a boil. Reduce heat; simmer, uncovered, for 30 minutes, stirring occasionally. Cool; process in batches in a blender or food processor until pureed. Return to the pan.

In a small skillet, saute red pepper in remaining butter until tender. Add to corn mixture. Stir in cream and remaining corn; heat through, stirring occasionally. Season with salt and pepper. **Yield:** 8 servings.

Lentil Spinach Soup

Lentils are packed with protein and are an easy change of pace from beans in soup. This quick-to-fix mixture tastes like it's been simmering all day. My husband and I like the zip it gets from the sausage.
—*Margaret Wilson, Hemet, California*

☑ Uses less fat, sugar or salt. Includes Nutritional Analysis and Diabetic Exchanges.

- 1/2 pound bulk Italian turkey sausage
- 1 small onion, chopped
- 4 cups water
- 1/2 cup dried lentils, rinsed
- 2 teaspoons chicken bouillon granules
- 1/8 teaspoon crushed red pepper flakes
- 1 package (10 ounces) fresh spinach, coarsely chopped
- 2 tablespoons shredded Parmesan cheese

In a large saucepan, cook sausage and onion until meat is no longer pink; drain. Stir in water, lentils, bouillon and red pepper flakes. Bring to a boil. Reduce heat; cover and simmer for 25-30 minutes or until lentils are tender. Stir in spinach. Cook 3-5 minutes longer or until spinach is tender. Sprinkle with cheese. **Yield:** 5 servings.

Nutritional Analysis: One serving (1 cup) equals 171 calories, 5 g fat (2 g saturated fat), 26 mg cholesterol, 823 mg sodium, 16 g carbohydrate, 7 g fiber, 16 g protein. **Diabetic Exchanges:** 2 lean meat, 1 starch.

Venison on Caraway Rolls

(Pictured on page 32)

When a family friend shared his hunting bounty with us, I looked for new ways to serve the venison.
—Dian Burge, Friedheim, Missouri

1-1/2 teaspoons active dry yeast
3/4 cup warm water (110° to 115°)
1-1/2 teaspoons sugar
2 tablespoons butter *or* margarine, softened
2 tablespoons nonfat dry milk powder
1 egg
1 teaspoon salt
2-1/2 to 3 cups all-purpose flour
1 egg white
1 teaspoon cold water
1 tablespoon rye flour
1/2 teaspoon coarse salt
1/2 teaspoon caraway seeds
VENISON BARBECUE:
1 venison roast (3 to 4 pounds)
1 cup water
1/2 cup ketchup
2 tablespoons onion soup mix
2 teaspoons prepared horseradish
1/2 teaspoon *each* garlic powder, dried oregano and pepper
3 teaspoons cornstarch
1 tablespoon cold water

In a mixing bowl, dissolve yeast in warm water. Add sugar; let stand for 5 minutes. Beat in butter, milk powder, egg, salt and enough all-purpose flour to form a soft dough. Turn onto a floured surface; knead until smooth and elastic, about 4-6 minutes. Place in a greased bowl, turning once to grease top. Cover and let rise in a warm place until doubled, about 40 minutes.

Punch dough down. Turn onto a lightly floured surface; divide into 12 pieces. Shape into 2-1/2-in. circles. Place 2 in. apart on greased baking sheets. Cover and let rise until doubled, about 20-25 minutes.

Beat egg white and cold water; brush over dough. Combine rye flour, coarse salt and caraway seeds; sprinkle over rolls. Bake at 425° for 9-12 minutes or until golden brown. Remove from pans to wire racks.

Place the venison roast in a Dutch oven. In a bowl, combine water, ketchup, soup mix, horseradish and seasonings; pour over roast. Cover and bake at 325° for 2-3 hours or until meat is tender, turning once.

Remove roast; let stand for 10 minutes. Shred meat with two forks; keep warm. Combine cornstarch and cold water until smooth; stir into pan drippings until blended. Bring to a boil; cook and stir for 2 minutes or until thickened. Return meat to the pan; heat through. Split rolls. Serve meat and gravy on rolls. **Yield:** 12 servings.

Beef Goulash Soup

(Pictured below)

Paprika, cayenne pepper and caraway spice up tender chunks of beef, potatoes and carrots in this tantalizing tomato-based soup. —Sharon Wilson Bickett
Chester, South Carolina

2 pounds boneless beef sirloin steak, cut into 1/2-inch cubes
1 large onion, chopped
1 large green pepper, chopped
2 tablespoons olive *or* vegetable oil
3 medium potatoes, peeled and cubed
3 medium carrots, chopped
4 cups beef broth
1 cup water
2 tablespoons paprika
1 tablespoon sugar
1 to 2 teaspoons salt
1/2 teaspoon pepper
1/4 teaspoon cayenne pepper
2 bay leaves
1 can (28 ounces) crushed tomatoes
1 can (6 ounces) tomato paste
2 tablespoons caraway seeds
Sour cream

In a Dutch oven over medium-high heat, cook and stir the beef, onion and green pepper in oil until meat is browned on all sides; drain. Stir in the next 10 ingredients. Bring to a boil. Reduce heat; cover and simmer for 25-30 minutes or until potatoes are tender.

Stir in the tomatoes, tomato paste and caraway seeds. Cover and simmer 25-30 minutes longer or until meat is tender. Discard bay leaves. Top servings with a dollop of sour cream. **Yield:** 16 servings.

Sausage Stromboli

(Pictured below)

I can't make this scrumptious hot sandwich often enough for my family. —Julie LeBar
Garden Grove, California

> 1 package (1/4 ounce) active dry yeast
> 1 teaspoon sugar
> 1 cup warm water (110° to 115°)
> 1/4 cup olive *or* vegetable oil
> 1/4 teaspoon salt, *divided*
> 2-1/2 to 3 cups all-purpose flour
> 3/4 pound bulk pork sausage
> 1 medium onion, chopped
> 1 can (8 ounces) tomato sauce
> 1/2 cup chopped green pepper
> 1 garlic clove, minced
> 1-1/2 teaspoons Italian seasoning
> Dash pepper
> 1 cup (8 ounces) sour cream
> 3 tablespoons whipped chive and onion cream cheese
> 1 cup (4 ounces) shredded cheddar cheese
> 1 cup (4 ounces) shredded mozzarella cheese
> 1 egg white, lightly beaten
> Fennel seed

In a mixing bowl, dissolve yeast and sugar in water; let stand for 5 minutes. Add the oil, 1/8 teaspoon salt and 2 cups flour; beat until smooth. Stir in enough remaining flour to form a soft dough. Turn onto a floured surface; knead until smooth and elastic, about 5 minutes. Place in a greased bowl, turning once to grease top. Cover and let rise in a warm place until doubled, about 1 hour.

Meanwhile, in a skillet, cook sausage and onion over medium heat until meat is no longer pink; drain. Add the tomato sauce, green pepper, garlic, Italian seasoning, pepper and remaining salt; set aside. Punch dough down. On a large greased baking sheet, roll dough into an 18-in. x 12-in. oval. Spread sausage mixture lengthwise down center.

Combine the sour cream and cream cheese; spread over sausage mixture. Sprinkle with cheeses. Fold one long side of dough over filling. Fold other long side over the top; pinch seam and ends to seal. With a sharp knife, cut slits in top of dough. Cover and let rise until doubled, about 30 minutes.

Brush top with egg white; sprinkle with fennel seed. Bake at 400° for 25-30 minutes or until lightly browned. Let stand for 10 minutes before slicing. **Yield:** 12 servings.

— 🥣 🥣 🥣 —

Chicken Rice Soup

This soothing soup hits the spot on chilly fall and winter days. I frequently simmer up big batches of this soup during the cooler months.
—Kevin Bruckerhoff, Columbia, Missouri

✓ Uses less fat, sugar or salt. Includes Nutritional Analysis and Diabetic Exchanges.

> 3 quarts water
> 4 bone-in chicken breast halves (about 3 pounds)
> 1-1/2 teaspoons salt
> 1/4 teaspoon pepper
> 1/4 teaspoon poultry seasoning
> 1 teaspoon chicken bouillon granules
> 3 medium carrots, chopped
> 2 celery ribs, chopped
> 1/2 cup uncooked long grain rice
> 1 small onion, chopped

In a large Dutch oven or soup kettle, place water, chicken, salt, pepper and poultry seasoning. Bring to a boil. Reduce heat; cover and simmer for 25-30 minutes or until chicken is tender.

With a slotted spoon, remove chicken from broth. When cool enough to handle, remove meat from bones; discard skin and bones. Cut chicken into bite-size pieces. Skim fat from broth; add chicken and remaining ingredients. Bring to a boil. Reduce heat; cover and simmer for 25-30 minutes or until vegetables and rice are tender. **Yield:** 10 servings.

Nutritional Analysis: One serving (1 cup) equals 128 calories, 1 g fat (trace saturated fat), 51 mg cholesterol, 543 mg sodium, 7 g carbohydrate, 1 g fiber, 21 g protein. **Diabetic Exchanges:** 2-1/2 very lean meat, 1/2 starch.

Country Potato Chowder

(Pictured on page 32)

This creamy comforting chowder is thick with potatoes, carrots, green beans and corn. —Sara Phillip
Topeka, Kansas

        6 bacon strips, diced
        1 medium onion, chopped
        3 celery ribs, chopped
    1/4 cup all-purpose flour
        1 quart half-and-half cream
        4 medium potatoes, peeled and cut into
            1/2-inch cubes
        2 cans (10-3/4 ounces *each*) condensed
            cream of celery soup, undiluted
        2 tablespoons dried parsley flakes
        1 tablespoon Worcestershire sauce
        1 teaspoon seasoned salt
    1/2 teaspoon pepper
        1 cup sliced carrots
        1 cup fresh *or* frozen green beans, cut into
            2-inch pieces
        1 can (14-3/4 ounces) cream-style corn

In a Dutch oven, cook bacon over medium heat until crisp; remove with a slotted spoon to paper towels. Drain, reserving 2 tablespoons drippings. In the drippings, saute onion and celery until tender. Sprinkle with flour and stir until blended. Gradually add cream. Stir in the potatoes, soup, parsley, Worcestershire sauce, seasoned salt and pepper. Bring to a boil; cook and stir for 1 minute. Reduce heat; cover and simmer for 25 minutes, stirring occasionally.

Add the carrots and beans. Cover and simmer 15 minutes longer or until the vegetables are tender. Stir in corn and reserved bacon; heat through. **Yield:** 12 servings.

'I Wish I Had That Recipe...'

"THE BEAN SOUP at the Sugar Bowl Restaurant in Gaylord, Michigan is outstanding!" report Marge and Ralph Weckler, who live in Grand Blanc. "We'd like to know how it is made. Can *Taste of Home* find out?"

Sugar Bowl owner Robert Doumas kindly shared the popular recipe. "This soup has been on our menu for about 25 years," he relates. "Customers tell us they love its flavor. A clear chicken broth makes it different from other bean soups."

The Sugar Bowl has been in the Doumas family—and in the same location—since 1919! It began as a small ice cream and candy shop, then changed to a restaurant serving light luncheons, and evolved into a full-service restaurant.

The Sugar Bowl is located at 216 West Main in Gaylord. The casual Family Room offers breakfast, lunch and dinner daily from 7 a.m. to 11 p.m. The Open Hearth, with tablecloth service, offers dinner from 5:30 p.m. to 11 p.m. For more information, call 1-989/732-5524 or visit *www.sugar-bowl.com.*

Navy Bean Soup

        1 pound dried navy beans
        2 quarts chicken broth
        2 tablespoons minced fresh parsley
        2 bay leaves
    1/4 teaspoon pepper
        1 medium onion, chopped
        1 medium carrot, chopped
        1 celery rib, chopped
        6 bacon strips, cooked and crumbled

Place beans in a Dutch oven or soup kettle; add water to cover by 2 in. Bring to a boil; boil for 2 minutes. Remove from the heat; cover and let stand for 1 hour. Drain and rinse beans, discarding liquid.

In a large saucepan, combine the broth, beans, parsley, bay leaves and pepper. Bring to a boil. Reduce heat; cover and simmer for 1 hour. Add onion, carrot and celery. Cover and simmer for 20-25 minutes or until vegetables and beans are tender. Stir in bacon. Discard bay leaves before serving. **Yield:** 8-10 servings.

Grilled Sandwiches Are Great

IT'S EASY to go beyond basic grilled cheese using these flavorful sandwich suggestions. Whether you rely on the stovetop, an electric skillet or a grill to prepare in-hand fare for your family, you'll find a recipe here that's sure to satisfy.

Sourdough Veggie Sandwiches
(Pictured below and on page 33)

This appealing grilled sandwich is quick and easy to assemble. —Billie Moss, El Sobrante, California

TIRED of the same old sandwich day after day? Try Toasted Reubens, Raspberry Chicken Sandwiches and Sourdough Veggie Sandwiches (shown above, from top).

- 2 tablespoons mayonnaise
- 4 slices sourdough bread
- 1 cup (4 ounces) shredded cheddar cheese
- 2 small zucchini, halved lengthwise
- 1 large tomato, thinly sliced
- 1/4 cup shredded carrot
- 1 to 2 tablespoons salted sunflower kernels
- 2 tablespoons butter *or* margarine, softened

Spread mayonnaise on one side of each slice of bread. On two slices, layer cheese, zucchini, tomato, carrot and sunflower kernels over mayonnaise. Top with remaining bread, mayonnaise side down. Spread butter over outsides of bread. In a large skillet, cook over medium heat until bread is lightly toasted and cheese is melted. **Yield:** 2 servings.

Toasted Reubens

(Pictured at left)

When New Yorkers taste these, they say they're like those served in the "Big Apple". —*Patty Kile, Greentown, Pennsylvania*

- 1/2 cup mayonnaise *or* salad dressing
- 3 tablespoons ketchup
- 2 tablespoons sweet pickle relish
- 1 tablespoon prepared horseradish
- 4 teaspoons prepared mustard
- 8 slices rye bread
- 1 pound thinly sliced deli corned beef
- 4 slices Swiss cheese
- 1 can (8 ounces) sauerkraut, rinsed and well drained
- 2 tablespoons butter *or* margarine

In a small bowl, combine the first four ingredients; set aside. Spread mustard on one side of four slices of bread. Layer with corned beef, cheese, sauerkraut and mayonnaise mixture; top with remaining bread.

In a large skillet, melt butter over medium heat. Cook sandwiches on both sides until bread is lightly toasted and cheese is melted. **Yield:** 4 servings.

Raspberry Chicken Sandwiches

(Pictured at left)

The raspberry barbecue sauce makes my grilled chicken sandwiches special. —*Kelly Thornberry, LaPorte, Indiana*

- 1 cup chili sauce
- 3/4 cup raspberry preserves
- 2 tablespoons red wine vinegar *or* cider vinegar
- 1 tablespoon Dijon mustard
- 6 boneless skinless chicken breast halves
- 2 tablespoons plus 1/2 cup olive *or* vegetable oil, *divided*
- 1/2 teaspoon salt
- 1/4 teaspoon pepper
- 24 slices French bread (1/2 inch thick)
- 12 slices Muenster cheese, halved
- Shredded lettuce

Coat grill rack with nonstick cooking spray before starting the grill. In a small saucepan, combine the first four ingredients. Bring to a boil. Reduce heat; simmer, uncovered, for 2 minutes. Set aside 1 cup for serving and remaining sauce for basting.

Flatten chicken breasts to 1/4-in. thickness. Cut in half widthwise; place in a large resealable plastic bag. Add 2 tablespoons oil, salt and pepper. Seal bag and turn to coat. Brush remaining oil over both sides of bread.

Grill chicken, uncovered, over medium heat for 5-7 minutes on each side or until juices run clear, basting frequently with raspberry sauce. Remove and keep warm.

Grill bread, uncovered, for 1-2 minutes or until lightly browned on one side. Turn bread; top each with a piece of cheese. Grill 1-2 minutes longer or until bottom of bread is toasted. Place a piece of chicken, lettuce and reserved raspberry sauce over half of the bread; top with remaining bread. **Yield:** 12 servings.

Grilled Deli Sandwiches

This outstanding sourdough sandwich is packed with a variety of meats, cheeses and sauteed vegetables. —*Pat Stevens, Granbury, Texas*

- 1 medium onion, sliced
- 1 cup sliced fresh mushrooms
- 1 cup julienned green pepper
- 1 cup julienned sweet red pepper
- 2 tablespoons vegetable oil
- 12 slices sourdough bread
- 1/2 pound *each* thinly sliced deli honey ham, smoked turkey and pastrami
- 6 bacon strips, cooked and crumbled
- 6 slices process American cheese
- 6 slices Swiss cheese

In a large skillet, saute the onion, mushrooms and peppers in oil until tender. Layer six slices of bread with ham, turkey, pastrami, bacon, vegetables and cheeses; top with remaining bread. Wrap each sandwich in foil. Grill, uncovered, over medium heat for 4-5 minutes on each side or until heated through. **Yield:** 6 servings.

Pita Burger

Similar to Greek gyros, the herbed ground beef patties are stuffed in pita bread with a yummy cucumber lettuce mixture. —Dorothy Wiedeman, Eaton, Colorado

✓ Uses less fat, sugar or salt. Includes Nutritional Analysis and Diabetic Exchanges.

    2 cups shredded lettuce
    1 medium cucumber, seeded and chopped
    1 cup (8 ounces) reduced-fat plain yogurt
    1 tablespoon sesame seeds, toasted
  1/2 cup chopped onion
    1 garlic clove, minced
    1 teaspoon dried oregano
  3/4 teaspoon salt
  1/2 teaspoon dried basil
  1/4 teaspoon dried rosemary, crushed
1-1/2 pounds lean ground beef
    6 whole pita breads, halved

In a bowl, combine the lettuce, cucumber, yogurt and sesame seeds; set aside. In another bowl, combine the onion, garlic and seasonings; crumble beef over top and mix well. Shape into six patties. Broil or grill until meat is no longer pink. Cut burgers in half; place each in a pita half with lettuce mixture. **Yield:** 6 servings.

Nutritional Analysis: One serving (2 filled pita halves) equals 409 calories, 12 g fat (5 g saturated fat), 44 mg cholesterol, 731 mg sodium, 40 g carbohydrate, 3 g fiber, 32 g protein. **Diabetic Exchanges:** 3-1/2 lean meat, 2-1/2 starch, 1 fat.

— 🍴 🍴 🍴 —

Salmon Chowder

After my husband and I caught four large salmon, my mother-in-law combined several recipes to create this delicious chowder. —Cindy St. Martin Portland, Oregon

    2 pounds red potatoes, peeled and cubed
    1 large onion, chopped
    1 can (49-1/2 ounces) chicken broth
    1 pound salmon steaks (bones removed), cut into 1-inch cubes
  1/2 pound bacon, cooked and crumbled
    2 cups milk
    1 cup half-and-half cream
    1 tablespoon butter *or* margarine
  1/2 teaspoon salt
Pepper to taste

In a soup kettle or Dutch oven, bring the potatoes, onion and broth to a boil. Reduce heat; cover and cook until potatoes are tender. Add salmon and bacon; cook over medium heat until fish flakes easily with a fork. Reduce heat; stir in milk, cream, butter, salt and pepper; heat through (do not boil). Thicken if desired. **Yield:** 14 servings.

— 🍴 🍴 🍴 —

Baked Ham Hoagies

(Pictured below)

For any holiday or gathering, I prefer quick-and-easy dishes since I work full-time. This main dish is fun because everyone can fix their own sandwich the way they like it. Adding cola to the ham while it bakes makes for moist, tasty slices. —Sundra Hauck Bogalusa, Louisiana

    1 boneless fully cooked ham (4 to 6 pounds)
  1/2 cup water
    1 can (12 ounces) regular cola
    2 tablespoons brown sugar
   15 to 20 hoagie buns, split
Lettuce leaves and sliced Colby-Monterey Jack cheese and tomatoes

Place ham in a roasting pan. Score the surface with shallow diagonal cuts, making diamond shapes. Add water to the pan. Cover and bake at 325° for 1-1/4 hours.

Pour cola over ham; sprinkle with brown sugar. Bake, uncovered, 30-45 minutes longer or until a meat thermometer reads 140° and ham is heated through. Let stand for 10 minutes before slicing. Serve on buns with lettuce, cheese and tomatoes. **Yield:** 15-20 servings.

minute. Gradually add cream. Bring to a boil; cook and stir for 1-2 minutes or until thickened. Stir into soup. Add parsley and potatoes; heat through. Garnish with cheese and green onions. **Yield:** 18 servings (4-1/2 quarts).

Venison Chili

This meaty chili is nicely seasoned and has gotten many "very good" responses from my friends. It's easy to make. —Gary Urness, Kenyon, Minnesota

  1 **pound boneless venison steak, cubed**
1/2 **cup chopped onion**
  2 **tablespoons olive *or* vegetable oil**
  1 **can (15 ounces) chili without beans**
1/2 **cup water**
1/2 **teaspoon garlic powder**
1/2 **teaspoon celery salt**

In a large saucepan, cook venison and onion in oil until meat is browned. Stir in the remaining ingredients. Bring to a boil. Reduce heat; cover and simmer for 1 hour or until meat is tender. **Yield:** 3-4 servings.

Fresh Tomato Cream Soup

Chunks of tomato and celery float in a rich broth in this deliciously different soup. Red pepper flakes add a bit of zip. —John Brink, Harrison, South Dakota

  8 **cups chopped fresh tomatoes***
  2 **teaspoons chicken bouillon granules**
1-1/4 **teaspoons salt**
1/2 **teaspoon pepper**
  2 **celery ribs, finely chopped**
1/2 **cup finely chopped onion**
  2 **garlic cloves, minced**
1/2 **teaspoon crushed red pepper flakes**
  6 **tablespoons butter *or* margarine, *divided***
1/4 **cup all-purpose flour**
  6 **cups milk, *divided***

In a large saucepan, simmer tomatoes, bouillon, salt and pepper for 30 minutes. Meanwhile, in a skillet, saute celery, onion, garlic and red pepper flakes in 2 tablespoons butter until tender; add to the tomatoes. In another saucepan, melt the remaining butter; stir in flour until smooth. Gradually add 2 cups milk. Bring to a boil; cook and stir for 2 minutes or until thickened and bubbly. Add tomato mixture. Stir in the remaining milk; heat through (do not boil). **Yield:** 9 servings.

*Editor's Note: Tomatoes can be peeled if desired.

Red Potato Soup

(Pictured above)

I love to entertain, and this recipe is one of my favorites to fix for guests. Onion, celery and bacon season the thin but creamy broth in this chunky potato soup, which always wins raves when I serve it. —Bev Bosveld
Waupun, Wisconsin

2-1/2 **pounds unpeeled small red potatoes, cut into 1-inch cubes**
  1 **large onion, diced**
  3 **celery ribs, diced**
  3 **bacon strips, diced**
  2 **quarts milk**
  4 **cups water**
  3 **tablespoons chicken bouillon granules**
  1 **teaspoon salt**
1/2 **teaspoon pepper**
3/4 **cup butter *or* margarine**
3/4 **cup all-purpose flour**
  1 **cup whipping cream**
1/2 **cup minced fresh parsley**
Shredded cheddar cheese and chopped green onions

Place potatoes in a saucepan and cover with water. Bring to a boil. Reduce heat; cover and cook for 10-12 minutes or until tender. Drain and set aside. In a soup kettle or Dutch oven, saute the onion, celery and bacon until vegetables are tender; drain well. Add the milk, water, bouillon, salt and pepper; heat through (do not boil).

In a saucepan, melt butter; stir in flour until smooth. Cook and stir over medium heat for 1

Side Dishes & Condiments

Turn to the complementary side dishes and condiments featured here for something special to serve alongside main courses.

———— 🥤 🥤 🥤 ————

ON THE SIDE. Clockwise from upper left: Italian Green Beans (p. 46); Hash Brown Casserole (p. 48); Bread and Butter Pickles and Spicy Plum Sauce (p. 53); Sage Dressing (p. 50); Fruit-Stuffed Acorn Squash (p. 57).

Bacon Potato Puff

(Pictured above)

If you're looking for ways to use up bacon, be sure to try this hearty and satisfying side dish. This company-worthy potato dish has down-home goodness.
—DeEtta Rasmussen, Ft. Madison, Iowa

1/2 pound sliced bacon, diced
4 eggs, *separated*
1/4 cup finely chopped onion
1/2 teaspoon ground mustard
1/8 teaspoon pepper
2 cups warm mashed potatoes (prepared with milk and butter)
1/2 cup shredded cheddar cheese
1/4 cup minced fresh parsley

In a skillet, cook bacon until crisp; remove to paper towels to drain. Discard drippings. In a mixing bowl, beat egg yolks until light, about 2 minutes. Beat in onion, mustard and pepper. Place potatoes in a bowl; fold in egg yolk mixture. Set aside 2 tablespoons bacon. Fold cheese, parsley and remaining bacon into potatoes. In a small mixing bowl, beat egg whites until stiff; fold into potato mixture.

Transfer to a greased 1-qt. baking dish. Sprinkle with reserved bacon. Bake, uncovered, at 325° for 45-50 minutes or until set and edges are golden brown. Serve immediately. **Yield:** 6-8 servings.

Walnut Stuffing

Toasted walnuts and other flavorful ingredients make this stuffing perfect alongside roasted turkey.
—Billie Moss, El Sobrante, California

1 large onion, chopped
2 garlic cloves, chopped
1/4 cup butter *or* margarine
4 cups soft bread crumbs
1-1/2 cups coarsely chopped walnuts, toasted
1/2 cup grated Parmesan cheese
2 teaspoons minced fresh rosemary *or* 3/4 teaspoon dried rosemary, crushed
1/2 teaspoon salt
1/4 teaspoon pepper
2 eggs *or* 1/2 cup egg substitute*
1/2 cup chicken broth

In a small skillet, saute onion and garlic in butter until tender. In a bowl, combine bread crumbs, walnuts, Parmesan cheese, rosemary, salt and pepper; stir in onion mixture. Beat eggs and broth; add to the bread mixture. Transfer to a greased 1-1/2-qt. baking dish. Cover and bake at 350° for 35-40 minutes. Uncover; bake 5-10 minutes longer or until browned. **Yield:** 6 servings.

***Editor's Note:** If the stuffing will be stuffed into poultry rather than baked in a baking dish, use egg substitute instead of eggs.

Lemon Curd

Lemon curd is a scrumptious spread for scones, biscuits or other baked goods. You can find it in larger grocery stores alongside the jams and jellies or with the baking supplies, but I like making it from scratch.
—Janaan Cunningham, Taste of Home Food Editor

3 eggs
1 cup sugar
1/2 cup lemon juice (about 2 lemons)
1/4 cup butter *or* margarine, melted
1 tablespoon grated lemon peel

In a heavy saucepan, beat eggs and sugar. Stir in lemon juice, butter and lemon peel. Cook and stir over medium-low heat for 15 minutes or until mixture is thickened and reaches 160°. Cover and store in the refrigerator for up to 1 week. **Yield:** 1-2/3 cups.

Versatile Meat Coating

I like to season chicken breasts, pork chops and other meats with this flavorful seasoning. It keeps well and lends a homemade, not packaged, flavor to meats. It's also great mixed with ground beef for hamburgers.
—Chris Nash, Berthoud, Colorado

3 cups finely crushed cornflakes
1 cup toasted wheat germ

1/2 cup sesame seeds, toasted
4 teaspoons dried parsley flakes
1 tablespoon paprika
1 teaspoon salt
1 teaspoon salt-free garlic and herb seasoning
1 teaspoon ground mustard
1/2 teaspoon onion salt
1/2 teaspoon celery salt
1/2 teaspoon pepper

In a resealable plastic bag or airtight container, combine all of the ingredients. Seal and shake well. Use to coat chicken, pork or fish. Store in the refrigerator for up to 6 months. **Yield:** 5-1/2 cups.

—— 🍴 🍴 🍴 ——

Pickled Baby Beets

Baby beets fresh from my garden are terrific pickled. In fact, I won a blue ribbon with this recipe at our county fair. We enjoy these beets all winter long.
—*Lucille Terry, Frankfort, Kentucky*

4-1/2 to 5 pounds small fresh beets
3 cups sugar
2 cups water
2 cups white vinegar
1 small onion, sliced
1/2 teaspoon canning salt
4-1/2 teaspoons mixed pickling spices

Remove and discard greens and all but 1/2 in. of the stems from the beets. Cook beets in boiling water for 35 minutes or until tender; drain. Peel and slice.

In a Dutch oven, combine the sugar, water, vinegar, onion and salt. Place pickling spices on a double thickness of cheesecloth; bring up corners of cloth and tie with string to form a bag. Add to pan. Bring to a boil. Add beets. Reduce heat; cover and simmer for 10 minutes.

Discard spice bag. With a slotted spoon, pack beets into pint jars to within 1/2 in. of top. Ladle vinegar mixture over beets, leaving 1/4-in. headspace. Adjust caps. Process for 30 minutes in a boiling-water bath. Remove jars to a wire rack to cool completely. **Yield:** 4 pints.

Red Handed!

Beets contain the pigment betacyanin, which gives them their red color. Betacyanin is difficult to remove from your hands, so wearing rubber or plastic gloves is recommended when working with beets.

Tomato Basil Fettuccine

(Pictured below)

The first time I tried this creamy pasta dish, my husband gave it a "gold star" rating. I sometimes add chopped cooked chicken. —*Martha Hightower Greenville, North Carolina*

✓ Uses less fat, sugar or salt. Includes Nutritional Analysis and Diabetic Exchanges.

8 ounces uncooked fettuccine
1/4 cup chopped onion
1/8 teaspoon crushed red pepper flakes
1 tablespoon butter *or* stick margarine
1 can (14-1/2 ounces) diced tomatoes, undrained
1/4 teaspoon salt
1/3 cup fat-free evaporated milk
1/4 cup chopped fresh basil
2 tablespoons grated Parmesan cheese

Cook fettuccine according to package directions. Meanwhile, in a large nonstick skillet, saute onion and red pepper flakes in butter until onion is tender. Add tomatoes and salt; cook and stir over medium-high heat until most of the liquid has evaporated. Remove from the heat; let stand for 1 minute. Gradually whisk in milk.

Drain fettuccine and place in a large bowl. Add the basil, Parmesan cheese and tomato mixture; toss to coat. **Yield:** 4 servings.

Nutritional Analysis: One serving equals 236 calories, 5 g fat (2 g saturated fat), 11 mg cholesterol, 507 mg sodium, 40 g carbohydrate, 3 g fiber, 10 g protein. **Diabetic Exchanges:** 2 starch, 1 lean meat, 1/2 fat.

Italian Green Beans

(Pictured on page 42)

Basil, oregano and Romano cheese give these beans their Italian accent. I serve them with broiled steak, pork roast, lamb chops or pork chops.
—*Andrea Ibzag, Gordon, Wisconsin*

1 small onion, chopped
2 tablespoons olive *or* vegetable oil
2 to 3 garlic cloves, minced
1 can (14-1/2 ounces) stewed tomatoes, coarsely mashed
1/2 cup water
3 tablespoons minced fresh oregano *or* 1 tablespoon dried oregano
4-1/2 teaspoons minced fresh basil *or* 1-1/2 teaspoons dried basil
1 teaspoon sugar
1 teaspoon salt
1/4 to 1/2 teaspoon coarsely ground pepper
2 pounds fresh green beans, cut into 1-inch pieces
2 tablespoons grated Romano *or* Parmesan cheese

In a small saucepan, saute onion in oil until tender. Add garlic; saute 1 minute longer. Add the tomatoes, water, oregano, basil, sugar, salt and pepper. Bring to a boil. Reduce heat; simmer, uncovered, for 40 minutes.

Meanwhile, place beans in a large saucepan and cover with water; bring to a boil. Cook, uncovered, for 8-10 minutes or until crisp-tender; drain. Add tomato mixture and cheese; cook for 5 minutes or until heated through. **Yield:** 10 servings.

———— 🝙 🝙 🝙 ————

Raisin Pear Chutney

We have so much fruit in the area that I just can't help putting up some of it. This hearty chutney is delicious with any meat. —*Ruth Andrewson, Peck, Idaho*

2 cups cider vinegar
1-1/4 cups packed brown sugar
3 pounds unpeeled ripe pears, diced
1 medium onion, chopped
1 cup raisins
2 teaspoons ground cinnamon
1 teaspoon ground cloves
1 garlic clove, minced
1/2 to 1 teaspoon cayenne pepper

In a large saucepan, bring vinegar and brown sugar to a boil. Stir in the remaining ingredients. Return to a boil. Reduce heat; simmer, uncovered, for 2 to 2-1/2 hours or until chutney reaches desired consistency.

Ladle into hot jars, leaving 1/4-in. headspace. Adjust caps. Process for 15 minutes in a boiling-water bath. Remove jars to a wire rack to cool completely. **Yield:** 2 pints.

———— 🝙 🝙 🝙 ————

Colorful Corn Saute

During harvest, I feed a number of hungry men. I try to provide a variety of hearty fare, using fresh produce whenever possible. I also rely on dishes like this corn saute, which was a prize-winner one year at the Kansas State Cornhusking Contest.
—*Karen Ann Bland, Gove, Kansas*

1 package (16 ounces) frozen corn
1/4 cup chopped celery
1/4 cup chopped green pepper
3 thin onion slices, separated into rings
1/4 cup butter *or* margarine
1 teaspoon salt
1/4 teaspoon dried oregano
1/4 teaspoon chili powder
2 medium tomatoes, chopped
1/2 cup half-and-half cream

In a large skillet, saute the corn, celery, green pepper and onion in butter until tender. Sprinkle with salt, oregano and chili powder. Stir in the tomatoes and cream. Bring to a boil; cook and stir for 1-2 minutes or until heated through. **Yield:** 4 servings.

———— 🝙 🝙 🝙 ————

Praline Sweet Potato Bake

I often serve this dish for Thanksgiving. It isn't overly sweet, and it's always popular with family and friends. I never serve it without someone wanting the recipe.
—*Kevin Bruckerhoff, Columbia, Missouri*

3 cups cold mashed sweet potatoes (about 2 pounds)
1/3 cup milk
1/4 cup packed brown sugar
1/4 cup butter *or* margarine, melted
1 egg
1 teaspoon vanilla extract
1/2 teaspoon salt
TOPPING:
1/3 cup packed brown sugar
1/3 cup chopped pecans
3 tablespoons all-purpose flour
3 tablespoons butter *or* margarine, melted

In a mixing bowl, beat the sweet potatoes, milk, brown sugar, butter, egg, vanilla and salt until fluffy. Transfer to a greased 1-1/2-qt. baking dish. Combine the brown sugar, pecans, flour and butter until blended; sprinkle over the top. Bake, uncovered, at 350° for 30-35 minutes or until golden brown. **Yield:** 4-6 servings.

— 🥄 🥄 🥄 —

Homemade Horseradish Sauce

A little of this fresh zippy relish goes a long way to liven up dark game meats, beef, sausage, chops and deli sandwiches.   —*Patricia Wolf, Lewes, Delaware*

> 6 tablespoons white wine vinegar *or* white vinegar
> 8 teaspoons water
> 2 tablespoons sugar
> 1 small jalapeno pepper, seeded and chopped*
> 1/8 teaspoon white pepper
> 1 cup finely shredded horseradish root

In a bowl, combine the first five ingredients; mix well. Stir in the horseradish. Cover and refrigerate overnight before serving. **Yield:** 1 cup.

*Editor's Note: When cutting or seeding hot peppers, use rubber or plastic gloves to protect your hands. Avoid touching your face.

— 🥄 🥄 🥄 —

Zippy Corn on the Cob

Dijon mustard and horseradish perk up this summertime favorite. You can prepare this sweet corn on the grill or in the oven.   —*Barb Sass, Burton, Ohio*

> 6 medium ears sweet corn
> 1/2 cup butter *or* margarine, melted
> 2 tablespoons Dijon mustard
> 1 tablespoon minced fresh parsley
> 2 teaspoons prepared horseradish
> 1/2 teaspoon salt
> 1/4 teaspoon pepper

Place ears of corn on a double thickness of heavy-duty foil. In a small bowl, combine the remaining ingredients; brush over corn. Fold foil around corn and seal tightly. Grill, covered, over medium heat for 25-30 minutes or until corn is tender, turning once. **Yield:** 6 servings.

Corn Kernel

When boiling corn on the cob, try adding a little milk to the water. This will bring out the sweetness of the corn.

Stuffed Baked Potatoes

(Pictured below)

My mom gave me the recipe for these twice-baked potatoes, and I altered them by adding garlic, bacon and green onions. They're perfect for a potluck or even an elegant meal. My two boys absolutely love them!
—*Kristyn Drews, Omaha, Nebraska*

> 5 medium baking potatoes
> 1/4 cup butter *or* margarine, softened
> 2 cups (8 ounces) shredded cheddar cheese, *divided*
> 3/4 cup sour cream
> 1 envelope ranch salad dressing mix
> 1 tablespoon snipped chives
> 1 garlic clove, minced
> Crumbled cooked bacon and chopped green onions

Bake potatoes at 400° for 1 hour or until tender. Reduce heat to 375°. Cut each potato in half lengthwise; scoop out the pulp, leaving a thin shell. In a large mixing bowl, beat the pulp with butter. Stir in 1 cup of cheese, sour cream, salad dressing mix, chives and garlic. Spoon into potato shells. Sprinkle with remaining cheese.

Place on a baking sheet. Bake for 15-20 minutes or until heated through. Top with bacon and green onions. **Yield:** 10 servings.

Two-Bean Tomato Bake

(Pictured below)

Parmesan cheese, basil and garlic spice up this mouth-watering medley of beans, mushrooms, onion and tomato. A crumb topping adds crunch to this veggie bake that's even more flavorful when you use your garden harvest. —Dorothy Rieke, Julian, Nebraska

  1-1/2 **pounds fresh green beans, cut into 2-inch pieces**
  1-1/2 **pounds fresh wax beans, cut into 2-inch pieces**
      5 **medium tomatoes, peeled and cubed**
   1/2 **pound fresh mushrooms, sliced**
    1 **medium sweet onion, chopped**
  10 **tablespoons butter** *or* **margarine,** *divided*
  1-1/2 **teaspoons minced garlic,** *divided*
  1-1/2 **teaspoons dried basil,** *divided*
  1-1/2 **teaspoons dried oregano,** *divided*
    1 **teaspoon salt**
  1-1/2 **cups soft bread crumbs**
   1/3 **cup grated Parmesan cheese**

Place beans in a large saucepan and cover with water; bring to a boil. Cook, uncovered, for 8-10 minutes or until crisp-tender. Drain; add the tomatoes and set aside.

In a skillet, saute mushrooms and onion in 4 tablespoons butter. Add 1 teaspoon garlic, 1 teaspoon basil, 1 teaspoon oregano and salt. Add to the bean mixture; toss to coat. Spoon into a greased 3-qt. baking dish.

Melt the remaining butter; toss with bread crumbs, Parmesan cheese and remaining garlic, basil and oregano. Sprinkle over bean mixture. Cover and bake at 400° for 20 minutes. Uncover; bake 15 minutes longer or until golden brown. **Yield:** 14-16 servings.

Pickled Asparagus

These tangy asparagus spears make a great addition to a relish tray. —Marie Hattrup, The Dalles, Oregon

  9 **quarts water,** *divided*
 16 **pounds fresh asparagus, trimmed**
  2 **quarts white vinegar**
  1 **cup canning salt**
  1 **tablespoon mixed pickling spices**
  1 **garlic clove, minced**

In a large kettle, bring 6 qts. of water to a boil. Cook asparagus in batches, uncovered, for 2-1/2 minutes. Remove and rinse in cold water.

In a Dutch oven, combine the vinegar, salt, pickling spices, garlic and remaining water; bring to a boil. Pack asparagus in quart jars to within 1/2 in. of top. Ladle boiling liquid over asparagus, leaving 1/4-in. headspace. Adjust caps. Process for 20 minutes in a boiling-water bath. Remove jars to wire racks to cool completely. **Yield:** 8 quarts.

Butternut Squash Supreme

To take advantage of delicious fall produce, I often prepare this rich-tasting side dish. —Marianna King Gastonia, North Carolina

  3 **pounds butternut squash, peeled, cubed**
  2 **eggs, beaten**
  1 **cup (4 ounces) shredded cheddar cheese**
  1 **medium onion, chopped**
 3/4 **cup milk**
  1 **teaspoon salt**
 1/4 **teaspoon pepper**
 1/2 **cup crushed butter-flavored crackers (about 12 crackers)**
  2 **tablespoons butter** *or* **margarine**

Place squash in a saucepan and cover with water; bring to a boil. Reduce heat; cover and simmer for 15-20 minutes or until very tender. Drain well and place in a large bowl; mash. In another bowl, combine the eggs, cheese, onion, milk, salt and pepper; add to the mashed squash and mix well.

Transfer to a greased 2-qt. baking dish. Sprinkle with cracker crumbs. Dot with butter. Bake, uncovered, at 350° for 40-45 minutes or until a knife comes out clean. **Yield:** 6-8 servings.

Hash Brown Casserole

(Pictured on page 42)

I first served this yummy casserole years ago at a family brunch for my husband's birthday. It was such

a hit that it became a mainstay at our family get-to-gethers. It makes a delicious supper, too, served with fruit salad and crusty bread. —Jan Huntington
Painesville, Ohio

    12 eggs
     1 can (12 ounces) evaporated milk
     1 teaspoon salt
    1/2 teaspoon pepper
    1/8 teaspoon cayenne pepper, optional
     1 package (30 ounces) frozen shredded
       hash brown potatoes, thawed
     2 cups (8 ounces) shredded cheddar cheese
     1 large onion, chopped
     1 medium green pepper, chopped
     1 cup cubed fully cooked ham

In a large bowl, combine the eggs, milk, salt, pepper and cayenne if desired. Stir in the potatoes, cheese, onion, green pepper and ham. Pour into a greased 13-in. x 9-in. x 2-in. baking dish. Bake, uncovered, at 350° for 45-50 minutes or until a knife inserted near the center comes out clean. **Yield:** 12-15 servings.

———— ▼ ▼ ▼ ————

Apricot Rhubarb Conserve

I originally made this conserve to use on breads and muffins, but I've also found it makes an excellent sweetener for my tea. —Laurae Fortner-Welch
Big Lake, Alaska

     8 ounces dried apricots, finely chopped
     6 cups sugar
     4 cups chopped fresh _or_ frozen rhubarb,
       thawed and undrained
    1/2 cup chopped orange pulp and peel
    1/2 cup chopped lemon pulp and peel
    1/2 cup chopped walnuts

Place the apricots in a bowl and cover with water; soak overnight. Drain and place the apricots in a large kettle. Add the sugar, rhubarb, orange and lemon. Cook over medium heat until a candy thermometer reads 220°, stirring frequently. Stir in the walnuts.

Ladle hot mixture into hot jars, leaving 1/4-in. headspace. Adjust caps. Process for 15 minutes in a boiling-water bath. Remove jars to wire racks to cool completely. **Yield:** 7 half-pints.

———— ▼ ▼ ▼ ————

Corny Garlic Mashed Potatoes

(Pictured above right)

I dreamed up this family favorite after dining on something similar in a restaurant. My family asks for these potatoes on special occasions, but I like them anytime. They're a nice change from regular mashed potatoes. —Patti Lacey, Lincoln, Nebraska

     1 whole garlic bulb
     1 tablespoon olive _or_ vegetable oil
     8 medium red potatoes, peeled and cut into
       chunks
    1/2 cup butter _or_ margarine
     1 cup (8 ounces) sour cream
     2 tablespoons milk
     1 tablespoon minced fresh parsley
     3 green onions, sliced
     1 can (11 ounces) whole kernel corn,
       drained
    Salt and pepper to taste
     1 cup (4 ounces) shredded cheddar cheese

Remove papery outer skin from garlic (do not peel or separate cloves). Brush with oil. Wrap in heavy-duty foil. Bake at 425° for 30-35 minutes or until softened. Cool for 10-15 minutes. Cut top off garlic head, leaving the root end intact. Squeeze softened garlic into a large bowl; set aside.

Place potatoes in a saucepan and cover with water. Bring to a boil. Reduce heat; cover and cook for 15-20 minutes or until tender. Drain and add to garlic. Add the butter, sour cream, milk and parsley; mash. Add the onions, corn, salt and pepper; mix well.

Spoon into a greased 11-in. x 7-in. x 2-in. baking dish. Sprinkle with the cheese. Bake, uncovered, at 350° for 25 minutes or until heated through. **Yield:** 8 servings.

Sage Dressing

(Pictured above and on page 42)

This moist hearty stuffing is nicely seasoned with sausage, sage and fresh mushrooms. —Betty Sitzman Wray, Colorado

- 1/2 pound bulk pork sausage
- 1 medium onion, chopped
- 2 celery ribs, chopped
- 1 cup sliced fresh mushrooms
- 2 teaspoons vegetable oil
- 6 cups cubed day-old bread
- 1/2 cup slivered almonds, toasted
- 1/2 cup chicken broth
- 1/4 cup butter *or* margarine, melted
- 1/4 cup minced fresh parsley
- 1/4 cup egg substitute
- 2 teaspoons rubbed sage
- 1/4 teaspoon salt
- 1/4 teaspoon pepper

In a large skillet over medium heat, cook the sausage, onion, celery and mushrooms in oil until meat is no longer pink; drain if necessary. In a large bowl, combine the remaining ingredients; add sausage mixture and toss to coat.

Transfer to a greased 11-in. x 7-in. x 2-in. baking dish. Cover and bake at 350° for 30 minutes. Uncover; bake 10-15 minutes longer or until lightly browned. **Yield:** 6 servings.

Creamy Chive Mashed Potatoes

Buttermilk and cream cheese lend a rich sour cream-like flavor to these wonderful whipped potatoes. —Bonnie Thompson, Rathdrum, Idaho

- 5 medium potatoes, peeled
- 1-1/2 teaspoons salt, *divided*
- 4 ounces cream cheese, softened
- 2 tablespoons butter *or* margarine, softened
- 2 tablespoons snipped chives
- 1/4 teaspoon pepper
- 1/4 to 1/2 cup buttermilk

Place potatoes in a saucepan; cover with water. Add 1 teaspoon salt. Bring to a boil. Reduce heat; cover and cook for 25-30 minutes or until tender. Drain.

In a large mixing bowl, mash the potatoes until smooth. Add cream cheese, butter, chives, pepper and remaining salt; gradually beat in the buttermilk. **Yield:** 4-5 servings.

Baked Vegetables

This delicious garden blend my older sister shared has become a tasty tradition at our family gatherings. —Janet Harper, Bremo Bluff, Virginia

✓ Uses less fat, sugar or salt. Includes Nutritional Analysis and Diabetic Exchanges.

- 2 medium potatoes, cut into 1/2-inch cubes
- 2 medium carrots, cut into 1/4-inch slices
- 1 cup cut fresh green beans
- 2 medium onions, chopped
- 2 garlic cloves, minced
- 2 tablespoons olive *or* canola oil
- 4 medium tomatoes, chopped
- 2 cups cauliflowerets
- 1 celery rib, thinly sliced
- 1 teaspoon salt
- 1/2 teaspoon dried thyme
- 1/4 teaspoon dried marjoram
- 1/8 teaspoon pepper
- 1 medium zucchini, cut into 1/4-inch slices
- 1 medium green pepper, chopped

In a saucepan, bring 1 in. of water to a boil. Add the potatoes, carrots and beans. Return to a boil. Reduce heat; cover and simmer for 10 minutes. Drain; place in a greased 2-1/2-qt. baking dish.

In a skillet, saute onions and garlic in oil until tender. Add tomatoes, cauliflower, celery and seasonings. Bring to a boil. Reduce heat; cover and simmer for 5 minutes. Spoon half over the potato mixture. Top with zucchini, green pepper and remaining tomato mixture. Cover and bake at 350° for 40-45 minutes or until vegetables are tender. Serve with a slotted spoon. **Yield:** 12 servings.

Nutritional Analysis: One serving (3/4 cup) equals 74 calories, 2 g fat (trace saturated fat), 0 cholesterol, 213 mg sodium, 13 g carbohydrate, 3 g fiber, 2 g protein. **Diabetic Exchanges:** 1 vegetable, 1/2 starch.

Caraway Sauerkraut Bake

If you're a sauerkraut lover, you'll savor this sweet and tangy variation that features stewed tomatoes and bacon. —Bernice Morris, Marshfield, Missouri

- 1/2 pound sliced bacon, diced
- 1 medium onion, chopped
- 2 cans (one 27 ounces, one 8 ounces) sauerkraut, rinsed and drained
- 1 can (14-1/2 ounces) stewed tomatoes, cut up
- 1 cup packed brown sugar
- 1 tablespoon caraway seeds

In a skillet, cook bacon and onion until bacon is crisp; drain. Add the sauerkraut, tomatoes, brown sugar and caraway seeds. Transfer to an ungreased 2-qt. baking dish. Bake, uncovered, at 350° for 30-35 minutes or until heated through. Serve with a slotted spoon. **Yield:** 8-10 servings.

Tomato Peach Chutney

As an avid gardener, I'm always looking for recipes to make use of my tomato harvest. —Charlene Moscicki, Wyandotte, Michigan

- 2-1/2 cups chopped seeded peeled fresh tomatoes
- 2 cups chopped peeled fresh peaches
- 1 cup chopped green pepper
- 1 cup packed brown sugar
- 3/4 cup sugar
- 3/4 cup white vinegar
- 1/2 cup golden raisins
- 1/2 cup chopped onion
- 1 teaspoon curry powder
- 1/2 teaspoon ground ginger

In a large saucepan, combine all ingredients. Cook over medium heat for 1 hour or until thickened, stirring frequently. Ladle hot chutney into hot jars, leaving 1/4-in. headspace. Adjust caps. Process for 20 minutes in a boiling-water bath. **Yield:** 1-1/2 pints.

Creamed New Potatoes

Thyme and tarragon give these saucy potatoes a fresh taste I really enjoy. —Lillian Julow Gainesville, Florida

- 2-1/2 pounds unpeeled small red potatoes, cut into 1-inch slices
- 1 teaspoon salt
- 1 package (8 ounces) cream cheese, cubed
- 1 cup buttermilk

'I Wish I Had That Recipe...'

SOMETIMES something as simple as a well-prepared sauce or condiment helps make a meal outstanding, as a letter from Mary Hopfner of St. Cloud, Minnesota indicates.

"The tartar sauce at O'Hara's Brew Pub and Restaurant in our town is absolutely delicious. Could *Taste of Home* learn their secret?"

We contacted owner Tim O'Hara, who was happy to share the ingredients for their popular sauce. "It's a flavorful blend with a little zip from mustard and a dash of Worcestershire," he says.

Located at 33rd. Ave and 3rd St. in St. Cloud, O'Hara's serves lunch and dinner Monday through Saturday 10 a.m. to midnight and Sunday 10 a.m. to 10 p.m. (brunch from 10 a.m. to 2 p.m.).

For reservations, call 1-320/251-9877. To see the menu, visit www.oharasbrewpub.com.

O'Hara's Tartar Sauce

- 1 quart mayonnaise
- 2 cups sweet pickle relish
- 1/2 cup finely chopped onion
- 2 tablespoons lemon juice
- 1 teaspoon sugar
- 1/4 teaspoon white pepper
- 1/4 teaspoon ground mustard
- 1/8 teaspoon Worcestershire sauce

In a bowl, combine all of the ingredients. Cover and refrigerate until serving. **Yield:** about 1-1/2 quarts.

- 1 bunch green onions, chopped
- 1 teaspoon dried thyme
- 1 teaspoon dried tarragon
- 1/4 teaspoon pepper
- 3 tablespoons minced fresh parsley

Place potatoes in a saucepan and cover with water; add salt. Bring to a boil. Reduce heat; cover and cook for 15-20 minutes or until tender.

Meanwhile, in another saucepan, combine the cream cheese and buttermilk; cook and stir over medium heat until cheese is melted and mixture is smooth. Remove from the heat; add the onions, thyme, tarragon and pepper. Drain potatoes and place in a serving bowl; add cream sauce and toss to coat. Sprinkle with parsley. **Yield:** 6 servings.

Capture Summer's Flavors

PRESERVE the great taste of the season's bounty when you can Bread and Butter Pickles, Spicy Plum Sauce and Sweet 'n' Spicy Chutney (shown above, from top).

YOU CAN SAVOR the flavor of summer all year with these tried-and-true recipes. Fresh-from-the-garden preserves are wonderful to have on hand…and make delightful gifts from your kitchen.

— 🍵 🍵 🍵 —

Bread and Butter Pickles

(Pictured at left and on page 42)

My mom always made these crisp pickles when we were kids, and she gave me the recipe. They're pleasantly tart and so good. —Karen Owen
Rising Sun, Indiana

    4 pounds cucumbers, sliced
    8 small onions, sliced
1/2 cup canning salt
    5 cups sugar
    4 cups white vinegar
    2 tablespoons mustard seed
    2 teaspoons celery seed
1-1/2 teaspoons ground turmeric
1/2 teaspoon ground cloves

In a large container, combine the cucumbers, onions and salt. Cover with crushed ice; mix well. Let stand for 3 hours. Drain; rinse and drain again.

In a large kettle, combine the sugar, vinegar and seasonings; bring to a boil. Add cucumber mixture; return to a boil. Ladle hot mixture into hot jars, leaving 1/4-in. headspace. Adjust caps. Process for 15 minutes in a boiling-water bath. Remove jars to a wire rack to cool completely. **Yield:** 4 pints.

— 🍵 🍵 🍵 —

Spicy Plum Sauce

(Pictured at left and on page 42)

This flavorful fruit sauce is delicious with pork, poultry or egg rolls. The pepper gives it a little kick.
—Suzanne Veverka, White Cloud, Michigan

    4 pounds fresh plums, pitted and quartered
    1 small onion, quartered
    1 garlic clove, peeled
3-1/2 cups sugar
    2 cups cider vinegar
    1 tablespoon ground ginger
    1 tablespoon ground mustard
    1 teaspoon ground cinnamon
    1 teaspoon crushed red pepper flakes
1/2 teaspoon ground cloves

In a blender or food processor, process the plums, onion and garlic in batches until smooth. Transfer to a large saucepan or Dutch oven. Stir in the remaining ingredients. Bring to a boil. Reduce heat;

simmer for 60-90 minutes or until reduced by a third.

Ladle hot mixture into hot jars, leaving 1/4-in. headspace. Adjust caps. Process for 15 minutes in a boiling-water bath. Remove jars to wire racks to cool completely. **Yield:** 9 half-pints.

— 🍵 🍵 🍵 —

Sweet 'n' Spicy Chutney

(Pictured at far left)

I make my own spicy sauce sweetened by pears and peaches, with a hint of cinnamon and cloves. It's a wonderful complement to sausage or hot dogs.
—Betty Lasselle, Center Conway, New Hampshire

    8 cups chopped seeded peeled tomatoes
       (about 10 large)
    6 large onions, finely chopped
    5 medium green peppers, finely chopped
    2 large sweet red peppers, finely chopped
    2 hot red peppers, seeded and chopped*
    4 cinnamon sticks
    2 tablespoons whole cloves
    6 medium ripe pears, peeled and chopped
    6 medium ripe peaches, peeled and
       chopped
    4 cups sugar
    2 cups white vinegar
    2 tablespoons salt

In a large kettle, bring tomatoes to a boil. Add onions and peppers. Place cinnamon and cloves on a double thickness of cheesecloth; bring up corners of cloth and tie with string to form a bag. Add to kettle. Cook until vegetables are tender. Stir in pears, peaches, sugar, vinegar and salt. Cook until fruit is very tender.

Discard spice bag. Ladle hot mixture into hot jars. Adjust caps. Process for 20 minutes in a boiling-water bath. Remove jars to wire racks to cool completely. **Yield:** 12 pints.

*****Editor's Note:** When cutting or seeding hot peppers, use rubber or plastic gloves to protect your hands. Avoid touching your face.

Canning Questions?

Check out *www.homecanning.com* (Alltrista home canning products) to find the basics on the boiling-water bath canning method. Or contact your county Extension Service home economist for canning information.

German-Style Green Beans

(Pictured below)

My mother-in-law introduced me to this quick down-home dish almost 50 years ago when I was a new bride. The tender green beans are topped with diced bacon and a classic sweet-sour glaze. Guests always ask for the recipe. —Vivian Steers
Central Islip, New York

  1 **pound fresh green beans, cut into 2-inch pieces**
  3 **bacon strips, diced**
  1 **medium onion, quartered and sliced**
  2 **teaspoons cornstarch**
1/4 **teaspoon salt**
1/4 **teaspoon ground mustard**
1/2 **cup water**
  1 **tablespoon brown sugar**
  1 **tablespoon cider vinegar**

Place beans in a saucepan and cover with water; bring to a boil. Cook, uncovered, for 8-10 minutes or until crisp-tender; drain and set aside. In a skillet, cook bacon over medium heat until crisp. Remove to paper towels. Drain, reserving 1 tablespoon drippings. In the same skillet, saute onion in drippings until tender.

In a small bowl, combine the cornstarch, salt, mustard and water until smooth. Stir into onion. Bring to a boil; cook and stir for 1-2 minutes or until thickened. Stir in brown sugar and vinegar. Add the beans; heat through. Sprinkle with bacon. **Yield:** 3-4 servings.

Spinach Feta Turnovers

These quick and easy turnovers are a favorite with my wife, who says they are delicious and melt in your mouth. —David Baruch, Weston, Florida

☑ Uses less fat, sugar or salt. Includes Nutritional Analysis and Diabetic Exchanges.

  2 **eggs *or* 1/2 cup egg substitute**
  1 **package (10 ounces) frozen leaf spinach, thawed, squeezed dry and chopped**
3/4 **cup crumbled feta cheese**
  2 **garlic cloves, minced**
1/4 **teaspoon pepper**
  1 **tube (10 ounces) refrigerated pizza crust**

In a bowl, whisk eggs; set aside 1 tablespoon. Combine the spinach, feta cheese, garlic, pepper and remaining beaten eggs. Unroll pizza dough; roll into a 12-in. square. Cut into four 3-in. squares; top each square with about 1/3 cup spinach mixture. Fold into a triangle and pinch edges to seal. Cut slits in top; brush with reserved egg. Place on a greased baking sheet. Bake at 425° for 8-10 minutes or until golden brown. **Yield:** 4 servings.

Nutritional Analysis: One turnover (prepared with egg substitute) equals 296 calories, 9 g fat (4 g saturated fat), 25 mg cholesterol, 904 mg sodium, 39 g carbohydrate, 3 g fiber, 15 g protein. **Diabetic Exchanges:** 2 starch, 2 lean meat, 1 vegetable.

Freezer Salsa

Kids in the home economics class at the school where I teach were making this salsa, and it smelled so good that I got the recipe. It's a great way to use up garden produce. —Deanna Richter, Elmore, Minnesota

  8 **cups diced seeded peeled tomatoes (about 10 large)**
  2 **medium green peppers, chopped**
  2 **large onions, chopped**
  2 **jalapeno peppers, seeded and finely chopped***
3/4 **cup tomato paste**
2/3 **cup condensed tomato soup, undiluted**
1/2 **cup white vinegar**
  2 **tablespoons sugar**
  2 **tablespoons salt**
4-1/2 **teaspoons garlic powder**
  1 **tablespoon cayenne pepper**

In a Dutch oven or large saucepan, combine all ingredients. Bring to a boil. Reduce heat; simmer, uncovered, for 45 minutes, stirring often. Pour into small freezer containers. Cool to room temperature, about 1 hour. Cover and freeze for up to 3 months. Stir before serving. **Yield:** 10 cups.

*Editor's Note: When cutting or seeding hot peppers, use rubber or plastic gloves to protect your hands. Avoid touching your face.

— 🍵 🍵 🍵 —

Asparagus with Orange Sauce

Pretty enough for company, this asparagus dish has a delightful citrus flavor. —Lucy Meyring
Walden, Colorado

1-1/2 pounds fresh asparagus, trimmed
    1 garlic clove, quartered
    3 tablespoons butter *or* margarine
  1/4 cup orange juice
    2 tablespoons grated orange peel
  1/4 teaspoon salt
  1/8 teaspoon pepper
    1 medium navel orange, peeled and
       sectioned

Place asparagus and a small amount of water in a skillet; bring to a boil. Cover and cook for 6-8 minutes or until crisp-tender. Meanwhile, in another skillet, saute garlic in butter for 1 minute; discard garlic. Stir in the orange juice, peel, salt and pepper; heat through.

Drain asparagus and place in a serving dish. Drizzle with orange sauce; garnish with orange segments. **Yield:** 6 servings.

— 🍵 🍵 🍵 —

Walnut Cream Pasta

I take advantage of the local walnut supply by fixing this change-of-pace pasta. —Kim Gilliland
Simi Valley, California

    1 package (12 ounces) fettuccine
    2 garlic cloves, minced
    3 tablespoons butter *or* margarine
  1/2 cup chicken broth
  1/4 cup sour cream
  1/4 cup whipping cream
  1/4 teaspoon salt
  1/8 teaspoon pepper
    1 cup grated Parmesan cheese
    1 cup finely chopped walnuts

Cook the fettuccine according to package directions. Meanwhile, in a small saucepan, saute garlic in butter for 1 minute. Gradually stir in broth. Reduce heat. In a bowl, combine the sour cream, whipping cream, salt and pepper; stir into broth mixture (do not boil). Drain fettuccine and place in a large serving bowl. Add the cream sauce, Parmesan cheese and walnuts; toss to coat. **Yield:** 6 servings.

Seasoned Potato Wedges

(Pictured above)

These baked wedges, seasoned with Parmesan cheese and served with a sour cream dip, make a nice alternative to french fries or baked potatoes. They go great with grilled steak, but my family enjoys them as snacks, too. —Karen Trewin, Decorah, Iowa

  1/3 cup all-purpose flour
  1/3 cup grated Parmesan cheese
    1 teaspoon paprika
    3 large baking potatoes (about 2-3/4
       pounds)
  1/3 cup milk
  1/4 cup butter *or* margarine, melted, ***divided***
SOUR CREAM DIP:
    2 cups (16 ounces) sour cream
    8 bacon strips, cooked and crumbled
    2 tablespoons snipped chives
  1/2 teaspoon garlic powder

In a large resealable plastic bag, combine the flour, Parmesan cheese and paprika. Cut each potato into eight wedges; dip in milk. Place in the bag, a few at a time, and shake to coat. Place in a greased 15-in. x 10-in. x 1-in. baking pan. Drizzle with 2 tablespoons butter. Bake, uncovered, at 400° for 20 minutes.

Turn the wedges; drizzle with the remaining butter. Bake 20-25 minutes longer or until potatoes are tender and golden brown. In a bowl, combine the dip ingredients. Serve with warm potato wedges. **Yield:** 6-8 servings.

Nutty Onion Green Beans

(Pictured above)

I never liked green beans until I tried this recipe. The beans, onion and chopped pecans are coated in a delicious orange-mustard sauce. Now I make it for my family on a regular basis.   *—Donna Buckley*
Western Springs, Illinois

    1/2 **pound fresh green beans, cut in half**
      1 **small red onion, sliced and separated into rings**
    1/3 **cup chopped pecans**
      3 **tablespoons butter *or* margarine**
      2 **tablespoons brown sugar**
      2 **tablespoons orange juice**
      1 **tablespoon Dijon mustard**
    1/2 **teaspoon salt**

Place beans in a saucepan and cover with water; bring to a boil. Cook, uncovered, for 8-10 minutes or until crisp-tender; drain and set aside.

In a skillet, cook onion and pecans in butter until onion is tender. In a small bowl, combine the brown sugar, orange juice, mustard and salt; stir into the onion mixture. Cook 2-3 minutes longer or until sauce begins to thicken. Stir in beans; heat through. **Yield:** 3-4 servings.

— ❦ ❦ ❦ —

Spiced Pineapple

A serving of this nicely seasoned pineapple is delicious alongside lamb chops or ham. It's an easy no-fuss side dish that adds a little something extra to make a meal stand out.   *—Chris Nash, Berthoud, Colorado*

      2 **cans (one 20 ounces, one 8 ounces) pineapple chunks**

1-1/4 **cups sugar**
    1/2 **cup cider vinegar**
      1 **cinnamon stick (3 inches)**
      6 to 8 **whole cloves**
Dash salt

Drain pineapple, reserving 1 cup juice (discard remaining juice or save for another use). In a saucepan, combine the sugar, vinegar, cinnamon, cloves, salt and reserved pineapple juice. Bring to a boil. Reduce heat; cover and simmer for 10 minutes.

Discard the cinnamon and cloves. Add the pineapple. Return to a boil; cook and stir for 2-3 minutes. Serve warm with a slotted spoon. **Yield:** 4-6 servings.

— ❦ ❦ ❦ —

Gingered Cranberry Chutney

This colorful chutney is a super side dish or condiment served with pork, ham or poultry. It also makes a nice holiday gift. My family enjoys the pears, cranberries and tongue-tingling spices in this chutney.
—Marion Lowery, Medford, Oregon

☑ Uses less fat, sugar or salt. Includes Nutritional Analysis and Diabetic Exchanges.

      1 **cup packed brown sugar**
    1/3 **cup red wine vinegar *or* cider vinegar**
    1/2 **teaspoon ground ginger *or* 1/4 cup sliced fresh gingerroot**
    1/8 **teaspoon cayenne pepper**
    1/8 **teaspoon salt**
      2 **pounds fresh pears, peeled and diced**
      1 **package (12 ounces) fresh *or* frozen cranberries, thawed**
    1/2 **teaspoon ground cinnamon**

In a large saucepan, combine the brown sugar, vinegar, ginger, cayenne and salt. Bring to a boil. Add pears. Reduce heat; cover and simmer for 10 minutes or until pears are tender. Strain, reserving liquid. Return liquid to pan. Discard gingerroot; set pears aside.

Stir cranberries into pan. Cook over medium heat until berries pop, about 3 minutes, stirring occasionally. Strain berries, reserving liquid. Return liquid to pan; set berries aside. Bring liquid to a boil; cook, uncovered, until liquid is reduced to 1/2 cup. Stir in pears, cranberries and cinnamon. Serve warm or cold. Store in the refrigerator. **Yield:** 3 cups.

Nutritional Analysis: One serving (1/4 cup) equals 129 calories, trace fat (trace saturated fat), 0 cholesterol, 32 mg sodium, 33 g carbohydrate, 3 g fiber, trace protein. **Diabetic Exchange:** 2 fruit.

Ultimate Scalloped Potatoes

This tasty variation on traditional scalloped potatoes is dressed up with garlic, Swiss cheese and Parmesan cheese. —Glenda Malan, Lake Forest, California

   1 teaspoon butter *or* margarine, softened
   1 cup whipping cream
  1/3 cup milk
   1 teaspoon salt
  1/2 teaspoon pepper
   2 garlic cloves, crushed
   6 medium potatoes
   1 cup (4 ounces) shredded Swiss cheese
  1/4 cup shredded Parmesan cheese

Grease a shallow 1-1/2-qt. baking dish with the butter; set aside. In a saucepan, combine cream, milk, salt, pepper and garlic. Cook just until bubbles begin to form around sides of pan. Remove from the heat; cool for 10 minutes.

Peel and thinly slice the potatoes; pat dry with paper towels. Layer half of the potatoes in prepared baking dish; top with half of the cream mixture and half of the cheeses. Repeat layers. Bake, uncovered, at 350° for 55-65 minutes or until potatoes are tender. Let stand for 5-10 minutes before serving. **Yield:** 6 servings.

— 🥄 🥄 🥄 —

Shepherd's Bean Pie

This pie is chock-full of fresh veggies, ham and a handful of almonds in a creamy Swiss cheese sauce. Topped with mashed potatoes, it makes a hearty side dish.
—Karen Cleveland, Spring Valley, Minnesota

1-1/4 pounds fresh green beans, cut into 2-inch pieces
1-1/4 pounds fresh wax beans, cut into 2-inch pieces
   3 medium carrots, cut into 2-inch julienne strips
  1/2 small onion, chopped
   1 teaspoon butter *or* margarine
   1 can (10-3/4 ounces) condensed cream of chicken soup, undiluted
  1/2 cup whipping cream
  1/2 cup chicken broth
3-1/4 teaspoons dill weed, *divided*
   6 ounces cubed fully cooked ham
1-1/2 cups (6 ounces) shredded Swiss cheese, *divided*
  1/4 cup slivered almonds
   7 cups hot mashed potatoes (prepared with milk and butter)

Place beans and carrots in a saucepan and cover with water; bring to a boil. Cook, uncovered, for 8-10 minutes or until crisp-tender; drain and set aside. In a small skillet, saute onion in butter for 3-4 minutes or until tender.

In a large bowl, whisk soup, cream, broth and 3 teaspoons of dill. Add the beans, carrots and onion; gently stir to coat. Transfer to a greased shallow 3-qt. baking dish. Top with the ham, 1 cup cheese and almonds. Spread mashed potatoes over the top.

Cover and bake at 350° for 30 minutes. Uncover; sprinkle with remaining cheese and dill. Bake 5-10 minutes longer or until heated through and the cheese is melted. **Yield:** 12-15 servings.

— 🥄 🥄 🥄 —

Fruit-Stuffed Acorn Squash

(Pictured below and on page 42)

Holiday meals are even more festive when I serve colorful acorn squash with a fruity filling tucked inside each half. —Peggy West, Georgetown, Delaware

   2 medium acorn squash
  1/4 teaspoon salt
   2 cups chopped unpeeled tart apples
  3/4 cup fresh *or* frozen cranberries
  1/4 cup packed brown sugar
   2 tablespoons butter *or* margarine, melted
  1/4 teaspoon ground cinnamon
  1/8 teaspoon ground nutmeg

Cut squash in half; discard seeds. Place squash cut side down in an ungreased 13-in. x 9-in. x 2-in. baking dish. Add 1 in. of hot water to the pan. Bake, uncovered, at 350° for 30 minutes. Drain water from pan; turn squash cut side up. Sprinkle with salt. Combine the remaining ingredients; spoon into squash. Bake 40-50 minutes longer or until squash is tender. **Yield:** 4 servings.

'I Wish I Had That Recipe...'

"DURING our meal at the Claudia Sanders Dinner House in Shelbyville, Kentucky, we had Breaded Tomatoes that were wonderfully rich and sweet," write Melissa and Tom Wyant of Mt. Sterling, Kentucky.

"We would love to re-create this dish at home. Could *Taste of Home* get the recipe for us?"

Owners Cherry and Tom Settle were happy to share the recipe for their popular old-fashioned side dish, which is a favorite with customers.

Located at 3202 Shelbyville Rd. (U.S. Hwy. 60), Claudia Sanders Dinner House serves Tuesday through Sunday from 11 a.m. to 9 p.m. For more information, call 1-502/633-5600.

Breaded Tomatoes

    1/2 cup chopped onion
      2 tablespoons butter *or* margarine
      2 tablespoons all-purpose flour
      2 cans (14-1/2 ounces *each*) diced
         tomatoes, undrained
    1/2 cup sugar
    1/2 cup vegetable oil
      1 teaspoon salt
    1/4 teaspoon pepper
      3 slices bread, toasted and cut into
         1/4-inch cubes

In saucepan, saute onion in butter until tender; stir in flour until blended. Add the tomatoes, sugar, oil, salt and pepper. Bring to a boil; cook and stir for 2 minutes or until slightly thickened. Stir in toast cubes. **Yield:** 6 servings.

Better-Than-Butter Sauce

This savory sauce dresses up any vegetable in a flavorful way. It has great taste and little fat and calories.
—Wendy Bohman, Howards Grove, Wisconsin

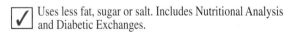
✓ Uses less fat, sugar or salt. Includes Nutritional Analysis and Diabetic Exchanges.

      2 teaspoons cornstarch
    1/2 teaspoon chicken bouillon granules
    1/4 teaspoon garlic powder
    1/4 teaspoon onion powder
    1/8 teaspoon dried tarragon
Dash pepper

    1/2 cup plus 2 tablespoons fat-free milk
      2 tablespoons water

In a saucepan, combine the first six ingredients. Stir in milk and water until smooth. Bring to a boil over medium heat; cook and stir for 1 minute or until thickened and bubbly. Serve over hot cooked vegetables. **Yield:** 10 tablespoons.
Nutritional Analysis: One serving (2 tablespoons) equals 14 calories, trace fat (trace saturated fat), 1 mg cholesterol, 110 mg sodium, 2 g carbohydrate, trace fiber, 1 g protein. **Diabetic Exchange:** Free food.

Creamy Hash Browns

No one will ever guess these saucy potatoes are a lighter side dish. They have good flavor and a nice zip.
—Shirley Kidd, New London, Minnesota

✓ Uses less fat, sugar or salt. Includes Nutritional Analysis and Diabetic Exchanges.

      1 package (28 ounces) frozen O'Brien hash
         brown potatoes
      1 cup (4 ounces) shredded reduced-fat
         cheddar cheese
      1 can (4 ounces) chopped green chilies
      1 can (10-3/4 ounces) reduced-fat
         reduced-sodium condensed cream of
         chicken soup, undiluted
      1 cup (8 ounces) reduced-fat sour cream

In a large bowl, combine the potatoes, cheese and chilies. Transfer to a 13-in. x 9-in. x 2-in. baking dish coated with nonstick cooking spray. Combine soup and sour cream; spread evenly over potato mixture. Bake, uncovered, at 350° for 50-55 minutes or until potatoes are tender. **Yield:** 10 servings.
Nutritional Analysis: One serving (1/2 cup) equals 140 calories, 4 g fat (3 g saturated fat), 16 mg cholesterol, 269 mg sodium, 19 g carbohydrate, 2 g fiber, 7 g protein. **Diabetic Exchanges:** 1 starch, 1 lean meat.

Favorite Beets

I make this recipe often. It dresses up beets with tangy flavor but lets their goodness come through. I prefer to eat mine warm, but my husband likes his cold.
—Lillian Castellini, Vineland, New Jersey

      5 medium fresh beets, peeled and sliced
      1 medium onion, sliced and separated into
         rings
    1/2 cup red wine vinegar *or* cider vinegar
      3 tablespoons vegetable oil

1/4 teaspoon salt
1/8 teaspoon pepper

Place beets in a large saucepan and cover with water. Bring to a boil. Reduce heat; cover and simmer for 10-12 minutes or until tender. Drain and place in a bowl; add onion. In a small bowl, combine the vinegar, oil, salt and pepper. Drizzle over beets and toss to coat. Serve immediately or refrigerate and serve chilled. **Yield:** 6 servings.

— ▼ ▼ ▼ —

Jalapeno Hush Puppies

Whenever we have a neighborhood fish fry, these hush puppies are part of the menu. They're crisp and golden with just a mild pepper flavor. —Mary Dixson
Decatur, Alabama

1 cup cornmeal
1/2 cup self-rising flour*
1 tablespoon sugar
1-1/2 teaspoons baking powder
1/2 teaspoon salt
1 egg, lightly beaten
1 cup milk
1/2 cup diced onion
1 tablespoon diced jalapeno pepper
Oil for deep-fat frying

In a bowl, combine the cornmeal, flour, sugar, baking powder and salt. Combine the egg, milk, onion and jalapeno; stir into dry ingredients just until moistened. In an electric skillet or deep-fat fryer, heat oil to 375°. Drop batter by tablespoonfuls into oil. Fry for 2 minutes or until golden brown, turning occasionally. Drain on paper towels. Serve warm. **Yield:** 3-1/2 to 4 dozen.

Editor's Note: As a substitute for 1/2 cup self-rising flour, place 3/4 teaspoon baking powder and 1/4 teaspoon salt in a 1/2-cup measuring cup. Add enough flour to measure 1/2 cup. When cutting or seeding hot peppers, use rubber or plastic gloves to protect your hands. Avoid touching your face.

— ▼ ▼ ▼ —

Green Bean Mushroom Pie

(Pictured at right)

Fresh green bean flavor stands out in this pretty lattice-topped pie. A flaky golden crust holds the savory bean, mushroom and cream cheese filling.
—Tara Walworth, Maple Park, Illinois

3 cups sliced fresh mushrooms
4 tablespoons butter *or* margarine, *divided*
2-1/2 cups chopped onions

6 cups cut fresh green beans (1-inch pieces)
2 teaspoons minced fresh thyme *or* 3/4 teaspoon dried thyme
1/2 teaspoon salt
1/4 teaspoon pepper
1 package (8 ounces) cream cheese, cubed
1/2 cup milk
CRUST:
2-1/2 cups all-purpose flour
2 teaspoons baking powder
1 teaspoon dill weed
1/4 teaspoon salt
1 cup cold butter *or* margarine
1 cup (8 ounces) sour cream
1 egg
1 tablespoon whipping cream

In a large skillet, saute mushrooms in 1 tablespoon butter until tender; drain and set aside. In the same skillet, saute onions and beans in remaining butter for 18-20 minutes or until beans are crisp-tender. Add the thyme, salt, pepper, cream cheese, milk and mushrooms. Cook and stir until the cheese is melted. Remove from the heat; set aside.

In a bowl, combine the flour, baking powder, dill and salt. Cut in butter until mixture resembles coarse crumbs. Stir in sour cream to form a soft dough. Divide dough in half. On a well-floured surface, roll out one portion to fit a deep-dish 9-in. pie plate; trim pastry even with edge.

Pour green bean mixture into crust. Roll out remaining pastry; make a lattice crust. Trim, seal and flute edge. In a small bowl, beat the egg and cream; brush over lattice top. Bake at 400° for 25-35 minutes or until golden brown. **Yield:** 8-10 servings.

Homemade Barbecue Sauces

FIRE UP the grill and add some sizzle to your steaks, ribs and chicken with these zesty from-scratch sauces.

— 🏆 🏆 🏆 —

Sweet 'n' Spicy BBQ Sauce

(Pictured below)

I developed this popular sauce to serve with a stromboli steak sandwich. It's also delicious on chicken and pork chops. —*Dorothy Ross, Jackson, Ohio*

- 2 cups packed brown sugar
- 2 cups ketchup
- 1 cup water
- 1 cup cider vinegar
- 1 cup finely chopped onion
- 1 can (8 ounces) tomato sauce
- 1 cup corn syrup
- 1 cup molasses
- 1 can (6 ounces) tomato paste
- 2 tablespoons Worcestershire sauce
- 1 tablespoon garlic-pepper blend
- 1 tablespoon liquid smoke, optional
- 1 tablespoon prepared mustard
- 1 teaspoon onion salt
- 1 teaspoon celery salt

In a large saucepan, combine all ingredients. Bring to a boil. Reduce heat; simmer, uncovered, for 15 minutes or until the flavors are blended. Remove from the heat; cool. **Yield:** about 2 quarts.

Jamaican Barbecue Sauce

(Pictured below)

This is a great sauce for ribs, whether grilled or baked in the oven. —*Lee Ann Odell, Boulder, Colorado*

- 1 bacon strip
- 1/2 cup chopped onion
- 2 tablespoons chopped green onion
- 1 tablespoon chopped jalapeno pepper*
- 1 cup ketchup
- 1/2 cup chicken broth
- 1/2 cup molasses
- 2 tablespoons cider vinegar
- 2 tablespoons lemon juice
- 1 tablespoon soy sauce
- 1 tablespoon Worcestershire sauce
- 1 tablespoon prepared mustard
- 1 tablespoon minced fresh thyme
- 1 teaspoon salt
- 1/2 teaspoon pepper
- 1/4 to 1/2 teaspoon ground cinnamon
- 1/4 to 1/2 teaspoon ground nutmeg

In a saucepan, cook bacon over medium heat until crisp. Discard bacon or save for another use. In the drippings, saute the onions and jalapeno until tender. Stir in the remaining ingredients. Bring to a boil. Remove from the heat; cool. **Yield:** 2 cups.

*Editor's Note: When cutting or seeding hot peppers, use rubber or plastic gloves to protect your hands. Avoid touching your face.

BRUSH ON Sweet 'n' Spicy BBQ Sauce, Jamaican Barbecue Sauce, Mustard Barbecue Sauce (shown below, from top).

Mustard Barbecue Sauce

(Pictured below left)

This isn't a thick sauce, but it coats meats very well. I use it on grilled barbecue ribs, and it's great with ham.
—*Cliff Mays, St. Albans, West Virginia*

        1 cup chicken *or* beef broth
        1 cup prepared mustard
    1/2 cup red wine vinegar *or* cider vinegar
    1/3 cup packed brown sugar
        3 tablespoons butter *or* margarine
        2 tablespoons Worcestershire sauce
        2 tablespoons tomato paste
        2 tablespoons molasses
        1 tablespoon garlic powder
        1 tablespoon onion powder
    1-1/2 teaspoons cayenne pepper
        1 teaspoon salt
    1/4 teaspoon pepper

In a large saucepan, combine all ingredients. Bring to a boil. Reduce heat; simmer, uncovered, for 15-20 minutes or until the flavors are blended. Remove from the heat; cool. **Yield:** 2-1/3 cups.

Bruce's Hot Barbecue Sauce

I've been making this barbecue sauce for 20 years and get requests for the recipe every summer. I'm always happy to share it. —*Bruce Fisher*
East Bloomfield, New York

        2 cans (15 ounces *each*) apricot halves, drained
        4 cups packed brown sugar
        4 cups cider vinegar
        1 can (29 ounces) tomato sauce
        2 cups ketchup
        1 cup maple syrup
        1 cup prepared mustard
    1/2 cup orange juice
    1/2 cup honey
    1/2 cup molasses
        3 tablespoons salt
        3 tablespoons chicken bouillon granules
        2 to 4 tablespoons crushed red pepper flakes
        2 tablespoons garlic powder
        2 tablespoons onion powder
        2 tablespoons Worcestershire sauce
        2 tablespoons soy sauce
        1 tablespoon pepper
        2 tablespoons liquid smoke, optional

In a blender or food processor, puree the apricots until smooth. Pour into a large soup kettle or Dutch oven; add the next 17 ingredients. Bring to a boil.

Reduce heat; simmer, uncovered, for 1 hour or until flavors are blended, stirring occasionally. Remove from the heat. Stir in liquid smoke if desired. Cool. Store in the refrigerator. **Yield:** 4 quarts.

Molasses Barbecue Sauce

This sauce has a bold molasses flavor with a hint of orange. It goes well with chicken, ribs and chops.
—*Sandi Pichon, Slidell, Louisiana*

        1 can (10-3/4 ounces) condensed tomato soup, undiluted
        1 can (8 ounces) tomato sauce
        1 cup molasses
    1/2 cup cider vinegar
    1/4 cup vegetable oil
        1 tablespoon dried minced onion
        1 tablespoon grated orange peel
        1 tablespoon Worcestershire sauce
        2 teaspoons ground mustard
    1-1/2 teaspoons paprika
        1 teaspoon seasoned salt
    1/2 teaspoon pepper
    1/4 teaspoon garlic powder

In a large saucepan, combine all ingredients. Bring to a boil. Reduce heat; simmer, uncovered, for 20 minutes or until the flavors are blended. Remove from the heat; cool. **Yield:** 3-1/2 cups.

Riverboat Barbecue Sauce

I gave my sauce this name because we live near the Ohio River and love to watch the riverboats go by. It is especially good on ribs or pork chops. —*Barb Loftin*
Florence, Kentucky

    1/2 cup maple syrup
    1/2 cup ketchup
    1/4 cup orange juice
        1 tablespoon dried minced onion
        1 tablespoon white vinegar
        1 tablespoon steak sauce
        1 teaspoon grated orange peel
        1 teaspoon prepared mustard
    1/2 teaspoon Worcestershire sauce
    1/4 teaspoon salt
    1/4 teaspoon pepper
    1/4 teaspoon hot pepper sauce
        3 whole cloves

In a small saucepan, combine all ingredients. Bring to a boil. Reduce heat; simmer, uncovered, for 15 minutes or until the flavors are blended. Remove from heat. Discard cloves. Cool. **Yield:** 1-1/3 cups.

Main Dishes

Whether your family is partial to pork, beef, poultry or fish, these hearty main dishes are sure to satisfy their taste buds.

SATISFYING SELECTIONS. Clockwise from upper left: Mixed Grill Kabobs (p. 78), Cheesy Crab Enchiladas (p. 81), Turkey Breast Florentine (p. 70), Green Bean Quiche (p. 69) and Catfish with Shrimp Salsa (p. 67).

turn pink and vegetables are crisp-tender. Add broth. Cook 1 minute longer or until heated through. Serve over rice. **Yield:** 4 servings.

Nutritional Analysis: One 1-cup serving (calculated without rice) equals 205 calories, 8 g fat (4 g saturated fat), 188 mg cholesterol, 563 mg sodium, 8 g carbohydrate, 2 g fiber, 25 g protein. **Diabetic Exchanges:** 3 lean meat, 1 vegetable.

Grilled Cornish Hens

I like experimenting with different foods and adapting them to my own tastes. These hens are one of my specialties, an entree I concocted by combining a few different recipes. The moist meat has a pleasant grilled flavor that's accented with cloves and ginger.
—*David Baruch, Weston, Florida*

1/4 cup butter *or* margarine, softened
2 green onions, finely chopped
2 tablespoons minced fresh parsley
1-1/2 teaspoons ground ginger *or* 2 tablespoons grated fresh gingerroot
3 garlic cloves, minced
1 teaspoon salt, *divided*
1/2 teaspoon pepper, *divided*
4 Cornish game hens (20 ounces *each*)

Coat grill rack with nonstick cooking spray before starting the grill. In a small bowl, combine the butter, onions, parsley, ginger, garlic, 1/2 teaspoon of salt and 1/4 teaspoon pepper. Rub mixture under the skin and over the top of each game hen. Sprinkle remaining salt and pepper inside the hen cavities.

Grill hens, uncovered, breast side up over medium heat for 25 minutes. Turn breast side down. Cover and grill 25-35 minutes longer or until a meat thermometer reads 180° and the meat juices run clear. **Yield:** 4 servings.

Garlic Shrimp Stir-Fry

(Pictured above)

This entree tastes wonderful and is pretty enough to serve to company. Most of the preparation can be done in advance. Tender shrimp, colorful sweet peppers and crunchy snow peas give it a variety of interesting textures and flavors.
—*Irene Lalevee*
River Vale, New Jersey

✓ Uses less fat, sugar or salt. Includes Nutritional Analysis and Diabetic Exchanges.

4 garlic cloves, minced
2 tablespoons butter *or* stick margarine
1 pound uncooked medium shrimp, peeled and deveined
6 ounces fresh snow peas
1/2 cup julienned sweet red pepper
1/2 cup julienned sweet yellow pepper
3 tablespoons minced fresh basil *or* 1 tablespoon dried basil
3 tablespoons minced fresh parsley
1/2 teaspoon salt
1/4 teaspoon pepper
1/4 cup chicken broth
Hot cooked rice

In a large skillet, saute garlic in butter until tender. Add the shrimp, peas, peppers, basil, parsley, salt and pepper. Stir-fry for 5 minutes or until shrimp

Vidalia Onion Tomato Pizza

For me, pizza is a staple of life. I worked at a pizza restaurant after college, and I've been trying ever since to re-create the wonderful pizza crust we served. This version, which my family loves, comes pretty close.
—*Herman Temple, Shawnee, Kansas*

1 package (1/4 ounce) active dry yeast
1/2 teaspoon sugar
1-1/2 cups warm water (110° to 115°)
3 tablespoons olive *or* vegetable oil, *divided*
1/2 teaspoon salt
4-1/3 cups all-purpose flour

2 cans (15 ounces *each*) pizza sauce, *divided*
2 large Vidalia *or* other sweet onions, thinly sliced
4 medium tomatoes, thinly sliced
2-1/2 cups (10 ounces) shredded mozzarella cheese
1-1/2 cups (6 ounces) shredded cheddar cheese

In a bowl, dissolve yeast and sugar in warm water. Add 2 tablespoons oil, salt and enough flour to form a soft dough. Turn onto a floured surface; knead until smooth and elastic, about 6-8 minutes. Place in a greased bowl, turning once to grease top. Cover and let rise in a warm place until doubled, about 1 hour.

Punch dough down. Turn onto a lightly floured surface; divide in half. Press dough onto the bottom and 1 in. up the sides of two greased 14-in. pizza pans. Spread 3/4 cup pizza sauce over each. Bake at 450° for 5 minutes. Meanwhile, in a skillet, saute onions in remaining oil until tender.

Arrange tomato slices over pizzas. Combine cheeses; sprinkle over tomatoes. Top with onions. Bake 10-15 minutes longer or until cheese is melted. Warm remaining pizza sauce; serve with pizza. **Yield:** 2 pizzas (8 slices each).

— ▼ ▼ ▼ —

Sweet 'n' Sour Halibut

(Pictured at right)

We live on the West Coast and catch a lot of halibut off our fishing boat. My family has always loved fresh fish, and this recipe is a favorite. The cubed halibut is cooked in a sweet-and-sour sauce along with pineapple, green pepper and tomatoes—yum!
—Willa Gilio, Cayucos, California

1 cup packed brown sugar
1 cup cider vinegar
1 cup apricot nectar
1/2 cup ketchup
1 teaspoon Worcestershire sauce
1 cup cubed green pepper
3 tablespoons all-purpose flour
4 tablespoons cold water, *divided*
1 tablespoon soy sauce
Dash salt and pepper
1-1/2 pounds halibut steaks, cut into 1-inch pieces
1 tablespoon cornstarch
2 medium tomatoes, seeded and cubed
2 cups pineapple chunks
Hot cooked linguine *or* rice

In a large saucepan, combine the first five ingredients; bring to a boil. Reduce heat; simmer, uncov-ered, for 30 minutes. Add the green pepper; cook 5 minutes longer; set aside.

In a bowl, combine the flour, 3 tablespoons water, soy sauce, salt and pepper. Add halibut; toss gently to coat. Transfer to a broiler pan. Broil 4 in. from the heat for 5-6 minutes or until fish flakes easily with a fork. Set aside and keep warm.

Combine cornstarch and remaining water until smooth; stir into green pepper mixture. Bring to a boil; cook and stir for 2 minutes or until thickened. Reduce heat to medium; add tomatoes and pineap-ple. Cook and stir for 4-5 minutes or until heated through. Serve with halibut over linguine or rice. **Yield:** 6 servings.

Sizes of Shrimp

Shrimp are sold in a variety of sizes. The most common sizes are jumbo shrimp, which average 21 to 25 per pound; large shrimp, 31 to 35 per pound; medium shrimp, 43 to 50 per pound; and tiny shrimp, which average more than 70 per pound.

Shrimp have a high water content and will re-duce from 1 pound to about 3/4 of a pound or less after cooking.

String Bean Chicken Skillet

(Pictured below)

I started to prepare a chicken stir-fry one day and discovered I was out of frozen snow peas. So I tossed in green beans instead with a few leftover wax beans for color. I've been making the recipe this way ever since.
—*Priscilla Gilbert*
Indian Harbour Beach, Florida

    1/2 pound fresh green beans, cut into 2-inch
        pieces
    1/2 pound fresh wax beans, cut into 2-inch
        pieces
      3 boneless skinless chicken breast halves
      2 tablespoons vegetable oil
      2 tablespoons plus 1-1/2 teaspoons corn
        starch
      3 tablespoons soy sauce
      1 can (8 ounces) pineapple chunks
      1 medium sweet red pepper, julienned
      1 small onion, thinly sliced
    1/4 teaspoon salt
    1/4 teaspoon ground ginger
Hot cooked rice

Place beans in a saucepan and cover with water; bring to a boil. Cook, uncovered, for 3 minutes; drain and set aside. Flatten chicken to 1/4-in. thickness; cut into 1/2-in. strips. In a large skillet, stir-fry chicken in oil for 2-4 minutes or until no longer pink. Remove with a slotted spoon.

In a small bowl, combine cornstarch and soy sauce until smooth. Drain the pineapple, reserving juice; set pineapple aside. Stir the juice into the soy sauce mixture; set aside.

In the skillet, stir-fry red pepper and onion for 5 minutes. Add the chicken, beans, pineapple, salt and ginger. Gradually stir in the soy sauce mixture. Bring to a boil; cook and stir for 2 minutes or until thickened. Serve with rice. **Yield:** 6 servings.

Country-Fried Venison

This is our favorite way to fix venison tenderloin. The marinade and coating eliminate the wild flavor in these tender mouth-watering steaks. —*Sandra Robinson*
Fair Grove, Missouri

      2 pounds venison tenderloin
    1/2 cup soy sauce
    1/2 cup Worcestershire sauce
    1/2 cup butter *or* margarine, melted
    1/2 to 2 teaspoons liquid smoke, optional
      1 egg, beaten
      1 cup buttermilk
      1 cup all-purpose flour
      2 teaspoons seasoned salt
      2 teaspoons vegetable oil

Cut tenderloin into eight steaks. In a large resealable plastic bag, combine the soy sauce, Worcestershire sauce, butter and liquid smoke if desired. Add steaks; seal bag and turn to coat. Refrigerate for 2 hours.

In a shallow bowl, combine egg and buttermilk. In another bowl, combine flour and seasoned salt. Drain steaks, discarding marinade. Dip steaks in buttermilk mixture, then roll in flour mixture. In a large skillet over medium-high heat, cook steaks in oil for 12-14 minutes, turning occasionally, or until a meat thermometer reads 160°. **Yield:** 8 servings.

—— 🎺 🎺 🎺 ——

Cheddar Salmon Quiche

My mother-in-law shared the recipe for this cheesy salmon dish. It dresses up convenient canned salmon in a very satisfying way. We enjoy this pretty quiche frequently during Lent. —*Jane Horn, Bellevue, Ohio*

      1 cup all-purpose flour
    1/4 teaspoon salt
      3 tablespoons cold butter *or* margarine
      3 tablespoons shortening
    1/4 cup milk
FILLING:
      1 can (14-3/4 ounces) salmon, drained,
        bones and skin removed
      1 cup (4 ounces) shredded cheddar cheese
    1/4 cup chopped green pepper
    1/4 cup chopped onion
      1 tablespoon all-purpose flour
    1/2 teaspoon salt
    1/8 teaspoon pepper
      3 eggs, beaten
1-1/4 cups milk

In a bowl, combine the flour and salt; cut in butter and shortening until crumbly. Stir in milk. On a floured surface, roll dough into a 10-in. circle.

Transfer to an ungreased 9-in. pie plate or quiche dish. Trim and flute edges. Bake at 350° for 10 minutes.

In a bowl, combine salmon, cheese, green pepper, onion, flour, salt and pepper; spoon into crust. Combine the eggs and milk; pour over salmon mixture. Bake for 50-55 minutes or until a knife inserted near the center comes out clean. Let stand for 10 minutes before cutting. **Yield:** 6 servings.

— 🍷 🍷 🍷 —

Venison and Beans

When I was first married, I had no idea how to cook game. I got this recipe from a friend, and now my husband thinks we should have it every night!
—Jill Kerr, York, Pennsylvania

1-1/2 **pounds ground venison**
   1 **medium onion, chopped**
   1 **can (16 ounces) pork and beans, undrained**
   1 **can (16 ounces) kidney beans, rinsed and drained**
   1 **can (15-1/2 ounces) great northern beans, rinsed and drained**
   1 **cup ketchup**
 1/3 **cup packed brown sugar**
   6 **bacon strips, cooked and crumbled**
   2 **tablespoons white vinegar**
   1 **tablespoon Worcestershire sauce**
 1/2 **teaspoon salt**
 1/4 **teaspoon ground mustard**

In a large skillet, cook venison and onion over medium heat until meat is no longer pink; drain. Stir in remaining ingredients. Transfer to a 2-qt. baking dish. Cover and bake at 350° for 35-40 minutes or until heated through. **Yield:** 8 servings.

— 🍷 🍷 🍷 —

Catfish with Shrimp Salsa

(Pictured above right and on page 62)

Catfish are plentiful in the freshwater lake where I live. This is one of my favorite recipes. Cajun seasoning, cumin and coriander spice up the fillets nicely. The colorful corn and shrimp salsa makes an excellent accompaniment. —Denise Wall
Ridgeway, South Carolina

   2 **tablespoons Cajun *or* blackened seasoning**
 1/2 **teaspoon ground cumin**
 1/2 **teaspoon ground coriander**
   4 **catfish fillets (6 ounces *each*)**
   2 **to 3 tablespoons vegetable oil**

SALSA:
   1 **medium green pepper, diced**
 3/4 **cup diced onion**
   1 **celery rib, diced**
   1 **jalapeno pepper, seeded and chopped***
   2 **garlic cloves, minced**
   1 **tablespoon butter *or* margarine**
1-1/2 **cups fresh *or* frozen corn**
   3 **plum tomatoes, seeded and chopped**
   2 **packages (5 ounces *each*) frozen cooked salad shrimp, thawed**
 1/2 **teaspoon Cajun *or* blackened seasoning**
Dash hot pepper sauce

Combine the Cajun seasoning, cumin and coriander; rub over catfish fillets. In a large skillet, fry fillets in oil over medium-high heat for 4-5 minutes on each side or until fish flakes easily with a fork. Remove and keep warm.

In the same skillet, saute the green pepper, onion, celery, jalapeno and garlic in butter until tender. Add the corn, tomatoes and shrimp; cook and stir for 4-5 minutes or until corn is tender. Stir in Cajun seasoning and hot pepper sauce. Serve with catfish. **Yield:** 4 servings.

*****Editor's Note:** When cutting or seeding hot peppers, use rubber or plastic gloves to protect your hands. Avoid touching your face.

In a saucepan, melt the remaining butter; stir in flour until smooth. Combine milk and reserved cooking liquid; gradually add to the saucepan. Add salt and remaining pepper. Bring to a boil; cook and stir for 2 minutes or until thickened. Remove from the heat; stir in cream and 1/4 cup Parmesan cheese. Stir 3/4 cup white sauce into the seafood mixture.

Spread 1/2 cup white sauce in a greased 13-in. x 9-in. x 2-in. baking dish. Top with three noodles; spread with half of the seafood mixture and 1-1/4 cups sauce. Repeat layers. Top with remaining noodles, sauce and Parmesan. Bake, uncovered, at 350° for 35-40 minutes or until golden brown. Let stand for 15 minutes before cutting. **Yield:** 12 servings.

Seafood Lasagna

(Pictured above)

This rich satisfying dish, adapted from a recipe given to me by a friend, is my husband's favorite. I usually serve it on his birthday. It's loaded with scallops, shrimp and crab in a creamy sauce. I consider this the "crown jewel" in my repertoire of recipes.
—Elena Hansen, Ruidoso, New Mexico

> 1 **green onion, finely chopped**
> 2 **tablespoons vegetable oil**
> 2 **tablespoons plus 1/2 cup butter *or* margarine, *divided***
> 1/2 **cup chicken broth**
> 1 **bottle (8 ounces) clam juice**
> 1 **pound bay scallops**
> 1 **pound uncooked small shrimp, peeled and deveined**
> 1 **package (8 ounces) imitation crabmeat, chopped**
> 1/4 **teaspoon white pepper, *divided***
> 1/2 **cup all-purpose flour**
> 1-1/2 **cups milk**
> 1/2 **teaspoon salt**
> 1 **cup whipping cream**
> 1/2 **cup shredded Parmesan cheese, *divided***
> 9 **lasagna noodles, cooked and drained**

In a large skillet, saute onion in oil and 2 tablespoons butter until tender. Stir in broth and clam juice; bring to a boil. Add the scallops, shrimp, crab and 1/8 teaspoon pepper; return to a boil. Reduce heat; simmer, uncovered, for 4-5 minutes or until shrimp turn pink and scallops are firm and opaque, stirring gently. Drain, reserving cooking liquid; set seafood mixture aside.

Green Chili Beef Burritos

Recipes that are leaner in fat and calories—like the one for these delicious burritos—helped me lose 30 pounds. The meat is so tender. —*Shirley Davidson Thornton, Colorado*

✓ Uses less fat, sugar or salt. Includes Nutritional Analysis and Diabetic Exchanges.

> 2 **boneless beef top sirloin roasts (3 pounds *each*)**
> 4 **cans (4 ounces *each*) chopped green chilies**
> 1 **medium onion, chopped**
> 3 **medium jalapeno peppers, seeded and chopped***
> 3 **garlic cloves, sliced**
> 3 **teaspoons chili powder**
> 1-1/2 **teaspoons ground cumin**
> 1 **teaspoon salt-free seasoning blend, optional**
> 1 **cup reduced-sodium beef broth**
> 24 **fat-free flour tortillas (7 inches), warmed**
> **Sliced tomatoes, shredded lettuce and reduced-fat cheddar cheese, optional**

Trim fat from roasts; cut meat into large chunks. Place in a 5-qt. slow cooker. Top with chilies, onion, jalapenos, garlic, chili powder, cumin and seasoning blend. Pour broth over all. Cover and cook on low for 8-9 hours.

Remove beef; cool slightly. Shred with two forks. Cool cooking liquid slightly; skim fat. In a blender, cover and process cooking liquid in small batches until smooth. Return liquid and beef to slow cooker; heat through. Place 1/3 cup beef mixture on each tortilla. Top with lettuce, tomatoes and cheese if desired. Fold in ends and sides. **Yield:** 2 dozen. **Nutritional Analysis:** One burrito (calculated without toppings) equals 362 calories, 9 g fat (3 g saturated fat), 109 mg cholesterol, 384 mg sodium, 27 g carbohydrate, 2 g fiber, 39 g protein. **Diabetic Exchanges:** 4-1/2 lean meat, 1-1/2 starch.

Editor's Note: When cutting or seeding hot peppers, use rubber or plastic gloves to protect your hands. Avoid touching your face.

—— 🦃 🦃 🦃 ——

Green Bean Quiche

(Pictured on page 62)

This colorful quiche is perfect for brunch or lunch. Each hearty slice is filled with green beans and mushrooms and topped with tomato and cheddar cheese.
—Lee Campbell, Bartow, Florida

  1 package (10 ounces) frozen cut green beans
1/2 cup water
1/2 cup chopped onion
  2 tablespoons butter *or* margarine
1/2 cup sliced fresh mushrooms
1/4 cup diced green pepper
1/2 cup mayonnaise*
1/4 cup sour cream
1/4 teaspoon salt
1/4 cup crushed saltines (about 8 crackers)
  6 eggs, beaten
  1 medium tomato, seeded and chopped
3/4 cup shredded sharp cheddar cheese

Place beans in a saucepan and cover with water; bring to a boil. Reduce heat. Cover and simmer for 6-8 minutes or until crisp-tender; drain and set aside. In a small skillet, saute onion in butter until tender. Add mushrooms and green pepper; saute until tender.

In a large bowl, combine the mayonnaise, sour cream and salt; stir in the beans, mushroom mixture and cracker crumbs. Gradually stir in eggs. Pour into a greased deep-dish 9-in. pie plate. Sprinkle with tomato and cheese. Bake at 350° for 25-30 minutes or until a knife inserted near the center comes out clean. **Yield:** 6 servings.

Editor's Note: Reduced-fat or fat-free mayonnaise may not be substituted for regular mayonnaise in this recipe.

—— 🦃 🦃 🦃 ——

Herbed Seafood Skewers

(Pictured at right)

I've made these well-seasoned kabobs many times, even over an open fire. They attracted the neighboring campers. *—Sharon Downs, Williston, Vermont*

☑ Uses less fat, sugar or salt. Includes Nutritional Analysis and Diabetic Exchanges

1/4 **cup canola oil**
1/4 **cup lemon juice**
  1 **garlic clove, minced**
  1 **teaspoon dried oregano**
  1 **teaspoon chicken bouillon granules**
1/2 **teaspoon dried basil**
1/2 **teaspoon salt**
3/4 **pound uncooked large shrimp, peeled and deveined**
1/2 **pound sea scallops**
  1 *each* **large green and sweet red pepper, cut into 1-inch pieces**
  1 **small zucchini, cut into 1/4-inch slices**
  1 **small yellow summer squash, cut into 1/4-inch slices**
Hot cooked rice, optional

In a bowl, combine the first seven ingredients. Divide marinade between two large resealable plastic bags. Add the shrimp and scallops to one; place vegetables in the other bag. Seal and turn to coat; refrigerate for 3-4 hours.

Drain shrimp and scallops; discard marinade. Drain vegetables, reserving marinade for basting. On eight metal or soaked wooden skewers, alternate the shrimp, scallops, peppers and squash. Grill, uncovered, over medium heat for 6 minutes or until shrimp turn pink, turning once and basting occasionally. Serve over rice if desired. **Yield:** 4 servings.

Nutritional Analysis: One serving (2 kabobs, calculated without rice) equals 217 calories, 10 g fat (1 g saturated fat), 120 mg cholesterol, 684 mg sodium, 10 g carbohydrate, 3 g fiber, 22 g protein. **Diabetic Exchanges:** 3 lean meat, 2 vegetable.

until blended. Gradually stir in milk. Bring to a boil; cook and stir for 2 minutes or until thickened. Remove from the heat.

Refrigerate 1/2 cup sauce. Add the spinach, mushrooms and crumbled bacon to the remaining sauce; spread over turkey breast. Starting at a short end, roll up and tuck in ends; tie with kitchen string. Place on a rack in a greased roasting pan. Brush with butter. Cover loosely with foil.

Bake at 350° for 1 hour. Remove foil. Cut remaining bacon strips in half; place over the turkey. Bake 25-35 minutes longer or until a meat thermometer reads 170°. Discard string. Let turkey stand for 10 minutes before slicing. Meanwhile, heat the reserved sauce; stir in cheese until melted. Serve with the turkey. **Yield:** 6-8 servings.

Leek Tart

This tart has a flaky pastry crust and tasty filling of leeks, bacon, eggs and cream. Satisfying and delicious, it makes a nice brunch dish, but you can serve it for any meal. —Anneliese Deising, Plymouth, Michigan

- 2 **cups all-purpose flour**
- 1/4 **teaspoon salt**
- 1/4 **teaspoon sugar**
- 1/2 **cup cold butter** *or* **margarine**
- 9 **to 11 tablespoons cold water**

FILLING:

- 1 **pound thick-sliced bacon, diced**
- 3-1/2 **pounds leeks (white portion only), sliced**
- 2 **tablespoons all-purpose flour**
- 4 **eggs**
- 1 **cup half-and-half cream**
- 1/2 **teaspoon salt**
- 1/4 **teaspoon pepper**
- 1/8 **teaspoon ground nutmeg**

In a bowl, combine the flour, salt and sugar; cut in butter until crumbly. Gradually add water, tossing with a fork until a ball forms. Cover and refrigerate for 30 minutes.

In a large skillet, cook bacon over medium heat until crisp. Using a slotted spoon, remove to paper towels. Drain, reserving 2 tablespoons of drippings. Saute leeks in drippings until tender; stir in the bacon. Stir in flour until blended; set aside.

On a floured surface, roll dough to 1/8-in. thickness. Transfer to an ungreased 10-in. springform pan, draping pastry edge over rim of pan. Spoon leek mixture into crust. Trim pastry to 1/4 in. above filling; press pastry against sides of pan. Bake at 400° for 10 minutes.

Meanwhile, in a bowl, beat the eggs, cream, salt, pepper and nutmeg. Pour over leek mixture. Bake

Turkey Breast Florentine

(Pictured above and on page 62)

A lovely dish for guests, this spinach-stuffed turkey breast looks beautiful when you slice it for serving. I've also spooned the filling into a pocket slit in a boneless center-cut pork roast with delicious results. —Shirley Goehring, Lodi, California

- 1 **turkey breast half (3 to 4 pounds), bone removed**
- 5 **bacon strips**
- 3/4 **cup chopped onion**
- 3 **tablespoons all-purpose flour**
- 3/4 **teaspoon dried tarragon**
- 1/2 **teaspoon salt**
- 1/4 **teaspoon pepper**
- 1-1/2 **cups milk**
- 1 **package (10 ounces) frozen chopped spinach, thawed and squeezed dry**
- 1 **jar (4-1/2 ounces) sliced mushrooms, drained**
- 1 **tablespoon butter** *or* **margarine, melted**
- 1/3 **cup cubed process cheese (Velveeta)**

Cut a lengthwise slit in turkey breast to within 1/2 in. of opposite side; open meat so it lies flat. Cover with plastic wrap and flatten to 1/2-in. thickness. Remove plastic wrap; set aside.

In a skillet, cook two bacon strips until crisp. Drain, reserving 2 tablespoons drippings. Crumble bacon; set aside. In the drippings, saute onion until tender. Stir in the flour, tarragon, salt and pepper

20-25 minutes longer or until a knife inserted near the center comes out clean. Serve warm. **Yield:** 10-12 servings.

Pork Chops with Zucchini Dressing

When my mom was in her 90s, I copied all her recipes and made a cookbook that I sent as a Christmas gift to my children, nieces and nephews. These tender pork chops were always one of my favorites.
—Marguery Saxe, Wilbraham, Massachusetts

  1 celery rib, chopped
  1 small onion, chopped
  2 tablespoons butter *or* margarine
  3 cups chopped zucchini
  3 cups bread cubes, toasted
  1 egg white, lightly beaten
  2 tablespoons minced fresh parsley *or* 2
     teaspoons dried parsley flakes
  1 teaspoon poultry seasoning
  6 bone-in pork loin chops (1/2 inch thick
     and about 2 pounds)
  2 teaspoons chicken bouillon granules
  2 tablespoons hot water

In a skillet, saute celery and onion in butter until tender. In a bowl, combine the zucchini, bread cubes, egg white, parsley and poultry seasoning. Stir in celery mixture. Cover and refrigerate.

Arrange pork chops in a greased 13-in. x 9-in. x 2-in. baking dish. Dissolve bouillon in hot water; drizzle over chops. Bake, uncovered, at 325° for 30 minutes. Top with zucchini dressing. Cover and bake 20 minutes longer or until meat juices run clear. **Yield:** 6 servings.

Sweet-and-Sour Chicken

(Pictured at right)

When a restricted diet became a necessity for me, I didn't want to give up my sweet-and-sour chicken, so I revamped my old recipe. It's still a satisfying main dish. —*Eva Marie Collins, Bolivar, Missouri*

☑ Uses less fat, sugar or salt. Includes Nutritional Analysis and Diabetic Exchanges.

1/2 pound boneless skinless chicken breasts,
     cut into 1/2-inch strips
  1 medium carrot, sliced
1/4 cup chopped onion
1-1/2 teaspoons canola oil
  1 small zucchini, sliced
  1 cup fresh *or* frozen snow peas, thawed
1/2 medium sweet red *or* green pepper, cut
     into strips
  3 tablespoons sugar
  2 tablespoons cornstarch
1/8 teaspoon pepper
  1 can (6 ounces) pineapple juice
  3 tablespoons ketchup
  2 tablespoons lemon juice
  2 tablespoons reduced-sodium soy sauce
  1 can (8 ounces) unsweetened pineapple
     chunks, drained
  2 cups hot cooked rice

In a nonstick skillet, cook the chicken, carrot and onion in oil until chicken is browned and carrot is crisp-tender. Add the zucchini, peas and red pepper; cook and stir until crisp-tender.

In a bowl, combine the sugar, cornstarch, pepper and pineapple juice until smooth. Stir in the ketchup, lemon juice and soy sauce. Pour over chicken and vegetables. Add pineapple. Bring to a boil; cook and stir for 2 minutes or until thickened. Serve over rice. **Yield:** 4 servings.

Nutritional Analysis: One serving (1 cup chicken mixture with 1/2 cup rice) equals 307 calories, 3 g fat (trace saturated fat), 33 mg cholesterol, 400 mg sodium, 52 g carbohydrate, 4 g fiber, 18 g protein. **Diabetic Exchanges:** 2 starch, 2 very lean meat, 1 fruit, 1 vegetable.

Pineapple-Glazed Fish

(Pictured below)

My son and our friends often spend a day fishing. This is one of my favorite ways to serve their catch.
—*JoAnn McGuane, Spring, Texas*

✓ Uses less fat, sugar or salt. Includes Nutritional Analysis and Diabetic Exchanges.

> 1 can (8 ounces) unsweetened sliced pineapple
> 1-1/2 teaspoons cornstarch
> 1/4 teaspoon ground ginger
> 2 tablespoons honey
> 2 tablespoons reduced-sodium soy sauce
> 1 tablespoon lemon juice
> 4 orange roughy *or* haddock fillets (6 ounces *each*)

Drain pineapple, reserving juice; set pineapple aside. In a small saucepan, combine the cornstarch and ginger; stir in pineapple juice until blended. Add the honey and soy sauce. Bring to a boil; cook and stir for 1-2 minutes or until thickened. Stir in the lemon juice. Pour half into a small bowl for serving.

Coat grill rack with nonstick cooking spray before starting the grill. Grill fillets, uncovered, over medium heat for 4-5 minutes. Spoon some of the glaze over fillets. Cook 4-5 minutes longer or until fish flakes easily with a fork. Meanwhile, grill pineapple slices for 4-6 minutes or until heated through, basting frequently with glaze and turning once. Serve fish with pineapple and reserved glaze. **Yield:** 4 servings.

Nutritional Analysis: One serving equals 190 calories, 1 g fat (trace saturated fat), 34 mg cholesterol, 415 mg sodium, 19 g carbohydrate, 1 g fiber, 26 g protein. **Diabetic Exchanges:** 4 very lean meat, 1 fruit.

Sausage-Peach Puff Pancake

My husband—who is not a big sweets eater—often requests this hearty dish. Peaches add a touch of fruity flavor to the savory sausage. It's a nice combination.
—*Nicole Clayton, Las Vegas, Nevada*

> 1/2 cup all-purpose flour
> 1 tablespoon sugar
> 1/8 teaspoon salt
> 2 eggs, beaten
> 1/2 cup milk
> 1 tablespoon butter *or* margarine
> **FILLING:**
> 8 to 10 pork sausage links, halved
> 1 can (16 ounces) sliced peaches, drained
> 1/3 cup pancake syrup
> **Dash ground nutmeg**

In a mixing bowl, combine the flour, sugar and salt. Whisk in eggs and milk until smooth. Place the butter in a 9-in. pie plate. Heat at 400° for 2-3 minutes or until melted. Pour batter into hot plate. Bake for 10-15 minutes or until edges are golden brown.

Meanwhile, in a skillet, cook the sausage over medium heat until no longer pink; drain. Stir in the peaches, syrup and nutmeg. Bring to a boil. Reduce heat; simmer, uncovered, for 7-10 minutes or until sausage and peaches are coated with syrup. Spoon into pancake. Serve immediately. **Yield:** 4-6 servings.

———— 🍴 🍴 🍴 ————

Sesame Pork Tenderloin

Pork tenderloin gets dressed up for company in this easy-to-fix yet special main dish. The meat is tender and flavorful. Sesame seeds and ginger go together so well. —*Sue Mackey, Galesburg, Illinois*

✓ Uses less fat, sugar or salt. Includes Nutritional Analysis and Diabetic Exchanges.

> 2 pork tenderloins (1 pound *each*)
> 1/2 cup soy sauce
> 3 tablespoons olive *or* canola oil
> 1/2 teaspoon ground ginger *or* 2 teaspoons minced fresh gingerroot
> 1 to 3 garlic cloves, minced
> 1/2 cup honey
> 1/4 cup packed brown sugar
> 1/3 cup sesame seeds, toasted

Place pork in a large resealable plastic bag. Add the soy sauce, oil, ginger and garlic; seal and turn to coat. Refrigerate for 4 hours or overnight, turning occasionally.

Drain and discard the marinade. Place pork tenderloins on a greased rack in a foil-lined shallow

roasting pan. Combine the honey and brown sugar; spoon over the top of the pork. Sprinkle with sesame seeds. Bake, uncovered, at 375° for 30-40 minutes or until a meat thermometer reads 160°. Let stand for 5-10 minutes before slicing. **Yield:** 8 servings.

Nutritional Analysis: One 4-ounce serving (prepared with reduced-sodium soy sauce) equals 284 calories, 6 g fat (2 g saturated fat), 74 mg cholesterol, 212 mg sodium, 25 g carbohydrate, trace fiber, 24 g protein. **Diabetic Exchanges:** 3 lean meat, 1-1/2 fruit.

Wild Turkey Rice Bake

Wild rice, turkey and vegetables are combined in a savory sauce and topped with golden crumbs in this hearty dish. Cooked wild turkey can be a little dry, but not when it's prepared this way. I never have leftovers. —Margaret Hill, Roanoke, Virginia

1 package (6 ounces) long grain and wild rice mix
1 teaspoon chicken bouillon granules
1 cup hot water
3-1/2 cups cubed fully cooked wild turkey
1-1/2 cups chopped celery
1 can (10-3/4 ounces) condensed cream of mushroom soup, undiluted
1 can (8 ounces) sliced water chestnuts, drained
1 jar (6 ounces) sliced mushrooms, drained
1/2 cup chopped onion
1/4 cup soy sauce
1 cup soft bread crumbs
2 tablespoons butter *or* margarine, melted

Prepare rice according to package directions; place in a large bowl. Dissolve bouillon in hot water; add to rice. Stir in the turkey, celery, soup, water chestnuts, mushrooms, onion and soy sauce.

Transfer to a greased 3-qt. baking dish. Toss bread crumbs and butter; sprinkle over the top. Bake, uncovered, at 350° for 55-60 minutes or until heated through. **Yield:** 8 servings.

Fowl Fact

According to history books, Christopher Columbus brought chickens to the New World in 1493. The turkey, however, is native to America and was introduced to Europe by Spanish explorers around the same time.

'I Wish I Had That Recipe...'

"ON A VISIT to Callaway Gardens in Pine Mountain, Georgia, I stopped for lunch at their Country Kitchen restaurant, where I ordered Southern Fried Chicken," writes Mary Shoshoo from Crown Point, Indiana.

"It was the most delicious fried chicken I've ever eaten. I hope *Taste of Home* can get the recipe."

We called Callaway Gardens and spoke with Executive Chef Thierry Connault. He related, "Our team of chefs conducted taste tests on several fried chicken recipes—changing, deleting and adding ingredients—until we came up with a recipe we thought tasted the most like down-home country fried chicken.

"We're delighted to share Callaway Gardens' Southern Fried Chicken recipe with *Taste of Home* readers."

Casual and quaint, with a wonderful view, the Country Kitchen is located in the Callaway Country Store on Highway 27. It opens for breakfast at 7:30 a.m. daily, serves lunch and offers dinner from 5 to 8 p.m. For more information, check out *www.callawaygardens.com* or call 1-800/225-5292.

Callaway Gardens' Southern Fried Chicken

2 cups all-purpose flour
6 tablespoons seasoned salt
1/4 cup salt-free seasoning blend
2 tablespoons paprika
1 tablespoon pepper
2 broiler/fryer chickens (3 to 4 pounds *each*), cut up
Oil for frying

In a large resealable plastic bag, combine the first five ingredients. Add chicken, a few pieces at a time, and shake to coat. In a large skillet, heat 1/4 in. of oil on medium-high; fry chicken in batches for 18-20 minutes or until juices run clear, turning once. **Yield:** 6-8 servings.

Grilled Salmon Steaks

(Pictured above)

This is a terrific way to fix salmon...and it's so easy to do. The marinade mellows the fish flavor, and the dill sauce is a wonderful complement. I once served this recipe to 12 people from the Pacific Northwest who declared it was the best salmon they'd ever eaten!
—Deb Essen,Victor, Montana

2 tablespoons white wine vinegar *or* cider vinegar
2 tablespoons sugar
1 tablespoon dill weed
3/4 teaspoon salt
1/8 to 1/4 teaspoon pepper, optional
4 salmon steaks (1 inch thick)
MUSTARD DILL SAUCE:
3 tablespoons mayonnaise
3 tablespoons Dijon mustard
3 tablespoons dill weed
1 tablespoon sugar
4 teaspoons white wine vinegar *or* cider vinegar
1/4 teaspoon pepper, optional

In a large resealable plastic bag, combine the first five ingredients. Add salmon; seal bag and turn to coat. Refrigerate for 1 hour, turning occasionally. In a small bowl, combine the sauce ingredients; cover and refrigerate.

Drain the salmon, discarding marinade. Grill salmon, covered, over medium-hot heat for 5 minutes. Turn; grill 7-9 minutes longer or until fish flakes easily with a fork. Serve with the mustard dill sauce. **Yield:** 4 servings.

Cooking Fish

If you are going to broil or grill fish, be sure to purchase steaks that are at least 1 inch thick. Fish dries out very quickly on the grill, so the thicker it is, the better. The skin should be left on fillets while they're grilling and removed after they are cooked.

Fish tends to cool rather quickly. For this reason, it should be served on warm plates or a warmed platter.

Turkey Puff Pancake

Your family or guests are sure to say "Wow!" when you present them with this dish that rises so high and browns so beautifully. I sometimes add water chestnuts for crunch.
—Patricia Millmann
Wauwatosa, Wisconsin

3/4 cup plus 2 tablespoons all-purpose flour, *divided*
2 eggs, beaten
Dash cayenne pepper
1 cup milk, *divided*
5 tablespoons butter *or* margarine, *divided*
1/2 cup chopped onion
3/4 cup sliced fresh mushrooms
3/4 cup turkey *or* chicken broth
1/4 teaspoon salt
1/4 teaspoon pepper
2 cups thinly sliced cooked turkey
1 to 2 tablespoons grated Parmesan cheese

Place 3/4 cup flour in a bowl. Whisk in eggs, cayenne and 3/4 cup milk until smooth. Place 3 tablespoons butter in a 9-in. pie plate. Heat at 400° for 3-4 minutes or until melted. Pour batter into hot plate. Bake for 15-18 minutes or until golden brown and center is set.

Meanwhile, in a skillet, saute onion in remaining butter until tender. Add mushrooms; saute until tender. Sprinkle with the remaining flour; cook and stir for 1 minute. Add broth and remaining milk. Bring to a boil; cook and stir for 2 minutes or until thickened. Stir in salt, pepper and turkey.

Spoon into center of pancake. Sprinkle with Parmesan cheese. Cut into wedges and serve immediately. **Yield:** 4-6 servings.

— 🍴 🍴 🍴 —

Beef in Onion Gravy

I double this super recipe to feed our family of four so I'm sure to have leftovers to send with my husband to

work for lunch. His co-workers tell him he's lucky to have someone who fixes him such special meals. It's our secret that it's an easy slow-cooker dinner!
—Denise Albers, Freeburg, Illinois

> 1 can (10-3/4 ounces) condensed cream of mushroom soup, undiluted
> 2 tablespoons onion soup mix
> 2 tablespoons beef broth
> 1 tablespoon quick-cooking tapioca
> 1 pound beef stew meat, cut into 1-inch cubes
> **Hot cooked noodles *or* mashed potatoes**

In a slow cooker, combine the soup, soup mix, broth and tapioca; let stand for 15 minutes. Stir in the beef. Cover and cook on low for 6-8 hours or until meat is tender. Serve over noodles or mashed potatoes. **Yield:** 3 servings.

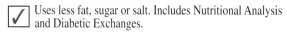

Pasta Pizza

My family often requests this meatless main dish, a tempting cross between pizza and spaghetti.
—Andrea Quick, Columbus, Ohio

✓ Uses less fat, sugar or salt. Includes Nutritional Analysis and Diabetic Exchanges.

> 8 ounces uncooked angel hair pasta
> 2 cups sliced fresh mushrooms
> 1/2 cup chopped green pepper
> 1/4 cup chopped onion
> 4 teaspoons olive *or* canola oil, *divided*
> 1 can (15 ounces) pizza sauce
> 1/4 cup sliced ripe olives
> 1/2 cup shredded part-skim mozzarella cheese
> 1/4 teaspoon Italian seasoning

Cook pasta according to package directions; drain. In a 10-in. ovenproof skillet, saute the mushrooms, green pepper and onion in 1 teaspoon oil until tender. Remove with a slotted spoon and keep warm. In the same skillet, heat remaining oil over medium-high. Spread pasta evenly in skillet to form a crust. Cook for 5-7 minutes or until lightly browned.

Turn crust onto a large plate. Reduce heat to medium; slide crust back into skillet. Top with pizza sauce, sauteed vegetables, olives, cheese and Italian seasoning. Bake at 400° for 10-12 minutes or until cheese is melted. **Yield:** 4 servings.

Nutritional Analysis: One serving equals 311 calories, 9 g fat (2 g saturated fat), 7 mg cholesterol, 376 mg sodium, 46 g carbohydrate, 4 g fiber, 14 g protein. **Diabetic Exchanges:** 3 starch, 1 fat, 1/2 lean meat.

Spicy Island Shrimp

(Pictured below)

My husband got this recipe while he was living on St. Croix Island. We've served the zippy shrimp dish on several holiday occasions. I'm amazed at how even those who claim not to care for shrimp come out of their shells and devour them when they're prepared this way! —Teresa Methe, Minden, Nebraska

> 1 large green pepper, chopped
> 1 large onion, chopped
> 1/2 cup butter *or* margarine
> 2-1/4 pounds uncooked large shrimp, peeled and deveined
> 2 cans (8 ounces *each*) tomato sauce
> 3 tablespoons chopped green onions
> 1 tablespoon minced fresh parsley
> 1 teaspoon salt
> 1 teaspoon pepper
> 1 teaspoon paprika
> 1/2 teaspoon garlic powder
> 1/2 teaspoon dried oregano
> 1/2 teaspoon dried thyme
> 1/4 to 1/2 teaspoon white pepper
> 1/4 to 1/2 teaspoon cayenne pepper
> **Hot cooked rice**

In a large skillet, saute the green pepper and onion in butter until tender. Reduce heat; add shrimp. Cook for 5 minutes. Stir in the tomato sauce, green onions, parsley and seasonings. Bring to a boil. Reduce heat; simmer, uncovered, for 20 minutes or until slightly thickened. Serve with rice. **Yield:** 6 servings.

Grilled Wild Turkey Breast

(Pictured below)

With only two ingredients, this is definitely the easiest recipe I have for cooking the wild turkey that my husband, Richard, brings home during spring hunting season. The grilled meat takes on a wonderful sweet smoky flavor. —Michelle Kaase, Tomball, Texas

> 1 bone-in wild turkey breast (about 1-1/2 pounds), split
> 1 bottle (8 ounces) fat-free honey Dijon salad dressing

Place turkey in a large resealable plastic bag; add salad dressing. Seal bag and turn to coat; refrigerate overnight, turning occasionally.

Drain and discard marinade. Grill turkey, covered, over indirect medium heat for 45-55 minutes or until juices run clear and a meat thermometer reads 170°. **Yield:** 2 servings.

— 🍷 🍷 🍷 —

Chicken Rosemary

My chicken dish is covered with sauteed mushrooms and onions and draped in a rich beefy sauce accented with rosemary. —Bob Wedemeyer
Lynnwood, Washington

> 4 bone-in chicken breast halves
> 1/4 cup all-purpose flour
> 5 tablespoons butter *or* margarine, *divided*
> 1 cup sliced fresh mushrooms
> 1/2 cup chopped onion
> 2 cans (14-1/2 ounces *each*) beef broth
> 1 tablespoon minced fresh rosemary *or* 1 teaspoon dried rosemary, crushed
Dash white pepper
> 1/4 cup cornstarch

1/4 cup cold water
Hot cooked fettuccine

Lightly coat chicken with flour. In a large skillet, brown chicken in 4 tablespoons butter. Transfer to a greased 13-in. x 9-in. x 2-in. baking dish. Cover and bake at 350° for 35-40 minutes or until juices run clear. Meanwhile, saute mushrooms and onion in the remaining butter until tender; set aside.

In a saucepan, bring broth to a boil over medium heat. Reduce heat; add rosemary and pepper. Simmer, uncovered, for 20 minutes or until reduced by half. Combine cornstarch and water until smooth; stir into broth. Bring to a boil; cook and stir for 2 minutes or until thickened. Stir in mushroom mixture. Serve chicken over fettuccine; top with mushroom sauce. **Yield:** 4 servings.

— 🍷 🍷 🍷 —

Quail with Mushroom Sauce

Succulent quail with a snappy sauce makes an impressive entree. This dish tastes wonderful over rice or toast points. Sometimes I'll use cinnamon toast to add flavor. —Chris Sendelbach, Henry, Illinois

> 2 tablespoons lemon juice
> 6 whole quail (5 to 6 ounces *each*)
> 1/8 teaspoon pepper
> 2 tablespoons vegetable oil
> 2 tablespoons butter *or* margarine
> 3 tablespoons all-purpose flour
> 1 tablespoon minced fresh parsley
> 1 teaspoon dried minced onion
> 2 cups chicken broth
> 1 jar (4-1/2 ounces) sliced mushrooms, drained
> 1/4 cup water
> 1/8 teaspoon hot pepper sauce
Hot cooked rice

Drizzle lemon juice over quail; sprinkle with pepper. In a large skillet, brown quail in oil and butter, turning frequently; remove and set aside.

Stir flour, parsley and onion into the drippings until blended. Gradually stir in broth, mushrooms, water and hot pepper sauce. Bring to a boil. Reduce heat; return quail to pan. Cover and simmer for 20-30 minutes or until meat is tender. Serve with rice. **Yield:** 6 servings.

— 🍷 🍷 🍷 —

Barbecued Lamb Chops

At Eastertime and for other holidays, I often get requests for these lamb chops. The moist and tender chops aren't difficult to make, but they taste special.

Even people who don't care for lamb like it prepared this way. —*Chris Nash, Berthoud, Colorado*

- **2 to 3 cups olive *or* vegetable oil**
- **1/4 cup chopped garlic**
- **4 teaspoons salt**
- **1 teaspoon minced fresh rosemary *or* 1/2 teaspoon dried rosemary, crushed**
- **1 teaspoon salt-free garlic and herb seasoning**
- **1 teaspoon pepper**
- **18 rib lamb chops (1 inch thick)**

In a large resealable plastic bag, combine the first six ingredients. Add lamb chops; seal bag and turn to coat. Refrigerate overnight, turning occasionally.

Drain and discard the marinade. Grill the lamb chops, uncovered, over medium heat for 2-4 minutes on each side or until meat reaches desired doneness (160° for medium-well, 170° for well-done). **Yield:** 9 servings.

Beefy Hash Brown Pizza

Hash brown potatoes form the crust for this fun pizza variation. When my children were growing up, this became a favorite Friday night treat. Now my grandchildren ask for it when they spend Friday nights with us. —*Betty Warren, Maryville, Tennessee*

- **5 cups frozen shredded hash brown potatoes, thawed**
- **1 can (10-3/4 ounces) cheddar cheese soup, undiluted**
- **1 egg, lightly beaten**
- **1/2 teaspoon salt**
- **1/4 teaspoon pepper**
- **2 pounds ground beef**
- **1 medium onion, chopped**
- **1 can (4 ounces) mushroom stems and pieces, drained**
- **1 can (15 ounces) pizza sauce**
- **4 cups (16 ounces) shredded pizza cheese, *divided***

In a bowl, combine the potatoes, soup, egg, salt and pepper. Spread mixture into a greased 15-in. x 10-in. x 1-in. baking pan. Bake at 400° for 20-25 minutes or until lightly browned.

Meanwhile, in a large skillet over medium heat, cook the beef, onion and mushrooms until meat is no longer pink; drain. Stir in pizza sauce; keep warm. Sprinkle 2 cups cheese over hot crust. Spread meat mixture over the top; sprinkle with remaining cheese. Bake 5-10 minutes longer or until cheese is melted. **Yield:** 6-8 servings.

Venison Roast

(Pictured above)

We've always cooked with venison...and this tender flavorful roast and gravy have been a favorite at our house for years. The children especially enjoy the sandwiches I make from the leftovers. —*Ruth McLaren, Shermans Dale, Pennsylvania*

- **1 venison roast (3 to 4 pounds)**
- **10 whole garlic cloves, peeled**
- **2 teaspoons dried rosemary, crushed**
- **1-1/2 teaspoons onion powder, *divided***
- **1 teaspoon garlic powder**
- **1 teaspoon dried thyme**
- **7 medium carrots, quartered**
- **5 small onions, quartered**
- **1 tablespoon beef bouillon granules**
- **1 teaspoon browning sauce, optional**
- **2 tablespoons cornstarch**
- **3 tablespoons cold water**

Cut 10 deep slits in roast; place a garlic clove in each slit. Pierce the roast in several places with a meat fork. In a small bowl, combine the rosemary, 1 teaspoon onion powder, garlic powder and thyme; rub over entire roast. Cover and refrigerate for 2 hours.

Add 1/2 in. of water to a roasting pan. Place the roast, carrots and onions in pan. Cover and bake at 325° for 2-1/2 to 3 hours or until a meat thermometer reads 160°.

Remove meat and vegetables to a serving platter; keep warm. Strain drippings into a measuring cup. In a saucepan, combine 3 cups drippings, bouillon, browning sauce if desired and remaining onion powder. Combine cornstarch and cold water until smooth; stir into drippings. Bring to a boil; cook and stir for 2 minutes or until thickened. Serve with roast. **Yield:** 8 servings.

Mixed Grill Kabobs

(Pictured above and on page 62)

These hearty kabobs combine beef and sausage, two of my favorite foods. Both the meat and vegetables are marinated before they're grilled, which makes this skewered meal extra flavorful. Be sure to fire up your grill and try these soon!
—Glenda Adams
Vanndale, Arkansas

>   3 cups pineapple juice
>   1 cup cider vinegar
>   1 cup vegetable oil
> 1/4 cup sugar
> 1/4 cup soy sauce
>   1 tablespoon browning sauce, optional
> 1/2 teaspoon garlic powder
> 1/4 teaspoon lemon-pepper seasoning
>   2 pounds beef tenderloin, cut into 1-inch cubes
>   1 pound fully cooked kielbasa *or* Polish sausage, cut into 1-inch chunks
>   3 to 4 medium tomatoes, quartered
>   3 to 4 medium green peppers, quartered
>   1 jar (4-1/2 ounces) whole mushrooms, drained
>   5 medium onions, quartered

In a large resealable plastic bag, combine the first eight ingredients. Add the meat and vegetables. Seal bag and turn to coat; refrigerate overnight.

Drain and discard marinade. Alternately thread beef, sausage and vegetables onto metal or soaked wooden skewers. Grill, covered, over medium-hot heat for 6-8 minutes. Turn kabobs; cook 6-8 minutes longer or until beef reaches desired doneness. **Yield:** 10-12 servings.

Rabbit Fricassee

I prefer rabbit cooked this way—moist and tasty, smothered in a homemade lemon sauce that's also a bit peppery. I've used this trusty recipe for as long as I can remember. —Audrey Thibodeau, Mesa, Arizona

>   1 dressed rabbit (about 3 pounds), cut into pieces
> 1/2 cup vegetable oil
>   2 tablespoons all-purpose flour
>   1 tablespoon butter *or* margarine, melted
>   1 teaspoon lemon juice
> 1/2 to 1 teaspoon hot pepper sauce
> 1/2 teaspoon celery salt
> 1/2 teaspoon salt
> 1/4 teaspoon pepper
>   1 egg
>   1 cup evaporated milk

In a skillet, cook rabbit in oil; drain. Cover rabbit with boiling water; cover and simmer for 30-40 minutes or until tender. Remove meat and keep warm. Bring cooking liquid to a boil; boil, uncovered, until reduced to 2 cups.

In a bowl, combine the flour and butter until smooth; gradually add a small amount of cooking liquid. Return to the skillet. Whisk in remaining liquid. Add lemon juice, hot pepper sauce, celery salt, salt and pepper. Bring to a boil, stirring constantly; cook and stir for 2 minutes.

Reduce heat. Combine the egg and milk; gradually whisk into sauce. Cook for 1 minute or until thickened and mixture reaches 160°. Pour over rabbit. **Yield:** 4 servings.

Sesame Sole

A friend regularly supplies our family with a fresh catch of fish. In this quick and easy recipe, sesame seeds add crunch and a tasty coating to the fillets.
—Nancy Zimmerman
Cape May Court House, New Jersey

>   2 teaspoons spicy brown *or* horseradish mustard
>   2 teaspoons tomato paste
> 1/2 teaspoon dried tarragon
> 1/4 teaspoon salt
>   4 sole *or* orange roughy fillets (6 ounces each)
> 1/4 cup buttermilk
> 1/2 cup sesame seeds
> 1/4 cup all-purpose flour
>   2 tablespoons vegetable oil

In a bowl, combine the mustard, tomato paste, tarragon and salt; spread on both sides of the fillets.

Place buttermilk in a shallow bowl. In another shallow bowl, combine sesame seeds and flour. Dip fillets in buttermilk, then coat with sesame seed mixture. Refrigerate for 30 minutes.

In a large skillet, heat oil over medium-high heat; fry fillets for 3-4 minutes on each side or until fish flakes easily with a fork. **Yield:** 4 servings.

Fisherman's Crispy Coating

My father is an avid fisherman and frequently acts as the chef on fishing trips he takes with his buddies. To please that group—and to get us kids to eat fish at home—he created this pleasantly mild crispy coating.
—*Tammi Freih, Lakewood, California*

> 1 egg
> 1 cup milk
> 1 cup crisp rice cereal, crushed
> 1/4 cup all-purpose flour
> 1/4 cup cornmeal
> 1-1/2 teaspoons lemon-pepper seasoning
> 1/4 teaspoon seasoned salt
> 1/8 teaspoon onion salt
> 1/8 teaspoon garlic salt
> 4 walleye *or* other whitefish fillets (1-3/4 to 2 pounds)

Oil for frying

In a shallow bowl, whisk together the egg and milk. In a large resealable plastic bag, combine the cereal, flour, cornmeal and seasonings. Dip the fish fillets into egg mixture, then coat with the cereal mixture.

In a large skillet, heat 1/4 in. of oil over medium-high heat. Fry the fillets for 5-7 minutes on each side or until fish flakes easily with a fork. **Yield:** 4 servings.

The Skinny on Skewers

To help prevent wooden skewers from burning or splinting, soak them in water for 15-30 minutes. Remove them from the water and then pile on the ingredients.

Items such as mushrooms, chunks of zucchini and pieces of meat may spin on kabobs, making it difficult to cook them evenly on all sides. To avoid this, pierce the food with two parallel skewers.

Not able to grill? Simply broil your kabobs in the oven 4-6 inches from the heat. Broil until poultry is no longer pink or until meat reaches the desired doneness.

Gingered Garlic Shrimp

(Pictured below)

Ginger and garlic nicely complement the tender shrimp in this delicious pasta dish. —*Rebecca Baird Salt Lake City, Utah*

> 3/4 teaspoon ground ginger *or* 1 tablespoon minced fresh gingerroot
> 2 garlic cloves, minced
> 2 tablespoons butter *or* margarine
> 2 tablespoons olive *or* vegetable oil
> 2 plum tomatoes, diced
> 3/4 cup chicken broth
> 3 teaspoons minced fresh parsley, *divided*
> 3 teaspoons minced fresh basil, *divided*
> 1-1/2 teaspoons cornstarch
> 1 tablespoon cold water
> 1/2 pound uncooked medium *or* large shrimp, peeled and deveined
> 2 cups cooked angel hair pasta

In a large skillet, saute ginger and garlic in butter and oil for 2-3 minutes or until tender. Stir in the tomatoes, broth, 1-1/2 teaspoons parsley and 1-1/2 teaspoons basil. Combine cornstarch and cold water until smooth; add to the skillet. Bring to a boil; cook and stir for 2 minutes or until thickened.

Reduce heat; add shrimp. Simmer, uncovered, for 2-3 minutes or until the shrimp turn pink. Add the pasta and remaining parsley and basil; toss to coat. **Yield:** 2 servings.

Beef Tenderloin with Potatoes

(Pictured below)

As an alternative to turkey or ham for the holidays one year, I decided to try this recipe. My family liked it so much, it's become a standard at our house. The meat is very tender and flavorful, and the potatoes get nicely browned. The marinade cooks into a terrific sauce. —Mrs. Clifford Davis, Fort Smith, Arkansas

- 2-1/4 **cups water**
- 1-1/2 **cups ketchup**
- 3 **envelopes (.7 ounce *each*) Italian salad dressing mix**
- 1 **tablespoon prepared mustard**
- 3/4 **teaspoon Worcestershire sauce**
- 1 **whole beef tenderloin (3 to 4 pounds), trimmed**
- 10 **medium potatoes, peeled and quartered**
- 1/2 **cup butter *or* margarine, melted**
- 1/2 **teaspoon salt**
- 1/4 **teaspoon pepper**

Combine the first five ingredients in a large resealable plastic bag. Pierce tenderloin in several places; place in bag and turn to coat. Seal and refrigerate for 8 hours or overnight.

Place potatoes in a saucepan and cover with water. Bring to a boil; cook for 10-15 minutes or until crisp-tender; drain. Toss with butter, salt and pepper.

Place tenderloin on a rack in a roasting pan. Pour marinade into a saucepan; bring to a rolling boil. Boil for 1 minute; pour over meat. Arrange the potatoes around meat.

Bake, uncovered, at 375° for 60-75 minutes,

basting occasionally, or until beef reaches desired doneness (for rare, a meat thermometer should read 140°; medium, 160°; well-done, 170°). Slice; serve with pan juices and potatoes. **Yield:** 10-12 servings.

Flounder Florentine

I discovered this recipe several years ago when I was looking for a way to dress up fish fillets. Even though we're not big fans of fish, we enjoy this dish. It's tasty, healthy and inexpensive. —Debbie Verbeck Florence, New Jersey

☑ Uses less fat, sugar or salt. Includes Nutritional Analysis and Diabetic Exchanges.

- 2 **packages (10 ounces *each*) frozen chopped spinach, thawed and drained**
- 1 **pound fresh *or* frozen flounder *or* sole fillets, thawed**
- 3 **tablespoons chopped onion**
- 2 **tablespoons butter *or* stick margarine**
- 3 **tablespoons all-purpose flour**
- 1/4 **teaspoon salt**
- 1/4 **teaspoon pepper**
- 1/8 **teaspoon ground nutmeg**
- 1-1/2 **cups fat-free milk**
- 1 **tablespoon grated Parmesan cheese**
- 1/4 **teaspoon paprika**

Sprinkle spinach in a 13-in. x 9-in. x 2-in. baking dish coated with nonstick cooking spray. Top with fillets.

In a saucepan, saute onion in butter until tender. Stir in the flour, salt, pepper and nutmeg until blended. Gradually add milk. Bring to a boil; cook and stir for 2 minutes or until thickened and bubbly. Pour over fillets; sprinkle with Parmesan cheese and paprika. Bake, uncovered, at 350° for 20 minutes or until fish flakes easily with a fork. **Yield:** 4 servings.

Nutritional Analysis: One serving equals 253 calories, 8 g fat (4 g saturated fat), 73 mg cholesterol, 480 mg sodium, 16 g carbohydrate, 5 g fiber, 30 g protein. **Diabetic Exchanges:** 3 lean meat, 2 vegetable, 1/2 fat-free milk.

Sesame Chicken

For flavorful, moist and tender chicken, try this marinade. The sesame seeds cling well to season the meat. We also like this mixture on chicken wings, beef short ribs and pork. —Julie Lake, Anchorage, Alaska

- 3/4 **cup soy sauce**
- 1/2 **cup packed brown sugar**

1/4 cup water
   3 tablespoons sesame seeds, toasted
   1 garlic clove, minced
Crushed red pepper flakes, optional
   4 bone-in chicken breast halves

In a large resealable plastic bag, combine the first six ingredients; add chicken. Seal bag and refrigerate overnight. Drain and discard marinade. Grill chicken, skin side down, uncovered, over medium heat for 15 minutes. Turn; grill 15-20 minutes longer or until the meat juices run clear. **Yield:** 4 servings.

Cinnamon Hotcakes

Since he was old enough to pull up a chair and help his dad in the kitchen, my son, Jory, has been interested in cooking. In fact, these fluffy pancakes are his own creation.
—_Deborah Hilpipre_
Eden Prairie, Minnesota

1-1/3 cups all-purpose flour
4-1/2 teaspoons brown sugar
1-1/4 teaspoons baking powder
   1 teaspoon ground cinnamon
   2 eggs
   1 cup milk
   2 tablespoons butter _or_ margarine, melted
Additional cinnamon
Maple syrup

In a bowl, combine the flour, brown sugar, baking powder and cinnamon. Combine eggs, milk and butter; stir into dry ingredients just until combined. Pour batter by 1/4 cupfuls onto a lightly greased hot griddle. Sprinkle with cinnamon. Turn when bubbles form on top of pancakes. Cook until second side is golden brown. Serve with syrup. **Yield:** 8 pancakes.

Cheesy Crab Enchiladas

(Pictured above right and on page 62)

While I was in college, my roommates and I loved the taste of ranch dressing—it was our condiment of choice for almost everything. So I created these rich delectable crab enchiladas, with ranch dressing mix as my secret ingredient. —_Kelly Mockler_
Madison, Wisconsin

   2 packages (8 ounces _each_) cream cheese, softened
   1 envelope ranch salad dressing mix
   3 tablespoons plus 1/4 cup milk, _divided_
   1 small red onion, diced
   2 garlic cloves, minced
   2 tablespoons butter _or_ margarine
   1 pound fresh, frozen _or_ canned crabmeat, flaked and cartilage removed
   2 cans (2-1/4 ounces _each_) sliced ripe olives, drained
   1 can (4 ounces) chopped green chilies
1/2 teaspoon pepper
1/4 teaspoon salt
   2 cups (8 ounces) shredded Monterey Jack cheese, _divided_
   8 flour tortillas (8 inches)
1/2 cup shredded Colby cheese
Chopped green onions and tomatoes, shredded lettuce and sliced ripe olives, optional

In a mixing bowl, combine cream cheese, dressing mix and 3 tablespoons milk until smooth. Set aside 3/4 cup for topping. In a skillet, saute onion and garlic in butter until tender. Stir in crab, olives, chilies, pepper and salt. Fold crab mixture and 1-1/2 cups Monterey Jack into remaining cream cheese mixture.

Spoon about 2/3 cup down the center of each tortilla. Roll up and place seam side down in a greased 13-in. x 9-in. x 2-in. baking dish. Combine the remaining milk and reserved cream cheese mixture until blended; pour over tortillas. Sprinkle with Colby and remaining Monterey Jack. Cover and bake at 350° for 25 minutes. Uncover; bake 5-10 minutes longer or until heated through. Serve with green onions, tomatoes, lettuce and olives if desired. **Yield:** 8 enchiladas.

1/2 teaspoon paprika
1/4 teaspoon salt
1/8 teaspoon pepper
  1 egg
  2 tablespoons milk
  4 orange roughy *or* catfish fillets (4 ounces *each*)

In a shallow bowl, combine the Parmesan cheese, flour, paprika, salt and pepper. In another bowl, beat egg and milk. Dip fish fillets into egg mixture, then coat with the Parmesan mixture. Arrange in a greased 13-in. x 9-in. x 2-in. baking dish. Bake, uncovered, at 350° for 25-30 minutes or until fish flakes easily with a fork. **Yield:** 4 servings.

Nutritional Analysis: One serving (prepared with 2% milk) equals 154 calories, 5 g fat (2 g saturated fat), 83 mg cholesterol, 392 mg sodium, 4 g carbohydrate, trace fiber, 22 g protein. **Diabetic Exchange:** 3 lean meat.

Ground Turkey Noodle Bake

Back in the 1950s, when my husband was diagnosed as diabetic, we had five children at home to feed. I made this casserole often...and it satisfied us all. We all agree it's still as delicious today as it was then.
—*Ruby Williams, Bogalusa, Louisiana*

☑ Uses less fat, sugar or salt. Includes Nutritional Analysis and Diabetic Exchanges.

  3 cups uncooked wide egg noodles
1/2 pound ground turkey
  1 medium onion, chopped
  1 can (15 ounces) tomato sauce
  1 teaspoon Italian seasoning
2/3 cup nonfat dry milk powder
1/2 cup water
  4 ounces reduced-fat cream cheese, cubed
  1 tablespoon minced fresh parsley
  1 garlic clove, minced
1-1/4 cups shredded part-skim mozzarella cheese

Cook noodles according to package directions. Meanwhile, in a large skillet, cook turkey and onion over medium heat until turkey is no longer pink; drain. Stir in tomato sauce and Italian seasoning. Bring to a boil. Reduce heat; cover and simmer for 10 minutes. In a saucepan, combine milk powder, water, cream cheese, parsley and garlic. Cook and stir over medium heat until cream cheese is melted.

Drain noodles; add to cream cheese mixture. Transfer to an 8-in. square baking dish coated with nonstick cooking spray. Top with turkey mixture. Sprinkle with mozzarella cheese. Bake, un-

Herbed Rib Roast

(Pictured above)

This spectacular roast is the star of any special meal my wife, Linda, and I host. A simple dry rub delicately seasons the tender juicy meat.   —*Ron Poole Saluda, North Carolina*

1/4 cup all-purpose flour
  2 tablespoons snipped fresh rosemary
  2 teaspoons seasoned salt
  2 teaspoons garlic pepper *or* seasoned pepper
  2 teaspoons ground mustard
  1 boneless beef rib roast (4 to 6 pounds), trimmed and tied

In a small bowl, combine the flour, rosemary, salt, garlic pepper and mustard; rub over roast. Place roast fat side up on a rack in a shallow roasting pan. Bake, uncovered, at 350° for 1-3/4 to 2-3/4 hours or until meat reaches desired doneness (for rare, a meat thermometer should read 140°; medium, 160°; well-done, 170°). Let stand for 10-15 minutes before slicing. **Yield:** 10-12 servings.

Baked Parmesan Fish

Here's an easy way to work an elegant fish dish into your menu. I sometimes sprinkle the golden fillets with slivered or sliced almonds before baking.
—*Carolyn Brinkmeyer, Centennial, Colorado*

☑ Uses less fat, sugar or salt. Includes Nutritional Analysis and Diabetic Exchanges.

1/3 cup grated Parmesan cheese
  2 tablespoons all-purpose flour

covered, at 375° for 15-20 minutes or until cheese is melted. **Yield:** 6 servings.

Nutritional Analysis: One serving equals 281 calories, 11 g fat (6 g saturated fat), 71 mg cholesterol, 676 mg sodium, 25 g carbohydrate, 2 g fiber, 21 g protein. **Diabetic Exchanges:** 2 fat, 1-1/2 starch, 1-1/2 lean meat.

Asparagus Beef Stir-Fry

Soy sauce and ginger boost the flavor in this savory stir-fry that features strips of beef and water chestnuts along with tender asparagus. —Marla Deakins
Salt Lake City, Utah

✓ Uses less fat, sugar or salt. Includes Nutritional Analysis and Diabetic Exchanges.

      6 teaspoons olive *or* canola oil, *divided*
      1 teaspoon sugar
  1/2 teaspoon salt
      1 teaspoon ground ginger *or* 3 teaspoons minced fresh gingerroot, *divided*
Dash pepper
      1 pound beef flank steak, thinly sliced
      2 tablespoons cornstarch
      1 cup beef broth
      3 tablespoons soy sauce
      1 tablespoon cider vinegar
1-1/2 pounds fresh asparagus, trimmed and cut into 2-inch pieces
      1 can (8 ounces) sliced water chestnuts, drained
  1/4 cup chopped green onions
      4 cups hot cooked rice

In a shallow glass container, combine 2 teaspoons of oil, sugar, salt, half of the ginger and pepper. Add beef and turn to coat. Let stand for 15 minutes. In a small bowl, combine the cornstarch, broth, soy sauce, vinegar and remaining ginger until blended; set aside.

In a large skillet or wok, brown beef in 2 teaspoons oil. Remove and keep warm. Add remaining oil; stir-fry asparagus for 3-5 minutes or until crisp-tender. Add water chestnuts and onions; stir-fry for 1 minute. Stir cornstarch mixture; add to the skillet. Bring to a boil, stirring constantly; cook and stir for 2 minutes or until thickened. Return beef to the pan; heat through. Serve over rice. **Yield:** 6 servings.

Nutritional Analysis: One serving (3/4 cup beef mixture with 3/4 cup rice, prepared with reduced-sodium soy sauce) equals 371 calories, 11 g fat (3 g saturated fat), 39 mg cholesterol, 718 mg sodium, 44 g carbohydrate, 4 g fiber, 23 g protein. **Diabetic Exchanges:** 3 lean meat, 2 starch, 2 vegetable.

'I Wish I Had That Recipe...'

"WHILE in the Great Smoky Mountains, we ate at Atrium Pancakes in Gatlinburg, Tennessee," recounts Janice Zook of White River Junction, Vermont.

"When I ordered the Baked Apple Pancake, I was warned it would take about a half hour. It was absolutely wonderful—and worth the wait! Can *Taste of Home* help me get the recipe?"

Debbie Smith, who owns Atrium Pancakes with husband Don, responded, "We're happy to hear that a customer is raving about our Baked Apple Pancake! The recipe originated when we changed our focus from a breakfast/lunch/dinner restaurant to one featuring breakfast all day.

"Deciding to serve pancakes for a specialty, we had to come up with some new and different ones. So Don got in the kitchen and started doing what he does best—cooking. A little of this…a little of that…try it this way…that way…and he came up with the Baked Apple Pancake."

The popular item is one of 25 varieties of pancakes and waffles on their breakfast menu. Homemade soups and salads are available for lunch.

Located at 423 Parkway, Atrium Pancakes is open daily from 7 a.m. to 2:30 p.m. For more information, call 1-865/430-3684.

Baked Apple Pancake

      1 cup pancake mix
  2/3 cup milk
      2 tablespoons vegetable oil
      1 egg, beaten
  1/4 cup butter *or* margarine
  1/3 cup packed brown sugar
      1 medium Golden Delicious apple, peeled and sliced
Maple syrup

In a bowl, combine pancake mix, milk, oil and egg. In an 8-in. ovenproof skillet, melt butter. Stir in brown sugar and apple slices; saute until sugar is dissolved. Pour batter over apple mixture. Cook, uncovered, over medium heat until bubbles form on top of pancake.

Bake, uncovered, at 350° for 12-17 minutes or until golden. Invert onto a serving platter. Serve with syrup. **Yield:** 1-2 servings.

Poached Perch with Broccoli

(Pictured below)

We live near Lake Erie and love to fish, and we consider this our favorite perch recipe. It's quick and easy to prepare and so delicious. Everyone who tastes it loves the tender fillets served with broccoli in a creamy garlic sauce. —Alyce Reed, Elyria, Ohio

    1 pound fresh broccoli, cut into spears
  3/4 cup water
    1 small onion, sliced
    1 bay leaf
    1 teaspoon salt
  1/2 teaspoon dried tarragon
    2 pounds perch fillets
GARLIC SAUCE:
    1 cup mayonnaise
    1 tablespoon lemon juice
    1 garlic clove, minced
  1/2 teaspoon ground mustard
  1/4 teaspoon salt
  1/4 teaspoon pepper

Place broccoli in a steamer basket. Place in a saucepan over 1 in. of water; bring to a boil. Cover and steam until crisp-tender; set aside and keep warm.

In a large skillet, combine the water, onion, bay leaf, salt and tarragon; bring to a boil. Reduce heat; add perch fillets in batches. Cover and cook until fish is firm and flakes easily with a fork. Remove fish and onions with a slotted spoon; keep warm. Discard bay leaf.

In a bowl, combine the sauce ingredients. Stir in 2-4 tablespoons cooking liquid until sauce reaches desired consistency. Arrange broccoli on a serving platter; top with fish, onions and garlic sauce. **Yield:** 4-6 servings.

— ⬛ ⬛ ⬛ —

Glazed Country Ribs

I'm the designated camp cook when my buddies and I go hunting and fishing. I started with a basic recipe, then modified it to suit my tastes. The ribs are melt-in-your-mouth tender and coated with a mild sweet sauce. —John Brink, Harrison, South Dakota

    2 pounds bone-in country-style pork ribs
1-3/4 teaspoons salt, *divided*
  1/4 teaspoon pepper, *divided*
  3/4 cup orange juice
    2 tablespoons lemon juice
  1/2 cup packed brown sugar
1-1/2 teaspoons garlic powder
    1 teaspoon grated lemon peel
  3/4 teaspoon ground ginger
  1/4 teaspoon ground cloves
    1 bay leaf

Place ribs on a rack in a foil-lined shallow roasting pan; sprinkle with 3/4 teaspoon salt and 1/8 teaspoon pepper. Bake, uncovered, at 400° for 30 minutes. Turn ribs. Reduce temperature to 350°; bake 30 minutes longer.

Meanwhile, in a saucepan, combine the orange juice, lemon juice, brown sugar, garlic powder, lemon peel, ginger, cloves, bay leaf and remaining salt and pepper; bring to a boil. Reduce heat; simmer, uncovered, for 15 minutes. Discard bay leaf.

Remove ribs from rack; drain drippings. Return ribs to pan; brush with sauce. Bake, uncovered, for 45-60 minutes or until tender, turning and basting often. **Yield:** 4 servings.

— ⬛ ⬛ ⬛ —

Marinated Venison Steaks

These venison steaks are so tender and tasty, they're even a hit with my kids. Someone who tried this dish once said, "Wow, if I could make venison taste like this, I'd make it all the time." —Janelle Inkens Tigard, Oregon

    6 boneless venison steaks (4 to 6 ounces each)
  1/2 cup white vinegar

1/2 cup ketchup
1/4 cup vegetable oil
1/4 cup Worcestershire sauce
4 garlic cloves, minced
1-1/2 teaspoons ground mustard
1/2 teaspoon salt
1/2 teaspoon pepper

Place venison in a large resealable plastic bag. In a bowl, combine all of the remaining ingredients. Pour half over the venison; seal bag and turn to coat. Refrigerate overnight. Refrigerate remaining marinade.

Drain and discard marinade from the steaks. Broil steaks 3-4 in. from the heat for 4 minutes. Turn; baste with reserved marinade. Broil 4 minutes longer, basting often, or until a meat thermometer reads 160° for medium or 170° for well-done. **Yield:** 6 servings.

Asparagus Swiss Quiche

Fresh asparagus stars along with bacon, onion and Swiss cheese in this hearty quiche that's perfect for breakfast or brunch. We even like it for a lighter supper on some days. *—Mary Ann Taylor Rockwell, Iowa*

10 bacon strips, diced
1/2 cup chopped onion
1 pound fresh asparagus, trimmed
1 cup (4 ounces) shredded Swiss cheese
1 tablespoon all-purpose flour
1/4 teaspoon salt
1/8 teaspoon pepper
1 unbaked pastry shell (9 inches)
3 eggs
1/2 cup half-and-half cream

In a skillet, cook bacon over medium heat until crisp. Remove with a slotted spoon to paper towels; drain, reserving 1 tablespoon drippings. In the drippings, saute onion until browned; drain.

Cut eight asparagus spears into 4-in.-long spears for garnish. Cut remaining asparagus into 1-in. pieces. In a saucepan, cook all of the asparagus in a small amount of boiling water until crisp-tender; drain.

In a bowl, toss the bacon, onion, asparagus pieces, cheese, flour, salt and pepper. Pour into pastry shell. In a bowl, beat eggs and cream; pour over bacon mixture. Top with asparagus spears. Bake at 400° for 30-35 minutes or until a knife inserted near the center comes out clean and crust is golden brown. Let stand for 10 minutes before cutting. **Yield:** 6-8 servings.

Stir-Fried Beef 'n' Beans

(Pictured above)

Garlic, ginger and soy sauce lend a robust flavor to this meaty marinated dish. My mother-in-law took cooking lessons while living in Japan and brought back this recipe. It has become a favorite of family and friends...even those who don't usually eat green beans. *—Kristine Lowry, Bowling Green, Kentucky*

1/4 cup cornstarch
1/2 cup soy sauce
2 tablespoons water
1 teaspoon ground ginger *or* 4 teaspoons minced fresh gingerroot
4 garlic cloves, minced
4 tablespoons vegetable oil, *divided*
1 pound boneless beef sirloin steak, cut into 1/4-inch strips
1/2 pound fresh green beans, cut in half lengthwise
1 teaspoon sugar
1/2 teaspoon salt
Hot cooked rice

In a bowl, combine the cornstarch, soy sauce, water, ginger, garlic and 2 tablespoons oil until smooth. Set aside 1/2 cup. Pour the remaining marinade into a large resealable plastic bag; add the beef. Seal bag and turn to coat; refrigerate for 25-30 minutes.

Drain and discard marinade from beef. In a wok or skillet, stir-fry beef in remaining oil for 4-6 minutes or until no longer pink. Remove and keep warm. In the same skillet, stir-fry the beans, sugar and salt for 15 minutes or until crisp-tender. Stir in the beef and reserved marinade. Bring to a boil; cook and stir for 1-2 minutes or until thickened. Serve over rice. **Yield:** 4 servings.

utes. Discard bay leaf. **Yield:** 6 servings.

Nutritional Analysis: One serving (1 cup) equals 302 calories, 4 g fat (1 g saturated fat), 43 mg cholesterol, 452 mg sodium, 45 g carbohydrate, 3 g fiber, 21 g protein. **Diabetic Exchanges:** 2-1/2 starch, 1-1/2 lean meat, 1 vegetable.

— 🛒 🛒 🛒 —

Sweet 'n' Saucy Meatballs

I got the recipe for these meatballs from one of my husband's parishioners, and I have modified it over the years. I usually double it to accommodate our big family of eight. —Kim Brandt, Lovell, Wyoming

   1 **pound lean ground beef**
   1 **egg**
1/2 **cup quick-cooking oats**
1-1/2 **cups water**
1-1/4 **cups ketchup**
   1 **cup sugar**

In a bowl, combine beef and egg. Sprinkle with oats; mix well. Shape into 1-1/2-in. balls. Place in a lightly greased 11-in. x 7-in. x 2-in. baking dish. Combine water, ketchup and sugar; pour over meatballs. Bake, uncovered, at 350° for 40-50 minutes or until meat is no longer pink. **Yield:** 4-6 servings.

— 🛒 🛒 🛒 —

Beef 'n' Bacon Lo Mein

This special dish is not tricky to fix, and it's very hearty. Even kids and my meat-and-potatoes husband like it. —Stephanie Francis, Yale, Iowa

1/2 **pound sliced bacon, diced**
1/2 **pound beef flank steak, cut into thin strips**
   2 **tablespoons vegetable oil, divided**
   1 **cup broccoli florets**
   1 **cup cauliflowerets**
   1 **medium carrot, cut into thin 2-inch strips**
   1 **small onion, cut into wedges**
   2 **garlic cloves, minced**
1/4 **teaspoon ground ginger or 1 teaspoon minced fresh gingerroot**
   1 **cup sliced fresh mushrooms**
   1 **can (8 ounces) sliced water chestnuts, drained**
   1 **tablespoon beef bouillon granules**
   1 **cup boiling water**
1/4 **cup soy sauce**
   3 **tablespoons cornstarch**
3/4 **cup cold water**
1/2 **pound thin spaghetti, cooked and drained**

In a large skillet, cook bacon until crisp; remove to paper towels to drain. Discard drippings. In the

Chicken Jambalaya

(Pictured above)

This is a great dish to serve at parties. It's just as good as, if not tastier than, the high-fat version. And it reheats well. —Lynn Desjardins Atkinson, New Hampshire

✓ Uses less fat, sugar or salt. Includes Nutritional Analysis and Diabetic Exchanges.

3/4 **pound boneless skinless chicken breasts, cubed**
   3 **cups reduced-sodium chicken broth**
1-1/2 **cups uncooked brown rice**
   4 **ounces reduced-fat smoked turkey sausage, diced**
1/2 **cup thinly sliced celery with leaves**
1/2 **cup chopped onion**
1/2 **cup chopped green pepper**
   2 **to 3 teaspoons Cajun or Creole seasoning**
   1 **to 2 garlic cloves, minced**
1/8 **teaspoon hot pepper sauce**
   1 **bay leaf**
   1 **can (14-1/2 ounces) no-salt-added diced tomatoes, undrained**

In a large nonstick skillet lightly coated with nonstick cooking spray, saute chicken for 2-3 minutes. Stir in the next 10 ingredients. Bring to a boil. Reduce heat; cover and simmer for 50-60 minutes. Stir in tomatoes; cover and simmer 10 minutes longer or until liquid is absorbed and rice is tender. Remove from the heat; let stand for 5 min-

same skillet, stir-fry beef in 1 tablespoon oil until no longer pink, about 2 minutes. Remove beef and pan juices; keep warm.

In the skillet, saute broccoli, cauliflower, carrot, onion, garlic and ginger in remaining oil for 3 minutes. Add mushrooms and water chestnuts; cook and stir 2 minutes longer. Dissolve bouillon in boiling water; stir into vegetables.

Stir in soy sauce and beef with pan juices. Combine cornstarch and cold water until smooth; add to skillet. Bring to a boil; cook and stir for 1-2 minutes or until thickened. Stir in bacon and spaghetti. Serve immediately. **Yield:** 4 servings.

— ☕ ☕ ☕ —

Turkey Potpie

A cornmeal crust with a hint of sage and a comforting turkey filling makes this savory potpie a satisfying supper. It's a delicious use for leftover turkey, especially around the holidays. —Joan Baskin
Black Creek, British Columbia

    1 small onion, chopped
    1 celery rib, chopped
  1/2 cup butter *or* margarine
  1/2 cup all-purpose flour
1-1/2 cups chicken broth
    1 cup milk
    1 teaspoon rubbed sage
    1 teaspoon lemon juice
  1/2 teaspoon salt
  1/8 teaspoon pepper
  1/8 teaspoon ground nutmeg
    3 cups diced cooked turkey
SAGE PASTRY:
  1/2 cup all-purpose flour
  1/2 cup cornmeal
  3/4 teaspoon rubbed sage
  1/4 teaspoon salt
  1/3 cup cold butter *or* margarine
    2 to 3 tablespoons cold water

In a large skillet, saute onion and celery in butter until tender. Stir in flour until blended. Gradually stir in broth, milk, sage, lemon juice, salt, pepper and nutmeg. Bring to a boil; cook and stir for 2 minutes or until thickened. Add turkey; cook and stir until heated through. Transfer to an ungreased 1-1/2-qt. baking dish; set aside.

In a bowl, combine the flour, cornmeal, sage and salt. Cut in butter until crumbly. Gradually add water, tossing with a fork until dough forms a ball. On a floured surface, roll pastry to fit top of baking dish; place over filling. Flute edges; cut slits in top. Bake at 425° for 18-20 minutes or until golden brown. **Yield:** 4-6 servings.

Coconut Fried Shrimp

(Pictured below)

These crisp and crunchy shrimp make a fun change-of-pace main dish. The coconut coating adds a little sweetness...and the tangy orange marmalade and honey sauce is great for dipping. It's impossible to stop munching these once you start! —Ann Atchison
O'Fallon, Missouri

1-1/4 cups all-purpose flour
1-1/4 cups cornstarch
6-1/2 teaspoons baking powder
  1/2 teaspoon salt
  1/4 teaspoon Cajun seasoning
1-1/2 cups cold water
  1/2 teaspoon vegetable oil
    1 pound uncooked large shrimp, peeled
      and deveined
2-1/2 cups flaked coconut
Additional oil for deep-fat frying
    1 cup orange marmalade
  1/4 cup honey

In a bowl, combine the first five ingredients. Stir in water and oil until smooth. Dip shrimp into batter, then coat with coconut. In an electric skillet or deep-fat fryer, heat oil to 375°. Fry shrimp, a few at a time, for 3 minutes or until golden brown. Drain on paper towels.

In a saucepan, heat marmalade and honey; stir until blended. Serve as a dipping sauce for the shrimp. **Yield:** 4 servings.

Breads, Rolls & Muffins

This bounty of breads, rolls and muffins will rise to the occasion.

BREADS CAN'T BE BEAT. Clockwise from upper left: Caraway Scones (p. 95), S'more Jumbo Muffins (p. 106), Buttermilk Dill Bread (p. 97), Cheddar English Muffins (p. 96) and Jelly Doughnuts (p. 91).

Molasses Oat Bread

(Pictured above)

This recipe has been passed down through my family from my Swedish great-grandmother. The slightly sweet bread receives high praise, even from my children, who are picky eaters. —*Patricia Finch Kelly Rindge, New Hampshire*

✓ Uses less fat, sugar or salt. Includes Nutritional Analysis and Diabetic Exchanges.

    4 cups boiling water
    2 cups old-fashioned oats
    1 cup molasses
    3 tablespoons canola oil
 1/4 cup sugar
    3 teaspoons salt
    1 package (1/4 ounce) active dry yeast
    9 to 10 cups all-purpose flour

In a mixing bowl, combine the first six ingredients. Cool to 110°-115°. Add yeast; mix well. Add enough flour to form a soft dough. Turn onto a floured surface; knead until smooth and elastic, about 6-8 minutes. Place in a greased bowl, turning once to grease top. Cover and let rise in a warm place until doubled, about 1-1/2 hours.

Punch dough down and divide into thirds; shape into loaves. Place in three greased 9-in. x 5-in. x 3-in. loaf pans. Cover and let rise until doubled, about 1 hour. Bake at 350° for 45-50 minutes or until golden brown. Remove from pans to wire racks to cool. **Yield:** 3 loaves (12 slices each).

Nutritional Analysis: One slice equals 183 calories, 2 g fat (trace saturated fat), 0 cholesterol, 200 mg sodium, 37 g carbohydrate, 1 g fiber, 4 g protein. **Diabetic Exchange:** 2-1/2 starch.

— 🛒 🛒 🛒 —

Honey Crunch Muffins

These muffins have lots of fun flavor, but they're not difficult to mix up. My granddaughter has helped me make them many times over the years.
    —*Mary Kilianek, Westmont, Illinois*

    1 cup granola cereal without raisins
1-1/3 cups all-purpose flour
 1/3 cup sugar
    2 teaspoons baking powder
 3/4 teaspoon baking soda
 1/2 teaspoon salt
    2 eggs, beaten
    1 cup plain yogurt
 1/4 cup vegetable oil
 1/2 teaspoon vanilla extract
 1/2 cup raisins
 1/2 cup chopped pecans
HONEY BUTTER:
 1/2 cup butter (no substitutes), softened
    4 to 5 tablespoons honey

In a bowl, combine the cereal, flour, sugar, baking powder, baking soda and salt. Combine the eggs, yogurt, oil and vanilla; stir into the dry ingredients just until moistened. Stir in raisins and pecans. Fill greased or paper-lined muffin cups three-fourths full.

Bake at 400° for 12-14 minutes or until a toothpick comes out clean. Cool for 5 minutes before removing from pan to a wire rack. In a small mixing bowl, beat butter and honey until smooth; serve with muffins. **Yield:** about 1 dozen.

— 🛒 🛒 🛒 —

Cinnamon Monkey Bread

Is it possible for four kids to cook together without total chaos in the kitchen? Yes, with the right recipe. This is a favorite with my bunch. They get to "play" with the dough as they roll pieces of refrigerated biscuits into balls. —*Lisa Combs, Greenville, Ohio*

    4 tubes (7-1/2 ounces *each*) refrigerated buttermilk biscuits
 1/2 cup sugar
    2 teaspoons ground cinnamon
 1/2 cup butter *or* margarine, melted
 1/2 cup packed brown sugar

Cut each biscuit into four pieces; shape into balls. In a small bowl, combine sugar and cinnamon.

Roll each ball in cinnamon-sugar. Arrange evenly in a greased 10-in. fluted tube pan. Sprinkle with remaining cinnamon-sugar. Combine butter and brown sugar; pour over the top. Bake at 350° for 35-40 minutes or until golden brown. Cool for 5 minutes before inverting bread onto a serving platter. **Yield:** 1 loaf.

----- 🛒 🛒 🛒 -----

Grandma's Rolls

I managed to coerce this recipe from my wife's grand-mother a few years ago. They're so good!
—*David Baruch, Weston, Florida*

✓ Uses less fat, sugar or salt. Includes Nutritional Analysis and Diabetic Exchanges.

> **2 packages (1/4 ounce *each*) active dry yeast**
> **1-1/4 cups warm water (110° to 115°)**
> **1 package (4.4 ounces) custard dessert mix***
> **1/4 cup butter *or* margarine, softened**
> **1 teaspoon salt**
> **3 to 3-1/2 cups all-purpose flour**

In a large mixing bowl, dissolve yeast in warm water. Add custard mix, butter, salt and 2 cups flour; beat until smooth. Stir in enough remaining flour to form a soft dough. Turn onto a lightly floured surface; knead 25-30 times. Roll into a 20-in. x 8-in. rectangle.

Cut rectangle in half lengthwise; with a long side facing you, fold bottom third to the center. Bring top of dough down to folded edge. Cut into 2-in. pieces. Place 3 in. apart on greased baking sheets. Repeat with second rectangle. Cover and let rise in a warm place until doubled, about 30 minutes. Bake at 400° for 7-10 minutes or until golden brown. **Yield:** 20 rolls.

Nutritional Analysis: One roll equals 114 calories, 3 g fat (1 g saturated fat), 6 mg cholesterol, 180 mg sodium, 20 g carbohydrate, 1 g fiber, 3 g protein. **Diabetic Exchange:** 1-1/2 starch.

***Editor's Note**: This recipe was tested with Jell-O Americana Custard Dessert.

----- 🛒 🛒 🛒 -----

Jelly Doughnuts

(Pictured at right and on page 88)

There's no need to run to the bakery for delicious jelly doughnuts! These sweet treats are lighter than air. I've been fixing them for 25 years for my husband, our two daughters and their families. They disappear almost as fast as I make them. —*Kathy Westendorf*
Westgate, Iowa

> **2 packages (1/4 ounce *each*) active dry yeast**
> **1/2 cup warm water (110° to 115°)**
> **1/2 cup warm milk (110° to 115°)**
> **1/3 cup butter *or* margarine, softened**
> **1-1/3 cups sugar, *divided***
> **3 egg yolks**
> **1 teaspoon salt**
> **3-3/4 cups all-purpose flour**
> **3 tablespoons jelly *or* jam**
> **1 egg white, beaten**
> **Oil for deep-fat frying**

In a mixing bowl, dissolve yeast in warm water. Add milk, butter, 1/3 cup sugar, egg yolks and salt; mix well. Stir in enough flour to form a soft dough (do not knead). Place in a greased bowl, turning once to grease top. Cover and let rise in a warm place until doubled, about 1-1/2 hours.

Punch dough down. Turn onto a lightly floured surface; knead about 10 times. Divide dough in half. Roll each portion to 1/4-in. thickness; cut with a floured 2-1/2-in. round cutter. Place about 1/2 teaspoon jelly in the center of half of the circles; brush edges with egg white. Top with remaining circles; press edges to seal tightly. Place on greased baking sheet. Cover and let rise until doubled, about 1 hour.

In an electric skillet, heat oil to 375°. Fry doughnuts, a few at a time, for 1-2 minutes on each side or until golden the brown. Drain on paper towels. Roll doughnuts in remaining sugar while warm. **Yield:** 16 doughnuts.

Rosemary Garlic Braid

(Pictured below)

This moist savory bread pairs nicely with a variety of main dishes. It's great with soup and makes a wonderful grilled ham and cheese sandwich. I came up with the recipe a few years ago when I wanted to use up the fresh rosemary in my garden. —Cori Oakley
Traverse City, Michigan

>   5 whole garlic bulbs
>   2 teaspoons olive oil
>   1/4 cup minced fresh rosemary *or* 4 teaspoons
>   dried rosemary, crushed
>   1 tablespoon chicken broth
>   9 to 9-1/2 cups bread flour
>   1/2 cup sugar
>   3 packages (1/4 ounce *each*) quick-rise
>   yeast
>   3 teaspoons salt
> 1-1/2 cups milk
>   1 cup water
>   3/4 cup butter *or* margarine, *divided*
>   1 egg
> 1-1/2 teaspoons garlic salt

Remove papery outer skin from garlic (do not peel or separate cloves). Cut top off garlic heads, leaving root end intact. Place cut side up in a small baking dish. Brush with oil; sprinkle with rosemary. Cover and bake at 425° for 30-35 minutes or until softened. Cool for 10 minutes; squeeze softened garlic into a bowl. Add broth; lightly mash.

In a large mixing bowl, combine 3 cups flour, sugar, yeast and salt. In a saucepan, heat milk, water and 1/2 cup butter to 120°-130°. Add to dry ingredients; beat just until moistened. Beat in egg and garlic paste until smooth. Stir in enough remaining flour to form a soft dough (dough will be sticky). Turn onto a floured surface; knead until smooth and elastic, about 6-8 minutes. Cover and let rest for 10 minutes.

Turn dough onto a lightly floured surface; divide into thirds. Divide each portion into three pieces; shape each into an 18-in. rope. Place three ropes on a greased baking sheet and braid; pinch ends to seal and tuck under. Repeat with remaining dough. Cover and let rise in a warm place until doubled, about 30 minutes.

Bake at 350° for 15 minutes. Melt remaining butter; add garlic salt. Brush over bread. Bake 10-15 minutes longer or until golden brown. Remove from pans to wire racks to cool. **Yield:** 3 loaves.

Zucchini Bread

I like this bread because it's lighter and fluffier than most zucchini breads. Plus, it's a great way to put that abundant vegetable to good use!
—Kevin Bruckerhoff, Columbia, Missouri

>   3 eggs
>   2 cups sugar
>   1 cup vegetable oil
>   2 teaspoons vanilla extract
>   1 teaspoon grated lemon peel
>   3 cups all-purpose flour
>   1 teaspoon baking soda
>   1 teaspoon baking powder
>   1 teaspoon salt
>   1 teaspoon ground cinnamon
>   2 cups shredded zucchini (about 2 medium)
>   1/2 cup chopped nuts

In a large mixing bowl, combine eggs and sugar. Beat in oil, vanilla and lemon peel. Combine the dry ingredients; gradually add to sugar mixture and mix well. Stir in zucchini and nuts. Pour into two greased 9-in. x 5-in. x 3-in. loaf pans.

Bake at 325° for 55-60 minutes or until a toothpick inserted near the center comes out clean. Cool for 10 minutes before removing from pans to wire racks. **Yield:** 2 loaves.

Quick Bread Basic

When making quick breads, be sure to blend the liquid and dry ingredients only until moistened. Overmixing can create a coarse, tough texture.

Trail Mix Muffins

(Pictured above)

These hearty muffins blend stick-to-your-ribs granola, fruit, nuts and chocolate chips. They're perfect for a breakfast on the go, or any time you need a lift.
—Patricia Jones, Hugo, Colorado

2-1/4 cups all-purpose flour
   1 cup granola cereal without raisins
  3/4 cup packed brown sugar
   2 teaspoons baking powder
  1/2 teaspoon salt
   2 eggs
   1 cup milk
  3/4 cup vegetable oil
   1 teaspoon vanilla extract
  1/2 cup miniature semisweet chocolate chips
  1/2 cup chopped dry roasted peanuts
  1/2 cup raisins
  1/2 cup chopped dried apricots

In a large bowl, combine the flour, cereal, brown sugar, baking powder and salt. In another bowl, beat the eggs, milk, oil and vanilla; stir into dry ingredients just until moistened. Fold in the chips, peanuts, raisins and apricots.

Fill greased or paper-lined muffin cups three-fourths full. Bake at 375° for 15-18 minutes or until a toothpick comes out clean. Cool for 5 minutes before removing from pans to wire racks. Serve warm. **Yield:** about 1-1/2 dozen.

mixture. Stir in walnuts.

Divide half of the batter between two 8-in. x 4-in. x 2-in. loaf pans coated with nonstick cooking spray. Spread each with filling; top with remaining batter. Bake at 350° for 40-45 minutes or until a toothpick inserted near the center comes out clean. Cool for 10 minutes before removing from pans to wire racks to cool completely. Refrigerate leftovers. **Yield:** 2 loaves (14 slices each).

Nutritional Analysis: One serving (2 slices) equals 107 calories, 3 g fat (1 g saturated fat), 11 mg cholesterol, 116 mg sodium, 19 g carbohydrate, 1 g fiber, 3 g protein. **Diabetic Exchanges:** 1 starch, 1/2 fat.

Ribbon Pumpkin Bread

(Pictured above)

No one will guess they're eating lighter when you serve moist slices of this pretty pumpkin bread with a ribbon of cream cheese inside. It makes a nice presentation at any autumn meal. —Beth Ask
Ulster, Pennsylvania

☑ Uses less fat, sugar or salt. Includes Nutritional Analysis and Diabetic Exchanges.

FILLING:
    6 ounces reduced-fat cream cheese
1/4 cup sugar
    1 tablespoon all-purpose flour
    2 egg whites
BATTER:
    1 cup cooked *or* canned pumpkin
1/2 cup unsweetened applesauce
    1 egg
    2 egg whites
    1 tablespoon canola oil
1-2/3 cups all-purpose flour
1-1/4 cups sugar
    1 teaspoon baking soda
1/2 teaspoon salt
1/2 teaspoon ground cinnamon
1/2 teaspoon ground cloves
1/3 cup chopped walnuts

For filling, combine the cream cheese, sugar, flour and egg whites in a bowl; set aside. In a mixing bowl, beat the pumpkin, applesauce, egg, egg whites and oil. Combine the flour, sugar, baking soda, salt, cinnamon and cloves; add to pumpkin

Nut-Filled Butterhorns

(Pictured below)

These rich flaky butterhorns were made on Good Friday morning or Christmas Eve morning when I was growing up. We used them to celebrate the end of Lent or Advent and the joy of family and friends coming together. They're so special, they're worth the bit of extra effort. —Michael Engerson
Hustisford, Wisconsin

    3 packages (1/4 ounce *each*) active dry yeast
1/4 cup warm milk (110° to 115°)
    2 tablespoons sugar
    2 cups butter *or* margarine, softened
    1 package (8 ounces) cream cheese, softened
    1 cup whipping cream

  1 cup (8 ounces) sour cream
  7 egg yolks
  1/8 teaspoon salt
  8 to 8-1/2 cups all-purpose flour
FILLING:
  6 egg whites
  1 teaspoon cream of tartar
  1 cup sugar, *divided*
  3 cups ground walnuts *or* pecans
  2 teaspoons ground cinnamon, optional
ICING:
  3 cups confectioners' sugar
  2 tablespoons butter *or* margarine,
    softened
  5 to 7 tablespoons milk
  1/2 teaspoon almond *or* vanilla extract,
    optional

In a large mixing bowl, dissolve yeast in warm milk. Add sugar; let stand for 5 minutes. Add butter, cream cheese, cream, sour cream, egg yolks, salt and 2-1/2 cups flour. Beat until smooth. Stir in enough remaining flour to form a soft dough. Turn onto a floured surface; knead until smooth and elastic, about 6-8 minutes. Place in a greased bowl, turning once to grease top. Cover and refrigerate overnight.

In a mixing bowl, beat egg whites until foamy. Add cream of tartar; beat until soft peaks form. Gradually add 2 tablespoons sugar, beating until glossy stiff peaks form. Fold in nuts.

Divide chilled dough into fourths. On a lightly floured surface, roll each portion into a 12-in. circle; spread a fourth of the filling over each circle. Add cinnamon if desired to remaining sugar; sprinkle over filling. Cut each into 12 wedges. Roll up wedges from the wide end; place pointed side down 3 in. apart on greased baking sheets. Curve ends to form a crescent shape.

Bake at 350° for 17-20 minutes or until golden brown. Remove from pans to wire racks to cool. Combine all of the icing ingredients; drizzle over rolls. **Yield:** 4 dozen.

Kneading Dough

To knead dough, turn it out onto a floured surface and shape it into a ball. Fold the top of the dough toward you. With palms, push with a rolling motion. Turn dough a quarter turn; repeat motion until dough is smooth and elastic. Add flour to surface only as needed.

If you're kneading dough on a pastry board, place a damp dishcloth underneath the board to prevent it from sliding.

Caraway Scones

(Pictured above and on page 88)

I like to serve these scrumptious scones alongside corned beef hash. They make a great addition to a soup and salad luncheon, too. —Brooke Staley
Mary Esther, Florida

✓ Uses less fat, sugar or salt. Includes Nutritional Analysis and Diabetic Exchanges.

  2 cups all-purpose flour
4-1/2 teaspoons sugar
  2 teaspoons baking powder
  2 teaspoons caraway seeds
  1/2 teaspoon salt
  1/4 cup cold butter *or* stick margarine
  1 egg
  2/3 cup milk

In a bowl, combine the first five ingredients. Cut in butter until mixture resembles coarse crumbs. In another bowl, whisk egg and milk; stir into dry ingredients just until moistened. Turn onto a floured surface; gently knead 6-8 times.

Transfer dough to a greased baking sheet; pat into an 8-in. circle. Cut into eight wedges, but do not separate. Bake at 400° for 17-22 minutes or until golden brown. Serve warm. **Yield:** 8 servings.

Nutritional Analysis: One scone (prepared with 2% milk) equals 197 calories, 7 g fat (4 g saturated fat), 44 mg cholesterol, 284 mg sodium, 28 g carbohydrate, 1 g fiber, 5 g protein. **Diabetic Exchanges:** 2 starch, 1 fat.

Cheddar English Muffins

(Pictured below and on page 88)

These chewy English muffins have a scrumptious mild cheese flavor that intensifies when they're split and toasted. My family really enjoys them.
—Marge Goral, Ridgefield, Connecticut

✓ Uses less fat, sugar or salt. Includes Nutritional Analysis and Diabetic Exchanges.

    3 to 3-1/4 cups bread flour
    1 tablespoon sugar
    1 package (1/4 ounce) active dry yeast
    1 teaspoon salt
    3/4 cup water (120° to 130°)
    2 tablespoons canola oil
    1 egg
    1 tablespoon cider vinegar
    1/2 cup shredded cheddar cheese
    4 tablespoons cornmeal, *divided*

In a mixing bowl, combine 2 cups flour, sugar, yeast and salt. Add water and oil; beat on medium speed for 2 minutes. Add egg and vinegar; beat on high for 2 minutes. Stir in cheese and enough remaining flour to form a stiff dough. Turn onto a floured surface; knead until dough is smooth and no longer sticky, about 2 minutes.

Roll dough to about 1/2-in. thickness. Cut with a 3-in. round cutter. Roll scraps if desired. Coat baking sheets with nonstick cooking spray and sprinkle with 2 tablespoons cornmeal. Place muffins 2 in. apart on prepared pans. Sprinkle tops with remaining cornmeal. Cover and let rise until doubled, about 1 hour.

Heat an ungreased griddle or electric skillet to 325°. Cook muffins for 20-25 minutes or until golden brown, turning every 5 minutes. Remove to wire racks to cool. Split with a fork and toast if desired. **Yield:** about 16 muffins.

Nutritional Analysis: One muffin equals 128 calories, 3 g fat (1 g saturated fat), 17 mg cholesterol, 173 mg sodium, 21 g carbohydrate, 1 g fiber, 5 g protein. **Diabetic Exchanges:** 1-1/2 starch, 1/2 fat.

Sugared Doughnut Holes

These tender tasty doughnut bites are easy to make. They're perfect as an after-school or anytime snack.
—Judy Jungwirth, Athol, South Dakota

    1-1/2 cups all-purpose flour
    1/3 cup sugar
    2 teaspoons baking powder
    1/2 teaspoon salt
    1/2 teaspoon ground nutmeg
    1 egg
    1/2 cup milk
    2 tablespoons butter *or* margarine, melted
Oil for deep-fat frying
Confectioners' sugar

In a bowl, combine the flour, sugar, baking powder, salt and nutmeg. In a small bowl, combine egg, milk and butter. Add to dry ingredients; mix well.

In an electric skillet or deep-fat fryer, heat oil to 375°. Drop dough by heaping teaspoonfuls, five or six at a time, into oil. Fry until browned, about 1-2 minutes, turning once. Drain on paper towels. Roll in confectioners' sugar. **Yield:** about 3 dozen.

Raspberry Coffee Cake

(Pictured at right)

My husband and I and our three children are missionaries in Spain. Special treats like this swirled bread are truly a taste of home for us. With a fruity filling and sweet glaze, it's hard to eat just one slice.
—Mary Bergman, Navarra, Spain

    1 tablespoon active dry yeast
    1/3 cup warm water (110° to 115°)
    1/2 cup warm sour cream (110° to 115°)
    1 egg
    1/4 cup butter *or* margarine, melted
    1/4 cup sugar
    1 teaspoon salt
2-1/4 to 2-1/2 cups all-purpose flour

FILLING:
- 1 package (8 ounces) cream cheese, softened
- 1 egg
- 1/2 cup sugar
- 1 teaspoon vanilla extract
- 1/8 teaspoon salt
- 1/2 cup raspberry jam

GLAZE:
- 1-1/4 cups confectioners' sugar
- 1 teaspoon vanilla extract
- 2 tablespoons milk

In a large bowl, dissolve yeast in warm water. Stir in sour cream, egg, butter, sugar and salt. Stir in enough flour to form a soft dough. Turn onto a floured surface; knead 20 times or until smooth. Place in a greased bowl, turning once to grease top. Cover and let rise in a warm place until doubled, about 1-1/4 hours.

In a mixing bowl, beat cream cheese, egg, sugar, vanilla and salt until smooth; set aside. Punch dough down. Turn onto a lightly floured surface; divide in half. Roll each portion into a 12-in. x 8-in. rectangle. Spread filling to within 1/2 in. of edges. Spoon jam lengthwise over half of filling. Roll up jelly-roll style, starting with the long side with the jam. Pinch seams to seal; tuck ends under.

Place loaves seam side down on a greased baking sheet. With a sharp knife, cut shallow slashes across the top of each. Cover and let rise until doubled, about 30 minutes. Bake at 375° for 15-20 minutes or until golden brown. Remove from pan to a wire rack. Combine glaze ingredients; drizzle over warm coffee cakes. **Yield:** 2 loaves.

Buttermilk Dill Bread

(Pictured above and on page 89)

This no-fuss bread machine recipe turns out a light golden loaf with a mild herb flavor. —Billie Moss
El Sobrante, California

☑ Uses less fat, sugar or salt. Includes Nutritional Analysis and Diabetic Exchanges.

- 1-1/4 cups warm 1% buttermilk (70° to 80°)
- 2 tablespoons butter *or* stick margarine, softened
- 2 tablespoons sugar
- 1-1/2 teaspoons dill weed
- 1/2 teaspoon salt
- 1/8 teaspoon white pepper
- 3 cups bread flour
- 2-1/4 teaspoons active dry yeast

In bread machine pan, place all ingredients in order suggested by manufacturer. Select basic bread setting. Choose crust color and loaf size if available. Bake according to bread machine directions (check dough after 5 minutes of mixing; add 1 to 2 tablespoons of water or flour if needed). **Yield:** 1-1/2 pounds (16 slices).

Nutritional Analysis: One slice equals 104 calories, 2 g fat (1 g saturated fat), 5 mg cholesterol, 109 mg sodium, 19 g carbohydrate, 1 g fiber, 4 g protein. **Diabetic Exchanges:** 1 starch, 1/2 fat.

Editor's Note: Warmed buttermilk will appeared curdled. If your bread machine has a time-delay feature, we recommend you do not use it for this recipe.

Potato Pan Rolls

(Pictured at right)

Beautiful color and light-as-a-feather texture make these rolls our family's favorite for holiday meals. I won the Reserve Champion award at a 4-H yeast bread competition with this recipe. —LeAnne Hofferichter
Floresville, Texas

        2 medium potatoes, peeled and quartered
1-1/2 cups water
        2 packages (1/4 ounce *each*) active dry
            yeast
        1 teaspoon sugar
    1/2 cup butter *or* margarine, melted
    1/2 cup honey
    1/4 cup vegetable oil
        2 eggs
        2 teaspoons salt
        6 to 7 cups all-purpose flour

In a saucepan, bring potatoes and water to a boil. Reduce heat; cover and simmer for 15-20 minutes or until tender. Drain, reserving 1 cup cooking liquid; cool liquid to 110°-115°. Mash potatoes; set aside 1 cup to cool to 110°-115° (save remaining potatoes for another use).

In a mixing bowl, dissolve yeast and sugar in reserved potato liquid; let stand for 5 minutes. Add reserved mashed potatoes, butter, honey, oil, eggs, salt and 1-1/2 cups flour; beat until smooth. Stir in enough remaining flour to form a soft dough. Turn onto a floured surface; knead until smooth and elastic, about 6-8 minutes. Place in a greased bowl, turning once to grease top. Cover and let rise in a warm place until doubled, about 1 hour.

Punch dough down and turn onto a floured surface; divide into 30 pieces. Shape each piece into a ball. Place 10 balls each in three greased 9-in. round baking pans. Cover and let rise until doubled, about 30 minutes. Bake at 400° for 20-25 minutes or until golden brown. Remove from pans to wire racks to cool. **Yield:** 2-1/2 dozen.

— ▆ ▆ ▆ —

Almond Bear Claws

(Pictured at right)

These bear claws are absolutely melt-in-your-mouth delicious! It's impossible to resist the delicate pastry, rich almond filling and pretty fanned tops sprinkled with sugar and almonds. —Aneta Kish
La Crosse, Wisconsin

1-1/2 cups cold butter *or* margarine, cut into
            1/2-inch pieces
        5 cups all-purpose flour

        1 package (1/4 ounce) active dry yeast
1-1/4 cups half-and-half cream
    1/4 cup sugar
    1/4 teaspoon salt
        2 eggs
        1 egg white
    3/4 cup confectioners' sugar
    1/2 cup almond paste, cubed
        1 tablespoon water
Coarse *or* granulated sugar
Sliced almonds

In a bowl, toss butter with 3 cups flour until well coated; refrigerate. In a mixing bowl, combine yeast and remaining flour. In a saucepan, heat cream, sugar and salt to 120°-130°. Add to yeast mixture with 1 egg; mix well. Stir in butter mixture just until moistened.

Turn onto a lightly floured surface; knead 10 times. Roll into a 21-in. x 12-in. rectangle. Starting at a short side, fold dough in thirds, forming a 12-in. x 7-in. rectangle. Cover and chill for 1 hour.

For filling, in a mixing bowl, beat egg white until foamy. Gradually add confectioners' sugar and almond paste; beat until smooth. Cut dough in half widthwise. Roll each portion into a 12-in. square; cut each square into three 12-in. x 4-in. strips. Spread about 2 tablespoons filling down center of each strip. Fold long edges together; seal edges and ends. Cut into three pieces.

Place on greased baking sheets with folded edge facing away from you. With scissors, cut strips four times to within 1/2 in. of folded edge; separate slightly. Repeat with remaining dough and filling. Cover and let rise in a warm place until doubled, about 1 hour. Lightly beat water and remaining egg; brush over dough. Sprinkle with sugar and almonds. Bake at 375° for 15 minutes or until golden brown. Remove from pans to wire racks to cool. **Yield:** 1-1/2 dozen.

Shaping Rolls

You can shape dough for rolls in a variety of ways. Instead of just making a traditional round dinner roll, try one of these techniques:

For crescent rolls, roll a portion of dough into a 12-inch circle. Cut into wedges. Roll up from the wide end.

For knot-shaped rolls, shape dough into 3-inch balls. Roll each ball into a rope. Tie a knot; tuck and pinch ends.

For cloverleaf rolls, shape dough into 1-1/2-inch balls. Place three of the balls in each greased muffin cup.

NOTHING is more inviting than the aroma of homemade breads like Potato Pan Rolls and Almond Bear Claws (shown above, from top) baking in the oven.

Punch dough down and turn onto a floured surface; divide in half. Roll one portion into a 15-in. x 10-in. rectangle. Combine filling ingredients; sprinkle half over dough. Roll up jelly-roll style, starting with a long side; pinch seams to seal. Place seam side down on a greased baking sheet; pinch ends together to form a ring. With a sharp knife, cut 1/2-in. slashes at 2-in. intervals. Repeat with remaining dough and filling.

Cover and let rise in a warm place until doubled, about 30 minutes. Brush each ring with egg; sprinkle with sesame seeds and Parmesan. Bake at 350° for 20-25 minutes or until golden brown. Remove from pans to wire racks. **Yield:** 2 loaves.

Candy Cane Coffee Cake

(Pictured below)

Dotted with dried apricots and maraschino cherries, this tender coffee cake has a festive flavor and look. I love to serve it at Christmastime for my family, fellow teachers and students. It makes a welcome holiday gift, too.
—Linda Hollingsworth, Quitman, Mississippi

   2 packages (1/4 ounce *each*) active dry yeast
1/2 cup warm water (110° to 115°)
   2 cups warm sour cream (110° to 115°)

Herbed Cheese Ring

(Pictured above)

This savory cheesy loaf is great sliced in thin wedges to go with soup, salads or casseroles. I've served it to large crowds and received many compliments. One year, I gave it to our neighbors for Christmas.
—Evelyn Bear, Kingston, Idaho

   1 package (1/4 ounce) active dry yeast
1/4 cup warm water (110° to 115°)
   1 cup warm milk (110° to 115°)
1/4 cup vegetable oil
   2 tablespoons honey
   1 egg
   1 teaspoon salt
   1 cup whole wheat flour
2-1/2 cups all-purpose flour
   1 teaspoon *each* dried oregano, basil and rosemary, crushed

FILLING:
1-1/2 cups (6 ounces) shredded cheddar cheese
1/2 teaspoon dried parsley flakes
1/4 teaspoon garlic powder
1/4 teaspoon paprika

TOPPING:
   1 egg, beaten
   2 teaspoons sesame seeds
   4 teaspoons grated Parmesan cheese

In a mixing bowl, dissolve yeast in warm water. Add milk, oil, honey, egg, salt, whole wheat flour, 1 cup all-purpose flour and herbs; beat until blended. Stir in enough remaining all-purpose flour to form a soft dough. Cover and refrigerate overnight.

6 tablespoons butter *or* margarine, *divided*
1/3 cup sugar
2 eggs
2 teaspoons salt
5-3/4 to 6-1/4 cups all-purpose flour
1-1/2 cups finely chopped dried apricots
1-1/2 cups finely chopped maraschino cherries
2 cups confectioners' sugar
2 tablespoons cold water
Additional cherries, halved

In a mixing bowl, dissolve yeast in warm water. Add sour cream, 4 tablespoons butter, sugar, eggs, salt and 2 cups flour; beat until smooth. Stir in enough remaining flour to form a soft dough. Turn onto a floured surface; knead until smooth and elastic, about 6-8 minutes. Place in a greased bowl, turning once to grease top. Cover and let rise in a warm place until doubled, about 1 hour.

Punch dough down. Turn onto a lightly floured surface; divide into thirds. Roll each portion into a 14-in. x 7-in. rectangle on a greased baking sheet. Combine apricots and cherries; spoon down the center of rectangle. On each long side, cut 3/4-in.-wide strips about 2 in. into center. Starting at one end, fold alternating strips at an angle across filling. Pinch ends to seal. Curve top.

Bake at 375° for 18-20 minutes or until golden brown. Melt remaining butter; brush over warm coffee cakes. Combine confectioners' sugar and cold water until smooth; drizzle over top. Garnish with cherries. **Yield:** 3 loaves.

------- 🥤 🥤 🥤 -------

Whole Grain Loaf

(Pictured at right)

This flavorful bread is eye-catching and chock-full of nutrients. I baked this beautiful bread on stage at the state fair and won Reserve Grand Champion.
—*Nancy Means, Moline, Illinois*

✓ Uses less fat, sugar or salt. Includes Nutritional Analysis and Diabetic Exchanges.

1 package (1/4 ounce) active dry yeast
1/2 cup warm water (110° to 115°)
1/2 cup reduced-fat small-curd cottage cheese
1/4 cup honey
2 tablespoons canola oil
1 teaspoon salt
1 egg
2 to 2-1/2 cups all-purpose flour
1/2 cup whole wheat flour
1/4 cup rye flour
1/4 cup quick-cooking oats
1/4 cup toasted wheat germ

Cornmeal
1 egg white
2 tablespoons cold water
1 tablespoon sesame seeds

In a mixing bowl, dissolve yeast in warm water. Add the cottage cheese, honey, oil, salt, egg and 1-1/2 cups all-purpose flour; beat until smooth. Gradually beat in whole wheat and rye flours, oats, wheat germ and enough remaining all-purpose flour to make a soft dough. Turn onto a floured surface; knead until smooth and elastic, about 8-10 minutes. Place in a greased bowl, turning once to grease top. Cover and let rise in a warm place until doubled, about 75 minutes.

Punch dough down; let rest for 10 minutes. Shape into a ball. Sprinkle a greased baking sheet with cornmeal. Transfer dough to prepared pan. Cover and let rise until doubled, about 30 minutes. Beat egg white and cold water; brush over dough. Sprinkle with sesame seeds. Bake at 350° for 25-30 minutes or until golden brown. Remove from pan to cool on wire rack. **Yield:** 1 loaf (16 slices).

Nutritional Analysis: One slice equals 120 calories, 1 g fat (trace saturated fat), trace cholesterol, 180 mg sodium, 23 g carbohydrate, 2 g fiber, 4 g protein. **Diabetic Exchange:** 1-1/2 starch.

Apricot Braids

(Pictured above)

These lovely yeast braids are light and tender and have a delightful apricot filling. They're very popular with family and friends. —Paula Wipf, Arlington, Virginia

2-1/4 cups chopped dried apricots
1-1/2 cups water, *divided*
1-1/2 cups packed brown sugar
5-1/2 to 6 cups all-purpose flour
   3/4 cup sugar
     3 packages (1/4 ounce *each*) active dry yeast
     1 teaspoon salt
   1/2 cup butter *or* margarine, softened
     3 eggs, beaten
GLAZE:
     1 cup confectioners' sugar
     1 to 2 tablespoons milk
   1/2 teaspoon vanilla extract

In a saucepan, bring apricots and 1/2 cup water to a boil. Reduce heat; cover and simmer until water is absorbed and fruit is tender, about 20 minutes. Transfer to a food processor; add brown sugar. Cover and process until smooth.

In a mixing bowl, combine 2 cups of flour, sugar, yeast and salt. In a saucepan, heat butter and remaining water to 120°-130°. Add to dry ingredients; beat just until moistened. Add eggs; beat until smooth. Stir in enough remaining flour to form a soft dough. Turn onto a floured surface; knead un-

til smooth and elastic, about 6-8 minutes. Place in a greased bowl, turning once to grease top. Cover and let rise in a warm place until doubled, about 40-45 minutes.

Punch dough down; divide into thirds. On greased baking sheets, roll out each portion into a 12-in. x 8-in. rectangle. Spread filling down the center of each rectangle. On each long side, cut 1-in.-wide strips about 2 in. into center. Starting at one end, fold alternating strips at an angle across filling. Pinch ends to seal. Cover and let rise for 30 minutes.

Bake at 375° for 20-25 minutes or until golden brown. Remove from pans to wire racks to cool. Combine glaze ingredients; drizzle over braids. **Yield:** 3 braids.

Baking Bread

If you're making several loaves of bread or a large batch of rolls at once, and they don't all fit on one baking sheet, put one sheet in the oven and the other in the refrigerator. If you bake two sheets at the same time, not enough air will circulate, and the bread or rolls will bake unevenly.

Resist opening the oven door during the first 15-20 minutes of baking time. It's not unusual for a loaf to increase in size by one-third during the first 15 minutes. This rise could be diminished by a sudden draft.

Raisin Apple Muffins

Apple, cinnamon and raisins combine to treat your taste buds in these tender muffins.
—Dorothy Schierbeek, Grand Rapids, Michigan

✓ Uses less fat, sugar or salt. Includes Nutritional Analysis and Diabetic Exchanges.

1-1/2 cups all-purpose flour
1/2 cup sugar
2 teaspoons baking powder
1 teaspoon ground cinnamon
1/2 teaspoon salt
1 egg
1/2 cup fat-free milk
1/4 cup canola oil
1 cup chopped peeled tart apple
1/4 cup raisins
CRUMB TOPPING:
2 tablespoons all-purpose flour
2 tablespoons quick-cooking oats
2 tablespoons brown sugar
1 teaspoon ground cinnamon
1 tablespoon cold butter *or* stick margarine

In a bowl, combine the flour, sugar, baking powder, cinnamon and salt. Combine the egg, milk and oil; stir into dry ingredients just until moistened. Fold in the apple and raisins. Coat muffin cups with nonstick cooking spray or use paper liners; fill two-thirds full with batter.

For topping, in a bowl, combine the flour, oats, brown sugar and cinnamon; cut in butter until crumbly. Sprinkle over batter. Bake at 375° for 15-20 minutes or until a toothpick comes out clean. Cool for 5 minutes before removing from pan to a wire rack. Serve warm. **Yield:** 1 dozen.

Nutritional Analysis: One muffin equals 180 calories, 6 g fat (1 g saturated fat), 21 mg cholesterol, 159 mg sodium, 29 g carbohydrate, 1 g fiber, 3 g protein. **Diabetic Exchanges:** 1 starch, 1 fruit, 1 fat.

———— ☕ ☕ ☕ ————

Italian Bread Wedges

(Pictured at right)

These savory wedges aren't hard to make, but they taste great. They're terrific served with soups, salads and pasta dishes. —Danielle McIntyre
Medicine Hat, Alberta

✓ Uses less fat, sugar or salt. Includes Nutritional Analysis and Diabetic Exchanges.

3 teaspoons active dry yeast
1 cup warm water (110° to 115°), *divided*
1 teaspoon sugar
2 tablespoons canola oil
1 teaspoon salt
2-1/2 to 3 cups all-purpose flour
TOPPING:
1/3 cup fat-free Italian salad dressing
1/4 teaspoon garlic powder
1/4 teaspoon dried oregano
1/4 teaspoon dried thyme
Dash pepper
1 cup (4 ounces) shredded part-skim mozzarella cheese
1/4 cup grated Parmesan cheese

In a mixing bowl, dissolve yeast in 1/4 cup warm water. Add sugar; let stand for 5 minutes. Add the oil, salt, remaining water and 2 cups of flour; beat until smooth. Stir in enough remaining flour to form a soft dough. Turn onto a floured surface; knead until smooth and elastic, about 6-8 minutes. Place in a greased bowl, turning once to grease top. Cover and let rise in a warm place until doubled, about 40 minutes.

Punch dough down. Turn onto a lightly floured surface. Pat dough flat. Let rest for 5 minutes. Press into a greased 14-in. pizza pan. Spread with salad dressing. Combine the garlic powder, oregano, thyme and pepper; sprinkle over dough. Top with cheeses. Bake at 450° for 15-20 minutes or until golden brown. Serve warm. **Yield:** 12 slices.

Nutritional Analysis: One slice equals 146 calories, 3 g fat (1 g saturated fat), 7 mg cholesterol, 359 mg sodium, 23 g carbohydrate, 1 g fiber, 6 g protein. **Diabetic Exchanges:** 1-1/2 starch, 1/2 lean meat.

Cherry Kringle

(Pictured below)

The dough in this recipe bakes into a golden tender pastry that surrounds a luscious cherry center. It makes four loaves, so I serve one and freeze the others.
—*Mary Christianson, Carmel, Indiana*

      1 package (1/4 ounce) active dry yeast
      1 cup warm milk (110° to 115°)
      4 cups bread flour
      2 tablespoons sugar
      1 teaspoon salt
  1/2 cup cold butter *or* margarine
  1/2 cup shortening
      2 eggs, lightly beaten
      4 cups cherry pie filling
ICING:
      2 cups confectioners' sugar
      2 to 3 tablespoons milk

In a mixing bowl, dissolve yeast in warm milk. In another bowl, combine flour, sugar and salt; cut in butter and shortening until crumbly. Add to yeast mixture. Add eggs; beat to form a very soft dough (do not knead). Cover and refrigerate for at least 8 hours.

Turn dough onto a lightly floured surface; divide into fourths. Roll each portion into a 14-in. x 11-in. rectangle; spread cherry pie filling down the center third of each rectangle. Starting at a long side, fold a third of the dough over filling; fold other third over top; pinch to seal. Pinch ends and tuck under. Place 2 in. apart on greased baking sheets.

Bake at 350° for 25 minutes or until golden brown. Remove from pans to wire racks to cool completely. Combine icing ingredients; drizzle over kringles. **Yield:** 4 loaves.

Country Sage Loaves

Sage is my favorite seasoning, so I'm always pleased to fix and serve these rugged golden loaves. They're crusty on the outside and chewy inside.
—*Geraldine Grisdale, Mount Pleasant, Michigan*

      1 package (1/4 ounce) active dry yeast
      1 cup warm water (110° to 115°)
      1 teaspoon sugar
  1/4 cup toasted wheat germ
      2 tablespoons vegetable oil
      1 tablespoon honey
      2 teaspoons rubbed sage
      1 teaspoon salt
  1/2 teaspoon dried rosemary, crushed
  1/2 teaspoon ground nutmeg
      2 to 2-1/2 cups all-purpose flour

In a mixing bowl, dissolve yeast in warm water. Stir in sugar; let stand for 5 minutes. Add the wheat germ, oil, honey, sage, salt, rosemary, nutmeg and 1-1/2 cups flour. Beat until smooth. Stir in enough remaining flour to form a soft dough. Turn onto a floured surface; knead until smooth and elastic, about 6-8 minutes. Place in a greased bowl, turning once to grease top. Cover and let rise in a warm place until doubled, about 45 minutes.

Punch dough down. Turn onto a lightly floured surface; divide in half. Shape each portion into two oval loaves. Place on a greased baking sheet. Cover and let rise until doubled, about 15 minutes. With a sharp knife, make three shallow slashes across the top of each loaf. Bake at 400° for 13-17 minutes or until golden brown. Remove from pan to wire racks to cool. **Yield:** 2 loaves.

Cardamom Wreath

(Pictured above right)

This lovely ring has a sweet spicy flavor, and the pretty shape makes it a special treat to serve at Christmas dinner with Cardamom Butter. I've been cooking since I was very young, and yeast breads are my favorite things to bake. —*Judy Wilson, Vermont, Illinois*

      2 packages (1/4 ounce *each*) active dry
          yeast
  1/3 cup warm water (110° to 115°)
  1/2 cup butter *or* margarine, softened
  3/4 cup sugar
      4 eggs
      1 can (12 ounces) evaporated milk
  1/4 cup sour cream
      1 tablespoon grated orange peel
2-1/4 teaspoons ground cardamom

2 teaspoons salt
7 to 7-1/2 cups all-purpose flour
1 tablespoon milk
Toasted sliced almonds
Coarse or granulated sugar
CARDAMOM BUTTER:
    2 cups butter (no substitutes), softened
   1/4 cup confectioners' sugar
1-1/2 teaspoons grated orange peel
    1 to 1-1/2 teaspoons ground cardamom
   1/2 teaspoon ground nutmeg

In a small bowl, dissolve yeast in warm water. In a mixing bowl, cream butter and sugar. Beat in 3 eggs, evaporated milk, yeast mixture, sour cream, orange peel, cardamom and salt; mix well. Beat in 6 cups flour until smooth. Stir in enough remaining flour to form a soft dough. Turn onto a floured surface; knead until smooth and elastic, about 6-8 minutes. Place in a greased bowl, turning once to grease top. Cover and let rise in a warm place until doubled, about 1 hour.

Punch dough down; turn onto a floured surface. Divide into six portions. Cover and let rest for 10 minutes. Shape each portion into a 24-in. rope. Place three ropes on a greased baking sheet and braid. Form into a ring; pinch ends tightly together. Repeat with remaining dough. Cover and let rise until almost doubled, about 45 minutes.

Beat milk and remaining egg; brush over wreaths. Sprinkle with almonds and sugar. Bake at 375° for 25-30 minutes or until golden brown. Remove from pans to wire racks to cool. In a mixing bowl, beat cardamom butter ingredients until blended. Serve with bread. **Yield:** 2 loaves (2 cups butter).

Gift of the Magi Bread
(Pictured below)

I make this extra-special banana bread only once a year to celebrate Christmas. It's loaded with scrumptious ingredients such as coconut, mandarin oranges, dates, cherries, chocolate chips and almonds.
—Sandra Bonow, Lewiston, Minnesota

1/2 cup butter *or* margarine, softened
   1 cup sugar
   2 eggs
   1 teaspoon vanilla extract
   2 cups all-purpose flour
   1 teaspoon baking soda
1/2 teaspoon salt
   1 cup mashed ripe bananas (about 2 medium)
   1 can (11 ounces) mandarin oranges, drained
   1 cup flaked coconut
   1 cup (6 ounces) semisweet chocolate chips
2/3 cup sliced almonds, *divided*
1/2 cup chopped maraschino cherries
1/2 cup chopped dates

In a mixing bowl, cream butter and sugar. Beat in eggs and vanilla. Combine the flour, baking soda and salt; add to the creamed mixture alternately with bananas. Stir in the oranges, coconut, chocolate chips, 1/2 cup almonds, cherries and dates.

Pour into two greased 8-in. x 4-in. x 2-in. loaf pans. Sprinkle with remaining almonds. Bake at 350° for 50-55 minutes or until a toothpick inserted near the center comes out clean. Cool for 10 minutes before removing from pans to wire racks to cool completely. **Yield:** 2 loaves.

Cinnamon Coffee Ring

(Pictured below)

Crunchy walnuts and yummy cinnamon lend old-fashioned flavor to this comforting coffee cake. Serve a generous slice with coffee for breakfast or with a glass of iced tea for dessert. —Merrill Powers
Spearville, Kansas

      1 cup butter *or* margarine, softened
2-3/4 cups sugar, *divided*
      4 eggs
      2 teaspoons vanilla extract
      3 cups all-purpose flour
      2 teaspoons baking powder
      1 teaspoon baking soda
      1 teaspoon salt
      2 cups (16 ounces) sour cream
      2 tablespoons ground cinnamon
  1/2 cup chopped walnuts

In a mixing bowl, cream butter and 2 cups sugar. Add eggs, one at a time, beating well after each addition. Add vanilla; mix well. Combine the flour, baking powder, baking soda and salt; add to creamed mixture alternately with sour cream.

Spoon a third of the batter into a greased and floured 10-in. tube pan. Combine the cinnamon, nuts and remaining sugar; sprinkle a third over batter. Repeat layers twice. Bake at 350° for 65-70 minutes or until a toothpick inserted near the center comes out clean. Cool for 10 minutes before removing from the pan to a wire rack. **Yield:** 10-12 servings.

S'more Jumbo Muffins

(Pictured above and on page 89)

My daughter loves marshmallows, graham crackers and chocolate, so I came up with this muffin just for her. My whole family gobbles them up! Each bite reminds us of camping out during the summer.
—Pam Ivbuls, Omaha, Nebraska

1-1/2 cups all-purpose flour
  1/2 cup graham cracker crumbs (about 8 squares)
  1/4 cup packed brown sugar
    1 teaspoon baking soda
  1/2 teaspoon salt
    1 egg
1-1/2 cups buttermilk
  1/4 cup vegetable oil
  3/4 cup semisweet chocolate chips
1-1/4 cups miniature marshmallows, *divided*

In a large bowl, combine the dry ingredients. Combine egg, buttermilk and oil; mix well. Stir into dry ingredients just until moistened. Fold in chocolate chips and 1 cup marshmallows.

Fill greased jumbo muffin cups three-fourths full. Sprinkle with remaining marshmallows. Bake at 375° for 18-20 minutes or until a toothpick comes out clean. Cool for 5 minutes before removing from pan to a wire rack. Serve warm. **Yield:** 6 muffins.

Sage Breadsticks

Sage is subtle but wonderful in these cheesy crisp breadsticks. They're a fun snack or terrific alongside a bowl of soup or salad.
—_Sue Wagner_
West Farmington, Ohio

✓ Uses less fat, sugar or salt. Includes Nutritional Analysis and Diabetic Exchanges.

      1 cup all-purpose flour
1-1/2 teaspoons baking powder
      1 teaspoon rubbed sage
   1/2 teaspoon salt
   1/2 cup finely shredded cheddar cheese
      2 tablespoons cold butter **or** stick margarine
   1/3 cup cold water

In a bowl, combine the flour, baking powder, sage and salt; stir in cheese. Cut in butter until crumbly. Gradually add water, tossing with a fork until dough forms a ball.

On a lightly floured surface, roll dough into a 12-in. x 10-in. rectangle. Cut in half lengthwise; cut each half widthwise into 1-in. strips. Twist each strip two to three times. Place 1 in. apart on greased baking sheets. Bake at 425° for 8-10 minutes or until golden brown. **Yield:** 2 dozen.
Nutritional Analysis: One serving (2 breadsticks, (prepared with reduced-fat cheese) equals 70 calories, 3 g fat (2 g saturated fat), 9 mg cholesterol, 186 mg sodium, 8 g carbohydrate, trace fiber, 2 g protein. **Diabetic Exchanges:** 1/2 starch, 1/2 fat.

———— 🥄 🥄 🥄 ————

Sesame Onion Braid

(Pictured at right)

Convenient onion soup mix gives this stunning braided loaf mild onion flavor. It's even more delicious spread with Caramelized Onion Butter. As a music professor/conductor, I sometimes share this treat with my musicians to give us all an energy boost!
—_Patrice Stribling Donald, Edwardsville, Illinois_

      1 package (1/4 ounce) active dry yeast
1-1/4 cups warm water (110° to 115°),
         divided
      1 cup warm sour cream (110° to 115°)
      3 eggs
      1 envelope onion soup mix
      2 tablespoons butter **or** margarine, softened
      2 tablespoons sugar
      2 teaspoons salt
   1/4 teaspoon baking soda
6-1/2 to 6-3/4 cups all-purpose flour
      1 tablespoon cold water
      3 tablespoons sesame seeds

CARAMELIZED ONION BUTTER:
      1 tablespoon diced onion
      6 tablespoons butter (no substitutes), softened, _divided_
      1 garlic clove, minced
      1 package (3 ounces) cream cheese, cubed
   1/2 teaspoon minced fresh parsley

In a mixing bowl, dissolve yeast in 1/4 cup warm water; let stand for 5 minutes. Add sour cream, 2 eggs, onion soup mix, butter, sugar, salt, baking soda and remaining warm water; mix well. Stir in enough flour to form a soft dough. Turn onto a floured surface; knead until smooth and elastic, about 6-8 minutes. Place dough in a greased bowl, turning once to grease top. Cover and let rise in a warm place until doubled, about 1 hour.

Punch dough down. Turn onto a lightly floured surface; divide into six portions. Shape each into a 15-in. rope. Place three ropes on a greased baking sheet; braid. Pinch ends to seal; tuck under. Repeat. Cover and let rise until doubled, about 1 hour. Beat cold water and remaining egg; brush over dough. Sprinkle with sesame seeds. Bake at 350° for 35-40 minutes or until golden brown.

In skillet over low heat, saute onion in 1 tablespoon butter until golden brown. Add garlic; cook 1-2 minutes longer or until golden. In a mixing bowl, beat the cream cheese, onion mixture, parsley and remaining butter until creamy. Serve with bread. **Yield:** 2 loaves (2/3 cup butter).

Cookies & Bars

A plate of fresh-baked cookies and bars is the perfect treat for bake sales, all kinds of parties and just plain snacking.

——— 🥄 🥄 🥄 ———

SMALL AND SWEET. Clockwise from upper left: Sugared Raisin Pear Diamonds (p. 113), Pumpkin Chip Cookies (p. 111), Peanut Butter Squares (p. 120), Honey Pecan Triangles (p. 115) and Frosted Raspberry Bars (p. 110)

Frosted Raspberry Bars

(Pictured below and on page 108)

While I was visiting a friend, her daughter gave me one of these tempting treats to try. After one bite, I knew I had to have the recipe. The cake-like bars with a fruity filling and creamy frosting are a sweet solution for any potluck or party. —Esther Horst
Augusta, Wisconsin

    1 cup butter (no substitutes), softened
1/4 cup sugar
    3 cups all-purpose flour
    3 teaspoons baking powder
    1 teaspoon salt
    2 eggs
1/2 cup milk
    1 teaspoon vanilla extract
    1 can (21 ounces) raspberry pie filling
FROSTING:
    1 tablespoon butter, softened
    1 tablespoon shortening
    1 ounce cream cheese, softened
    2 tablespoons marshmallow creme
1/2 cup plus 1 tablespoon confectioners'
      sugar
    1 tablespoon milk

In a mixing bowl, cream butter and sugar. Combine the flour, baking powder and salt. Combine the eggs, milk and vanilla. Add the dry ingredients to creamed mixture alternately with egg mixture; mix well. Divide dough in half; chill for 2 hours or until firm.

Roll out one portion of dough into a 15-in. x 10-in. x 1-in. rectangle; carefully transfer to a greased 15-in. x 10-in. x 1-in. baking pan. Spread with raspberry filling. Roll out remaining dough to 1/4-in. thickness. Cut into 1/2-in.-wide strips; make a lattice crust over filling. Bake at 350° for 30 minutes or until golden brown. Cool on a wire rack.

In a mixing bowl, beat the butter, shortening, cream cheese and marshmallow creme until smooth. Add the confectioners' sugar and milk; mix well. Drizzle over bars. Refrigerate until set before cutting. **Yield:** about 2 dozen.

— 🥣 🥣 🥣 —

Orange Spritz Cookies

Brown sugar gives these spritz cookies a lovely light caramel tint. This variation has a rich buttery short-bread taste and texture with a hint of orange flavor.
—Sean Fleming, St. Charles, Illinois

1/2 cup butter (no substitutes), softened
    1 package (3 ounces) cream cheese,
      softened
1/2 cup packed brown sugar
    2 teaspoons grated orange peel
1/2 teaspoon orange *or* vanilla extract
1-1/2 cups all-purpose flour
1/4 teaspoon salt
Colored sugar

In a mixing bowl, cream the butter, cream cheese and brown sugar. Beat in orange peel and extract. Combine flour and salt; gradually add to creamed mixture.

Using a cookie press fitted with the disk of your choice, press cookies 1 in. apart onto ungreased baking sheets. Sprinkle with colored sugar. Bake at 375° for 6-9 minutes or until lightly browned. Cool for 2 minutes before removing to wire racks. **Yield:** about 5-1/2 dozen.

— 🥣 🥣 🥣 —

Frosted Cocoa Cookies

Almond flavor in the chocolate frosting accents these soft cookies nicely. My husband and two sons gobble them up quickly.
—Diane Moran
Rhame, North Dakota

    1 cup shortening
    2 cups sugar
    4 eggs
    2 teaspoons vanilla extract
3-1/2 cups all-purpose flour
    1 cup baking cocoa
    2 teaspoons baking soda
    1 teaspoon salt
FROSTING:
    3 cups confectioners' sugar
1/3 cup baking cocoa
1/3 cup butter *or* margarine, softened
1/4 teaspoon almond extract
    3 to 4 tablespoons milk

In a large mixing bowl, cream shortening and sugar. Add eggs, one at a time, beating well after each addition. Beat in vanilla. Combine the flour, cocoa, baking soda and salt; gradually add to creamed mixture. Roll into 1-1/2-in. balls. Place 2 in. apart on ungreased baking sheets. Bake at 350° for 13-16 minutes or until set. Remove to wire racks to cool.

For frosting, in a mixing bowl, combine the confectioners' sugar, cocoa, butter and extract. Add enough milk to achieve spreading consistency. Frost cooled cookies. **Yield:** 3-1/2 dozen.

— 🍵 🍵 🍵 —

Pumpkin Chip Cookies

(Pictured above and on page 108)

These cookies are my favorite. They disappear quickly from my dessert trays. The subtle pumpkin and cinnamon flavors pair nicely with chocolate chips.
—*Tami Burroughs, Salem, Oregon*

1-1/2 cups butter (no substitutes), softened
    2 cups packed brown sugar
    1 cup sugar
    1 can (15 ounces) solid-pack pumpkin
    1 egg
    1 teaspoon vanilla extract
    4 cups all-purpose flour
    2 cups quick-cooking oats
    2 teaspoons baking soda
    2 teaspoons ground cinnamon
    1 teaspoon salt
    2 cups (12 ounces) semisweet chocolate
      chips

In a large mixing bowl, cream butter and sugars. Beat in the pumpkin, egg and vanilla. Combine the flour, oats, baking soda, cinnamon and salt; gradually add to creamed mixture. Stir in chocolate chips. Drop by tablespoonfuls 2 in. apart onto ungreased baking sheets. Bake at 350° for 10-12 minutes or until lightly browned. Remove to wire racks to cool. **Yield:** 10 dozen.

Molasses Raisin Cookies

These old-fashioned mildly sweet cookies are dotted with walnuts and raisins. We like them soft right from the oven. Later, they crisp up and are perfect for dunking. —*Denise Hymel, Gramercy, Louisiana*

  3/4 cup shortening
    1 cup packed brown sugar
  1/4 cup molasses
    2 eggs
2-1/4 cups all-purpose flour
    1 teaspoon baking soda
    1 teaspoon ground ginger
    1 teaspoon ground cinnamon
  1/2 teaspoon salt
  1/2 teaspoon ground cloves
  1/2 cup raisins
  1/2 cup chopped walnuts

In a mixing bowl, cream shortening and brown sugar. Beat in molasses. Add eggs, one at a time, beating well after each. Combine flour, baking soda, ginger, cinnamon, salt and cloves; gradually add to creamed mixture. Stir in raisins and nuts.

Drop by rounded tablespoonfuls 2 in. apart onto greased baking sheets. Bake at 375° for 8-10 minutes or until edges are lightly browned. Remove to wire racks to cool. **Yield:** about 3-1/2 dozen.

— 🍵 🍵 🍵 —

Welsh Tea Cakes

These longtime family favorites are crisp on the outside, slightly chewy in the center and full of currants. The dough is not overly sweet, so sprinkling the tops with sugar enhances the flavor and gives them a nice look. —*Wendy Lehman, Huron, Ohio*

2-1/2 cups all-purpose flour
    1 cup cold butter (no substitutes)
  3/4 cup sugar
  1/4 cup quick-cooking oats
  1/2 teaspoon salt
  1/2 teaspoon ground nutmeg
    2 eggs
  1/4 cup milk
    1 cup dried currants
Additional sugar, optional

Place flour in a bowl; cut in butter until mixture resembles coarse crumbs. Add the sugar, oats, salt and nutmeg. Stir in the eggs and milk. Add currants.

On a heavily floured surface, roll out dough to 1/4-in. thickness. Cut with a floured 2-1/2-in. round cookie cutter. Place 2 in. apart on greased baking sheets. Sprinkle with sugar if desired. Bake at 350° for 12-16 minutes or until lightly browned. Remove to wire racks to cool. **Yield:** 3 dozen.

Apricot Meringue Bars

(Pictured above)

Each year for our family picnic, I'm expected to bring these wonderful treats. Their sweet apricot filling and delicate meringue topping make them everyone's favorite. I wouldn't dream of hosting a get-together without serving these bars.

—Krissy Fossmeyer, Huntley, Illinois

> 3 cups all-purpose flour
> 1 cup sugar, *divided*
> 1 cup cold butter (no substitutes)
> 4 eggs, *separated*
> 1 teaspoon vanilla extract
> 2 cans (12 ounces *each*) apricot filling
> 1/2 cup chopped pecans

In a bowl, combine flour and 1/2 cup sugar; cut in butter until crumbly. Add egg yolks and vanilla; mix well. Press into a greased 15-in. x 10-in. x 1-in. baking pan. Bake at 350° for 12-15 minutes or until lightly browned. Spread apricot filling over crust.

In a small mixing bowl, beat the egg whites until soft peaks form. Gradually add the remaining sugar, beating until stiff peaks form. Spread over apricot layer; sprinkle with pecans. Bake for 25-30 minutes or until lightly browned. Cool on a wire rack. Cut into bars. Refrigerate leftovers. **Yield:** 32 bars.

Frosted Pumpkin Cranberry Bars

With tangy dried cranberries tucked inside and a creamy browned butter frosting, these mildly spiced pumpkin bars are doubly delightful. It's a good thing the recipe makes lots because once you taste one, you won't be able to resist going back for more!

—Barbara Nowakowski, Mesa, Arizona

> 1-1/2 cups all-purpose flour
> 1-1/4 cups sugar
> 2 teaspoons baking powder
> 2 teaspoons ground cinnamon
> 1 teaspoon baking soda
> 1/2 teaspoon ground ginger
> 3 eggs
> 1 can (15 ounces) solid-pack pumpkin
> 3/4 cup butter (no substitutes), melted
> 3/4 cup chopped dried cranberries
> **BROWN BUTTER FROSTING:**
> 1/2 cup butter
> 4 cups confectioners' sugar
> 1 teaspoon vanilla extract
> 4 to 6 tablespoons milk

In a bowl, combine the first six ingredients. In another bowl, whisk the eggs, pumpkin and butter; stir into dry ingredients until well combined. Stir in cranberries. Spread into a greased 15-in. x 10-in. x 1-in. baking pan. Bake at 350° for 20-25 minutes or until a toothpick inserted near the center comes out clean. Cool on a wire rack.

For frosting, heat butter in a saucepan over medium heat until golden brown, about 7 minutes. Remove from the heat; cool for 5 minutes. Stir in confectioners' sugar, vanilla and enough milk to achieve spreading consistency. Spread over bars before cutting. **Yield:** about 4 dozen.

Granola Cookie Bars

My wife and I love to experiment with new recipes. These oat-based bars are chock-full of tasty ingredients like chocolate chips, coconut and raisins.

—Brian Fox, Fergus Falls, Minnesota

> 1/2 cup butter *or* margarine, softened
> 1-1/2 cups sugar
> 1-1/2 cups packed brown sugar
> 4 eggs
> 2 teaspoons vanilla extract
> 1 teaspoon water
> 4 cups old-fashioned oats
> 3 cups all-purpose flour
> 2 teaspoons salt
> 2 cups (12 ounces) semisweet chocolate chips

1 cup flaked coconut
1 cup raisins

In a mixing bowl, cream butter and sugars. Add eggs, one at a time, beating well after each. Beat in vanilla and water. Combine oats, flour and salt; gradually add to the creamed mixture. Stir in chocolate chips, coconut and raisins.

Press into a greased 15-in. x 10-in. x 1-in. baking pan. Bake at 350° for 22-27 minutes or until golden brown. Cool on a wire rack. Cut into bars. **Yield:** 4 dozen.

— 🏆 🏆 🏆 —

Rich Butterscotch Bars

My husband works second shift, so I spend a few nights a week baking just for fun. He takes half of my sweets to his co-workers, who frequently ask for these tasty bars. —Kathryn Roth, Jefferson, Wisconsin

1 package (10 to 11 ounces) butterscotch chips
1/2 cup butter (no substitutes)
2 cups graham cracker crumbs (about 32 squares)
1 package (8 ounces) cream cheese, softened
1 can (14 ounces) sweetened condensed milk
1 egg
1 teaspoon vanilla extract
1 cup chopped pecans

In a large microwave-safe bowl, heat the chips and butter on high for 1-1/2 to 2 minutes or until chips are melted, stirring every 30 seconds until smooth. Add the cracker crumbs; set aside 2/3 cup. Press the remaining crumb mixture into a greased 13-in. x 9-in. x 2-in. baking pan.

In a small mixing bowl, beat cream cheese until smooth. Add the milk, egg and vanilla; mix well. Stir in pecans. Pour over the crust. Sprinkle with reserved crumb mixture. Bake at 325° for 30-35 minutes or until a toothpick inserted near the center comes out clean. Cool on a wire rack. Store in the refrigerator. **Yield:** 3 dozen.

— 🏆 🏆 🏆 —

Sugared Raisin Pear Diamonds

(Pictured at right and on page 108)

With their tender golden crust and tempting pear and raisin filling, these fabulous bars stand out on any buffet table. —Jeanne Allen, Rye, Colorado

2-1/2 cups plus 4-1/2 teaspoons all-purpose flour, *divided*

1/4 cup plus 6 tablespoons sugar, *divided*
1/2 teaspoon salt
3/4 cup cold butter (no substitutes)
1/2 teaspoon grated lemon peel
1/2 cup half-and-half cream
6 cups diced peeled ripe pears (about 7)
6 tablespoons golden raisins
1/4 cup lemon juice
1/8 to 1/4 teaspoon ground cinnamon
1 egg, lightly beaten
Additional sugar

In a bowl, combine 2-1/2 cups flour, 1/4 cup sugar and salt. Cut in butter and lemon peel until mixture resembles coarse crumbs. Gradually add cream, tossing with a fork, until dough forms a ball. Divide in half.

Roll out one portion onto lightly floured waxed paper or pastry cloth into a 16-in. x 11-1/2-in. rectangle. Transfer to an ungreased 15-in. x 10-in. x 1-in. baking pan. Bake at 350° for 10-15 minutes or until lightly browned. Cool on a wire rack. Increase temperature to 400°.

In a bowl, combine the pears, raisins, lemon juice, cinnamon, and remaining flour and sugar. Spread over crust. Roll out remaining dough into a 16-in. x 12-in. rectangle; place over filling. Trim and seal edges. Brush top with egg; sprinkle with additional sugar. Bake for 30-34 minutes or until golden brown. Cool on a wire rack. Cut into diamond-shaped bars. **Yield:** about 2 dozen.

Fudgy Mint Squares

(Pictured above)

I've had this recipe since I was in junior high school. No one can resist the fudgy brownie base, cool minty cheesecake filling and luscious chocolate glaze.
—Heather Campbell, Lawrence, Kansas

  10 **tablespoons butter (no substitutes), *divided***
   3 **squares (1 ounce *each*) unsweetened chocolate, chopped**
   3 **eggs**
1-1/2 **cups sugar**
   2 **teaspoons vanilla extract**
   1 **cup all-purpose flour**
   1 **package (8 ounces) cream cheese, softened**
   1 **tablespoon cornstarch**
   1 **can (14 ounces) sweetened condensed milk**
   1 **teaspoon peppermint extract**
   4 **drops green food coloring, optional**
   1 **cup (6 ounces) semisweet chocolate chips**
1/2 **cup whipping cream**

In a microwave-safe bowl, melt 8 tablespoons butter and unsweetened chocolate; cool slightly. In a mixing bowl, beat 2 eggs, sugar and vanilla. Add the chocolate mixture; mix until blended. Gradually beat in flour. Spread into a greased 13-in. x 9-in. x 2-in. baking pan. Bake at 350° for 15-20 minutes or until top is set.

In a mixing bowl, beat cream cheese and remaining butter. Add cornstarch; beat until smooth. Gradually beat in milk and remaining egg. Add ex-tract and food coloring if desired. Pour over crust. Bake for 15-20 minutes or until center is almost set. Cool on a wire rack.

Meanwhile, in a heavy saucepan, combine chocolate chips and cream. Cook and stir over medium heat until chips are melted. Cool for 30 minutes or until lukewarm, stirring occasionally. Pour over cream cheese layer. Chill for 2 hours or until set before cutting. **Yield:** about 4 dozen.

— 🍶 🍶 🍶 —

Blueberry Lattice Bars

(Pictured below)

Our area has an annual blueberry festival, so I am always looking for new recipes to enter in the cooking contest. These bars won a blue ribbon one year.
—Debbie Ayers, Baileyville, Maine

   1 **cup butter (no substitutes), softened**
1/2 **cup sugar**
   1 **egg**
2-3/4 **cups all-purpose flour**
1/2 **teaspoon vanilla extract**
1/4 **teaspoon salt**
FILLING:
   3 **cups fresh *or* frozen blueberries**
   1 **cup sugar**
   3 **tablespoons cornstarch**

In a mixing bowl, cream butter and sugar. Add the egg, flour, vanilla and salt; mix well. Cover and refrigerate for 2 hours. Meanwhile, in a saucepan, bring the blueberries, sugar and cornstarch to a boil. Cook and stir for 2 minutes or until thickened.

Roll two-thirds of the dough into a 14-in. x 10-in. rectangle. Place in a greased 13-in. x 9-in. x 2-in. baking dish. Top with filling. Roll out remaining dough to 1/4-in. thickness. Cut into 1/2-in.-wide strips; make a lattice crust over filling. Bake at 375° for 30-35 minutes or until top is golden brown. Cool on a wire rack. Cut into bars. **Yield:** 2 dozen.

Oatmeal Raisin Cookies

The first time I made these sweet chewy cookies, I didn't tell my family they were low in fat. Their reaction when they found out? "No way!" —Julie Hauser Sheridan, California

✓ Uses less fat, sugar or salt. Includes Nutritional Analysis and Diabetic Exchanges.

      1 cup raisins
  1/4 cup water
      3 egg whites
      1 tablespoon molasses
      1 cup sugar
      1 cup packed brown sugar
1-1/2 teaspoons vanilla extract
      1 cup all-purpose flour
  1/2 cup nonfat dry milk powder
1-1/2 teaspoons baking powder
1-1/2 teaspoons ground cinnamon
2-1/2 cups quick-cooking oats

In a food processor or blender, combine the raisins, water, egg whites and molasses. Cover and process for 10-15 seconds or until the raisins are finely chopped. Transfer to a mixing bowl. Beat in sugars and vanilla. Combine the flour, milk powder, baking powder and cinnamon; gradually add to raisin mixture. Stir in oats.

Drop by tablespoonfuls 2 in. apart onto baking sheets coated with nonstick cooking spray. Bake at 350° for 8-10 minutes or until edges are golden brown. Remove to wire racks to cool. **Yield:** 44 cookies.

Nutritional Analysis: One cookie equals 77 calories, trace fat (trace saturated fat), trace cholesterol, 24 mg sodium, 18 g carbohydrate, 1 g fiber, 1 g protein. **Diabetic Exchange:** 1 starch.

Potato Chip Cookies

These treats get their crunch from potato chips and pecans. My grandson, Cameron, enjoys helping make these deliciously different cookies, which are a family favorite. —Dona McCloskey, Minerva, Ohio

  2 cups butter (no substitutes), softened
  1 cup sugar
  4 cups all-purpose flour
  2 teaspoons vanilla extract
  1 cup crushed potato chips
  1 cup chopped pecans

In a large mixing bowl, cream butter and sugar. Gradually add flour, beating until combined. Beat in the vanilla. Stir in potato chips and nuts. Cover and refrigerate for 1 hour.

Drop dough by tablespoonfuls 2 in. apart onto ungreased baking sheets. Bake at 350° for 12-15 minutes or until golden brown. Remove to wire racks to cool. **Yield:** 5 dozen.

Honey Pecan Triangles
(Pictured below and on page 109)

I've been stirring up batches of these tasty bar cookies for many years, and they're a big hit wherever I share them. They have all the goodness of pecan pie. —Debbie Fogel, East Berne, New York

  2 teaspoons plus 1/2 cup butter (no substitutes), softened, *divided*
  1/2 cup packed brown sugar
  1 egg yolk
1-1/2 cups all-purpose flour
TOPPING:
  1 cup packed brown sugar
  1/2 cup butter
  1/4 cup honey
  1/2 cup whipping cream
  4 cups chopped pecans

Line a 13-in. x 9-in. x 2-in. baking pan with foil; butter the foil with 2 teaspoons butter. In a mixing bowl, cream remaining butter with brown sugar. Add egg yolk; mix well. Gradually add flour. Press into prepared pan. Bake at 350° for 15 minutes or until golden brown.

Meanwhile, in a saucepan, combine the brown sugar, butter and honey. Bring to a boil over medium heat; cook and stir for 3 minutes. Remove from the heat; stir in cream and pecans. Pour over crust. Bake for 30 minutes or until hot and bubbly. Cool completely on a wire rack.

Use foil to lift the bars out of the pan and place on a cutting board. Carefully remove foil. Cut into 24 bars; cut each in half diagonally. **Yield:** 4 dozen.

Easter Sugar Cookies

(Pictured above)

Cream cheese contributes to the rich taste of these melt-in-your-mouth cookies. They have such nice flavor, you can skip the frosting and sprinkle them with colored sugar for a change. —Julie Brunette
Green Bay, Wisconsin

   1 cup butter (no substitutes), softened
   1 package (3 ounces) cream cheese, softened
   1 cup sugar
   1 egg yolk
1/2 teaspoon vanilla extract
1/4 teaspoon almond extract
2-1/4 cups all-purpose flour
1/2 teaspoon salt
1/4 teaspoon baking soda
Tinted frosting *or* colored sugar

In a mixing bowl, cream butter, cream cheese and sugar. Beat in egg yolk and extracts. Combine the flour, salt and baking soda; gradually add to creamed mixture. Cover and refrigerate for 3 hours or until easy to handle.

On a lightly floured surface, roll out dough to 1/8-in. thickness. Cut with a 2-1/2-in. cookie cutter dipped in flour. Place 1 in. apart on ungreased baking sheets. Bake at 375° for 8-10 minutes or until edges begin to brown. Cool for 2 minutes before removing from pans to wire racks. Decorate as desired. **Yield:** 4 dozen.

Giant Pizza Cookie

My husband and I were taking care of our two grandsons, Nathan and Brandon, and their mom left the ingredients for this fun dessert. The boys loved pressing the dough into the pan, spreading the frosting and adding the candy "pizza" toppings. They were so proud to serve yummy wedges to their parents when they returned. —Ruth Shefcyk, Lake Orion, Michigan

1/2 cup butter *or* margarine, softened
1/2 cup packed brown sugar
   1 egg
1/2 teaspoon vanilla extract
   1 cup all-purpose flour
3/4 cup old-fashioned oats
1/2 teaspoon baking soda
1/4 teaspoon salt
   1 cup (6 ounces) semisweet chocolate chips
TOPPING:
   1 cup prepared chocolate frosting
2/3 cup M&M miniature baking bits
   3 ounces white candy coating, grated
1/2 cup chopped gumdrops
   1 piece (10 to 12 inches) strawberry Fruit by the Foot

In a mixing bowl, cream the butter and brown sugar. Beat in egg and vanilla. Combine the flour, oats, baking soda and salt; gradually add to creamed mixture. Stir in the chocolate chips. Spread onto a greased 12-in. pizza pan. Bake at 350° for 14-16 minutes or until golden brown. Cool on a wire rack.

Spread frosting over cookie. Sprinkle with M&M's, candy coating and gumdrops. For "pepperoni", cut circles in strawberry fruit roll; arrange on top of the pizza. Cut into wedges. **Yield:** 10-12 servings.

— 🍴 🍴 🍴 —

Sesame Seed Cookies

These golden cookies are light inside, chewy outside and really showcase the flavor of sesame. Just one cookie is never enough! —Joan Humphreys
Ellicott City, Maryland

1/2 cup shortening
1/2 cup butter *or* margarine, softened
   2 cups sugar
   5 eggs
   1 teaspoon vanilla extract
3-1/2 cups all-purpose flour
   5 teaspoons baking powder
1/2 teaspoon salt
   3 tablespoons milk
   5 tablespoons sesame seeds, toasted

In a large mixing bowl, cream the shortening, butter and sugar. Add eggs, one at a time, beating well after each addition. Beat in vanilla. Combine the flour, baking powder and salt; gradually add to creamed mixture.

Drop by tablespoonfuls 3 in. apart onto greased baking sheets. Brush with milk; sprinkle with sesame seeds. Bake at 400° for 8-10 minutes or until golden brown. Remove to wire racks to cool. **Yield:** about 5-1/2 dozen.

Decorated Butter Cookies

Tender, crisp and flavorful, these versatile cookies can be decorated to suit any season or occasion.
— _Doris Schumacher, Brookings, South Dakota_

    1 **cup butter (no substitutes), softened**
1/2 **cup sugar**
1/2 **cup packed brown sugar**
    1 **egg**
    1 **teaspoon vanilla extract**
    2 **cups all-purpose flour**
    2 **teaspoons cream of tartar**
    1 **teaspoon baking soda**
1/8 **teaspoon salt**
Colored sugar, ground nuts _and/or_ chocolate _or_ colored sprinkles

In a mixing bowl, cream butter and sugars. Beat in egg and vanilla. Combine the flour, cream of tartar, baking soda and salt; gradually add to creamed mixture. Cover and refrigerate for 1 hour.

Roll into 1-in. balls. Place 2 in. apart on ungreased baking sheets. Flatten with a glass dipped in sugar; sprinkle with colored sugar, nuts or sprinkles. Bake at 350° for 10-12 minutes or until lightly browned. Remove to wire racks to cool. **Yield:** 4 dozen.

Chewy Macaroons

My family loves these delicious cookies on special occasions. With only three ingredients, they're a snap to make. — _Marcia Hostetter, Canton, New York_

5-1/3 **cups flaked coconut**
    1 **can (14 ounces) sweetened condensed milk**
    2 **teaspoons vanilla extract**

In a bowl, combine all ingredients. Drop 2 in. apart onto greased baking sheets. Bake at 350° for 10-12 minutes or until lightly browned. With a spatula dipped in water, immediately remove to wire racks to cool. **Yield:** 4-1/4 dozen.

Candy Cereal Treats

(Pictured below)

These scrumptious bars travel well and are loved by kids of all ages. — _Janet Shearer, Jackson, Michigan_

1/2 **cup butter _or_ margarine, softened**
2/3 **cup packed brown sugar**
    2 **egg yolks**
    1 **teaspoon vanilla extract**
1-1/2 **cups all-purpose flour**
1/2 **teaspoon baking powder**
1/2 **teaspoon salt**
1/4 **teaspoon baking soda**
    3 **cups miniature marshmallows**
TOPPING:
2/3 **cup corn syrup**
1/4 **cup butter _or_ margarine**
    1 **package (10 ounces) peanut butter chips**
    2 **teaspoons vanilla extract**
    2 **cups crisp rice cereal**
    1 **cup salted peanuts**
    1 **cup plain M&M's**

In a mixing bowl, cream butter and brown sugar. Beat in egg yolks and vanilla. Combine the flour, baking powder, salt and baking soda; gradually add to the creamed mixture until mixture resembles coarse crumbs (do not overmix).

Press into a greased 13-in. x 9-in. x 2-in. baking pan. Bake at 350° for 12-14 minutes or until golden brown. Immediately sprinkle with marshmallows; bake 2-3 minutes longer or until marshmallows are puffed. Cool on a wire rack.

For topping, combine the corn syrup, butter and peanut butter chips in a saucepan. Cook and stir over medium heat until chips are melted and mixture is smooth. Remove from the heat; stir in the vanilla, cereal, nuts and M&M's. Spread over crust. Cool before cutting. **Yield:** 2 dozen.

Apple Pie Bars

(Pictured below)

This is only one of the many wonderful recipes that my mother handed down to me. These delicious bars, with their flaky crust and scrumptious fruity filling, are the perfect way to serve apple pie to a crowd.
—Janet English, Pittsburgh, Pennsylvania

    4 cups all-purpose flour
    1 teaspoon salt
    1 teaspoon baking powder
    1 cup shortening
    4 egg yolks
    2 tablespoons lemon juice
    8 to 10 tablespoons cold water
FILLING:
    7 cups finely chopped peeled apples
    2 cups sugar
  1/4 cup all-purpose flour
    2 teaspoons ground cinnamon
Dash ground nutmeg
GLAZE:
    1 cup confectioners' sugar
    1 tablespoon milk
    1 tablespoon lemon juice

In a large bowl, combine the flour, salt and baking powder. Cut in the shortening until mixture resembles coarse crumbs. In a small bowl, whisk the egg yolks, lemon juice and water; gradually add to the flour mixture, tossing with a fork until dough forms a ball. Divide in half. Refrigerate for 30 minutes.

Roll out one portion of dough between two large sheets of waxed paper into a 17-in. x 12-in. rectangle. Transfer to an ungreased 15-in. x 10-in. x 1-

in. baking pan. Press pastry onto the bottom and up the sides of pan; trim pastry even with top edge.

In a bowl, toss the apples, sugar, flour, cinnamon and nutmeg; spread over crust. Roll out remaining pastry to fit top of pan; place over filling. Trim edges; brush edges between pastry with water or milk; pinch to seal. Cut slits in top. Bake at 375° for 45-50 minutes or until golden brown. Cool on a wire rack. Combine glaze ingredients until smooth; drizzle over bars before cutting. **Yield:** about 2 dozen.

— 🏆 🏆 🏆 —

Orange Cheesecake Bars

On the last day of first grade, our teacher treated the class to little cups with orange sherbet and vanilla ice cream swirled together. It was the best thing I'd ever tasted! I tried to capture that same flavor when I created these rich creamy layered bars.
—Connie Faulkner, Moxee, Washington

    2 cups crushed vanilla wafers (about 40)
  1/4 cup butter (no substitutes), melted
    3 packages (8 ounces *each*) cream cheese, softened
    1 can (14 ounces) sweetened condensed milk
    3 eggs
    2 teaspoons vanilla extract
    2 tablespoons orange juice concentrate
    1 teaspoon grated orange peel
    1 teaspoon orange extract
    5 drops yellow food coloring
    3 drops red food coloring

In a bowl, combine the wafer crumbs and butter. Press into a greased 13-in. x 9-in. x 2-in. baking pan. In a mixing bowl, beat the cream cheese until smooth. Add the milk, eggs and vanilla; beat just until combined. Pour half over crust.

Add the orange juice concentrate, orange peel, extract and food coloring to the remaining cream cheese mixture; beat until combined. Pour over first layer. Bake at 325° for 45-50 minutes or until center is almost set. Cool on a wire rack. Refrigerate for at least 2 hours before cutting. **Yield:** 3 dozen.

— 🏆 🏆 🏆 —

Surprise Package Cookies

Each of these cookies has a chocolate mint candy inside. They're my very favorite cookie and are always part of our Christmas cookie trays. They also make a great gift wrapped up in a pretty tin. Either way, these pleasing cookies are well received.
—Loraine Meyer, Bend, Oregon

    1 cup butter (no substitutes), softened
    1 cup sugar
  1/2 cup packed brown sugar
    2 eggs
    1 teaspoon vanilla extract
    3 cups all-purpose flour
    1 teaspoon baking powder
  1/2 teaspoon salt
  65 mint Andes candies

In a mixing bowl, cream butter and sugars. Add eggs, one at a time, beating well after each addition. Beat in vanilla. Combine the flour, baking powder and salt; gradually add to creamed mixture. Cover and refrigerate for 2 hours or until easy to handle. With floured hands, shape a tablespoonful of dough around 42 candies, forming rectangular cookies.

    Place 2 in. apart on greased baking sheets. Bake at 375° for 10-12 minutes or until the edges are golden brown. Remove to wire racks to cool. Meanwhile, in a microwave or saucepan, melt the remaining mint candies; drizzle over cookies. **Yield:** 3-1/2 dozen.

Greek Holiday Cookies

These buttery golden twists are a traditional treat in Greece, where they are usually made for Easter and other celebrations. One side of my family is Greek, and I enjoy making foods that keep me in touch with my heritage. —Nicole Moskou, St. Petersburg, Florida

1-1/2 cups butter (no substitutes), softened
1-1/4 cups sugar
    4 eggs
    2 tablespoons orange juice
    1 tablespoon vanilla extract
5-1/4 cups all-purpose flour
1-1/2 teaspoons baking powder
  3/4 teaspoon baking soda

In a large mixing bowl, cream the butter and sugar. Add 2 eggs, one at a time, beating well after each addition. Beat in the orange juice and vanilla. Combine the flour, baking powder and baking soda; gradually add to the creamed mixture. Cover and refrigerate for 1 hour or until dough is easy to handle.

    Roll dough into 1-1/4-in. balls. Shape each ball into a 6-in. rope; fold in half and twist twice. Place 2 in. apart on ungreased baking sheets. In a small bowl, beat remaining eggs; brush over dough. Bake at 350° for 7-12 minutes or until edges are golden brown. Remove to wire racks to cool. **Yield:** about 6-1/2 dozen.

Chocolate Chip Graham Bars

(Pictured above)

These moist chewy bars are a satisfying snack any time of day. Packed with oats, chocolate chips, crunchy peanuts and graham cereal, they have something for everyone. —Sandi Michalski, Macy, Indiana

  3/4 cup butter (no substitutes), softened
  3/4 cup sugar
  3/4 cup packed brown sugar
    2 eggs
    1 teaspoon vanilla extract
1-1/2 cups all-purpose flour
1-1/2 cups Golden Grahams cereal, crushed
  3/4 cup plus 2 tablespoons quick-cooking oats, _divided_
    1 teaspoon baking soda
  1/2 teaspoon baking powder
  1/2 teaspoon salt
    1 cup salted peanuts, _divided_
    1 cup (6 ounces) semisweet chocolate chips, _divided_

In a large mixing bowl, cream butter and sugars. Add eggs, one at a time, beating well after each addition. Beat in vanilla. Combine the flour, cereal, 3/4 cup oats, baking soda, baking powder and salt; gradually add to creamed mixture. Stir in 3/4 cup peanuts and 2/3 cup chocolate chips.

    Spread into a greased 13-in. x 9-in. x 2-in. baking pan. Coarsely chop remaining peanuts; sprinkle over the top with remaining oats and chips. Bake at 350° for 25-30 minutes or until golden brown. Cool on a wire rack. Cut into bars. **Yield:** 2 dozen.

Peanut Butter Squares

(Pictured above and on page 109)

I grew up in Lancaster County, Pennsylvania and spent a lot of time in the kitchen with my mom and grandmother preparing Pennsylvania Dutch classics. This scrumptious recipe, which combines two of our favorite flavors, is one I adapted. —Rachel Keller
Roanoke, Virginia

> 3/4 cup cold butter (no substitutes), cubed
> 2 squares (1 ounce *each*) semisweet chocolate
> 1-1/2 cups graham cracker crumbs (about 24 squares)
> 1 cup flaked coconut
> 1/2 cup chopped salted peanuts
> 1/4 cup toasted wheat germ
> **FILLING:**
> 2 packages (8 ounces *each*) cream cheese, softened
> 3/4 cup sugar
> 2/3 cup chunky peanut butter
> 1 teaspoon vanilla extract
> **TOPPING:**
> 4 squares (1 ounce *each*) semisweet chocolate
> 1/4 cup butter

In a microwave-safe bowl, heat butter and chocolate on high for 1 minute; stir. Microwave 30-60 seconds longer or until melted; stir until smooth. Stir in the cracker crumbs, coconut, peanuts and wheat germ. Press into a greased 13-in. x 9-in. x 2-in. dish. Cover and refrigerate for at least 30 minutes.

In a small mixing bowl, combine filling ingredients; mix well. Spread over crust. Cover and refrigerate for at least 30 minutes.

In a microwave-safe bowl, heat chocolate and butter on high for 45 seconds; stir. Microwave 30 seconds longer or until melted; stir until smooth. Pour over filling. Cover and refrigerate for at least 30 minutes or until the topping is set. Cut into squares. Refrigerate leftovers. **Yield:** 4 dozen.

Editor's Note: This recipe was tested in an 850-watt microwave.

— 🍺 🍺 🍺 —

Low-Fat Chocolate Cookies

These cake-like cookies have a mild cocoa flavor. They're so good, no one misses the fat.
—Mary Houchin, Swansea, Illinois

✓ Uses less fat, sugar or salt. Includes Nutritional Analysis and Diabetic Exchanges.

> 1/2 cup unsweetened applesauce
> 1/3 cup canola oil
> 3 egg whites
> 3/4 cup sugar
> 3/4 cup packed brown sugar
> 2 teaspoons vanilla extract
> 2-2/3 cups all-purpose flour
> 1/2 cup baking cocoa
> 1 teaspoon baking soda
> 1/2 teaspoon salt
> 1/4 cup miniature semisweet chocolate chips

In a large mixing bowl, combine the applesauce, oil and egg whites. Beat in sugars and vanilla. Combine the flour, cocoa, baking soda and salt; gradually add to applesauce mixture. Cover and refrigerate for 2 hours or until slightly firm.

Drop dough by rounded teaspoonfuls 2 in. apart onto baking sheets coated with nonstick cooking spray. Sprinkle with chocolate chips. Bake at 350° for 8-10 minutes or until set. **Yield:** 44 cookies.

Nutritional Analysis: One cookie equals 78 calories, 2 g fat (trace saturated fat), trace cholesterol, 63 mg sodium, 14 g carbohydrate, 1 g fiber, 1 g protein. **Diabetic Exchange:** 1 starch.

— 🍺 🍺 🍺 —

Peanut Chocolate Whirls

The mouth-watering combination of chocolate and peanut butter is irresistible in these tender swirl cookies. My daughters and I have such fun making and

sharing these yummy snacks with family and friends.
—Joanne Woloschuk, Yorkton, Saskatchewan

  1/2 **cup shortening**
  1/2 **cup creamy peanut butter**
    1 **cup sugar**
    1 **egg**
    2 **tablespoons milk**
    1 **teaspoon vanilla extract**
1-1/4 **cups all-purpose flour**
  1/2 **teaspoon baking soda**
  1/2 **teaspoon salt**
    1 **cup (6 ounces) semisweet chocolate chips**

In a mixing bowl, cream shortening, peanut butter and sugar. Add egg, milk and vanilla. Combine the flour, baking soda and salt; gradually add to creamed mixture. Turn onto a lightly floured surface; roll into a 16-in. x 12-in. rectangle.

Melt chocolate chips; cool slightly. Spread over dough to within 1/2 in. of edges. Tightly roll up jelly-roll style, starting with a long side. Wrap in plastic wrap. Refrigerate for up to 30 minutes.

Unwrap and cut into 1/4-in. slices. Place 1 in. apart on ungreased baking sheets. Bake at 350° for 8-10 minutes or until lightly browned. Remove to wire racks to cool. **Yield:** about 3 dozen.

— 🍴 🍴 🍴 —

Old-Fashioned Tea Cookies

These buttery, rich-tasting treats help me and the ladies in my card club overcome the dark days of winter. It's nice to end our card parties on a sweet note.
—Peggy Tucker, Fulton, Mississippi

  3/4 **cup butter (no substitutes), softened**
    1 **cup sugar**
    1 **egg**
    2 **teaspoons vanilla extract**
2-1/2 **cups self-rising flour***
Confectioners' sugar

In a mixing bowl, cream butter and sugar. Beat in the egg and vanilla. Gradually add flour. Roll dough into 1-in. balls. Place 2 in. apart on ungreased baking sheets; flatten slightly with fingers. Bake at 325° for 17-20 minutes or until edges are golden brown. Cool for 2 minutes before removing to wire racks to cool completely. Dust with confectioners' sugar. **Yield:** 4 dozen.

*Editor's Note: As a substitute for *each cup* of self-rising flour, place 1-1/2 teaspoons baking powder and 1/2 teaspoon salt in a 1-cup measuring cup. Add all-purpose flour to measure 1 cup.

As a substitute for *1/2 cup* self-rising flour, place 3/4 teaspoon baking powder and 1/4 teaspoon salt in a 1/2-cup measuring cup. Add all-purpose flour to measure 1/2 cup.

Cherry Cocoa Shortbread Squares

(Pictured below)

Whenever there is a potluck at work or a family gathering, I'm asked to bring these delectable bars. I found the recipe years ago and have made it countless times since.
—Bettie Martin, Oneida, Wisconsin

  1/2 **cup plus 2 tablespoons butter (no substitutes), softened, *divided***
  1/4 **cup sugar**
    1 **cup all-purpose flour**
    2 **tablespoons baking cocoa**
    2 **cups confectioners' sugar**
    2 **tablespoons milk**
  1/2 **teaspoon vanilla extract**
   18 **maraschino cherries, halved**
GLAZE:
    1 **square (1 ounce) unsweetened chocolate**
1-1/2 **teaspoons butter**

In a mixing bowl, cream 1/2 cup butter and sugar. Beat in flour and cocoa (mixture will be crumbly). Spread into a greased 9-in. square baking pan. Bake at 350° for 15 minutes or until surface is set. Cool on a wire rack for 15 minutes.

Meanwhile, in a mixing bowl, combine confectioners' sugar and remaining butter; beat in milk and vanilla until smooth. Spread over crust. Pat cherries dry with a paper towel; arrange over frosting and press down gently.

In a microwave-safe bowl, melt chocolate and butter; stir until smooth. Drizzle over cherries. Refrigerate until glaze has hardened. Cut into squares. **Yield:** 3 dozen.

Cakes & Pies

Expect a bunch of compliments when you bake these pretty cakes and pies that are as delicious as they are eye-catching.

BLUE-RIBBON WORTHY. Clockwise from upper left: Chocolate Mallow Pie (p. 137), Strawberry Poke Cake (p. 132), Strawberry Custard Torte (p. 136), Tiramisu Toffee Torte (p. 124) and Spiced Peach Pie (p. 133).

Fresh Raspberry Pie

(Pictured below)

I've never baked a berry pie that keeps its shape when it's sliced like this one. Even the next day—if there's any left—it still looks fresh. —*Kaye Hopkins*
Spokane, Washington

1-1/4 cups all-purpose flour
   3 tablespoons confectioners' sugar
  1/2 cup cold butter *or* margarine
FILLING:
   1 cup sugar
   3 tablespoons plus 2 teaspoons cornstarch
1-1/2 cups cold water
   3 tablespoons corn syrup
  1/4 cup strawberry gelatin powder
  1/2 teaspoon vanilla extract
   1 quart fresh raspberries

In a bowl, combine flour and confectioners' sugar; cut in butter until crumbly. Press onto the bottom and up the sides of an ungreased 9-in. pie plate. Bake at 350° for 18-22 minutes or until edges are golden brown. Cool on a wire rack.

In a saucepan, combine sugar and cornstarch. Stir in water until smooth; stir in corn syrup. Bring to a boil; cook and stir for 2 minutes or until thickened. Remove from the heat; stir in gelatin and vanilla until gelatin is dissolved. Cool to room temperature, about 30 minutes.

Add the raspberries; gently stir to coat. Spoon into crust. Refrigerate until set, about 3 hours. **Yield:** 6-8 servings.

— 🍷 🍷 🍷 —

Tiramisu Toffee Torte

(Pictured below left and on page 122)

Tiramisu is Italian for "pick-me-up", and this treat truly lives up to its name. It's worth every bit of effort to see my husband's eyes light up when I put a piece of this delicious torte in front of him. —*Donna Gonda*
North Canton, Ohio

   1 package (18-1/4 ounces) white cake mix
   1 cup strong brewed coffee, room temperature
   4 egg whites
   4 Heath candy bars (1.4 ounces *each*), chopped
FROSTING:
   4 ounces cream cheese, softened
  2/3 cup sugar
  1/3 cup chocolate syrup
   2 teaspoons vanilla extract
   2 cups whipping cream
   6 tablespoons strong brewed coffee, room temperature
   1 Heath candy bar (1.4 ounces), chopped

Line two greased 9-in. round baking pans with waxed paper and grease the paper; set aside. In a mixing bowl, beat the cake mix, coffee and egg whites on low speed until moistened. Beat on high for 2 minutes. Fold in chopped candy bars. Pour into prepared pans.

Bake at 350° for 25-30 minutes or until a toothpick inserted near the center comes out clean. Cool for 10 minutes before removing from pans to wire racks. When cool, split each cake into two horizontal layers.

For frosting, in a chilled mixing bowl, beat the cream cheese and sugar until smooth. Beat in the chocolate syrup and vanilla. Add the whipping cream. Beat on high speed until light and fluffy, about 5 minutes.

Place one cake layer on a serving plate; drizzle with 2 tablespoons of coffee. Spread with 3/4 cup frosting. Repeat twice. Top with fourth cake layer. Frost top and sides of cake with remaining frosting.

WRAP UP dinner with Tiramisu Toffee Torte and Fresh Raspberry Pie (shown below, from top).

Refrigerate overnight. Garnish with chopped candy bar. Store in the refrigerator. **Yield:** 12-14 servings.

— 🥄 🥄 🥄 —

Chocolate Beet Cake

The first time I baked this cake, my son loved its moistness, and he couldn't taste the beets.
—Peggy Van Arsdale, Crosswicks, New Jersey

     1 cup grated peeled uncooked beets
       (about 2 medium)
     2 teaspoons lemon juice
     4 eggs
 1-1/4 cups butter *or* margarine, melted
   1/2 cup milk
     2 tablespoons honey
     2 teaspoons vanilla extract
 2-1/2 cups all-purpose flour
     2 cups sugar
   1/2 cup baking cocoa
     2 teaspoons baking soda
     1 teaspoon salt
FROSTING:
     1 package (3 ounces) cream cheese,
       softened
   1/4 cup whipping cream
     1 teaspoon vanilla extract
 3-3/4 cups confectioners' sugar
 Dash salt
   1/4 cup finely chopped walnuts, optional

In a small bowl, toss beets with lemon juice; set aside. In a mixing bowl, beat the eggs, butter, milk, honey and vanilla. Combine the flour, sugar, cocoa, baking soda and salt; add to egg mixture and beat just until blended. Stir in beet mixture.

Pour into a greased 13-in. x 9-in. x 2-in. baking dish. Bake at 350° for 35-40 minutes or until a toothpick inserted near the center comes out clean. Cool on a wire rack.

For frosting, in a mixing bowl, beat the cream cheese, cream and vanilla until smooth. Beat in confectioners' sugar and salt. Spread over cooled cake. Sprinkle with nuts if desired. **Yield:** 12-15 servings.

— 🥄 🥄 🥄 —

Chocolate Macaroon Cupcakes

A delightful coconut and ricotta cheese filling is hidden inside these cupcakes. *—Dolores Skrout*
Summerhill, Pennsylvania

☑ Uses less fat, sugar or salt. Includes Nutritional Analysis and Diabetic Exchanges.

     2 egg whites
     1 egg

   1/3 cup unsweetened applesauce
     1 teaspoon vanilla extract
 1-1/4 cups all-purpose flour
     1 cup sugar
   1/3 cup baking cocoa
   1/2 teaspoon baking soda
   3/4 cup 1% buttermilk
FILLING:
     1 cup fat-free ricotta cheese
   1/4 cup sugar
     1 egg white
   1/3 cup flaked coconut
   1/2 teaspoon coconut *or* almond extract
     2 teaspoons confectioners' sugar

In a mixing bowl, combine the egg whites, egg, applesauce and vanilla. Combine the flour, sugar, cocoa and baking soda; gradually add to egg white mixture alternately with buttermilk. Spoon half of the batter into 18 muffin cups coated with nonstick cooking spray.

In another mixing bowl, beat the ricotta cheese, sugar and egg white until smooth. Stir in coconut and extract. Spoon 1 tablespoonful in the center of each muffin cup. Fill muffin cups two-thirds full with remaining batter.

Bake at 350° for 28-33 minutes or until a toothpick inserted in cupcake comes out clean. Cool for 5 minutes before removing from pans to wire racks; cool completely. Dust with confectioners' sugar. **Yield:** 1-1/2 dozen.

Nutritional Analysis: One cupcake equals 121 calories, 1 g fat (1 g saturated fat), 14 mg cholesterol, 75 mg sodium, 24 g carbohydrate, 1 g fiber, 4 g protein. **Diabetic Exchange:** 1-1/2 starch.

— 🥄 🥄 🥄 —

Creamy Watermelon Pie

My family loves this pie. Cubes of sweet watermelon "float" in a creamy filling made from condensed milk and whipped topping with a hint of lime. It's a nice change from more traditional fruit pies.
—Brent Harrison, Nogales, Arizona

     1 can (14 ounces) sweetened condensed
       milk
   1/4 cup lime juice
 1-2/3 cups whipped topping
     2 cups cubed seeded watermelon
     1 graham cracker crust (9 inches)
 Watermelon balls and fresh mint, optional

In a bowl, combine milk and lime juice; fold in whipped topping and cubed watermelon. Pour into crust. Refrigerate for at least 2 hours before slicing. Garnish with watermelon balls and mint if desired. **Yield:** 6-8 servings.

Jeweled Gelatin Torte

(Pictured above)

My mother made this special torte for all our holiday dinners when I was young. I love the colorful stained-glass look of the Jell-O cubes and the dainty ladyfingers in this elegant dessert. —Kimberly Adams
Falmouth, Kentucky

 1 package (3 ounces) cherry gelatin
 3 cups boiling water, *divided*
 2 cups cold water, *divided*
 1 package (3 ounces) lime gelatin
 1 package (3 ounces) orange gelatin
 1 cup pineapple juice
 1 package (3 ounces) lemon gelatin
 1/4 cup sugar
 36 ladyfingers
 1 carton (8 ounces) frozen whipped topping, thawed
Citrus slices and fresh mint, optional

In a small bowl, dissolve cherry gelatin in 1 cup boiling water; stir in 1/2 cup cold water. Pour into a 9-in. x 5-in. x 3-in. loaf pan coated with nonstick cooking spray. Repeat with lime and orange gelatin, using two more loaf pans. Refrigerate until firm, about 1-1/2 hours.

In a small saucepan, bring pineapple juice to a boil. Stir in lemon gelatin and sugar until dissolved. Stir in remaining cold water. Refrigerate until syrupy, about 45 minutes. Meanwhile, line the sides and bottom of a 9-in. springform pan with ladyfingers; set aside.

Cut cherry, lime and orange gelatin into 1/2-in.

cubes. Pour lemon gelatin mixture into a large bowl; fold in whipped topping. Gently fold in gelatin cubes. Pour into prepared pan. Refrigerate until set. Garnish with citrus and mint if desired. **Yield:** 10-12 servings.

Oat-Topped Rhubarb Pie

For many years we had a bountiful rhubarb crop, and this pie was one way I could get my three sons to eat it. We look forward to this tasty springtime treat.
—Marion Lipinsky, Winnipeg, Manitoba

Pastry for single-crust pie (9 inches)
 1-1/2 cups packed brown sugar
 1/3 cup water
 4 tablespoons plus 1-1/2 teaspoons quick-cooking tapioca
 4-1/2 cups fresh *or* frozen chopped rhubarb, thawed
TOPPING:
 1 cup old-fashioned oats
 1/2 cup packed brown sugar
 1/4 cup cold butter *or* margarine

Line a 9-in. pie plate with pastry. Trim pastry to 1/2 in. beyond edge of plate. Flute edges; set aside. In a bowl, toss brown sugar, water, tapioca and rhubarb; let stand for 15 minutes. Pour into crust. For topping, combine oats and brown sugar in a bowl. Cut in butter until crumbly. Sprinkle over filling.

Cover edges loosely with foil. Bake at 375° for 45 minutes. Remove foil. Bake 10-15 minutes longer or until browned and bubbly. Cool for 3 hours before cutting. **Yield:** 6-8 servings.

Walnut Molasses Pie

This pie is a family favorite I frequently prepare for Sunday dinner at my mother's. Somewhat like pecan pie, this treat is scrumptious and nutty with a sweet molasses flavor. —Betty Jones, Collinston, Louisiana

 3 eggs
 3/4 cup light corn syrup
 2/3 cup sugar
 1/3 cup butter *or* margarine, melted
 1/4 cup molasses
 1 teaspoon vanilla extract
 1-1/2 cups chopped walnuts
 1 unbaked pastry shell (9 inches)

In a bowl, whisk the eggs, corn syrup, sugar, butter, molasses and vanilla until blended; stir in walnuts. Pour into pastry shell. Cover edges with foil.

Bake at 350° for 25 minutes; remove foil. Bake

12-17 minutes longer or until top of pie is set and crust is golden. Cool on wire rack. Refrigerate for 1-2 hours before cutting. **Yield:** 6-8 servings.

— 🧇 🧇 🧇 —

Pecan Torte

Even though the holidays always seem to be more pie-oriented, this cake steals the show at our family celebrations. It looks magnificent and tastes simply scrumptious! —Lois Thayer, Hutchinson, Kansas

    3 cups finely chopped toasted pecans,
      divided
  1/2 cup butter *or* margarine, softened
  1/2 cup shortening
    2 cups sugar
    5 eggs, *separated*
    2 teaspoons vanilla extract
    2 cups all-purpose flour
    1 teaspoon baking soda
    1 cup buttermilk
  3/4 cup dark corn syrup
FILLING:
  1/2 cup packed brown sugar
  1/3 cup cornstarch
  1/8 teaspoon salt
1-1/2 cups half-and-half cream
  3/4 cup dark corn syrup
    4 egg yolks, beaten
    3 tablespoons butter *or* margarine
    1 teaspoon vanilla extract
  1/2 cup coarsely chopped pecans

Sprinkle 2/3 cup pecans each into three greased 9-in. round baking pans; set aside. In a mixing bowl, cream butter, shortening and sugar. Add egg yolks, one at a time, beating well after each addition. Beat in vanilla. Combine flour and baking soda; add to creamed mixture alternately with buttermilk. Stir in remaining pecans.

In a small mixing bowl, beat egg whites until stiff peaks form; fold into batter. Pour into prepared pans. Bake at 350° for 25-30 minutes or until a toothpick inserted near the center comes out clean. Cool for 10 minutes before removing from pans to wire racks. Brush with corn syrup; cool completely.

For filling, in a heavy saucepan, combine the brown sugar, cornstarch and salt. Gradually stir in cream until smooth. Add the corn syrup. Bring to a boil over medium heat, stirring constantly; cook and stir for 1-2 minutes or until thickened. Remove from the heat. Stir a small amount of hot filling into egg yolks; return all to pan, stirring constantly. Bring to a gentle boil; cook and stir for 3 minutes. Remove from heat; stir in butter and vanilla. Cover and refrigerate until cool, about 4 hours.

Place one cake layer, pecan side up, on a serving plate; spread with about 2/3 cup filling. Repeat layers twice. Sprinkle with pecans. **Yield:** 12-14 servings.

— 🧇 🧇 🧇 —

Double Chocolate Pie

(Pictured below)

If you thought your days of luscious chocolate pies were over, think again! This light pudding pie is a rich and creamy treat. —Carol LaNaye Burnette Sylvan Springs, Alabama

✓ Uses less fat, sugar or salt. Includes Nutritional Analysis and Diabetic Exchanges.

1-1/2 cups cold fat-free milk, *divided*
    1 package (1.4 ounces) sugar-free instant chocolate fudge pudding mix
    1 carton (8 ounces) fat-free frozen whipped topping, thawed, *divided*
    1 reduced-fat graham cracker crust (8 inches)
    1 package (1 ounce) sugar-free instant white chocolate *or* vanilla pudding mix
Semisweet chocolate curls and shavings, optional

In a bowl, whisk 3/4 cup milk and chocolate pudding mix for 2 minutes or until thickened. Fold in 1-3/4 cups whipped topping. Spread into crust. In another bowl, whisk the remaining milk and the white chocolate pudding mix for 2 minutes or until slightly thickened. Fold in remaining whipped topping. Spread over chocolate layer. Refrigerate for 4 hours or until set. Garnish with chocolate curls if desired. **Yield:** 8 servings.

Nutritional Analysis: One piece (calculated without garnish) equals 191 calories, 3 g fat (1 g saturated fat), 1 mg cholesterol, 426 mg sodium, 34 g carbohydrate, trace fiber, 3 g protein. **Diabetic Exchanges:** 2 starch, 1 fat.

Almond Fudge Cake

(Pictured above)

People are amazed that this moist and tender cake is a light dessert. I love the rich chocolate flavor and fruity sauce. —*Mike Pickerel, Columbia, Missouri*

✓ Uses less fat, sugar or salt. Includes Nutritional Analysis and Diabetic Exchanges.

1-3/4 cups all-purpose flour
1-1/2 cups sugar
  3/4 cup baking cocoa
1-1/2 teaspoons baking powder
1-1/2 teaspoons baking soda
  1/2 teaspoon salt
    4 egg whites
    1 cup fat-free milk
  1/2 cup unsweetened applesauce
    1 teaspoon almond extract
  3/4 cup boiling water
  1/4 cup miniature semisweet chocolate chips
RASPBERRY SAUCE:
    2 cups fresh *or* frozen unsweetened
      raspberries
    1 tablespoon sugar
    1 teaspoon lemon juice
  3/4 cup reduced-fat whipped topping
   12 fresh raspberries

In a mixing bowl, combine the first six ingredients. Add the egg whites, milk, applesauce, extract and water; beat until well blended (batter will be thin). Pour into a 9-in. springform pan coated with nonstick cooking spray. Sprinkle with chips. Place pan on a baking sheet.

Bake at 325° for 55-60 minutes or until a toothpick inserted near the center comes out clean. Cool for 30 minutes. Carefully run a knife around edge of pan to loosen; remove sides of pan. Cool completely.

For sauce, puree the raspberries in a food processor or blender; strain to remove seeds. Stir in sug-

ar and lemon juice. Spoon sauce onto dessert plates; top with cake wedges. Garnish each with 1 tablespoon whipped topping and a raspberry. **Yield:** 12 servings.

Nutritional Analysis: One serving equals 241 calories, 2 g fat (1 g saturated fat), 0 cholesterol, 314 mg sodium, 51 g carbohydrate, 4 g fiber, 5 g protein.

Tart Cherry Cake

Dotted with cherries and topped with a rich butter sauce, this cake is good simple country cooking.
—*Lavonn Bormuth, Westerville, Ohio*

    1 cup all-purpose flour
    1 cup sugar
    1 teaspoon baking soda
  1/2 teaspoon salt
    1 egg, beaten
    1 can (14-1/2 ounces) pitted tart cherries,
      drained
BUTTER SAUCE:
    1 cup sugar
  1/2 cup butter (no substitutes), cubed
  1/2 cup evaporated milk
    1 teaspoon vanilla extract

In a large bowl, combine the flour, sugar, baking soda and salt. Combine the egg and cherries; add to dry ingredients. Stir until well combined and batter no longer appears dry. Pour into a greased 8-in. square baking dish. Bake at 350° for 30-35 minutes or until golden brown and a toothpick inserted near the center comes out clean. Cool on a wire rack.

Combine the sugar, butter and milk in a small saucepan. Bring to a boil over medium heat, stirring occasionally. Cook and stir for 5 minutes or until thickened. Remove from the heat; stir in vanilla. Serve warm over cake. **Yield:** 9 servings.

Editor's Note: The cake contains no liquid, butter or shortening.

Sweetheart Fudge Pie

If your sweetie is a chocolate fan, this pie is a perfect way to declare your devotion. —*Kim Marie Van Rheenen Mendota, Illinois*

    1 unbaked pastry shell (9 inches)
  1/4 cup butter *or* margarine, softened
  3/4 cup packed brown sugar
    3 eggs
    2 cups (12 ounces) semisweet chocolate
      chips, melted
    2 teaspoons instant coffee granules

1/4 teaspoon vanilla *or* rum extract
1 cup coarsely chopped walnuts
1/4 cup all-purpose flour
1 cup whipping cream
2 tablespoons confectioners' sugar
3 tablespoons chopped red maraschino
cherries

Line pastry shell with a double thickness of heavy-duty foil. Bake at 450° for 5 minutes. Remove foil; set crust aside. In a small mixing bowl, cream butter and brown sugar. Add eggs, one at a time, beating well after each addition. Add chocolate, coffee and extract. Stir in walnuts and flour. Pour into crust. Bake at 375° for 28-30 minutes. Cool completely.

In a small mixing bowl, beat cream and confectioners' sugar until stiff peaks form; fold in cherries. Spread over pie. **Yield:** 12-14 servings.

— 🍵 🍵 🍵 —

Gingerbread Cake

This dark moist cake combines the old-fashioned flavors of ginger and molasses. The recipe was passed down to me from a dear aunt. —*Ila Alderman Galax, Virginia*

1/3 cup shortening
1/2 cup sugar
1 egg
3/4 cup water
1/2 cup molasses
1-1/2 cups all-purpose flour
1 teaspoon ground ginger
1/2 teaspoon baking soda
1/4 teaspoon salt
Whipped topping

In a mixing bowl, cream shortening and sugar. Beat in egg. Combine water and molasses. Combine the flour, ginger, baking soda and salt; add to creamed mixture alternately with molasses mixture. Pour into a greased 8-in. square baking pan.

Bake at 350° for 28-32 minutes or until a toothpick inserted near the center comes out clean. Serve warm with whipped topping. **Yield:** 9 servings.

— 🍵 🍵 🍵 —

Easy-Does-It Fruitcake

(Pictured at right)

These miniature loaves are chock-full of tempting fruit and nuts. The glaze makes them extra moist and tasty. They are wonderful to give as gifts and fun to serve to holiday guests. —*Romaine Wetzel Lancaster, Pennsylvania*

1 cup butter *or* margarine, softened
1-1/4 cups packed brown sugar
4 eggs
3 cups all-purpose flour, *divided*
1 pound chopped candied fruit
2 packages (8 ounces *each*) pitted dates, chopped
1 package (15 ounces) raisins
1 cup chopped walnuts
1 cup chopped pecans *or* almonds
1 teaspoon baking soda
1 teaspoon salt
1 teaspoon ground cinnamon
1 teaspoon ground cloves
1/4 cup orange juice
GLAZE:
1 cup confectioners' sugar
2 tablespoons milk

In a mixing bowl, cream butter and brown sugar. Add eggs, one at a time, beating well after each. In a large bowl, combine 1/4 cup flour, candied fruit, dates, raisins and nuts; toss until well coated. Set aside. Combine the baking soda, salt, cinnamon, cloves and remaining flour; gradually add to creamed mixture alternately with orange juice. Stir in fruit and nut mixture; mix well.

Spoon into five greased 5-3/4-in. x 3-in. x 2-in. baking pans (pans will be full). Bake at 325° for 1 hour. Cover with foil; bake 10-15 minutes longer or until a toothpick inserted near the center comes out clean. Let stand for 10 minutes before removing from pans to wire racks. In a bowl, combine glaze ingredients. With a pastry brush, brush glaze over warm loaves. Cool completely. **Yield:** 5 loaves.

Cocoa Angel Food Cake

This delicious chocolaty cake is so simple, I've made it hundreds of times. —Lorraine Olson
Madison, Minnesota

✓ Uses less fat, sugar or salt. Includes Nutritional Analysis and Diabetic Exchanges.

12 egg whites
3/4 cup cake flour
1-1/2 cups sugar, *divided*
1/4 cup baking cocoa
1 teaspoon cream of tartar
1/4 teaspoon salt

Let egg whites stand at room temperature for 30 minutes. Sift the flour, 1/2 cup sugar and cocoa together five times; set aside. In a mixing bowl, beat egg whites, cream of tartar and salt on high speed until soft peaks form. Add the remaining sugar, 2 tablespoons at a time, beating well after each addition. Gradually fold in sifted dry ingredients.

Spoon into an ungreased 10-in. tube pan. Bake at 350° for 35-40 minutes or until the top springs back when lightly touched and cracks feel dry. Immediately invert pan; cool completely. Loosen sides of cake from pan and remove. **Yield:** 12 servings.
Nutritional Analysis: One piece equals 150 calories, trace fat (0 saturated fat), 0 cholesterol, 104 mg sodium, 33 g carbohydrate, 1 g fiber, 5 g protein. **Diabetic Exchange:** 2 starch.

Nutmeg Pear Cake

I've been in love with baking since I was in seventh grade. I especially enjoy making this pear cake for my husband and our two children. With its apple cider sauce, it tastes like autumn. —Kim Rubner
Worthington, Iowa

3 cups all-purpose flour
1-1/2 teaspoons ground nutmeg
1 teaspoon baking soda
1 teaspoon ground cinnamon
3/4 teaspoon salt
1/2 teaspoon baking powder
2 cups sugar
1 cup vegetable oil
3 eggs, beaten
1/2 cup apple cider
3 teaspoons vanilla extract
1 can (29 ounces) pear halves, drained and mashed
1 cup chopped pecans
APPLE CIDER SAUCE:
3/4 cup butter *or* margarine
2/3 cup sugar

1/3 cup packed brown sugar
2 tablespoons cornstarch
2/3 cup apple cider
1/3 cup whipping cream
1/3 cup lemon juice

In a large bowl, combine the first six ingredients. In another bowl, whisk the sugar, oil, eggs, cider and vanilla. Add to the dry ingredients and stir well. Stir in pears and pecans. Pour into a greased and floured 10-in. fluted tube pan. Bake at 350° for 65-70 minutes or until a toothpick inserted near the center comes out clean. Cool for 10 minutes before removing from pan to a wire rack.

For sauce, combine butter and sugars in a saucepan. Cook over low heat for 2-3 minutes or until sugar is dissolved. Combine the cornstarch and cider until smooth; add to sugar mixture. Stir in the cream and lemon juice. Bring to a boil; cook and stir for 1-2 minutes or until thickened. Serve warm with cake. **Yield:** 12-15 servings.

Zucchini Carrot Cake

My family has quite a sweet tooth, but I like to serve treats like this that are good for them, too. —Layla Payton, Midwest City, Oklahoma

✓ Uses less fat, sugar or salt. Includes Nutritional Analysis and Diabetic Exchanges.

1 cup whole wheat flour
1 cup all-purpose flour
2-1/2 teaspoons ground cinnamon
2 teaspoons baking soda
3/4 teaspoon ground nutmeg
1/4 teaspoon ground cloves
1/2 cup 1% buttermilk
1 cup unsweetened applesauce
1-1/2 cups shredded carrots
1/2 cup shredded zucchini
1 teaspoon vanilla extract
6 egg whites
1-1/3 cups sugar
FROSTING:
1 carton (8 ounces) reduced-fat cream cheese spread
1 jar (7-1/2 ounces) marshmallow creme
1 teaspoon orange juice
1/2 teaspoon vanilla extract

In a large mixing bowl, combine the first six ingredients. Gradually add buttermilk, applesauce, carrots, zucchini and vanilla. In small mixing bowl, beat egg whites until soft peaks form; gradually beat in sugar, 1 tablespoon at a time, until sugar is dissolved. Gently fold into batter.

Pour into a 13-in. x 9-in. x 2-in. baking dish

coated with nonstick cooking spray. Bake at 350° for 30-40 minutes or until a toothpick inserted near the center comes out clean. Cool on a wire rack. For frosting, in a mixing bowl, beat cream cheese, marshmallow creme, orange juice and vanilla just until combined. Frost cake. **Yield:** 12 servings.

   Nutritional Analysis: One piece equals 291 calories, 4 g fat (2 g saturated fat), 11 mg cholesterol, 325 mg sodium, 59 g carbohydrate, 3 g fiber, 7 g protein. **Diabetic Exchanges:** 2 starch, 2 fruit.

— 🍴 🍴 🍴 —

Toffee Apple Pie

Fruit trees in my yard provide me with the main ingredient for this lovely pie. A scoop of vanilla or cinnamon ice cream is terrific on top.   —_Dixie Helders Roberts, Wisconsin_

   5 **cups sliced peeled Granny Smith apples**
1/2 **cup sugar**
1/2 **cup packed brown sugar**
   1 **Heath candy bar (1.4 ounces), chopped**
   2 **tablespoons cornstarch**
   1 **tablespoon butter _or_ margarine, melted**
   1 **teaspoon ground cinnamon**
Dash ground nutmeg
   1 **unbaked pastry shell (9 inches)**
TOPPING:
1/3 **cup all-purpose flour**
   2 **tablespoons brown sugar**
1/4 **teaspoon ground cinnamon**
   2 **tablespoons cold butter _or_ margarine**
1/4 **cup chopped nuts**
   1 **Heath candy bar (1.4 ounces), chopped**

In a bowl, combine the first eight ingredients. Spoon into pie shell. For topping, combine the flour, brown sugar and cinnamon; cut in butter until mixture resembles coarse crumbs. Add nuts and candy bar. Sprinkle over pie. Bake at 375° for 30-35 minutes or until topping is browned and apples are tender. **Yield:** 6-8 servings.

— 🍴 🍴 🍴 —

Raspberry Cheesecake Pie

(Pictured above right)

Topped with bright berries, this pretty pie has a creamy fresh-tasting filling that is not overly sweet.
   —_Beverly Coyde, Gasport, New York_

   1 **unbaked pastry shell (10 inches)**
   1 **cup (8 ounces) small-curd cottage cheese**
   2 **tablespoons milk**
   2 **packages (8 ounces _each_) cream cheese, softened**

1/2 **cup sugar**
   2 **tablespoons all-purpose flour**
1/4 **teaspoon vanilla extract**
   3 **eggs**
1-1/2 **cups fresh raspberries, _divided_**
   1 **cup whipping cream, whipped**

Line unpricked pastry shell with a double thickness of aluminum foil. Bake at 450° for 8 minutes or until lightly browned. Cool on a wire rack. Reduce heat to 350°.

   In a blender, combine cottage cheese and milk; cover and process until smooth. In a mixing bowl, beat cream cheese and sugar until smooth. Beat in cottage cheese mixture, flour and vanilla. Beat in eggs just until blended. Pour into pastry shell (pie will be full). Sprinkle with 1/2 cup raspberries; gently press into filling with the back of a spoon.

   Bake at 350° for 30-35 minutes or until the center is almost set (cover edges loosely with foil if browning too quickly). Cool on a wire rack for 1 hour. Refrigerate for at least 1 hour. Top with whipped cream and remaining raspberries. Store in the refrigerator. **Yield:** 10 servings.

🥄 _Pie Pointer_

Pies containing dairy products, like milk, sour cream, cream cheese, cottage cheese, yogurt or whipped cream, should be refrigerated as soon as possible after they've been prepared or about 1 hour after baking.

Strawberry Poke Cake

(Pictured above and on page 122)

That classic spring treat strawberry shortcake takes on a wonderful new twist with this recipe. Strawberry gelatin and strawberries liven up each pretty slice of this lovely layered cake that's made from a convenient boxed mix.
—*Mary Jo Griggs*
West Bend, Wisconsin

      1 package (18-1/4 ounces) white cake mix*
1-1/4 cups water
  1/4 cup vegetable oil
      2 eggs
      1 package (16 ounces) frozen sweetened sliced strawberries, thawed
      2 packages (3 ounces *each*) strawberry gelatin
      1 carton (12 ounces) frozen whipped topping, thawed, *divided*
Fresh strawberries, optional

In a mixing bowl, beat cake mix, water, oil and eggs on low speed until moistened. Beat on medium for 2 minutes. Pour into two greased and floured 9-in. round baking pans. Bake at 350° for 25-35 minutes or until a toothpick inserted near the center comes out clean. Cool for 10 minutes; remove from pans to wire racks to cool completely.

Using a serrated knife, level top of each cake if necessary. Return layers, top side up, to two clean 9-in. round baking pans. Pierce cakes with a meat fork at 1/2-in. intervals. Drain juice from strawberries into a 2-cup measuring cup; refrigerate berries. Add water to juice to measure 2 cups; pour into a saucepan. Bring to a boil; stir in gelatin until dissolved. Chill for 30 minutes. Gently spoon over each cake layer. Chill for 2-3 hours.

Dip bottom of one pan in warm water for 10 seconds. Invert cake onto a serving platter. Top with reserved strawberries and 1 cup whipped topping. Place second cake layer over topping. Frost cake with remaining whipped topping. Chill for at least 1 hour. Garnish with fresh berries if desired. Refrigerate leftovers. **Yield:** 10-12 servings.

*Editor's Note: This cake was tested with Pillsbury white cake mix.

Peppermint Angel Torte

My mom gave me this fantastic recipe more than 40 years ago. We always called it "celebration cake". Carrying on her tradition, I serve it for Christmas and Valentine's Day.
—*Jan Harris*
Murrieta, California

      8 egg whites
      1 teaspoon cream of tartar
      1 teaspoon almond extract
      1 teaspoon vanilla extract
  1/4 teaspoon salt
1-1/4 cups sugar
      1 cup cake flour
      1 carton (8 ounces) frozen whipped topping, thawed
  1/2 cup crushed peppermint candies, *divided*

Place egg whites in a mixing bowl; let stand at room temperature for 30 minutes. Add cream of tartar, extracts and salt; beat on high speed until soft peaks form. Gradually add sugar, beating until sugar is dissolved and stiff peaks form. Gradually fold in flour, 1/4 cup at a time.

Gently spoon into a greased 10-in. tube pan; cut through batter with a knife to remove air pockets. Bake at 350° for 35-40 minutes or until cake springs back when lightly touched. Immediately invert pan; cool completely.

Run a knife around sides of cake and remove from pan. Slice cake into three layers. Place the bottom layer on a serving plate. Top with 1/2 cup of whipped topping; sprinkle with 2 tablespoons crushed candies. Repeat. Top with remaining cake layer. Spread remaining whipped topping over the entire cake. Sprinkle with remaining candies. Refrigerate for at least 2 hours before serving. **Yield:** 10-12 servings.

Editor's Note: Peppermint candies will melt on the whipped topping and form a pink syrup.

— 🍶 🍶 🍶 —

Crunchy-Topped Spice Cake

The recipe originally called for making the cake from scratch. I much prefer this version.
—Laurine Lockwood, McGregor, Minnesota

        3 eggs
    1/2 cup butter *or* margarine, melted
        1 can (15 ounces) solid-pack pumpkin
        1 package (18-1/4 ounces) spice cake mix
    1-1/2 cups finely chopped walnuts, *divided*
        1 cup butterscotch chips

In a mixing bowl, combine the eggs, butter and pumpkin. Add cake mix; beat on medium speed for 2 minutes. Stir in 3/4 cup walnuts. Pour into a greased 13-in. x 9-in. x 2-in. baking pan. Sprinkle with butterscotch chips and remaining nuts.

Bake at 350° for 35-40 minutes or until a toothpick inserted near the center comes out clean. Cool on a wire rack. **Yield:** 12-15 servings.

— 🍶 🍶 🍶 —

Chocolate Oat Snack Cake

A sprinkling of walnuts and chips tops this sweet treat.
—Bonnie Spaulding, Litchfield, New Hampshire

    1-3/4 cups boiling water
        1 cup quick-cooking oats
    1/2 cup butter *or* margarine, softened
        1 cup sugar
        1 cup packed brown sugar
        2 eggs
    1-3/4 cups all-purpose flour
        2 tablespoons baking cocoa
        1 teaspoon baking soda
    1/2 teaspoon salt
        1 package (11-1/2 ounces) milk
            chocolate chips, *divided*
        1 cup chopped walnuts

In a bowl, combine water and oats; let stand for 10 minutes. In a large mixing bowl, cream butter and sugars. Add the eggs, one at a time, beating well after each addition. Beat in oat mixture. Combine the flour, cocoa, baking soda and salt; gradually add to creamed mixture. Stir in 1 cup chips.

Pour into a greased 13-in. x 9-in. x 2-in. baking pan. Sprinkle with walnuts and remaining chips. Bake at 350° for 40-45 minutes or until a toothpick comes out clean. Cool on a wire rack. **Yield:** 12-16 servings.

Spiced Peach Pie

(Pictured below and on page 122)

Chilled peach pie is a delectable change of pace from the traditional baked fruit pie.
—Lois Dunlop
Venice, Florida

        1 can (15 ounces) sliced peaches
        2 tablespoons brown sugar
    1/4 teaspoon ground ginger
        1 cinnamon stick (3 inches)
        1 package (3 ounces) peach gelatin
        4 ounces cream cheese, softened
        2 tablespoons butter *or* margarine, softened
    1/8 teaspoon ground nutmeg
        1 pastry shell (9 inches), baked
        1 carton (8 ounces) frozen whipped
            topping, thawed
Fresh mint, optional

Drain syrup from peaches into a 2-cup measuring cup. Add enough water to measure 1-1/3 cups. Chop peaches and set aside. In a saucepan, combine the syrup, brown sugar, ginger and cinnamon stick. Bring to a boil. Reduce heat; cook and stir for 5 minutes. Remove from the heat. Discard cinnamon stick. Stir gelatin into syrup mixture until dissolved. Add peaches. Refrigerate until partially set, about 40 minutes.

In a mixing bowl, beat cream cheese, butter and nutmeg until smooth. Spread over the bottom and up the sides of the crust. Pour gelatin mixture over cream cheese layer. Chill until serving. Spread with whipped topping. Garnish with mint if desired. **Yield:** 6-8 servings.

Chocolate Chip Caramel Cake

(Pictured below)

When I want to serve a treat that's pretty and delicious, I make this scrumptious cake. —Michele VanDewerke Roseboom, New York

>   1 package (18-1/4 ounces) white cake mix
> 1-1/2 cups vanilla yogurt
>   4 egg whites
>   1 teaspoon baking soda
>   1/2 teaspoon baking powder
>   1 cup miniature semisweet chocolate chips

CARAMEL TOPPING:

>   1/4 cup butter *or* margarine
>   1/3 cup packed brown sugar
>   2 to 3 tablespoons evaporated milk
>   1/2 teaspoon vanilla extract
>   1 cup confectioners' sugar
>   1/4 cup chopped pecans

CHOCOLATE DRIZZLE:

>   1/4 cup semisweet chocolate chips
>   1/2 teaspoon shortening

In a large mixing bowl, combine the first five ingredients. Beat on medium speed for 2 minutes. Stir in chocolate chips. Spread into a well-greased and floured 10-in. fluted tube pan. Bake at 350° for 50-55 minutes or until a toothpick inserted near the center comes out clean. Cool for 10 minutes; invert onto a wire rack to cool completely.

For topping, combine the butter and brown sugar in a saucepan; bring to a boil, stirring constantly. Boil for 2 minutes. Stir in milk and vanilla. Return to a boil; remove from the heat and cool slightly. Add sugar; beat on high with a portable mixer for 30 seconds or until thickened. Drizzle over cake. Sprinkle with nuts.

In a microwave, melt chocolate and shortening; stir until smooth. Drizzle over top. **Yield:** 12-16 servings.

Six-Layer Coconut Cake

I found this recipe when going through my grandmother's old files. It is simply the best.
—Angela Leinenbach, Mechanicsville, Virginia

>   1 cup butter *or* margarine, softened
>   3 cups sugar
>   3 teaspoons vanilla extract
>   4 cups cake flour
>   1 teaspoon baking soda
>   1/2 teaspoon baking powder
>   1/2 teaspoon salt
>   2 cups buttermilk
>   6 egg whites

FILLING:

>   1/2 cup sugar
>   2 tablespoons cornstarch
>   1 cup orange juice
>   4 eggs, lightly beaten
>   1/4 cup butter *or* margarine
>   2 tablespoons grated orange peel
>   1 teaspoon orange extract

FROSTING:

>   1 cup sugar
>   2 egg whites
>   1/2 cup water
>   1/4 teaspoon salt
>   1/8 teaspoon cream of tartar
>   1/4 teaspoon vanilla extract
>   2 cups flaked coconut

In a mixing bowl, cream butter and sugar until light and fluffy. Add vanilla. Combine flour, baking soda, baking powder and salt; add to creamed mixture alternately with buttermilk. In another mixing bowl, beat egg whites until stiff peaks form; gently fold into batter. Pour into three greased and floured 9-in. round baking pans. Bake at 350° for 25-30 minutes or until a toothpick comes out clean. Cool for 10 minutes; remove from pans to wire racks to cool completely.

In a saucepan, combine sugar and cornstarch. Gradually stir in orange juice until smooth. Bring to a boil; cook and stir for 2 minutes or until thickened. Remove from the heat. Gradually stir 1/2 cup into eggs; return all to pan, stirring constantly. Bring to a gentle boil; cook and stir for 2 minutes. Remove from the heat. Stir in butter, orange peel and extract. Cover and refrigerate.

In a heavy saucepan, combine sugar, egg whites, water, salt and cream of tartar. With a portable mixer, beat on low speed for 1 minute. Continue beating on low speed over low heat until frosting reaches 160°, about 12 minutes. Pour into a large mixing bowl; add vanilla. Beat on high until frosting forms stiff peaks, about 7 minutes.

Split each cake in half horizontally. Place one layer on a serving plate; spread with 1/3 cup filling. Repeat four times. Top with remaining cake layer. Spread frosting over top and sides. Sprinkle with coconut. Store in the refrigerator. **Yield:** 12-14 servings.

Editor's Note: We recommend that you test your candy thermometer before each use by bringing water to a boil; the thermometer should read 212°. Adjust your recipe temperature up or down based on your test. A stand mixer is recommended for beating the frosting after it reaches 160°.

— 🥄 🥄 🥄 —

Walnut Toffee Tart

There's no sweeter way to enjoy the flavor of walnuts than this scrumptious tart. —Patricia Green
Yuba City, California

    2 **cups all-purpose flour**
    3 **tablespoons sugar**
 3/4 **cup cold butter *or* margarine**
    2 **egg yolks, lightly beaten**
 1/4 **cup cold milk**
FILLING:
1-1/2 **cups sugar**
1-1/2 **cups whipping cream**
 1/2 **teaspoon ground cinnamon**
 1/4 **teaspoon salt**
    2 **cups coarsely chopped walnuts**

In a bowl, combine flour and sugar. Cut in butter until mixture resembles coarse crumbs. Combine egg yolks and milk; stir into flour mixture until blended. With lightly floured hands, press dough onto the bottom and 1 in. up the sides of a 12-in. tart pan with removable bottom.

Line unpricked shell with a double thickness of heavy-duty foil. Place pan on a 15-in. x 10-in. x 1-in. baking pan. Bake at 375° for 12-15 minutes or until edges are lightly browned.

Meanwhile, in a saucepan, combine the sugar, cream, cinnamon and salt. Bring to a boil over medium heat, stirring constantly. Remove from the heat; stir in walnuts. Remove foil from pastry shell; pour filling into pastry. Bake for 20-25 minutes or until golden brown. Cool on a wire rack. Store in the refrigerator. **Yield:** 8-10 servings.

— 🥄 🥄 🥄 —

Raisin Meringue Pie

I taught myself to cook early on in our marriage. Since I got home from work first, I took it upon myself to start supper. This pie is a treat for both the eyes and stomach. —John Brink, Harrison, South Dakota

    1 **cup packed brown sugar**
    2 **tablespoons all-purpose flour**

    1 **cup (8 ounces) sour cream**
    3 **eggs, *separated***
 1/2 **teaspoon *each* ground nutmeg, cinnamon and allspice**
 1/4 **teaspoon salt**
    1 **cup chopped raisins**
 1/4 **teaspoon cream of tartar**
    6 **tablespoons sugar**
    1 **pastry shell (9 inches), baked**

In a heavy saucepan, combine brown sugar and flour. Stir in sour cream, egg yolks, spices and salt until smooth. Cook and stir over medium heat until mixture comes to a boil. Remove from the heat. Stir in raisins; cover and set aside.

In a mixing bowl, beat egg whites and cream of tartar on medium speed until foamy, about 1 minute. Gradually beat in sugar, 1 tablespoon at a time, on high until stiff glossy peaks form and sugar is dissolved, about 3 minutes. Pour hot raisin filling into pastry shell. Spread meringue evenly over filling; seal edges to crust.

Bake at 350° for 15 minutes or until golden brown. Cool on a wire rack for 1 hour. Refrigerate for at least 2 hours before serving. **Yield:** 6-8 servings.

— 🥄 🥄 🥄 —

Lemon Tea Cakes

Whenever I serve these lovely bite-size glazed cakes, they get rave reviews. —Charlene Crump
Montgomery, Alabama

1-1/2 **cups butter (no substitutes), softened**
    1 **package (8 ounces) cream cheese, softened**
2-1/4 **cups sugar**
    6 **eggs**
    3 **tablespoons lemon juice**
    2 **teaspoons lemon extract**
    1 **teaspoon vanilla extract**
1-1/2 **teaspoons grated lemon peel**
    3 **cups all-purpose flour**
GLAZE:
5-1/4 **cups confectioners' sugar**
 1/2 **cup plus 3 tablespoons milk**
3-1/2 **teaspoons lemon extract**

In a mixing bowl, cream butter, cream cheese and sugar. Add eggs, one at a time, beating well after each. Beat in lemon juice, extracts and peel. Gradually add flour.

Fill greased miniature muffin cups two-thirds full. Bake at 325° for 10-15 minutes or until cakes pull away from sides. Cool for 5 minutes; remove from pans to wire racks to cool. Combine glaze ingredients. Dip tops of cakes into glaze; place on waxed paper to dry. **Yield:** 8-1/2 dozen.

cook and stir for 2 minutes. Remove from the heat. Stir in butter and vanilla. Cover and refrigerate until chilled.

Place half of the whipped topping in a bowl; add strawberries. Split each cake into two horizontal layers; place one layer on a serving plate. Spread with half of the strawberry mixture. Top with a second cake layer; spread with custard. Add third layer; spread with remaining strawberry mixture. Top with remaining cake and whipped topping. Refrigerate overnight. Garnish with strawberries and mint if desired. **Yield:** 12 servings.

Strawberry Custard Torte

(Pictured above and on page 122)

This elegant dessert is as beautiful as it is delicious. Not only is it ultra easy to prepare, but it's a make-ahead recipe, so there's no last-minute fussing when company is coming.   —Brenda Bodnar, Euclid, Ohio

    1 package (18-1/4 ounces) yellow cake mix
1/3 cup sugar
    1 tablespoon cornstarch
1/8 teaspoon salt
    1 cup milk
    2 egg yolks, lightly beaten
    1 tablespoon butter *or* margarine
    1 teaspoon vanilla extract
    1 carton (8 ounces) frozen whipped
        topping, thawed
    1 package (12 ounces) frozen sweetened
        sliced strawberries, thawed and drained
Sliced fresh strawberries and mint leaves,
    optional

Prepare and bake cake according to package directions, using two greased and floured 9-in. round baking pans. Cool for 10 minutes; remove from pans to wire racks to cool completely.

In a saucepan, combine the sugar, cornstarch and salt; gradually stir in milk until smooth. Bring to a boil over medium heat; cook and stir for 2 minutes or until thickened. Remove from the heat. Stir a small amount of hot filling into egg yolks; return all to pan, stirring constantly. Bring to a gentle boil;

Almond Brittle Torte

I brought this impressive cake to my bridge club potluck—and now they want it every time we meet. Homemade brittle makes it extra special.
—Marrian Storm, Athol, Idaho

1-1/2 cups sugar
  1/2 cup water
  1/2 cup light corn syrup
  1/4 teaspoon instant coffee granules
    3 teaspoons baking soda
    1 cup slivered almonds
CAKE:
    8 eggs, *separated*
  1/4 cup water
    3 teaspoons lemon juice
    1 teaspoon vanilla extract
1-1/2 cups cake flour
1-1/2 cups sugar, *divided*
    1 teaspoon cream of tartar
    1 teaspoon salt
3-1/2 cups whipping cream, whipped

Line a 13-in. x 9-in. x 2-in. baking pan with foil; butter the foil and set aside. In a saucepan, combine the sugar, water, corn syrup and coffee granules. Bring to a boil over medium-high heat, stirring constantly, until a candy thermometer reads 290°. Sprinkle with baking soda, stirring constantly (mixture will foam). Stir in the almonds. Pour into prepared pan. Cool completely.

In a large mixing bowl, combine the egg yolks, water, lemon juice and vanilla; mix well. Combine flour and 3/4 cup sugar; add to egg yolk mixture and mix well. In a small mixing bowl, beat egg whites, cream of tartar and salt until soft peaks form. Beat in remaining sugar, 1 tablespoon at a time. Fold into the batter. Pour into an ungreased 10-in. tube pan. Bake at 350° for 50-55 minutes or until cake springs back when lightly touched. Cool on a wire rack.

Remove cake from pan. Split horizontally into

four layers. Place bottom layer on a serving plate; spread with about 3/4 cup whipped cream. Break almond brittle into small pieces; sprinkle some over cream. Repeat layers twice. Spread remaining whipped cream over top and sides of cake; sprinkle with remaining brittle. Refrigerate until serving. **Yield:** 12-16 servings.

Editor's Note: Almond brittle will melt on the whipped cream and form a syrup.

A Nutty Idea

Toasting nuts before using them in recipes intensifies their flavor and adds even more crunch. Simply bake at 350° for 10 to 15 minutes, stirring occasionally.

Apricot Meringue Pie

(Pictured below right)

My sister-in-law wanted to create an apricot pie recipe, so we experimented until we came up with a combination of ingredients we liked. The meringue sits nice and high, while the sweet apricots retain a little of their chewy texture. It's yummy! —Olive Rumage
Jacksboro, Texas

    12 ounces dried apricots, chopped
  1-1/2 cups water
  2-1/2 cups sugar, *divided*
      3 tablespoons cornstarch
    1/4 teaspoon salt
      4 eggs, *separated*
      2 tablespoons butter *or* margarine
    1/4 teaspoon cream of tartar
      1 pastry shell (9 inches), baked

In a saucepan, bring apricots and water to a boil. Reduce heat; simmer, uncovered, for 10 minutes or until apricots are softened. In a bowl, combine 2 cups sugar, cornstarch and salt; stir into apricot mixture. Bring to a boil. Reduce heat; cook and stir for 1 minute or until thickened. Remove from the heat; stir a small amount of hot filling into yolks. Return all to pan, stirring constantly. Bring to a gentle boil; cook and stir 1 minute longer or until glossy and clear. Remove from the heat; stir in butter. Keep warm.

In a mixing bowl, beat egg whites and cream of tartar on medium speed until soft peaks form. Gradually beat in remaining sugar, 1 tablespoon at a time, on high until stiff glossy peaks form and sugar is dissolved. Pour hot filling into crust. Spread meringue evenly over filling, sealing edges to crust.

Bake at 325° for 25-30 minutes or until golden brown. Cool on a wire rack for 1 hour. Chill for at least 3 hours before serving. Refrigerate leftovers. **Yield:** 6-8 servings.

Chocolate Mallow Pie

(Pictured on page 122)

This rich and fudgy cream cheese pie should serve eight, but it never does because so many folks request a second slice! This is the best chocolate pie recipe I've found. —Louise Genn, Cosmopolis, Washington

  1-1/4 cups crushed cream-filled
          chocolate sandwich cookies
          (about 14 cookies)
    1/4 cup butter *or* margarine, melted
      2 tablespoons sugar
      2 packages (one 8 ounces, one
          3 ounces) cream cheese, softened
    1/2 cup chocolate syrup
  1-1/3 cups semisweet chocolate chips, melted
      1 carton (8 ounces) frozen whipped
          topping, thawed
      2 cups miniature marshmallows
Chocolate curls, optional

In a bowl, combine the cookie crumbs, butter and sugar. Press onto the bottom and up the sides of a 9-in. pie plate. Bake at 375° for 8-10 minutes or until set; cool completely on a wire rack.

In a mixing bowl, beat cream cheese and chocolate syrup until blended. Beat in melted chips. Set aside 1/4 cup of whipped topping. Fold marshmallows and remaining whipped topping into chocolate mixture. Spoon into crust. Refrigerate for at least 8 hours or overnight. Garnish with reserved whipped topping and chocolate curls if desired. **Yield:** 8 servings.

Just Desserts

If you're sweet on desserts, you'll love this tempting selection of creamy parfaits, luscious cheesecakes, confections and more.

DEVOTED TO DESSERTS. Clockwise from upper left: Strawberry Graham Dessert (p. 141); Orange Cream Cheesecake (p. 140); Apple-Honey Dutch Baby (p. 157); Butter Pecan Sauce (p. 153); Blueberry Peach Parfaits and Rhubarb Gingersnap Parfaits (p. 152).

Orange Cream Cheesecake

(Pictured below and on page 138)

I love serving this impressive-looking cheesecake with its pretty layers and silky-smooth texture. The combination of orange gelatin, cream cheese and whipped topping is simply irresistible.
—Madonna Faunce, Boise, Idaho

2 cups graham cracker crumbs
1 teaspoon ground cinnamon
1 teaspoon grated orange peel
1/2 cup butter _or_ margarine, melted
FILLING:
   1 package (3 ounces) orange gelatin
   3 packages (8 ounces _each_) cream cheese, softened

COOL AND REFRESHING gelatin dishes like Orange Cream Cheesecake and Strawberry Graham Dessert (shown below, from top) are popular with young and old alike.

1-1/4 cups sugar
    1 can (5 ounces) evaporated milk
    1 teaspoon lemon juice
1/3 cup orange juice concentrate
    1 teaspoon vanilla extract
    1 carton (8 ounces) frozen whipped
        topping, thawed
TOPPING:
    2 cups whipped topping
1/4 cup sugar
Lemon slices, orange peel strips, kumquats and
    lemon balm for garnish, optional

Combine the cracker crumbs, cinnamon, orange peel and butter. Press onto the bottom of a greased 10-in. springform pan. Refrigerate for at least 30 minutes.

Prepare gelatin according to package directions. Set aside 1/2 cup at room temperature. Chill remaining gelatin until slightly thickened, about 80 minutes.

Meanwhile, in a mixing bowl, beat the cream cheese and sugar for 2 minutes. Gradually beat in the milk and lemon juice. Beat on medium-high speed 2 minutes longer. Gradually beat in the orange juice concentrate, vanilla and room-temperature gelatin. Fold in the whipped topping. Pour over prepared crust.

In a mixing bowl, beat whipped topping and sugar. Beat in refrigerated gelatin (mixture will be thin). Chill for 30 minutes. Gently spoon over filling (pan will be full). Refrigerate for 8 hours or overnight. Garnish with lemon slices, orange peel strips, kumquats and lemon balm if desired. **Yield:** 10-12 servings.

— 🥄 🥄 🥄 —

Strawberry Graham Dessert

(Pictured at left and on page 138)

My mother passed the recipe for this luscious layered dessert on to me...and my family has enjoyed it for years. These days, I often make this special treat for my granddaughter. It's a fun way to dress up Jell-O, and kids love it. —Audrey Huckell, Wabigoon, Ontario

    1 cup graham cracker crumbs (about 16
        squares)
    2 tablespoons butter *or* margarine, melted
    1 package (3 ounces) strawberry gelatin
    1 cup boiling water
    1 package (16 ounces) frozen sweetened
        sliced strawberries, thawed
    1 tablespoon lemon juice
    4 ounces cream cheese, softened
1/2 cup confectioners' sugar
    1 teaspoon vanilla extract

Dash salt
    1 cup whipping cream, whipped
Fresh strawberries and mint, optional

In a small bowl, combine cracker crumbs and butter; set aside 1 tablespoon for topping. Press the remaining crumb mixture onto the bottom of a greased 8-in. square baking dish. Bake at 325° for 10-14 minutes or until golden brown. Cool on a wire rack.

In a bowl, dissolve gelatin in boiling water; stir in strawberries and lemon juice. Refrigerate until partially set, about 1-1/2 hours.

In a small mixing bowl, beat the cream cheese, sugar, vanilla and salt until smooth. Fold in whipped cream. Spread half over cooled crust. Cover and refrigerate remaining cream mixture. Pour gelatin mixture over filling; refrigerate until firm. Top with remaining cream mixture. Sprinkle with reserved crumb mixture. Refrigerate overnight. Garnish with fresh berries and mint if desired. **Yield:** 9 servings.

— 🥄 🥄 🥄 —

Fabulous Fudge Cheesecake

This fudgy cheesecake is particularly popular with my two children. It's also a favorite with guests at the cheesecake party my wife and I host every year.
    —Scott Fox, Pelican Rapids, Minnesota

    1 cup vanilla wafer crumbs
1/2 cup confectioners' sugar
1/3 cup baking cocoa
1/3 cup butter *or* margarine, melted
FILLING:
    3 packages (8 ounces *each*) cream cheese,
        softened
    1 can (14 ounces) sweetened condensed
        milk
    2 teaspoons vanilla extract
    2 cups semisweet chocolate chips, melted
        and cooled
    4 eggs

In a small bowl, combine wafer crumbs, confectioners' sugar and cocoa; stir in butter. Press onto the bottom of a greased 9-in. springform pan; set aside. In a mixing bowl, beat cream cheese, milk and vanilla until smooth. Add melted chocolate; mix until blended. Add eggs; beat on low speed just until combined. Pour over crust. Place pan on a baking sheet.

Bake at 325° for 40-45 minutes or until center is almost set. Cool on a wire rack for 10 minutes. Carefully run a knife around edge of pan to loosen; cool 1 hour longer. Refrigerate overnight. **Yield:** 10-12 servings.

Chocolate Dessert Cups

(Pictured at far right)

This elegant party dessert is tailor-made for Christmas. Making the chocolate cups is a bit time-consuming—but they look so pretty on a holiday platter.
—Ellen Govertsen, Wheaton, Illinois

1 cup (6 ounces) semisweet chocolate chips
1 tablespoon shortening
8 scoops peppermint ice cream
Miniature candy canes

In a microwave or saucepan, melt the chocolate chips and shortening. Brush evenly on the inside of eight paper or foil muffin cup liners. Chill until hardened, about 25 minutes. Remove liners. Fill chocolate cups with ice cream. Garnish with candy canes. **Yield:** 8 servings.

———— 🍵 🍵 🍵 ————

Orange Chocolate Fondue

(Pictured at far right)

Invite your family and friends to dip cubes of pound cake and pieces of fruit into this rich, luscious fondue for a special treat during the holiday season.
—Mary Jean DeVries, Grandville, Michigan

1/2 cup milk chocolate chips
3 squares (1 ounce *each*) bittersweet chocolate
1/2 cup whipping cream
3 tablespoons orange juice concentrate
1 frozen pound cake (16 ounces), thawed and cut into 1-inch cubes
Sliced bananas and star fruit, orange segments, sweet cherries *or* strawberries *or* fruit of your choice

In a heavy saucepan over low heat, cook and stir the chocolate chips, bittersweet chocolate and cream until smooth. Stir in the orange juice concentrate. Transfer to a fondue pot and keep warm. Serve with cake and fruit. **Yield:** 1-1/3 cups.

———— 🍵 🍵 🍵 ————

Chocolate-Filled Meringue

(Pictured at far right)

This is my favorite dessert for the Christmas season. It has a nutty, chewy crust and dark chocolate filling that's not too sweet. I'm proud to serve this impressive-looking treat, and my guests love the rich taste.
—Joan Totton, Stanfield, Oregon

3 egg whites
1/2 teaspoon vanilla extract
1/4 teaspoon cream of tartar
1/4 teaspoon salt
1/2 cup sugar
1/4 cup confectioners' sugar
3/4 cup finely chopped pecans
1 cup (6 ounces) semisweet chocolate chips, optional
FILLING:
2 milk chocolate candy bars (1.55 ounces *each*)
1 square (1 ounce) unsweetened chocolate
1/4 cup water
1 teaspoon vanilla extract
1 cup whipping cream, whipped
Additional whipped cream, optional

In a mixing bowl, beat egg whites, vanilla, cream of tartar and salt until soft peaks form. Gradually add sugars, beating until stiff peaks form. Fold in pecans. Grease the bottom and sides of a 9-in. pie plate, leaving the top edge ungreased. Spread meringue onto the bottom and up the sides of prepared plate. Build up top edge. Bake at 350° for 20-30 minutes or until lightly browned. Cool on a wire rack.

If chocolate stars are desired, melt chocolate chips in a microwave or saucepan. Transfer chocolate to a small heavy-duty resealable plastic bag; cut a small hole in one corner of bag. On a waxed paper-lined baking sheet, pipe chocolate into star shapes. Refrigerate until firm, about 15 minutes. When ready to serve, carefully remove stars with a metal spatula.

For filling, in a heavy saucepan, combine candy bars, unsweetened chocolate and water. Cook and stir over low heat until melted. Pour into a large bowl; cool to room temperature. Stir in vanilla. Fold in whipped cream; pour into the crust. Top with additional whipped cream and chocolate stars if desired. **Yield:** 6-8 servings.

———— 🍵 🍵 🍵 ————

Plum Bumble

Since this recipe was published in our local newspaper in 1976, I've served it numerous times to family and friends. Similar to a fruit cobbler, it is always a favorite at all sorts of gatherings.
—Arlis Enburg
Rock Island, Illinois

1 cup plus 5 teaspoons sugar, *divided*
1/4 cup cornstarch
3 cups sliced fresh plums (about 1-1/4 pounds)
3/4 cup pineapple tidbits
2 tablespoons butter *or* margarine, *divided*
1/2 teaspoon ground cinnamon

1 tube (7-1/2 ounces) refrigerated buttermilk biscuits, separated and quartered

In a bowl, combine 1 cup sugar, cornstarch, plums and pineapple. Transfer to a greased shallow 2-qt. baking dish; dot with 1 tablespoon butter. Bake, uncovered, at 400° for 15 minutes.

Meanwhile, melt the remaining butter. In a small bowl, combine the cinnamon and remaining sugar. Place biscuit pieces over the hot plum mixture; brush with melted butter and sprinkle with the cinnamon-sugar mixture. Bake 25-30 minutes longer or until the biscuits are golden brown. **Yield:** 6 servings.

FESTIVE DESSERTS such as Chocolate-Filled Meringue, Orange Chocolate Fondue and Chocolate Dessert Cups (shown below, clockwise from top left) put the finishing touches on great holiday meals.

Berry Cream Dessert

(Pictured above)

When I was in high school, my friend's mom used to make this light dessert. Now I fix it for my own family.
—Deb Sandoval, Colorado Springs, Colorado

✓ Uses less fat, sugar or salt. Includes Nutritional Analysis and Diabetic Exchanges.

1 package (3 ounces) strawberry gelatin
1 package (3 ounces) raspberry gelatin
2 cups boiling water
2 cups cold water
1 carton (8 ounces) strawberry yogurt
1 carton (8 ounces) raspberry yogurt
2 cups sliced fresh *or* frozen unsweetened strawberries
1 carton (12 ounces) frozen whipped topping, thawed
Additional fresh strawberries, optional

In a large bowl, dissolve strawberry and raspberry gelatin in boiling water. Stir in cold water and strawberry and raspberry yogurt until blended. Chill until syrupy, about 1 hour.

Fold in strawberries and whipped topping. Spoon into individual dishes. Chill until firm, about 4 hours. Garnish with fresh berries if desired. **Yield:** 16 servings.

Nutritional Analysis: One 3/4-cup serving (prepared with sugar-free gelatin, reduced-fat yogurt and reduced-fat whipped topping; calculated without garnish) equals 95 calories, 3 g fat (3 g saturated fat), 2 mg cholesterol, 46 mg sodium, 13 g carbohydrate, 1 g fiber, 2 g protein. **Diabetic Exchanges:** 1 fruit, 1/2 fat.

Danish Rhubarb Pudding

This delicious pudding my grandmother used to make is one of my favorite traditional Danish desserts.
—Kay Sundheim, Nashua, Montana

6 cups chopped fresh *or* frozen rhubarb, thawed
6 cups water
2 cups sugar
1/4 cup cornstarch
3 tablespoons cold water

In a saucepan, bring rhubarb and water to a boil. Reduce heat; simmer, uncovered, for 10-15 minutes or until rhubarb is tender. Drain, reserving liquid; discard pulp. Measure 4 cups liquid; return to the pan.

Add sugar; bring to a boil. Combine cornstarch and cold water until smooth; stir into rhubarb liquid. Cook and stir for 1-2 minutes or until slightly thickened. Pour into individual dishes. Refrigerate for at least 4 hours before serving. **Yield:** 8 servings.

Lime Sherbet

You don't need an ice cream maker to churn out this pretty light green refresher. *—Carolyn Hannay, Antioch, Tennessee*

✓ Uses less fat, sugar or salt. Includes Nutritional Analysis and Diabetic Exchanges.

1 package (3 ounces) lime gelatin
1 cup boiling water
3 cups 1% milk
1/2 cup sugar
1/4 cup lemon juice

In a bowl, dissolve gelatin in boiling water. Add the milk, sugar and lemon juice; stir until sugar is dissolved. Pour into a freezer container; freeze for 4 hours or until frozen. Remove from the freezer and let stand for 10 minutes or until slightly softened. Beat with a mixer until light and fluffy. Refreeze for at least 1 hour. **Yield:** about 1 quart.

Nutritional Analysis: One serving (1 cup) equals 260 calories, 2 g fat (1 g saturated fat), 11 mg cholesterol, 156 mg sodium, 54 g carbohydrate, trace fiber, 9 g protein. **Diabetic Exchanges:** 2 starch, 1-1/2 fruit.

first appear separated; continue stirring until fully blended). Remove from the heat; stir in the marshmallow creme and extracts until well blended. Stir in nuts.

Spread into prepared pan. Refrigerate until set. Lift out of pan and remove foil; cut into squares. Store in the refrigerator. **Yield:** about 4-1/2 pounds.

— 🍷 🍷 🍷 —

Triple Sherbet Dessert

(Pictured below)

For a special, refreshing and lovely treat, try this sherbet dessert. Our children requested this dessert many times over the years. —Mrs. Howard Hinseth
Minneapolis, Minnesota

  1 package (14-1/2 ounces) coconut
     macaroon cookies, crumbled
  1 carton (12 ounces) frozen whipped
     topping, thawed
1/2 cup chopped pecans, optional
1/2 cup flaked coconut
  1 pint *each* orange, lemon and lime sherbet,
     softened

In a bowl, combine the cookie crumbs, whipped topping, pecans and coconut. Spread half into a 13-in. x 9-in. x 2-in. dish. Spread with orange sherbet; freeze for 10-15 minutes. Repeat with lemon and lime layers. Top with the remaining cookie mixture. Cover and freeze until firm. **Yield:** 12-16 servings.

Four-Chip Fudge

(Pictured above)

I stir up this wonderful creamy fudge every Christmas. My friend Marlene gave me the recipe years ago, and I've passed it on to everyone who tries it. Flavored with four different kinds of chips, this is the best fudge I've ever tasted! —Delores Wigginton
Prudenville, Michigan

1-1/2 teaspoons plus 3/4 cup butter (no
     substitutes), *divided*
  1 can (14 ounces) sweetened condensed
     milk
  3 tablespoons milk
  1 package (12 ounces) semisweet
     chocolate chips
  1 package (11-1/2 ounces) milk chocolate
     chips
  1 package (10 ounces) peanut butter chips
  1 cup butterscotch chips
  1 jar (7 ounces) marshmallow creme
1/2 teaspoon almond extract
1/2 teaspoon vanilla extract
  1 cup chopped walnuts

Line a 13-in. x 9-in. x 2-in. pan with foil and grease the foil with 1-1/2 teaspoons of butter; set aside. In a large heavy saucepan, melt the remaining butter over low heat. Add the next six ingredients. Cook and stir constantly until smooth (mixture will

Carefully run a knife around the edge of pan to loosen; cool 1 hour longer. Refrigerate until completely cooled.

In a saucepan over low heat, melt chocolate chips, cream and honey; stir until smooth. Remove from the heat; cool for 5 minutes. Remove sides of springform pan. Pour topping over cheesecake. Chill for at least 4 hours or until topping is set. Refrigerate leftovers. **Yield:** 12 servings.

Blueberry Swirl Cheesecake

My wife, Gail, and I host an annual cheesecake party. For the event's 10th anniversary, we prepared 10 family favorites, including this fruity creation.
—Scott Fox, Pelican Rapids, Minnesota

  1 package (12 ounces) frozen blueberries, thawed
  1 tablespoon sugar
  1 tablespoon water
1-1/2 teaspoons cornstarch
CRUST:
1-1/4 cups graham cracker crumbs
  1/4 cup sugar
  1/3 cup butter *or* margarine, melted
FILLING:
  3 packages (8 ounces *each*) cream cheese, softened
  1 can (14 ounces) sweetened condensed milk
  3 eggs
  1/4 cup lemon juice

In a food processor or blender, process the blueberries, sugar, water and cornstarch until blended. Transfer to a heavy saucepan; bring to a boil. Reduce heat; cook and stir over medium heat for 2 minutes or until thickened. Set aside 6 tablespoons for filling. Refrigerate the remaining sauce for topping.

Combine crust ingredients. Press onto the bottom of a greased 9-in. springform pan; set aside. In a mixing bowl, beat the cream cheese and milk until smooth. Add eggs; beat on low just until combined. Add lemon juice; beat just until blended. Pour half of the filling over crust; top with half of the reserved blueberry sauce. Repeat layers. Cut through filling with a knife to swirl blueberry sauce. Place pan on a baking sheet.

Bake at 325° for 40-45 minutes or until center is almost set. Cool on a wire rack for 10 minutes. Carefully run a knife around the edge of pan to loosen; cool 1 hour longer. Refrigerate overnight. Remove sides of pan. Serve with chilled blueberry sauce. **Yield:** 12 servings.

Chocolate Cheesecake

(Pictured above)

This luscious cheesecake has a hint of almond in the creamy chocolate filling. Honey sweetens the rich chocolate topping.
—Lori Coulthard
Laramie, Wyoming

1-1/4 cups graham cracker crumbs (about 20 squares)
  1/2 cup sugar
  1/4 cup baking cocoa
  6 tablespoons butter *or* margarine, melted
FILLING:
  3 packages (8 ounces *each*) cream cheese, softened
  3/4 cup sugar
  3 eggs
  1 cup (6 ounces) semisweet chocolate chips, melted
  1 teaspoon almond extract
  1/2 teaspoon vanilla extract
TOPPING:
  1/4 cup semisweet chocolate chips
  1/3 cup whipping cream
  1 tablespoon honey

In a bowl, combine cracker crumbs, sugar and cocoa; stir in butter. Press onto the bottom and 1 in. up the sides of a greased 9-in. springform pan; set aside. In a small mixing bowl, beat cream cheese and sugar until smooth. Add eggs; beat on low speed just until combined. Stir in melted chocolate and extracts just until blended. Pour into crust.

Bake at 350° for 45-50 minutes or until center is almost set. Cool on a wire rack for 10 minutes.

Gingered Pear Sorbet

(Pictured below)

During the hot summer here in Florida, we enjoy this refreshing sorbet. Sometimes I dress up servings with berries, mint leaves or crystallized ginger.
—*Donna Cline, Pensacola, Florida*

  1 **can (29 ounces) pear halves**
1/4 **cup sugar**
  2 **tablespoons lemon juice**
1/8 **teaspoon ground ginger**
Yellow food coloring, optional

Drain pears, reserving 1 cup syrup (discard remaining syrup or save for another use); set pears aside. In a saucepan, bring sugar and reserved syrup to a boil. Remove from the heat; cool.

In a blender, process the pears, lemon juice and ginger until smooth. Add cooled syrup and food coloring if desired; cover and process until pureed. Pour into an 11-in. x 7-in. x 2-in. dish. Cover and freeze for 1-1/2 to 2 hours or until partially frozen.

Return mixture to blender; cover and process until smooth. Place in a freezer container; cover and freeze for at least 3 hours. Remove from the freezer 20 minutes before serving. **Yield:** 3 cups.

Khrustyky

This crisp, dainty pastry dusted with confectioners' sugar has an eggy flavor similar to cream puffs. I honor my Ukrainian heritage by serving khrustyky on Christmas Eve as part of the traditional feast of 12 dishes. Each dish symbolizes one of the apostles.
—*Carol Funk, Richard, Saskatchewan*

    2 **eggs**
    3 **egg yolks**
    1 **tablespoon whipping cream**
    1 **tablespoon vanilla extract**
    2 **tablespoons sugar**
1-1/2 **cups all-purpose flour**
  1/2 **teaspoon salt**
Oil for deep-fat frying
Confectioners' sugar

In a mixing bowl, beat the eggs, egg yolks, cream and vanilla. Beat in sugar. Combine flour and salt; stir into the egg mixture just until smooth (dough will be soft). Divide into four portions.

On a well-floured surface, roll out one portion to 1/8-in. thickness. Cut into 1-1/2-in. strips; cut strips diagonally into three pieces. Cut a 1-1/2-in. slit lengthwise into the center of each piece; pull one end of strip through slit to make a loop. Cover shaped pieces while rolling out and cutting the remaining dough.

In an electric skillet or deep-fat fryer, heat 2-3 in. of oil to 375°. Fry pastries, a few at a time, until golden brown, turning once. Drain on paper towels. Dust with confectioners' sugar while warm. **Yield:** 1-1/2 dozen pastries.

Choice Cheesecake

Cheesecakes require even heat in order to rise properly. For this reason, it's important not to open the oven door during the first 30 minutes of baking time. Drafts can cause a cheesecake to fall or crack.

Cracks don't ruin a cheesecake! Disguise scars with a topping such as slighly sweetened sour cream or whipping cream, fresh berries or your favorite jam.

COOL, CREAMY Vanilla Custard Ice Cream and Caramel Cheesecake (shown above, from top) are "dairy" delightful.

Vanilla Custard Ice Cream

(Pictured above)

This ice cream is a classic and scrumptious use for milk and whipping cream. It is the most wonderful custard I've ever tasted, and my family and guests have loved it for years. —*Margaret Gage Roseboom, New York*

> 2 eggs, beaten
> 2 cups milk
> 3/4 cup sugar
> 1/8 teaspoon salt
> 2 cups whipping cream
> 2 tablespoons vanilla extract
> Colored sprinkles

In a large saucepan, combine the eggs, milk, sugar and salt. Cook and stir over medium-low heat until mixture reaches 160° and is thick enough to coat a metal spoon. Cool. Stir in cream and vanilla.

Fill cylinder of ice cream freezer two-thirds full; freeze according to manufacturer's directions. Refrigerate remaining mixture until ready to freeze. Allow to ripen in ice cream freezer or firm up in re-frigerator freezer for 2-4 hours before serving. Garnish with colored sprinkles. **Yield:** 1-1/2 quarts.

Caramel Cheesecake

(Pictured at left)

This caramel-topped cheesecake is a divine way to savor the goodness of cream cheese. It always gets rave reviews whenever I serve it to friends and family alike. —*Rena Fields, Sackets Harbor, New York*

> 2 cups vanilla wafer crumbs (about 32 wafers)
> 3 tablespoons sugar
> 1/3 cup butter *or* margarine, melted
> **FILLING:**
> 3 packages (8 ounces *each*) cream cheese, softened
> 1/2 cup sugar
> 2 tablespoons all-purpose flour
> 3 eggs
> 1 teaspoon vanilla extract
> **CARAMEL SAUCE:**
> 1 can (5 ounces) evaporated milk
> 1 package (14 ounces) caramels*
> 1 cup chopped walnuts

In a bowl, combine crumbs and sugar; stir in butter. Press onto the bottom and 3/4 in. up the sides of a greased 10-in. springform pan; set aside. In a mixing bowl, beat cream cheese and sugar until smooth. Add flour; beat well. Beat in eggs on low speed just until combined. Stir in vanilla. Pour into prepared crust. Place pan on a baking sheet.

Bake at 375° for 30-35 minutes or until center is almost set. Cool on a wire rack for 10 minutes. Carefully run a knife around edge of pan to loosen; cool 1 hour longer. Refrigerate overnight. Remove sides of pan.

In a saucepan over low heat, stir milk and caramels until caramels are melted. Stir in nuts. Cool to room temperature. Drizzle over cheesecake slices. Refrigerate leftovers. **Yield:** 12-16 servings.

*Editor's Note: This recipe was tested with Hershey caramels.

Chocolate Chip Dutch Baby

I modified a traditional Dutch baby recipe given to me by a friend to come up with this version my family thinks is terrific. You'll be surprised at how easy it is to make. —*Mary Thompson, Faribault, Minnesota*

> 1/4 cup miniature semisweet chocolate chips
> 1/4 cup packed brown sugar

1/2 cup all-purpose flour
2 eggs
1/2 cup half-and-half cream
1/8 teaspoon ground nutmeg
Dash cinnamon
3 tablespoons butter *or* margarine, cubed
Maple syrup and additional butter *or* margarine, optional

In a small bowl, combine chocolate chips and brown sugar; set aside. In a mixing bowl, beat flour, eggs, cream, nutmeg and cinnamon until smooth. Place butter in a 9-in. pie plate. Heat at 425° for 4-6 minutes or until melted. Pour batter into hot plate. Sprinkle with chocolate chip mixture. Bake for 15-20 minutes or until top edges are golden brown. Serve immediately with syrup and butter if desired. **Yield:** 4-6 servings.

Molasses Taffy

(Pictured above)

When I was growing up, we'd have taffy pulling parties. The more experienced taffy pullers could make the long strips of shiny candy pop as they worked it into rope-like streamers. —Sherrill Bennett
Rayville, Louisiana

7 tablespoons butter (no substitutes), softened, *divided*
2 cups molasses
1 cup sugar
3/4 cup water
1/2 teaspoon vanilla extract
1/8 teaspoon baking soda

Butter a 15-in. x 10-in. x 1-in. pan with 3 tablespoons butter; set aside. In a heavy saucepan over medium heat, bring the molasses, sugar and water to a boil. Cook and stir until a candy thermometer reads 245° (firm-ball stage), stirring occasionally.

Add vanilla, baking soda and remaining butter. Cover and cook for 3 minutes. Uncover and cook until the thermometer reads 260° (hard-ball stage), stirring occasionally. Remove from the heat; pour into prepared pan. Cool on a wire rack for 15 minutes or until cool enough to handle.

With buttered fingers, quickly pull half of the taffy until firm but pliable. Pull and shape into a 1/2-in. rope; cut into 1-1/4-in. pieces. Repeat with remaining taffy. Wrap each piece in foil, colored candy wrappers or waxed paper. **Yield:** about 12-1/2 dozen.

Editor's Note: We recommend that you test your candy thermometer before each use by bringing water to a boil; the thermometer should read 212°. Adjust your recipe temperature up or down based on your test.

— 🍴 🍴 🍴 —

Peanut Clusters

(Pictured below)

My husband, Greg, likes to mix up these treats with the kids. With three simple ingredients I usually have on hand, it's easy to make a batch in a matter of minutes. —Deb Darr, Falls City, Oregon

4 ounces milk chocolate candy coating
4 ounces white candy coating
1 can (16 ounces) salted peanuts (about 2-1/2 cups)

In a microwave, melt candy coatings, stirring often until blended. Stir in the peanuts until coated. Drop by tablespoonfuls onto a waxed paper-lined baking sheet. Refrigerate until serving. **Yield:** about 3 dozen.

SPRING GATHERINGS will be something sweet when you serve Rich Chocolate Cheesecake, Chocolate-Filled Meringues and Peanut Butter Berry Delights (shown above, clockwise from top).

Rich Chocolate Cheesecake

(Pictured above)

With seven children and 15 grandchildren, I favor desserts that serve a bunch. Here's a special treat that will easily satisfy the chocolate cravings of up to 16 hungry people. —Mary Walker, Berlin, Maryland

1-1/2 cups crushed chocolate wafers (about 24 wafers)
  1/4 cup butter *or* margarine, melted
  2 tablespoons sugar
  1/4 cup finely chopped almonds
FILLING:
  3 packages (8 ounces *each*) cream cheese, softened
3/4 cup sugar
  3 eggs
1/3 cup strong brewed coffee
  1 teaspoon vanilla extract
3/4 cup baking cocoa

1 cup (6 ounces) semisweet chocolate chips
TOPPING:
    1 cup (8 ounces) sour cream
    2 tablespoons brown sugar
    1 teaspoon vanilla extract
    1/2 cup sliced almonds

In a bowl, combine the wafer crumbs, butter, sugar and almonds. Press onto the bottom and 1 in. up the sides of a 9-in. springform pan; set aside. In a mixing bowl, beat cream cheese and sugar until smooth. Add eggs; beat on low speed just until combined. Stir in coffee and vanilla; mix well. Beat in cocoa just until blended. Stir in chocolate chips. Pour into prepared crust. Place pan on a baking sheet. Bake at 375° for 30-35 minutes or until center is almost set.

Remove from the oven; increase temperature to 425°. Combine the sour cream, brown sugar and vanilla until smooth. Spread over warm cheesecake; sprinkle with nuts. Bake for 10 minutes or until lightly browned.

Cool on a wire rack for 10 minutes. Carefully run a knife around edge of pan to loosen; cool 1 hour longer. Chill overnight. Remove sides of pan. Refrigerate leftovers. **Yield:** 16 servings.

Peanut Butter Berry Delights

(Pictured at left)

These cream-filled, chocolate-dipped berries make a fun snack for a shower or a pretty party dessert that inspires compliments. —Rose Harman, Hays, Kansas

  1/2 cup creamy peanut butter*
    5 tablespoons milk chocolate chips, melted and cooled
    2 tablespoons whipped topping
  20 to 25 large fresh strawberries
    5 squares (1 ounce *each*) semisweet chocolate, melted

Line a baking sheet with waxed paper; set aside. In a small bowl, combine the peanut butter, melted milk chocolate and whipped topping.

Beginning at the right of the stem, cut each strawberry in half diagonally. Scoop out the white portion from the larger half of each berry. Spread or pipe peanut butter mixture between the two halves; press gently. Place on prepared pan; refrigerate for 15 minutes or until set. Dip bottom half of berries in semisweet chocolate. Place on pan. Refrigerate for 15-20 minutes or until set. **Yield:** 20-25 servings.

*Editor's Note: Reduced-fat or generic brands of peanut butter are not recommended for this recipe.

Chocolate-Filled Meringues

(Pictured at far left)

These lovely delicate meringue shells are easy to make, and their crisp texture is a perfect complement to the creamy chocolate filling. —Mary Lou Wayman
Salt Lake City, Utah

    2 egg whites
  1/4 teaspoon cream of tartar
  1/4 teaspoon vanilla extract
Dash salt
  1/2 cup sugar
FILLING:
    1 package (8 ounces) cream cheese, softened
    1 cup confectioners' sugar
  1/4 cup baking cocoa
    1 cup whipped topping
    1 package (10 ounces) frozen sweetened sliced strawberries, thawed

Place egg whites in a small mixing bowl; let stand at room temperature for 30 minutes. Beat on medium speed until foamy. Add cream of tartar, vanilla and salt; beat until soft peaks form. Gradually add sugar, 1 tablespoon at a time, beating until stiff peaks form.

Line a baking sheet with parchment paper. Spoon meringue into six mounds on paper. Using the back of a spoon, shape into 3-in. cups. Bake at 300° for 35 minutes. Turn off oven and do not open door; let meringues dry for 1 hour. Cool on a wire rack.

For filling, in a mixing bowl, beat cream cheese, confectioners' sugar and cocoa until smooth and fluffy. Fold in whipped topping. Process the strawberries in a blender or food processor until pureed. To serve, spoon filling into meringue shells. Top with strawberry sauce. **Yield:** 6 servings.

Gingersnap Ice Cream

It's easy to dress up plain vanilla ice cream for the holidays by spicing it with a little molasses and ginger. A friend gave me this simple recipe. —Carolyn Hayes
Marion, Illinois

    2 cups vanilla ice cream, softened
    2 tablespoons molasses
    1 teaspoon ground ginger
  1/2 cup crushed crisp gingersnaps (about 8 cookies)

In a bowl, combine the ice cream, molasses and ginger just until blended; stir in cookie crumbs. Cover and freeze for 4 hours or until firm. **Yield:** 6 servings.

Cool Off...with Perfect Parfaits

IN FRENCH, the word "parfait" means "perfect", which is how many people perceive these lovely layered desserts. Whether they feature ice cream and a sweet topping or another whipped or creamy filling and fruit, there's no better way to beat the summer heat than with a cool parfait.

Check out these delightful recipes, then grab a spoon and dig in!

REFRESHING Blueberry Peach Parfaits, Rhubarb Gingersnap Parfaits and Butter Pecan Sauce (shown above, clockwise from top left) are cool treats on hot days.

Blueberry Peach Parfaits

(Pictured below left and on page 138)

We have peach trees and blueberry bushes, so combining those fresh fruits with a thick old-fashioned custard sauce is an extraordinary summer treat.
—Suzanne Cleveland, Lyons, Georgia

 1/2 cup sugar
  3 tablespoons cornstarch
 1/4 teaspoon salt
  2 cups milk
  2 eggs, lightly beaten
1-1/2 teaspoons vanilla extract
  2 medium ripe peaches, peeled and sliced
1-1/2 cups fresh blueberries
Whipped cream

In a saucepan, combine the sugar, cornstarch and salt. Stir in milk until smooth. Bring to a boil over medium heat; cook and stir for 2 minutes or until thickened. Remove from the heat. Stir a small amount of hot mixture into eggs; return all to the pan, stirring constantly. Bring to a gentle boil; cook and stir for 2 minutes. Remove from the heat; stir in vanilla. Cover and refrigerate until chilled.

In six parfait glasses, layer 2 rounded tablespoons of custard, two to three peach slices and 2 tablespoons blueberries; repeat layers. Top with whipped cream. **Yield:** 6 servings.

Rhubarb Gingersnap Parfaits

(Pictured at left and on page 138)

I created this recipe to showcase one of my favorite garden plants—rhubarb. My four children are grown, but I enjoy fixing this colorful dessert for my grandchildren. —Diane Halferty, Corpus Christi, Texas

  4 cups chopped fresh *or* frozen rhubarb
   (about 1 pound)
 1/2 cup sugar
 3/4 cup whipping cream
  3 tablespoons confectioners' sugar
 1/3 cup sour cream
 1/8 teaspoon almond extract
  2 tablespoons coarsely crushed gingersnaps

In a large saucepan, bring rhubarb and sugar to a boil over medium heat, stirring constantly. Reduce heat; simmer, uncovered, until rhubarb is tender and mixture is reduced to 1-1/3 cups. Remove from the heat. Cool for 30 minutes. Cover and refrigerate.

In a mixing bowl, beat the whipping cream until soft peaks form. Beat in confectioners' sugar. Add sour cream and extract; beat until stiff peaks form. In four parfait glasses, place about 2 tablespoons rhubarb mixture and 1/4 cup cream mixture; repeat layers. Sprinkle with gingersnaps. Refrigerate until serving. **Yield:** 4 servings.

— 🍷 🍷 🍷 —

Butter Pecan Sauce

(Pictured at far left and on page 138)

It's hard to beat the homemade goodness of this buttery smooth pecan sauce over ice cream.
—*Kim Gilliland, Simi Valley, California*

  1/2 **cup plus 2 tablespoons packed brown**
      sugar
    2 **tablespoons sugar**
    4 **teaspoons cornstarch**
  3/4 **cup whipping cream**
    1 **tablespoon butter *or* margarine**
  1/2 **cup chopped pecans, toasted**
Vanilla ice cream *or* flavor of your choice

In a heavy saucepan, combine the sugars and cornstarch. Gradually stir in cream until smooth. Bring to a boil over medium heat, stirring constantly; cook and stir for 2-3 minutes or until slightly thickened. Remove from the heat; stir in butter until melted. Add the pecans. Serve warm over ice cream. **Yield:** 1-1/2 cups.

— 🍷 🍷 🍷 —

German Chocolate Sundaes

This terrific topping is a real treat over chocolate ice cream. It's fun and fancy at the same time and much cooler to make on hot days than a German chocolate cake. —*DeEtta Rasmussen, Fort Madison, Iowa*

  1/2 **cup sugar**
  1/2 **cup evaporated milk**
  1/4 **cup butter *or* margarine**
    2 **egg yolks, beaten**
  2/3 **cup flaked coconut**
  1/2 **cup chopped pecans**
    1 **teaspoon vanilla extract**
Chocolate ice cream
Chocolate syrup, toasted coconut and additional
      chopped pecans, optional

In a heavy saucepan, combine the sugar, milk, butter and egg yolks. Bring to a boil over medium heat, stirring constantly; cook and stir for 2 minutes or until thickened. Remove from the heat. Stir in the coconut, pecans and vanilla. Stir until sauce is cooled slightly. Serve over ice cream. Top with chocolate syrup, coconut and pecans if desired. **Yield:** 1-1/4 cups.

— 🍷 🍷 🍷 —

Hot Fudge Sauce

The big chocolate flavor of this heavenly sauce over ice cream and a brownie is sure to satisfy the craving of any sweet tooth. —*Priscilla Weaver*
      Hagerstown, Maryland

    1 **can (14 ounces) sweetened condensed**
      milk
    4 **squares (1 ounce *each*) semisweet**
      chocolate
    2 **tablespoons butter (no substitutes)**
    1 **teaspoon vanilla extract**

In a heavy saucepan, combine the milk, chocolate and butter. Cook and stir over medium-low heat until chocolate is melted. Remove from the heat; stir in vanilla. **Yield:** about 1-1/2 cups.

— 🍷 🍷 🍷 —

Black Cherry Cream Parfaits

This dessert is light and cool, but incredibly decadent-tasting. My mom used to make it on special days, and I still use the recipe often.
—*Margaret Schmieder, Sparks, Nevada*

    2 **packages (3 ounces *each*) black cherry**
      gelatin
    2 **cups boiling water**
    2 **cups black cherry soda, chilled**
    1 **cup whipping cream**
  1/2 **cup confectioners' sugar**
    1 **can (15 ounces) pitted dark sweet**
      cherries, drained
  1/2 **cup chopped walnuts**

In a bowl, dissolve gelatin in boiling water. Stir in soda; refrigerate for 2 hours or until partially set.

In a mixing bowl, beat cream until it begins to thicken. Add confectioners' sugar; beat until soft peaks form. Stir cherries and walnuts into gelatin; fold in whipped cream. Spoon into parfait glasses. Refrigerate until firm. **Yield:** 10 servings.

Keeping Cream

Refrigerate whipping cream in the coldest part of your refrigerator; use by the sell-by date printed on the carton.

Lime Coconut Cheesecake

(Pictured below)

This dessert is ideal for warm-weather entertaining. The cheesecake's delicate lime flavor is complemented by a chewy coconut crust. —Inge Schermerhorn
East Kingston, New Hampshire

- 1-1/2 cups flaked coconut
- 3 tablespoons ground macadamia nuts *or* almonds
- 3 tablespoons butter *or* margarine, melted
- 1 envelope unflavored gelatin
- 1/4 cup cold water
- 3/4 cup sugar
- 2 packages (8 ounces *each*) cream cheese, softened
- 1/4 cup lime juice
- 1 tablespoon grated lime peel

Green food coloring

1-1/2 cups whipping cream, whipped

Additional whipped cream and toasted coconut, optional

In a bowl, combine coconut and nuts; stir in butter. Press onto the bottom of a greased 9-in. springform pan. Bake at 350° for 10-15 minutes or until crust is golden brown around the edges. Cool on a wire rack.

In a saucepan, sprinkle gelatin over cold water; let stand for 1 minute. Stir in sugar; cook over low heat until sugar and gelatin are dissolved. Remove from the heat. In a mixing bowl, beat cream cheese until smooth. Gradually beat in gelatin mixture. Add lime juice and peel; beat until blended. Tint pale green with food coloring. Fold in whipped cream. Pour over crust. Refrigerate for 5 hours or overnight.

Carefully run a knife around the edge of pan to loosen. Remove sides of the pan. Garnish with whipped cream and coconut if desired. **Yield:** 10-12 servings.

— 🥄 🥄 🥄 —

Creamy Peach Dessert

My comforting dessert is full of old-fashioned flavor. It stars fresh peaches, so it's super made in summer when the fruit is at its juicy best. —Christine Wilson
Sellersville, Pennsylvania

- 1/2 cup milk
- 3 tablespoons butter *or* margarine, melted
- 1 egg
- 3/4 cup all-purpose flour
- 1 package (3 ounces) cook-and-serve vanilla pudding mix
- 1 teaspoon baking powder
- 1/2 teaspoon salt
- 4 to 5 medium ripe peaches, peeled and sliced

TOPPING:

- 2 packages (8 ounces *each*) cream cheese, softened
- 3/4 cup plus 1 tablespoon sugar, *divided*
- 1/3 cup half-and-half cream
- 1/2 teaspoon ground cinnamon

In a mixing bowl, beat the milk, butter and egg. Combine the flour, pudding mix, baking powder and salt; add to milk mixture. Beat on medium speed for 2 minutes. Pour into a greased 8-in. square baking dish. Top with peaches.

In a small mixing bowl, beat the cream cheese, 3/4 cup sugar and half-and-half cream. Drop by tablespoonfuls over the peaches. Combine the cinnamon and remaining sugar; sprinkle over the top. Bake at 350° for 55-60 minutes or until puffed and golden brown. Cool on wire rack for 1 hour. Refrigerate for at least 2 hours before cutting. **Yield:** 9 servings.

— 🥄 🥄 🥄 —

Raisin Cheese Blintzes

Milk, butter and cottage cheese combine delightfully in these blintzes. When I was a child, my mother served them often for Sunday brunch or for dessert, and they tasted so good.
—Lauren Kargen
Williamsville, New York

4 eggs
1 cup milk
3 tablespoons butter *or* margarine, melted
1 teaspoon sugar
Dash salt
1 cup all-purpose flour
Additional butter *or* margarine
FILLING:
2 cups raisins
4 cups (32 ounces) small-curd cottage cheese
1/2 cup sugar
1 tablespoon ground cinnamon
Dash salt
Butter *or* margarine
Sour cream and blueberry *or* strawberry pie filling

In a bowl, whisk eggs, milk, butter, sugar and salt. Beat in flour until smooth; let stand for 10 minutes. Melt 1 teaspoon butter in a 10-in. nonstick skillet; pour 1/4 cup batter into center of skillet. Lift and tilt pan to evenly coat bottom. Cook until top appears dry. Remove crepe to paper towel. Repeat with remaining batter, adding butter to skillet as needed.

Place the raisins in a saucepan; cover with water. Bring to a boil. Reduce heat; cook, uncovered, for 5 minutes. Drain. In a bowl, combine the cottage cheese, sugar, cinnamon, salt and raisins. Spoon about 1/2 cup down the center of each crepe; fold ends and sides over filling. In a skillet, cook the blintzes in butter until heated through. Top with sour cream and blueberry pie filling if desired. **Yield:** 9 servings.

Get Creative with Crepes

Crepes, which are made from a smooth egg batter, are used in both savory and sweet dishes. They are very versatile.

They can be eaten plain with a sprinkling of powdered sugar on top. They are also the perfect accompaniment to fruits—just roll some up with the berries of your choice, sprinkle with cinnamon and sugar, and you have a quick dessert. For another delectable dessert, try filling a chocolate crepe with ice cream, then top it with hot fudge and whipped cream.

It's important to let crepe batter rest before cooking—the resting process relaxes the gluten in the flour, resulting in more tender crepes.

Crepes used for blintzes are made from the same batter but are browned on one side only.

Pineapple Coconut Squares

(Pictured above)

I don't remember where I got this recipe, but I'm glad I have it.—Elaine Anderson, Aliquippa, Pennsylvania

✓ Uses less fat, sugar or salt. Includes Nutritional Analysis and Diabetic Exchanges.

2 tablespoons butter *or* stick margarine, melted
3 tablespoons sugar
1 egg
1 cup all-purpose flour
1 teaspoon baking powder
2 cans (8 ounces *each*) unsweetened crushed pineapple, drained
TOPPING:
1 tablespoon butter *or* stick margarine, melted
1 cup sugar
2 eggs
2 cups flaked coconut

In a mixing bowl, beat butter and sugar. Beat in egg. Combine flour and baking powder; stir into egg mixture. Press into a 9-in. square baking dish coated with nonstick cooking spray. Spread pineapple over crust; set aside.

For topping, in a mixing bowl, beat butter and sugar. Beat in eggs. Stir in coconut. Spread over pineapple. Bake at 325° for 35-40 minutes or until golden brown. **Yield:** 16 servings.

Nutritional Analysis: One serving equals 192 calories, 7 g fat (5 g saturated fat), 46 mg cholesterol, 79 mg sodium, 30 g carbohydrate, 1 g fiber, 3 g protein. **Diabetic Exchanges:** 2 starch, 1 fat.

til golden brown. Remove to a wire rack. Immediately split puffs open; remove tops and set aside. Discard soft dough inside. Cool puffs.

In a mixing bowl, beat the milk, pudding mix and extract on low speed for 2 minutes. Let stand for 5 minutes. Fold in whipped cream. Fill cream puffs; replace tops.

In a heavy saucepan, combine glaze ingredients. Cook and stir over low heat until chocolate is melted and mixture is smooth. Drizzle over cream puffs. Chill for at least 1 hour before serving. Refrigerate leftovers. **Yield:** 1 dozen.

Vanilla Cream Puffs

(Pictured above)

I turn out batches of these yummy morsels. The puffs are filled with a tasty almond-vanilla cream, and there's a hint of cinnamon in the chocolate glaze.
—Mike Kennon, Raleigh, North Carolina

    1 cup water
1/2 cup butter (no substitutes)
1/4 teaspoon salt
    1 cup all-purpose flour
    4 eggs
FILLING:
1-1/2 cups cold milk
    1 package (5.1 ounces) instant vanilla
        pudding mix
1/2 to 1 teaspoon almond extract
    2 cups whipping cream, whipped
CHOCOLATE GLAZE:
    6 tablespoons semisweet chocolate chips
1-1/2 teaspoons shortening
3/4 teaspoon corn syrup
1/4 teaspoon ground cinnamon

In a large saucepan, bring water, butter and salt to a boil. Add flour all at once and stir until a smooth ball forms. Remove from the heat; let stand for 5 minutes. Add eggs, one at a time, beating well after each addition. Continue beating until mixture is smooth and shiny.

Drop by 1/4 cupfuls 3 in. apart onto a greased baking sheet. Bake at 400° for 30-35 minutes or un-

Pear Crisp with Lemon Sauce

Everyone loves the crunchy oat topping and sweet pear filling in this fruity crisp. The tartness of the lemon sauce goes nicely with the pears. —Rachel Franklin
Hockley, Texas

    2 tablespoons plus 1/4 cup all-purpose
        flour, *divided*
    1 tablespoon sugar
    1 teaspoon grated lemon peel, *divided*
    5 cups sliced peeled ripe pears (about
        2 pounds)
1/2 cup old-fashioned oats
1/4 cup packed brown sugar
1/8 teaspoon ground cardamom
    3 tablespoons cold butter *or* margarine
1/4 cup sliced almonds
LEMON SAUCE:
1/4 cup sugar
    2 teaspoons cornstarch
1/2 cup cold water
    1 egg yolk, beaten
    1 tablespoon butter *or* margarine
    1 tablespoon lemon juice
1/4 teaspoon grated lemon peel

In a large bowl, combine 2 tablespoons flour, sugar and 1/4 teaspoon of lemon peel. Add pears; gently toss to coat. Transfer to a greased 8-in. square baking dish. Combine the oats, brown sugar, cardamom and remaining flour and lemon peel; mix well. Cut in butter until mixture resembles coarse crumbs. Stir in almonds. Sprinkle over pears. Bake at 375° for 35-40 minutes or until pears are tender and topping is golden brown.

For lemon sauce, combine sugar and cornstarch in a saucepan. Gradually stir in water until smooth. Bring to a boil over medium heat; cook and stir for 1 minute or until thickened. Remove from the heat. Stir a small amount of hot mixture into egg yolk; return all to pan, stirring constantly. Bring to a gentle boil over medium heat. Cook and stir 1 minute longer. Remove from the heat; stir in butter, lemon juice and peel. Serve with warm pear crisp. **Yield:** 9 servings.

— 🍴 🍴 🍴 —

Apple-Honey Dutch Baby

(Pictured below and on page 138)

I love to make this treat on Sunday morning. It's so impressive when it's served warm right out of the oven...and the honey and apple filling is yummy! It also makes a scrumptious dessert. —Kathy Fleming
Lisle, Illinois

  3/4 **cup all-purpose flour**
    1 **tablespoon sugar**
    3 **eggs**
  3/4 **cup milk**
    2 **tablespoons butter** *or* **margarine**
TOPPING:
    2 **large apples, sliced**
    1 **tablespoon butter** *or* **margarine**
  1/2 **cup honey**
    2 **to 3 teaspoons lemon juice**
  1/2 **teaspoon ground cardamom**
    1 **teaspoon cornstarch**
    2 **teaspoons cold water**

In a mixing bowl, whisk the flour, sugar, eggs and milk until smooth. Place butter in a 10-in. oven-proof skillet. Heat at 400° for 3-4 minutes or until melted; tilt pan to coat bottom and sides. Pour

batter into hot skillet. Bake for 16-20 minutes or until edges are lightly browned.

Meanwhile, in a saucepan, saute apples in butter until lightly browned. Stir in honey, lemon juice and cardamom. Combine cornstarch and water until smooth; add to apple mixture. Bring to a boil; cook and stir for 2 minutes or until thickened. Spoon into pancake. Serve immediately. **Yield:** 4 servings.

— 🍴 🍴 🍴 —

Coconut Custard

My family always thought baked custard was a treat...and I especially like this coconut version.
—Ruth Peterson, Jenison, Michigan

    4 **eggs**
  1/3 **cup sugar**
  1/2 **teaspoon salt**
  1/2 **teaspoon vanilla extract**
    3 **cups milk**
    1 **cup flaked coconut**
Dash ground nutmeg
MELBA SAUCE:
    5 **teaspoons cornstarch**
  1/3 **cup cold water**
    2 **cups fresh** *or* **frozen raspberries, thawed**
  2/3 **cup sugar**
  1/4 **teaspoon salt**

In a bowl, beat eggs. Add sugar, salt and vanilla. Gradually add milk; mix well. Stir in coconut. Place six ungreased 10-oz. ramekins or custard cups in a 13-in. x 9-in. x 2-in. baking dish. Fill each with about 3/4 cup coconut mixture. Sprinkle with nutmeg. Fill larger pan with boiling water to a depth of 1 in. Bake at 325° for 30-40 minutes or until center is just set (mixture will jiggle). Remove ramekins from pan to a wire rack.

In a saucepan, combine cornstarch and water until smooth. Add raspberries, sugar and salt. Bring to a boil; cook and stir for 2 minutes or until thickened. Remove from the heat; strain if desired. Cool. Serve over custard. **Yield:** 6 servings.

Baked Custard Basics

Baked custards are generally baked in a water bath—the water acts as insulation and diffuses the oven heat so the mixture will set properly without separating.

Don't beat the mixture for custard until foamy or the surface of the baked custard will be pock-marked.

Assemble Santa's Workshop!

USING RECIPES from two *Taste of Home* field editors, our staff crafted this festive Santa's workshop.

Mary Kay Morris from Cokato, Minnesota shared the recipe for the gingerbread, saying, "I recommend it, as does my sister."

The *non-edible* icing comes from Iola Egle of Mc-Cook, Nebraska. "It's the 'glue' I've used to mortar together more than 75 gingerbread houses."

🛷 🛷 🛷

Santa's Workshop

1 cup shortening
1 cup sugar
1 cup molasses
2 eggs
5 cups all-purpose flour
1 tablespoon ground ginger
1 tablespoon ground cinnamon
2 teaspoons baking powder
1 teaspoon baking soda
1 teaspoon salt
1 teaspoon ground nutmeg
1 teaspoon ground cloves
Cookie cutters—3-inch reindeer and
   4-inch Santa
ICING AND ASSEMBLY:
   8 egg whites

12 cups confectioners' sugar
Red, green and black paste food coloring
   1 yellow Fruit Roll-Up
Pastry tips—star tips #25 and #9027, round tip
   #2 and leaf tip #67
   1 package (1.65 ounces) watermelon/wild
      cherry Nerds
   2 packages (.5 ounce *each*) miniature
      Chiclets
  12 Cracklin' Oat Bran squares
  32 dark chocolate thin mints
Covered display base—22 inches x 16 inches
  13 pieces red rope licorice (four 5 inches,
      one 8 inches and eight 2 inches)
   2 starlight mints
   1 stick red Fruit Stripe gum
   1 piece red shoestring licorice (9 inches)
   5 leaf-shaped spearmint gumdrops
   2 sugar ice cream cones

In a mixing bowl, cream shortening and sugar. Beat in molasses and eggs. Combine dry ingredients; gradually add to creamed mixture. Divide dough into eighths. Chill for 2 hours or until easy to handle.

With lightly floured rolling pin, roll out one portion of dough directly onto a greased baking sheet to 1/4-in. thickness. Cut into a 7-in. x 5-in. rectangle for side piece. Remove scraps; repeat.

Roll a second portion into an 8-1/2-in. x 5-1/2-in. rectangle for roof piece; repeat.

Roll out two portions of dough to 1/4-in. thickness. Position shop pattern on dough. With a sharp knife, cut out one shop front. Repeat for shop back. Remove scraps. On shop front, score door and window outlines. Bake at 350° for 10-14 minutes or until lightly browned. Cool for 5 minutes; while warm, place pattern over baked dough and recut. Cool on wire racks.

Roll out scraps; cut out two reindeer and one Santa. Bake at 350° for 8-10 minutes or until edges begin to brown. Cool on wire racks. Use the remaining dough for cutout cookies.

To make icing: Prepare three batches, *one at a time.* In a mixing bowl, beat two egg whites until frothy. Gradually add 3 cups confectioners' sugar; beat on medium speed for 4-7 minutes or until icing forms peaks. Cover icing between uses. Prepare fourth batch of icing; tint a fourth red, a fourth green and 1/4 cup black.

To decorate front: Place shop front on waxed paper. Cut Fruit Roll-Up into a 3-in. x 2-1/2-in. rectangle and a 1-1/4-in. square. Spread with white icing; position rectangle over shop front window and square over door window. Insert #25 tip into pastry bag; fill two-thirds full with white icing.

Pipe small stars around door and windows. With #2 tip, pipe windowpanes. On large window, pipe triangle of icing in bottom corner of each pane. Attach red Chiclet with icing for doorknob.

For wreath, trace 2-in. circle below roof peak. Pipe 1-in.-wide strip of white icing around inside edge of circle. Place green and red Nerds on icing for wreath.

Using green icing and #2 tip, pipe a thin line on sides and top of large window; attach Chiclets for lights. Let dry.

For side windows: For each window, form a rectangle with six cereal squares on waxed paper; pipe between squares with white icing. Let dry. Attach to sides of house with white icing. Pipe a thin line of green icing along top and sides of windows; attach Chiclets for lights. Let dry.

For roof: Spread a thin layer of white icing over the roof pieces. Cut two mint wafers in half diagonally; place the cut edges against bottom edge of roof. Continue placing wafers on the diagonal, cutting as needed at edges; pipe white icing between for mortar. Let dry.

To assemble: Pipe icing along base and sides of front section and one side section. Position at right angles to each other and place on display board. Press firmly into place; prop with small cans. Pipe icing along inside edge for added stability. Repeat with second side section and back. Pipe icing along each outside corner; press 5-in.

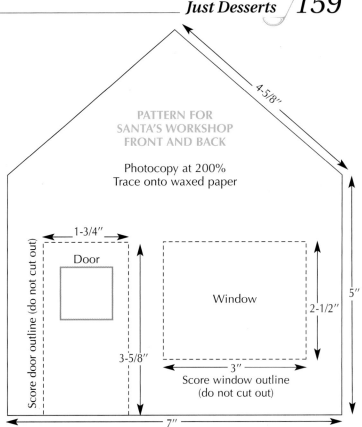

PATTERN FOR
SANTA'S WORKSHOP
FRONT AND BACK

Photocopy at 200%
Trace onto waxed paper

Score door outline (do not cut out)

1-3/4"

Door

Window

2-1/2"

3-5/8"

3"

Score window outline
(do not cut out)

4-5/8"

5"

7"

licorice pieces into each corner. Let dry.

Pipe icing along top edge of shop. Position one roof piece; repeat. Pipe icing along top edge between roof pieces; press 8-in. licorice into icing. Place a starlight mint at front and back roof peaks. Using #9027 tip, pipe stars along front and side edges of roof for snow. Add lights with green icing and Chiclets.

To decorate Santa: Frost Santa with red, white and black icing. For skis, cut gum in half lengthwise, tapering ends. Position in an "X" shape; pipe icing between skis, holding until stable. Attach red Chiclets on skis with icing; let dry.

To decorate reindeer: Frost reindeer with white, red, black and green icing; let dry. Attach with icing to roof, holding until secure. With red icing, attach shoestring licorice from one collar to the other.

Finishing touches: For bushes, pipe thin lines of green icing on gumdrops; decorate with Chiclets. For trees, use #67 tip with green icing; beginning at bottom of ice cream cones, pipe frosting in rows. Add Chiclet lights. Place on waxed paper to harden.

Working in small sections, frost base with icing for snow. For path, place 2-in. licorice pieces side by side in a curve. Position bushes, trees, Santa and skis on base and secure with icing.

Editor's Note: Icing is for *decorative purposes only* because of the uncooked egg whites. If gingerbread house will be eaten, substitute a royal icing recipe using meringue powder.

Use of a coupler ring will allow you to easily change pastry tips between decorating steps.

Potluck Pleasers

Your contribution to the potluck table will be the first to go if it's one of the crowd-pleasing dishes found in this chapter.

GREAT FOR GATHERINGS. Clockwise from upper left: Giant Focaccia Sandwich (p. 178), Sour Cream Fan Rolls (p. 166), Pepperoni Pizza Salad (p. 178), Chocolate Chip Cake (p. 175) and Four-Pasta Beef Bake (p. 176).

Irish Soda Bread

(Pictured above)

This round loaf is moist with a wonderful texture and flavor. Golden raisins peek out of every slice.
—Ann Lauver, Lititz, Pennsylvania

> 1 package (1/4 ounce) active dry yeast
> 1/2 cup warm water (110° to 115°)
> 3 tablespoons sugar, *divided*
> 1 cup warm buttermilk (110° to 115°)*
> 2 tablespoons butter *or* margarine, softened
> 1/2 teaspoon salt
> 1/2 teaspoon baking soda
> 3-1/2 to 4 cups all-purpose flour
> 3/4 cup golden raisins

In a mixing bowl, dissolve yeast in warm water. Add 1 tablespoon sugar; let stand for 5 minutes. Beat in the buttermilk, butter, salt, baking soda, 1 cup flour and remaining sugar until smooth. Stir in raisins and enough remaining flour to form a soft dough. Turn onto a floured surface; knead until smooth and elastic, about 6-8 minutes. Place in a greased bowl, turning once to grease top. Cover and let rise in a warm place until doubled, about 40 minutes.

Punch dough down. Turn onto a lightly floured surface; knead for 2 minutes. Shape into a round loaf. Place on a greased baking sheet. With a sharp knife, cut a 1/4-in.-deep cross on top of loaf. Cover and let rise until doubled, about 30 minutes. Bake at 350° for 30-35 minutes or until golden brown. Remove from pan to cool on a wire rack. **Yield:** 1 loaf.

   *Editor's Note: Warmed buttermilk will appear curdled.

Cherry Orange Punch

I've served this punch at ladies luncheons and as a breakfast beverage for a crowd. The sweet tangy flavor complements many foods. It's a fun change from plain red punch. —Lorene Corbett, Arnold, Nebraska

> 6 cups water
> 2 cans (12 ounces *each*) frozen orange juice concentrate, thawed
> 3/4 cup maraschino cherry juice *or* grenadine syrup
> 3/4 cup sugar
> 1 liter ginger ale, chilled

In a gallon container, combine the first four ingredients; mix well. Chill. Just before serving, stir in ginger ale. **Yield:** 4 quarts.

Lemon Meringue Dessert

This dessert is a great way to serve lemon meringue pie without rolling out enough pie crusts to feed a crowd. The crust presses into the pan. —Joyce Ashe
Gloversville, New York

> 2-1/2 cups all-purpose flour
> 1/4 cup sugar
> 1 cup cold butter *or* margarine
> 1/2 cup finely chopped walnuts
> **FILLING:**
> 4 packages (2.9 ounces *each*) cook-and-serve lemon pudding mix
> 2-1/2 cups sugar, *divided*
> 9 cups water, *divided*
> 8 eggs, *separated*
> 1/2 teaspoon cream of tartar

In a bowl, combine flour and sugar. With a pastry blender, cut in butter until crumbly. Stir in walnuts. Press into two greased 13-in. x 9-in. x 2-in. baking dishes. Bake at 350° for 17-20 minutes.

Meanwhile, in a large kettle or Dutch oven, combine pudding mixes, 2 cups sugar, 1 cup water and egg yolks. Stir in remaining water until smooth. Whisk over medium heat until mixture comes to a full boil. Set aside and keep warm.

In a large mixing bowl, beat egg whites and cream of tartar on medium speed until soft peaks form. Gradually beat in remaining sugar, 1 tablespoon at a time, on high until stiff glossy peaks form and sugar is dissolved. Spread hot pudding over crust. Evenly spread meringue over filling, sealing edges to pan.

Bake at 350° for 15 minutes or until the meringue is golden brown. Cool on wire racks for 1 hour. Refrigerate. Cut with a moistened knife. **Yield:** 2 desserts (12-15 servings each).

Polynesian Chicken

Seasoned with ginger, almonds and colorful fruit, this chicken is a special main dish for a crowd. I dreamed up this economical recipe one day when chicken thighs were on sale. I served it to guests and they loved it.
—_Marilou Robinson, Portland, Oregon_

  1 **cup all-purpose flour**
  2 **teaspoons salt**
  1 **teaspoon coarsely ground pepper**
 20 **chicken leg quarters, skin removed**
1/3 **cup vegetable oil**
  2 **cups orange juice**
1-1/2 **cups pineapple juice**
1/4 **teaspoon ground ginger** _or_ **1 teaspoon minced fresh gingerroot**
  1 **can (20 ounces) pineapple chunks, drained**
  2 **cans (11 ounces** _each_**) mandarin oranges, drained**
  1 **cup sliced almonds, toasted**
Hot cooked rice

In a large resealable plastic bag, combine the flour, salt and pepper. Add the chicken, one piece at a time, and shake to coat. In a large skillet, brown chicken in oil in batches; drain. Place chicken in two greased 13-in. x 9-in. x 2-in. baking dishes.

In a saucepan, bring orange juice, pineapple juice and ginger to a boil. Pour over chicken. Top with pineapple, oranges and almonds. Cover and bake at 350° for 30-45 minutes or until chicken juices run clear. Serve over hot cooked rice. **Yield: 20 servings.**

Baked Oatmeal

My mom liked this recipe because it was quick and easy and made enough to fill up all seven of us hungry kids. Now I prepare it for my own family of five.
—_Kathy Smith, Butler, Indiana_

 12 **cups quick-cooking oats**
  2 **cups sugar**
  2 **cups packed brown sugar**
  4 **teaspoons salt**
  2 **teaspoons baking powder**
  4 **cups milk**
  2 **cups vegetable oil**
  8 **eggs, lightly beaten**
Additional milk

In a large bowl, combine the first eight ingredients. Pour into two greased 13-in. x 9-in. x 2-in. baking dishes. Bake, uncovered, at 350° for 30-35 minutes or until set. Serve with additional milk. **Yield: 18 servings.**

Vidalia Onion Spinach Salad

(Pictured below)

Sweet onions and spinach make a delightful combination in this unique salad. Onions also star in the tangy Dijon dressing and in the homemade croutons.
—_Lois Fetting, Nelson, Wisconsin_

CROUTONS:
  4 **cups soft bread crumbs**
1/3 **cup finely chopped Vidalia** _or_ **other sweet onion**
  1 **tablespoon dried parsley flakes**
  6 **tablespoons butter** _or_ **margarine, melted**
  1 **egg, lightly beaten**
Oil for frying
DRESSING:
1/3 **cup chopped Vidalia** _or_ **other sweet onion**
1/3 **cup cider vinegar**
1/3 **cup honey**
  1 **teaspoon Dijon mustard**
1/2 **cup plus 2 tablespoons olive** _or_ **vegetable oil**
  1 **teaspoon poppy seeds**
SALAD:
 16 **cups torn fresh spinach**
1/2 **pound sliced bacon, cooked and crumbled**
  1 **medium Vidalia** _or_ **other sweet onion, sliced and separated into rings**

In a bowl, combine the bread crumbs, onion and parsley. Stir in butter and egg; mix well. Shape into 1/2-in. balls. In an electric skillet, heat 1 in. of oil to 375°. Fry croutons for 10-15 seconds, turning to brown all sides. Drain on paper towels.

For dressing, combine onion, vinegar, honey and mustard in a blender or food processor; cover and process until smooth. While processing, gradually add oil in a steady stream. Stir in poppy seeds. In a salad bowl, toss the spinach, bacon, onion rings and croutons. Serve with dressing. **Yield: 16 servings.**

Pistachio Mallow Salad

This fluffy salad is a real treat since it's creamy but not overly sweet. It's easy to mix up, and the flavor gets better the longer it stands. It's perfect for St. Patrick's Day, served in a green bowl. —Pattie Ann Forssberg
Logan, Kansas

- 1 carton (16 ounces) frozen whipped topping, thawed
- 1 package (3.4 ounces) instant pistachio pudding mix
- 6 to 7 drops green food coloring, optional
- 3 cups miniature marshmallows
- 1 can (20 ounces) crushed pineapple, undrained
- 1/2 cup chopped pistachios *or* walnuts

In a large bowl, combine whipped topping, pudding mix and food coloring if desired. Fold in the marshmallows and pineapple. Cover and refrigerate for at least 2 hours. Just before serving, sprinkle with nuts. **Yield:** 12 servings.

— 🍸 🍸 🍸 —

Corn Pudding Squares

I coordinate a Wednesday night dinner at my church. Many of the dishes that our cooking crews prepare, like these corn-filled bread squares, are family favorites adapted to feed a large group. —Kim McLaughlin
South Charleston, West Virginia

- 2 cans (15-1/4 ounces *each*) whole kernel corn, undrained
- 2 cans (14-3/4 ounces *each*) cream-style corn
- 2 cups (16 ounces) sour cream
- 1 cup butter *or* margarine, melted
- 2 packages (8-1/2 ounces *each*) corn bread/muffin mix
- 3 eggs

In a large mixing bowl, combine all ingredients; beat just until combined. Pour into two greased 13-in. x 9-in. x 2-in. baking dishes. Bake at 350° for 40-45 minutes or until a toothpick inserted near the center comes out clean. Cool for 15 minutes on wire racks before cutting. Serve warm. **Yield:** 24 servings.

Buffet Table Tip

Dishes set on a buffet table tend to move around when people scoop food from them. To prevent this, just set a damp dish towel under the dishes.

Confetti Cabbage Coleslaw

For a tart crisp salad, try this slaw. It's perfect for a gathering since you make it well in advance.
—Sue Ross, Casa Grande, Arizona

- 10 pounds cabbage, shredded
- 2 tablespoons salt
- 6 cups sugar
- 3 cups cider vinegar
- 1-1/2 cups water
- 2 tablespoons mustard seed
- 2 tablespoons celery seed
- 1 bunch celery, chopped
- 4 medium carrots, shredded
- 1 medium sweet red pepper, diced
- 1 medium green pepper, diced

In a large bowl, combine the cabbage and salt; let stand for 2 hours. In a large saucepan, combine the sugar, vinegar, water, mustard seed and celery seed. Bring to a boil over medium heat; stir until the sugar is dissolved. Remove from the heat; cool completely.

Drain cabbage if desired. Add celery, carrots and peppers. Add dressing and toss to coat. Cover and refrigerate for 2 hours or freeze for up to 3 months. Serve with a slotted spoon. **Yield:** 50-60 servings.

— 🍸 🍸 🍸 —

Spaghetti and Meatballs

My mother got this recipe from our Italian neighbors in the 1950s. It's been a big hit at our church community dinners, where we sometimes make three or four batches of this wonderful sauce. —Monica Crouch
Trotwood, Ohio

- 4 garlic cloves, minced
- 2 tablespoons dried parsley flakes
- 2 tablespoons olive *or* vegetable oil
- 3 cans (28 ounces *each*) tomato puree
- 2 cans (28 ounces *each*) tomato sauce
- 2 cans (12 ounces *each*) tomato paste
- 2 to 3 tablespoons sugar
- 1 tablespoon Italian seasoning
- 1-1/2 teaspoons dried basil
- 1-1/2 teaspoons dried oregano
- 1 teaspoon salt
- 1/4 teaspoon pepper

MEATBALLS:
- 3 eggs
- 1/3 cup water
- 1 small onion, finely chopped
- 2 cups soft bread crumbs
- 2 cups grated Parmesan *or* Romano cheese, *divided*
- 2 garlic cloves, minced
- 1 teaspoon Italian seasoning

1 teaspoon dried parsley flakes
1 teaspoon salt
1/2 teaspoon pepper
1/2 teaspoon dried oregano
1/2 teaspoon dried basil
3 pounds lean ground beef

In two or three large soup kettles or Dutch ovens, saute garlic and parsley in oil for 1 minute. Add tomato puree, sauce, paste and seasonings. Bring to a boil. Reduce heat; simmer, uncovered, for 2-1/2 hours.

For meatballs, in a large bowl, combine the eggs, water, onion, bread crumbs, 1 cup Parmesan cheese, garlic and seasonings; mix well. Crumble beef over mixture and mix well. Shape into 1-1/2-in. balls. Place 1 in. apart in ungreased 15-in. x 10-in. x 1-in. baking pans. Bake, uncovered, at 375° for 15-18 minutes or until no longer pink.

Stir the remaining Parmesan into spaghetti sauce; simmer 30 minutes longer. Drain meatballs on paper towels; add to sauce. **Yield:** 20-24 servings.

Toffee Chip Cookies

These cookies combine several mouth-watering flavors. The generous size of the batch gives me plenty of scrumptious cookies to have on hand and extras to send to our sons at college.
—_Kay Frances Ronnenkamp, Albion, Nebraska_

1 cup butter _or_ margarine, softened
1/2 cup vegetable oil
1 cup sugar
1 cup packed brown sugar
1 teaspoon vanilla extract
2 eggs
3-1/2 cups all-purpose flour
1 teaspoon cream of tartar
1 teaspoon baking soda
1 teaspoon salt
3 cups crisp rice cereal
1 cup quick-cooking oats
1 cup flaked coconut
1 cup chopped pecans
1 cup English toffee bits _or_ almond
  brickle chips

In a large mixing bowl, cream butter, oil, sugars and vanilla. Add eggs, one at a time, beating well after each addition. Combine the flour, cream of tartar, baking soda and salt; add to creamed mixture. Stir in remaining ingredients.

Drop by tablespoonfuls 2 in. apart onto ungreased baking sheets. Bake at 350° for 10-12 minutes or until lightly browned. Remove to wire racks to cool. **Yield:** 12 dozen.

Glazed Corned Beef

(Pictured above)

I serve this delicious entree each St. Patrick's Day, even though my family is Dutch, not Irish. The meat is so tender and tasty topped with a simple tangy glaze. Leftovers make excellent Reuben sandwiches.
—_Perlene Hoekema, Lynden, Washington_

1 corned beef brisket (3 to 4 pounds),
  trimmed
1 medium onion, sliced
1 celery rib, sliced
1/4 cup butter _or_ margarine
1 cup packed brown sugar
2/3 cup ketchup
1/3 cup white vinegar
2 tablespoons prepared mustard
2 teaspoons prepared horseradish

Place corned beef and contents of seasoning packet in a Dutch oven; cover with water. Add onion and celery. Bring to a boil. Reduce heat; cover and simmer for 2-1/2 hours or until meat is tender. Drain and discard liquid and vegetables. Place beef on a rack in a shallow roasting pan; set aside.

In a saucepan, melt the butter over medium heat. Stir in the remaining ingredients. Cook and stir until sugar is dissolved. Brush over beef. Bake, uncovered, at 350° for 25 minutes. Let stand for 10 minutes before slicing. **Yield:** 12 servings.

Crispy Fried Chicken

(Pictured at far right)

This Sunday dinner staple is first fried and then baked to a crispy golden brown. I love fixing it for family and friends. —Donna Kuhaupt, Slinger, Wisconsin

1-1/2 cups all-purpose flour
1/2 cup cornmeal
1/4 cup cornstarch
 1 tablespoon salt
 2 teaspoons paprika
 1 teaspoon dried oregano
 1 teaspoon rubbed sage
 1 teaspoon pepper
 2 eggs
1/4 cup water
 2 broiler/fryer chickens (3 to 4 pounds *each*), cut up
Vegetable oil for frying

In a large resealable plastic bag, combine the flour, cornmeal, cornstarch, salt, paprika, oregano, sage and pepper. In a shallow bowl, beat eggs and water. Dip chicken in egg mixture; place in the bag, a few pieces at a time, and shake until coated.

In an electric skillet, heat 1 in. of oil to 375°. Fry chicken, a few pieces at a time, for 3-5 minutes on each side or until golden and crispy. Place in two ungreased 15-in. x 10-in. x 1-in. baking pans. Bake, uncovered, at 350° for 25-30 minutes or until chicken is tender and juices run clear. **Yield:** 12 servings.

Show-Off Salad

(Pictured at far right)

People tell me they can't stay away from this fresh-tasting salad, with its layers of lettuce, green pepper, cucumber, macaroni, hard-cooked eggs, ham and more. —C. Neomi Drummond, Des Moines, Iowa

 2 cups uncooked elbow macaroni
 1 tablespoon vegetable oil
 3 cups shredded lettuce
 1 medium green pepper, chopped
 1 medium cucumber, peeled, seeded and diced
 3 hard-cooked eggs, sliced
 1 cup shredded red cabbage
 1 small red onion, chopped
 2 medium carrots, shredded
 1 cup diced fully cooked ham, optional
 1 package (10 ounces) frozen peas, thawed
 1 cup (4 ounces) shredded Colby-Monterey Jack *or* Monterey Jack cheese

 1 cup mayonnaise *or* salad dressing
1/2 cup sour cream
1/2 cup chopped green onions, *divided*
 1 tablespoon spicy brown *or* horseradish mustard
 1 teaspoon sugar
Salt and pepper to taste

Cook macaroni according to package directions; drain and rinse in cold water. Drizzle with oil; toss to coat. Place lettuce in a shallow 3-qt. dish; top with the green pepper, cucumber, macaroni, eggs, cabbage, red onion, carrots, ham if desired, peas and cheese.

In a small bowl, combine the mayonnaise, sour cream, 1/4 cup of green onions, mustard, sugar, salt and pepper; spread over the top. Cover and refrigerate overnight. Just before serving, sprinkle with remaining green onions. **Yield:** 16-18 servings.

Sour Cream Fan Rolls

(Pictured at right and on page 160)

I received this recipe from an E-mail pen pal in Canada. The dough is so easy to work with, and it makes the lightest yeast rolls. —Carrie Ormsby
West Jordan, Utah

 2 tablespoons active dry yeast
 1 cup warm water (110° to 115°)
 2 tablespoons plus 1/2 cup sugar, *divided*
 2 cups warm sour cream (110° to 115°)
 2 eggs, lightly beaten
 6 tablespoons butter *or* margarine, melted
1-1/2 teaspoons salt
1/4 teaspoon baking powder
 7 to 8 cups all-purpose flour

In a bowl, dissolve yeast in water. Add 2 tablespoons sugar; let stand for 5 minutes. In a large mixing bowl, combine the sour cream, eggs, butter, salt and remaining sugar. Stir in baking powder, yeast mixture and 4 cups of flour until smooth. Stir in enough remaining flour to form a soft dough. Turn onto a floured surface; knead until smooth and elastic, about 6-8 minutes. Place in a greased bowl, turning once to grease top. Cover and let rise in a warm place until doubled, about 1 hour.

Punch dough down. Turn onto a lightly floured surface; divide in half. Roll each portion into a 23-in. x 9-in. rectangle. Cut into 1-1/2-in. strips. Stack five strips together; cut into 1-1/2-in. pieces and place cut side up in a greased muffin cup. Cover and let rise until doubled, about 20 minutes. Bake at 350° for 20-25 minutes or until golden. Cool on wire racks. **Yield:** about 2-1/2 dozen.

White Cake with Raspberry Sauce

(Pictured below)

Raspberries folded into a thick strawberry glaze turn a boxed cake mix into a festive finale to any meal.
—Cynthia Ford, Powder Springs, Georgia

1 package (18-1/4 ounces) white cake mix
4 ounces cream cheese, softened
1 cup confectioners' sugar
1 cup whipping cream, whipped
1 carton (16 ounces) strawberry glaze
1/2 cup water
2-1/2 cups fresh *or* frozen unsweetened raspberries

Prepare and bake cake according to package directions, using a 13-in. x 9-in. x 2-in. baking pan.

In a small mixing bowl, beat cream cheese and confectioners' sugar until smooth. Fold in whipped cream. Spread over cooled cake. Refrigerate until serving. Just before serving, combine strawberry glaze and water in a bowl; gently fold in raspberries. Serve over cake. **Yield:** 12-15 servings.

DELICIOUS DISHES like Crispy Fried Chicken, Show-Off Salad, Sour Cream Fan Rolls and White Cake with Raspberry Sauce (shown below, clockwise from top) will guarantee an appetizing picnic or potluck.

Hot Cranberry Citrus Drink

(Pictured above)

This lovely rosy drink is not too sweet or tart. I sometimes serve this hot beverage at Christmas or at brunch gatherings as an alternative to coffee, tea or cold juice.
—Shari Donaldson, Cummings, Kansas

   1 package (12 ounces) fresh *or*
      frozen cranberries
2-1/2 quarts water
   2 cups orange juice
   1 cup sugar
   1 cup pineapple juice
   2 tablespoons lemon juice
   3 cinnamon sticks (3 inches)

In a large saucepan, bring cranberries and water to a boil. Reduce heat; simmer for 5-7 minutes or until the berries pop. Stir in the remaining ingredients; return to a boil. Reduce heat; simmer, uncovered, for 25-30 minutes. Strain through cheesecloth; discard pulp and cinnamon sticks. Serve warm. **Yield:** 3 quarts.

— 🍷 🍷 🍷 —

Marinated Potato Salad

I fix this flavorful potato salad when we're entertaining at home or to take to picnics and potluck suppers. I get lots of compliments and recipe requests.
—Ethel Selway, Middletown, Delaware

 12 medium potatoes
1-1/2 cups vegetable oil
 1/2 cup plus 2-1/2 teaspoons white
     vinegar, *divided*

4-1/4 teaspoons sugar, *divided*
   1 teaspoon salt
 1/2 teaspoon paprika
   8 celery ribs, chopped
   2 medium onions, chopped
   8 radishes, sliced
   2 medium green peppers, chopped
   5 hard-cooked eggs, chopped
2-1/2 cups mayonnaise *or* salad dressing
   1 tablespoon milk
   1 tablespoon Dijon mustard
 1/2 teaspoon pepper

Place potatoes in a large saucepan or Dutch oven; cover with water. Bring to a boil; cook until tender, about 35 minutes. Drain and cool. In a jar with a tight-fitting lid, combine the oil, 1/2 cup vinegar, 2 teaspoons sugar, salt and paprika; shake well. Peel and cube potatoes; place in a large bowl. Add celery, onions and radishes. Add dressing and toss to coat. Cover and refrigerate overnight.

Stir in green peppers and eggs. In a bowl, combine the mayonnaise, milk, mustard, pepper, and remaining vinegar and sugar. Pour over potato salad and toss to coat. **Yield:** 28-32 servings.

— 🍷 🍷 🍷 —

Tamale Casserole

I served this casserole at a large Mexican-themed party I hosted. With its zippy tomato and ground beef sauce, it was a big hit. *—Elaine Daniels*
Santa Ana, California

   7 pounds ground beef
   6 medium onions, chopped
   2 celery ribs, chopped
   3 garlic cloves, minced
   2 cans (14-1/2 ounces *each*) diced
      tomatoes, undrained
   2 cans (12 ounces *each*) tomato paste
   2 cans (15-1/4 ounces *each*) whole kernel
      corn, drained
   2 cans (4-1/2 ounces *each*) mushroom
      stems and pieces, drained
   3 cans (2-1/4 ounces *each*) sliced ripe
      olives, drained
2-1/4 to 2-3/4 cups water
   2 to 3 tablespoons chili powder
   1 tablespoon seasoned salt
 1/2 to 1 teaspoon crushed red pepper flakes
   1 teaspoon pepper
   3 jars (13-1/2 ounces *each*) tamales, papers
      removed and halved
   2 cups (8 ounces) shredded cheddar cheese

In several Dutch ovens, cook the beef, onions, celery and garlic until meat is no longer pink; drain.

Stir in tomatoes and tomato paste. Add the corn, mushrooms and olives. Stir in water and seasonings. Bring to a boil; remove from the heat.

Spoon into three greased 13-in. x 9-in. x 2-in. baking dishes. Top with the tamales. Cover and bake at 350° for 50-60 minutes. Sprinkle with cheese. Bake 5-10 minutes longer or until cheese is melted. **Yield:** 3 casseroles (8-10 servings each).

— ☕ ☕ ☕ —

Fruity Gelatin Salad

This pretty side dish is ideal for big holiday dinners. It's refreshing, sweet and tart and has just the right amount of tang.   —Sarah Baumann, Saginaw, Texas

    2 packages (6 ounces _each_) cherry gelatin
    2 cups boiling water
    2 packages (10 ounces _each_)
        frozen sweetened sliced strawberries
    2 cans (20 ounces _each_)
        crushed pineapple, undrained
    2 cans (16 ounces _each_) whole-berry
        cranberry sauce

In two large bowls, dissolve gelatin in boiling water. Stir in strawberries until berries are separated. Stir in the pineapple and cranberry sauce until blended. Transfer to two 13-in. x 9-in. x 2-in. dishes. Refrigerate until firm. **Yield:** 36-40 servings.

— ☕ ☕ ☕ —

Chocolate Mincemeat Bars

What would the holidays be without mincemeat for dessert? Even people who say they don't care for the taste will love these moist chocolate bars.
    —Darlene Berndt, South Bend, Indiana

  1/2 cup shortening
    1 cup sugar
    3 eggs
    2 cups all-purpose flour
    2 teaspoons baking soda
1-3/4 cups mincemeat
    2 cups (12 ounces) semisweet chocolate
        chips
Confectioners' sugar

In a mixing bowl, cream shortening and sugar. Add eggs, one at a time, beating well after each addition. Combine flour and baking soda; gradually add to the creamed mixture. Beat in mincemeat. Stir in chocolate chips.

Spread into a greased 15-in. x 10-in. x 1-in. baking pan. Bake at 375° for 20-25 minutes or until golden brown. Cool on a wire rack. Dust with confectioners' sugar. **Yield:** 3 dozen.

Blarney Stones

(Pictured below)

When I was in high school, I worked for an Irish family...and they made these yummy treats each year for St. Patrick's Day. The sweet frosting and salty peanuts are an irresistible combination.   —Bridget Jones
Veyo, Utah

    4 eggs
1-3/4 cups sugar
    1 teaspoon vanilla extract
1-3/4 cups all-purpose flour
    3 teaspoons baking powder
  1/2 teaspoon salt
    1 cup milk
  1/4 cup butter _or_ margarine, melted
FROSTING:
    2 pounds confectioners' sugar (about
        7-1/2 cups)
  2/3 cup milk
    2 teaspoons vanilla extract
  1/8 teaspoon salt
    6 cups finely chopped peanuts

In a mixing bowl, beat the eggs, sugar and vanilla until thick and lemon-colored, about 4 minutes. Combine the flour, baking powder and salt; add to the egg mixture. Beat on low speed just until combined.

Add the milk and butter; mix well. Pour into a greased 13-in. x 9-in. x 2-in. baking pan. Bake at 350° for 30-35 minutes or until a toothpick inserted near the center comes out clean. Cool on a wire rack. Cut into squares. Cover and freeze overnight.

For frosting, in a mixing bowl, combine confectioners' sugar, milk, vanilla and salt; beat until smooth. Frost the top and sides of frozen cake squares; roll in peanuts. Place on wire racks to dry. **Yield:** 2 dozen.

Spinach with Hot Bacon Dressing

This dish is popular in Pennsylvania Dutch country. It takes a little time to make, but it's worth the effort. Sometimes I serve the dressing over other greens or even potato salad. —Romaine Wetzel
Lancaster, Pennsylvania

        1 cup sugar
        3 tablespoons cornstarch
  1-1/2 teaspoons celery seed
        1 teaspoon salt
      3/4 teaspoon ground mustard
        2 cups milk
      3/4 cup cider vinegar
      1/2 cup butter *or* margarine, cubed
        3 eggs, lightly beaten
        4 bacon strips, cooked and crumbled
        3 hard-cooked eggs, chopped
Torn fresh spinach

In a saucepan, combine the sugar, cornstarch, celery seed, salt and mustard. Gradually stir in milk and vinegar. Add butter. Cook and stir until mixture comes to a boil; cook and stir for 1-2 minutes or until thickened and bubbly.

Stir a small amount of hot liquid into beaten eggs; return all to the pan. Cook and stir 1 minute longer. Stir in bacon and hard-cooked eggs. Serve immediately over spinach. **Yield:** about 4 cups.

— 🏆 🏆 🏆 —

Fruit Cocktail Cake

This is a moist yummy dessert with bits of fruit inside and a crunchy brown sugar-walnut mixture on top. It's perfect for potlucks. —Mrs. James Patterson
Spokane, Washington

        8 cups all-purpose flour
        5 cups sugar
        2 tablespoons baking powder
        1 tablespoon baking soda
        1 tablespoon salt
        5 eggs, lightly beaten
        2 tablespoons vanilla extract
        5 cans (15-1/4 ounces *each*) fruit cocktail
TOPPING:
        2 cups packed brown sugar
        2 cups chopped walnuts
        2 tablespoons all-purpose flour

In a large mixing bowl, combine flour, sugar, baking powder, baking soda and salt. Add eggs and vanilla; mix well. Drain fruit cocktail, reserving the syrup. Add syrup to dry ingredients; mix well. Fold in fruit cocktail. Pour into four greased 13-in. x 9-in. x 2-in. baking dishes.

Combine the topping ingredients; sprinkle over

batter. Bake at 350° for 40-45 minutes or until a toothpick inserted near the center comes out clean. Cool on wire racks. **Yield:** 4 cakes (16 servings each).

— 🏆 🏆 🏆 —

Pancakes for a Crowd

Every time I make these pancakes, I'm reminded of Lansford, North Dakota, a lovely little town where I used to live. The country club there sponsored an annual breakfast that featured these tasty pancakes.
—Penelope Hamilton, Riverside, California

       40 cups all-purpose flour
        3 cups sugar
  1-1/2 cups baking powder
  1-1/2 cups baking soda
      3/4 cup salt
       28 eggs
        2 gallons milk
        1 gallon buttermilk
       64 ounces vegetable oil

In several large bowls, combine the flour, sugar, baking powder, baking soda and salt. Combine the eggs, milk, buttermilk and oil; stir into dry ingredients just until blended. Pour batter by 1/3 cupfuls onto a greased hot griddle. Turn when bubbles form on top; cook until second side is golden brown. **Yield:** 70-80 servings (5 gallons of batter).

— 🏆 🏆 🏆 —

Chicken Spaghetti Bake

This casserole is always a hit at church and anywhere else I serve it. For variety, I sometimes substitute different cheeses, spiral pasta or cooked turkey for the chicken. —Renee Quintero, Mission, Texas

        3 packages (two 16 ounces, one 7 ounces) thin spaghetti
      1/2 cup olive *or* vegetable oil, *divided*
        2 large onions, chopped
        2 large green peppers, chopped
        3 medium zucchini, thinly sliced
   6 to 8 garlic cloves, minced
        3 jars (26 ounces *each*) spaghetti sauce
        3 cans (8 ounces *each*) tomato sauce
        1 can (7 ounces) sliced ripe olives, drained
        9 cups cubed cooked chicken
        1 can (10-3/4 ounces) condensed cream of mushroom soup, undiluted
        6 cups (24 ounces) shredded cheddar cheese

Cook spaghetti according to package directions; rinse and drain. Toss with 1/4 cup oil; set aside. In a Dutch oven, saute the onions, green peppers, zucchini and garlic in remaining oil until crisp-tender. Stir in the spaghetti sauce, tomato sauce and olives; bring to a boil. Reduce heat; simmer, uncovered, for 20 minutes. Stir in chicken and soup.

Place 2-1/4 cups spaghetti each in three greased 13-in. x 9-in. x 2-in. baking dishes. Top each with 4 cups sauce and 1 cup cheese. Layer with 2-1/4 cups spaghetti and 2 cups sauce. Cover and bake at 350° for 40-45 minutes. Sprinkle with remaining cheese. Bake 5 minutes longer or until cheese is melted. Let stand 10 minutes before serving. **Yield:** 3 casseroles (10-12 servings each).

— 🍽 🍽 🍽 —

Sausage Egg Bake

(Pictured below)

This hearty egg dish is wonderful for any meal of the day. I fix it frequently for special occasions, too, because it's easy to prepare and really versatile. For a change, use spicier sausage or substitute a flavored cheese blend. —Molly Swallow, Blackfoot, Idaho

> 1 **pound bulk Italian sausage**
> 2 **cans (10-3/4 ounces *each*) condensed cream of potato soup, undiluted**
> 9 **eggs**
> 3/4 **cup milk**
> 1/4 **teaspoon pepper**
> 1 **cup (4 ounces) shredded cheddar cheese**

In a skillet, cook sausage over medium heat until no longer pink; drain. Stir in soup. In a mixing bowl, beat eggs, milk and pepper; stir in sausage mixture.

Transfer to a lightly greased 11-in. x 7-in. x 2-in. baking dish. Sprinkle with cheese. Bake, uncovered, at 375° for 40-45 minutes or until a knife inserted near the center comes out clean. **Yield:** 12 servings.

Glazed Raisin Sheet Cake

This dessert is full of plump raisins and cinnamon. I like it because it's quick and easy to make.
—Betty Bonker, Egg Harbor, Wisconsin

> 1-1/2 **cups raisins**
> 1-1/4 **cups boiling water**
> 1 **cup butter *or* margarine, softened**
> 1-1/2 **cups sugar**
> 2 **eggs**
> 3-1/2 **cups all-purpose flour**
> 2 **teaspoons ground cinnamon**
> 1-1/2 **teaspoons baking soda**
> 1/2 **teaspoon salt**
> **GLAZE:**
> 1-1/2 **cups confectioners' sugar**
> 1 **tablespoon butter *or* margarine, softened**
> 3 **to 4 tablespoons milk**

Place raisins in a bowl; cover with boiling water and let stand for 5 minutes. Drain, reserving 1 cup liquid; set raisins and liquid aside.

In a mixing bowl, cream butter and sugar. Add eggs; mix well. Combine flour, cinnamon, baking soda and salt; add to creamed mixture alternately with reserved raisin liquid. Fold in raisins. Pour into a greased 15-in. x 10-in. x 1-in. baking pan.

Bake at 375° for 16-20 minutes or until a toothpick comes out clean. Cool on a wire rack for 5 minutes. Meanwhile, in a mixing bowl, combine the glaze ingredients. Pour over warm cake; spread evenly. Cool before cutting. **Yield:** 24 servings.

— 🍽 🍽 🍽 —

Home-Style Meat Loaf

This recipe makes five moist meat loaves that are great for large gatherings. —Allison Craig
Ormstown, Quebec

> 5 **eggs**
> 4 **cups milk**
> 4 **cups dry bread crumbs**
> 2-1/2 **cups shredded carrots**
> 1-1/4 **cups chopped onions**
> 5 **teaspoons salt**
> 4 **teaspoons pepper**
> 10 **pounds ground beef**
> 5 **pounds ground pork**

In five large bowls, combine the first seven ingredients. Crumble meat over top; mix well. Shape into five loaves; place each in an ungreased 13-in. x 9-in. x 2-in. baking dish. Bake, uncovered, at 350° for 75-85 minutes or until meat is no longer pink and a meat thermometer reads 160°. Drain; let stand for 10 minutes before cutting. **Yield:** 5 meat loaves (12 servings each).

Winter Fruit Salad

(Pictured below)

For a flavorful and attractive side dish, try this refreshing salad. I fix it ahead to give the flavors a chance to blend, which also eliminates last-minute fuss. Family members and guests always tell me how much they enjoy it.
—*Ruby Williams*
Bogalusa, Louisiana

    6 large red apples, sliced
    2 tablespoons lemon juice
    4 bunches watercress, stems removed
    2 pounds seedless red grapes, separated into small bunches
    2 small red onions, halved and thinly sliced
HONEY LEMON DRESSING:
  1/2 cup lemon juice
  1/4 cup vegetable oil
    2 to 3 tablespoons honey
  1/2 teaspoon salt
  1/8 teaspoon pepper
Lemon slices and fresh mint, optional

In a bowl, toss apples and lemon juice. Arrange watercress on a large serving platter. Top with the grapes, onions and apples.

In a jar with a tight-fitting lid, combine lemon juice, oil, honey, salt and pepper; shake well. Drizzle 1/2 cup over salad. Cover and refrigerate salad and remaining dressing until serving. Serve remaining dressing on the side. Garnish with lemon and mint if desired. **Yield:** 12 servings (about 1 cup dressing).

Seafood Soup

Hosting a huge holiday gathering this season? This special soup is great any time of year, but it's always a hit on New Year's Eve. It has the perfect blend of flavors to work well as an entree or first course.
—*Victor Miller, Levittown, Pennsylvania*

4-1/2 quarts chicken broth
   10 packages (8 ounces *each*) imitation crabmeat
    2 medium onions, diced
1-1/2 cups butter *or* margarine
  1/4 cup all-purpose flour
    5 pounds sea scallops
    3 pounds cooked medium shrimp, peeled and deveined
1-1/4 teaspoons dried thyme
    1 teaspoon dried parsley
    4 cups whipping cream
Salt and pepper to taste

In a large kettle, bring broth and crab to a boil. Reduce heat; cover and simmer for 20 minutes or until crab breaks into pieces when stirred. Meanwhile, in a large skillet, saute onions in butter until tender. Stir in flour until blended. Stir into crab mixture; return to a simmer.

Add scallops, shrimp, thyme and parsley. Simmer, uncovered, for 5-7 minutes or until scallops turn opaque. Add the cream, salt and pepper; cook and stir until heated through (do not boil). **Yield:** 48 servings (12 quarts).

——— 🍷 🍷 🍷 ———

Beef Stew for a Crowd

Beef stew always seems to be popular at a large gathering. Everyone likes this hearty combination of beef, potatoes, carrots, celery and onion in a savory tomato-beef broth. —*Jackie Holland, Gillette, Wyoming*

✓ Uses less fat, sugar or salt. Includes Nutritional Analysis and Diabetic Exchanges.

2-1/2 pounds beef stew meat, cut into 1/2-inch cubes
    3 tablespoons canola oil
    3 quarts water
    2 cans (15 ounces *each*) tomato sauce
  1/4 cup beef bouillon granules
    1 teaspoon salt, optional
  1/2 teaspoon pepper
3-1/2 pounds potatoes, peeled and cubed
    4 medium carrots, sliced
    3 celery ribs, sliced
    2 medium onions, coarsely chopped
  3/4 cup all-purpose flour
1-1/2 cups cold water

In a soup kettle, brown the beef in oil; drain. Stir in the water, tomato sauce, bouillon, salt if desired and pepper. Bring to a boil. Reduce heat; cover and simmer for 1-1/2 hours or until the meat is tender.

Add the potatoes, carrots, celery and onions. Return to a boil. Reduce heat; cover and simmer for 25-30 minutes or until the vegetables are tender. Combine flour and cold water until smooth; gradually stir into stew. Bring to a boil; cook and stir for 2 minutes or until thickened. **Yield:** 22 servings (5-1/2 quarts).

Nutritional Analysis: One 1-cup serving (prepared with lean stew meat and without salt) equals 183 calories, 6 g fat (2 g saturated fat), 32 mg cholesterol, 739 mg sodium, 22 g carbohydrate, 3 g fiber, 13 g protein. **Diabetic Exchanges:** 1-1/2 lean meat, 1 starch, 1 vegetable.

Walnut Chip Cookies

No one can resist these rich cookies with their double dose of sweetness. Melted chocolate is mixed into the dough, then chocolate chips, oats and walnuts are added. Yum! —Joy Hanje, Gaylord, Michigan

> 2 cups butter *or* margarine, softened
> 2 cups sugar
> 2 cups packed brown sugar
> 4 eggs
> 2 squares (1 ounce *each*) unsweetened chocolate, melted
> 2 teaspoons vanilla extract
> 5 cups quick-cooking oats
> 4 cups all-purpose flour
> 2 teaspoons baking soda
> 2 teaspoons baking powder
> 1 teaspoon salt
> 4 cups (24 ounces) semisweet chocolate chips
> 3 cups chopped walnuts

In a large mixing bowl, cream butter and sugars. Add the eggs, one at a time, beating well after each addition. Beat in melted chocolate and vanilla. Place half of the oats at a time in a blender or food processor; cover and process until powdery. Combine the oats, flour, baking soda, baking powder and salt; gradually add to the creamed mixture.

Transfer to a larger bowl if necessary. Stir in chocolate chips and nuts. Roll into 1-1/4-in. balls. Place 2 in. apart on lightly greased baking sheets. Bake at 375° for 7-9 minutes or until edges are firm (do not overbake). Remove to wire racks to cool. **Yield:** about 12 dozen.

Buttermilk Chocolate Bread

(Pictured above)

I serve this rich cake-like bread often at Christmastime. It makes a great brunch item, but it also goes well on a dinner buffet. This recipe won me a "Best in Category" award in a local cooking contest.
—Patrice Bruwer, Grand Rapids, Michigan

> 1/2 cup butter *or* margarine, softened
> 1 cup sugar
> 2 eggs
> 1-1/2 cups all-purpose flour
> 1/2 cup baking cocoa
> 1/2 teaspoon salt
> 1/2 teaspoon baking powder
> 1/2 teaspoon baking soda
> 1 cup buttermilk
> 1/3 cup chopped pecans
> **CHOCOLATE HONEY BUTTER:**
> 1/2 cup butter (no substitutes), softened
> 2 tablespoons honey
> 2 tablespoons chocolate syrup

In a mixing bowl, cream the butter and sugar. Add eggs, one at a time, beating well after each addition. Combine the flour, cocoa, salt, baking powder and baking soda; add to creamed mixture alternately with buttermilk. Fold in pecans.

Pour into a greased 9-in. x 5-in. x 3-in. loaf pan. Bake at 350° for 55-60 minutes or until a toothpick inserted near the center comes out clean. Cool for 10 minutes before removing from pan to a wire rack.

In a small mixing bowl, beat butter until fluffy. Add honey and chocolate syrup; mix well. Serve with the bread. **Yield:** 1 loaf (1/2 cup butter).

FALL GATHERINGS call for flavorful stick-to-your-ribs fare like Chocolate Chip Cake, Super-Duper Chili, Fresh Vegetable Salad and Mexican Corn Bread (shown above, clockwise from top right).

Super-Duper Chili

(Pictured above)

This chili is thick and hearty with a pleasant zip that makes it very popular at potluck meals.
—*Elizabeth Mays, Nunnelly, Tennessee*

1 **pound bulk pork sausage**
1 **pound ground beef**
2 **cans (15-1/2 ounces *each*) hot chili beans**
1 **jar (16 ounces) salsa**
1 **can (16 ounces) kidney beans, rinsed and drained**

1 can (15 ounces) pinto beans, rinsed and
  drained
1 can (14-1/2 ounces) diced tomatoes,
  undrained
1 can (10-3/4 ounces) condensed cream of
  mushroom soup, undiluted
1 can (8 ounces) tomato sauce
8 ounces process cheese (Velveeta), cubed
1-1/2 teaspoons chili powder
1/2 teaspoon cayenne pepper

In a soup kettle or Dutch oven, cook the sausage
and beef over medium heat until no longer pink;
drain. Stir in the remaining ingredients. Bring to a
boil. Reduce heat; cover and simmer for 30 minutes or until heated through. **Yield:** 14 servings (3-
1/2 quarts).

Mexican Corn Bread

(Pictured at left)

_My corn bread goes great with soups or stews. It's so
moist and sweet, it doesn't need any butter. Chopped
green chilies and jalapeno pepper add some kick._
—Sandy Gaulitz, Spring, Texas

2 packages (8-1/2 ounces _each_) corn
  bread/muffin mix
1 medium onion, chopped
2 cups (8 ounces) shredded cheddar cheese
1 can (14-3/4 ounces) cream-style corn
1-1/2 cups (12 ounces) sour cream
4 eggs, beaten
1 can (4 ounces) chopped green chilies
1/3 cup vegetable oil
1 tablespoon finely chopped jalapeno
  pepper*

In a bowl, combine corn bread mix and onion.
Combine the remaining ingredients; add to the
corn bread mixture just until moistened. Pour into
a greased 13-in. x 9-in. x 2-in. baking dish. Bake at
350° for 50-55 minutes or until lightly browned
and edges pull away from sides of pan. Serve warm.
Refrigerate leftovers. **Yield:** 18-24 servings.

*Editor's Note: When cutting or seeding hot peppers, use rubber or plastic gloves to protect your
hands. Avoid touching your face.

Fresh Vegetable Salad

(Pictured at left)

_For a colorful and refreshing side dish, give this veg-
gie salad a try. The dressing has a mild mustard flavor._
—Harriet Stichter, Milford, Indiana

2 cups sliced celery
2 cups thinly sliced cauliflower
2 cups halved cherry tomatoes
2 cups thinly sliced carrots
2 cups sliced cucumber
1 medium onion, thinly sliced and separated
  into rings
3/4 cup olive _or_ vegetable oil
1/2 cup minced fresh parsley
3 tablespoons white wine vinegar _or_ cider
  vinegar
1 teaspoon salt
1 teaspoon ground mustard
1/8 teaspoon pepper
1 garlic clove, minced

In a large serving bowl, combine the celery, cauliflower, tomatoes, carrots, cucumber and onion. In
a jar with a tight-fitting lid, combine the remaining ingredients. Pour over vegetables and toss
gently. Cover and refrigerate for at least 2 hours or
overnight. Serve with a slotted spoon. **Yield:** 12-
14 servings.

Chocolate Chip Cake

(Pictured at far left and on page 160)

_This cake is perfect for transporting to a dinner be-
cause you don't have to worry about any sticky frosting—it's plenty moist and yummy without it. Not only
does my cake make a pretty presentation on a buffet
table, it's also one of the first desserts to dissappear!_
—Abigail Crawford, Lake Butler, Florida

1 package (18-1/4 ounces) yellow cake mix
1 package (3.4 ounces) instant vanilla
  pudding mix
1 cup milk
1 cup vegetable oil
4 eggs
1 cup miniature semisweet chocolate chips
5 tablespoons grated German sweet
  chocolate, _divided_
2 tablespoons confectioners' sugar

In a mixing bowl, combine cake and pudding mixes, milk, oil and eggs. Beat on low speed until
moistened. Beat on medium for 2 minutes. Stir in
chocolate chips and 3 tablespoons grated chocolate. Pour into a greased and floured 10-in. fluted
tube pan.

Bake at 350° for 55-65 minutes or until a toothpick inserted near the center comes out clean. Cool
for 10 minutes before removing from pan to a
wire rack to cool completely. Combine confectioners' sugar and remaining grated chocolate;
sprinkle over cake. **Yield:** 12 servings.

Four-Pasta Beef Bake

(Pictured above and on page 160)

This hearty casserole looks and tastes a lot like lasagna, but it's quicker to prepare since you don't have to layer it. It disappears fast when I share it at a gathering. Served with rolls and a salad, it makes an easy and satisfying supper. —Harriet Stichter
Milford, Indiana

> 8 cups uncooked pasta (four different shapes)
> 2 pounds ground beef
> 2 medium green peppers, chopped
> 2 medium onions, chopped
> 2 cups sliced fresh mushrooms
> 4 jars (26 ounces *each*) meatless spaghetti sauce
> 2 eggs, lightly beaten
> 4 cups (16 ounces) shredded mozzarella cheese

Cook pasta according to package directions. Meanwhile, in a large skillet, cook the beef, green peppers, onions and mushrooms over medium heat until meat is no longer pink; drain.

Drain pasta and place in a large bowl; stir in the beef mixture, two jars of spaghetti sauce and eggs. Transfer to two greased 13-in. x 9-in. x 2-in. baking dishes. Top with remaining sauce; sprinkle with cheese. Bake, uncovered, at 350° for 25-30 minutes or until heated through. **Yield:** 2 casseroles (8-10 servings each).

Brunswick Stew

Festivals in North Carolina wouldn't be the same without this popular stew. A thick hearty blend of meats, vegetables and seasonings in a savory tomato-based broth, it's a special main dish for a crowd.
—Judi Brinegar, Liberty, North Carolina

> 4 large onions, halved and thinly sliced
> 1/4 cup butter *or* margarine
> 1 broiler/fryer chicken (3 to 4 pounds), cut up
> 2 quarts water
> 2 cans (28 ounces *each*) crushed tomatoes
> 1-3/4 cups ketchup
> 1 can (6 ounces) tomato paste
> 1 can (10-3/4 ounces) condensed tomato soup, undiluted
> 2 medium jalapeno peppers, seeded and chopped*
> 1 tablespoon salt
> 1 teaspoon Worcestershire sauce
> 1 teaspoon hot pepper sauce
> 1 teaspoon pepper
> 2 pounds ground beef, cooked and drained
> 1 pound cubed fully cooked ham
> 1 package (16 ounces) frozen cut green beans
> 1 package (16 ounces) frozen butter beans
> 1 package (16 ounces) frozen corn
> 6 cups hot mashed potatoes (prepared without milk and butter)

In a large stockpot, saute onions in butter until tender. Add chicken and water. Bring to a boil. Reduce heat; cover and simmer for 1 hour.

Remove chicken; when cool enough to handle, remove meat from bones. Discard bones and dice meat. Skim fat from broth; return chicken to broth. Add the next 14 ingredients; bring to a boil. Reduce heat; cover and simmer for 1 hour or until vegetables are tender. Stir in potatoes; heat through. **Yield:** about 8 quarts (25-30 servings).

*Editor's Note: When cutting or seeding hot peppers, use rubber or plastic gloves to protect your hands. Avoid touching your face.

Tangy Strawberry Punch

A super summertime drink, this punch is tart and sweet. I like to serve it at showers, parties and other occasions. Kids really like it, too. —Shirley Hughes
Gadsden, Alabama

> 2 cans (46 ounces *each*) unsweetened pineapple juice

2 quarts water
6 cups sugar
6 envelopes (.19 ounce *each*) unsweetened
  strawberry lemonade soft drink mix
2 liters ginger ale, chilled
1 can (8 ounces) crushed pineapple,
  optional

In a large container, combine pineapple juice, water, sugar and drink mix. Stir until sugar is dissolved. Freeze. Remove from the freezer 1-2 hours before serving. Stir in the ginger ale and crushed pineapple if desired. Serve immediately. **Yield:** 35-40 servings (about 7-1/2 quarts).

——— 🍶 🍶 🍶 ———

Ranch French Bread

(Pictured above)

Golden on the outside and tender on the inside, these lovely loaves get a fun flavor boost from ranch dressing. One slice always prompts a second helping or more, so this bread never lasts long.
      —Cherri Schmidt, Grand Island, Nebraska

2 packages (1/4 ounce *each*) active dry
  yeast
1/2 cup warm water (110° to 115°)
1/2 cup sugar, *divided*
2 cups warm buttermilk (110° to 115°)*
1/2 cup butter *or* margarine, softened
3 eggs

1 to 2 envelopes original ranch salad
  dressing mix
2 teaspoons salt
8 to 9 cups all-purpose flour
Additional butter *or* margarine, melted

In a mixing bowl, dissolve yeast in warm water. Add 1 teaspoon sugar; let stand for 5 minutes. Add the buttermilk, butter, eggs, ranch dressing mix, salt, 4 cups flour and remaining sugar; beat until smooth. Stir in enough remaining flour to form a soft dough. Turn onto a floured surface; knead until smooth and elastic, about 6-8 minutes. Place in a greased bowl, turning once to grease top. Cover and let rise in a warm place until doubled, about 1 hour.

Punch dough down. Turn onto a lightly floured surface; divide into fourths. Roll each portion into a 14-in. x 12-in. rectangle. Roll up jelly-roll style, starting with a long side; pinch seams to seal and tuck ends under. Place seam side down on two greased baking sheets. With a sharp knife, make five shallow slashes across the top of each loaf. Cover and let rise in a warm place until doubled, about 30 minutes.

Bake at 350° for 20-25 minutes or until golden brown. Brush with melted butter. Remove from pans to wire racks to cool. **Yield:** 4 loaves.

*Editor's Note: Heated buttermilk will appear curdled.

——— 🍶 🍶 🍶 ———

Marbled Chocolate Bars

*With only four ingredients, these scrumptious chocolate bars with pockets of rich cream cheese are perfect for taking to a potluck. They're quick to assemble, don't need frosting and are easy to transport and serve. Best of all, folks love them!   —Margery Bryan
Royal City, Washington*

1 package (18-1/4 ounces)
  German chocolate cake mix
1 package (8 ounces) cream cheese,
  softened
1/2 cup sugar
3/4 cup milk chocolate chips, *divided*

Prepare cake batter according to package directions. Pour into a greased 15-in. x 10-in. x 1-in. baking pan. In a small mixing bowl, beat cream cheese and sugar. Stir in 1/4 cup of the chocolate chips. Drop by tablespoonfuls over the batter. Cut through batter with a knife to swirl the cream cheese mixture. Sprinkle with the remaining chocolate chips.

Bake at 350° for 25-30 minutes or until a toothpick inserted near the center comes out clean. Cool on a wire rack. Cut into bars. **Yield:** 3 dozen.

Giant Focaccia Sandwich

(Pictured at far right and on page 160)

A flavorful Italian flat bread made with oats and molasses turns this sandwich into something special.
—Marina Gelling, Rowlett, Texas

OAT FOCACCIA:
5-1/2 cups all-purpose flour
  1 cup quick-cooking oats
  2 packages (1/4 ounce *each*) active dry yeast
  2 teaspoons salt
2-1/4 cups water
  1/2 cup molasses
  1 tablespoon butter *or* margarine
  1 egg, lightly beaten
  1 tablespoon dried minced onion
  1 tablespoon sesame seeds
  1 teaspoon garlic salt
SANDWICH FILLING:
  6 tablespoons mayonnaise
  2 tablespoons prepared mustard
  6 to 8 lettuce leaves
  3/4 to 1 pound thinly sliced fully cooked ham
  6 to 8 thin slices Swiss *or* cheddar cheese
  4 slices red onion, separated into rings
  1 medium green pepper, sliced
  2 medium tomatoes, thinly sliced

In a large mixing bowl, combine the flour, oats, yeast and salt. In a saucepan, heat water, molasses and butter to 120°-130°. Add to dry ingredients; beat just until moistened. Place in a greased bowl; turn once to grease top. Cover and let rise in a warm place until doubled, about 45 minutes.

Press dough onto a greased 14-in. pizza pan. Cover and let rise until doubled, about 30 minutes. Brush with egg. Sprinkle with onion, sesame seeds and garlic salt. Bake at 350° for 30-35 minutes or until golden brown. Remove to a wire rack to cool.

Split the focaccia in half horizontally; spread mayonnaise and mustard on cut sides. On bottom half, layer lettuce, ham, cheese, onion, green pepper and tomatoes. Replace top half. Chill until serving. Cut into wedges. **Yield:** 12 servings.

---❦ ❦ ❦---

BLT Macaroni Salad

(Pictured at far right)

This pleasing pasta salad is like eating a BLT in a bowl. It's a real crowd-pleaser! —Norene Wright
Manilla, Indiana

  2 cups uncooked elbow macaroni
  5 green onions, finely chopped
  1 large tomato, diced
1-1/4 cups diced celery
1-1/4 cups mayonnaise
  5 teaspoons white vinegar
  1/4 teaspoon salt
  1/8 to 1/4 teaspoon pepper
  1 pound bacon, cooked and crumbled

Cook macaroni according to package directions; drain and rinse in cold water. In a large bowl, combine the macaroni, green onions, tomato and celery. In a small bowl, combine mayonnaise, vinegar, salt and pepper. Pour over macaroni mixture and toss to coat. Cover and chill for at least 2 hours. Just before serving, add bacon. **Yield:** 12 servings.

---❦ ❦ ❦---

Pepperoni Pizza Salad

(Pictured at right and on page 160)

This salad is so popular at potlucks that I always bring home an empty bowl. —Cathy Riebschlager
Hordville, Nebraska

 10 plum tomatoes, chopped
  3 green peppers, cut into 1-inch pieces
  2 cups (8 ounces) shredded mozzarella cheese
  1 package (3-1/2 ounces) sliced pepperoni
  1 can (2-1/4 ounces) sliced ripe olives, drained
  1/4 cup chopped onion
  1/3 cup tomato juice
  1/4 cup red wine vinegar *or* cider vinegar
  1/4 cup olive *or* vegetable oil
  1 garlic clove, minced
  1/2 teaspoon dried basil
  1/4 teaspoon pepper
  3/4 cup seasoned salad croutons

In a large bowl, combine the tomatoes, green peppers, cheese, pepperoni, olives and onion. In a small bowl, combine the tomato juice, vinegar, oil, garlic, basil and pepper; mix well. Pour over tomato mixture and toss to coat. Cover and refrigerate for several hours. Just before serving, sprinkle with croutons. **Yield:** 12-14 servings.

---❦ ❦ ❦---

Lemon Cream Dessert

(Pictured at right and on front cover)

My friend and I enjoy trying out new dishes on our husbands. They love this easy yet yummy layered lemon dessert. —Laurel Adams, Danville, Kentucky

1-1/2 cups sugar
  1/3 cup plus 1 tablespoon cornstarch

1-1/2 cups cold water
  3 egg yolks, lightly beaten
  3 tablespoons butter *or* margarine, cubed
  2 teaspoons grated lemon peel
1/2 cup lemon juice
CRUST:
  1 cup all-purpose flour
  1 cup finely chopped walnuts
1/2 cup cold butter *or* margarine
TOPPING:
  1 package (8 ounces) cream cheese, softened
  1 cup confectioners' sugar
  2 cups cold milk
  2 packages (3.4 ounces *each*) instant vanilla pudding mix
  1 teaspoon vanilla extract
  1 carton (16 ounces) frozen whipped topping, thawed

In a small saucepan, combine sugar and cornstarch; gradually stir in water until smooth. Bring to a boil; cook and stir for 1 minute. Remove from the heat. Stir a small amount of hot filling into egg yolks; return all to the pan, stirring constantly. Bring to a gentle boil; cook and stir for 1 minute. Remove from the heat; stir in butter and lemon peel. Gently stir in lemon juice. Refrigerate until cool.

In a bowl, combine flour and nuts. Cut in butter until mixture resembles crumbs. Press into a greased 13-in. x 9-in. x 2-in. baking dish. Bake at 350° for 15-20 minutes or until golden brown. Cool on a wire rack.

In a mixing bowl, beat cream cheese and sugar until smooth; spread over crust. Spread with lemon mixture. In another mixing bowl, beat milk and pudding mixes on low for 2 minutes; beat in vanilla. Fold in half of the whipped topping. Spread over lemon layer. Spread with remaining whipped topping. Chill for at least 4 hours. **Yield:** 18-24 servings.

WARM-WEATHER DISHES like Pepperoni Pizza Salad, Giant Focaccia Sandwich, Lemon Cream Dessert and BLT Macaroni Salad (shown below, clockwise from top) will make your next gathering a delight.

Cooking for One or Two

These small-serving recipes that are big on taste will fill the bill when cooking for one or two is the order of the day.

—— 🝢 🝢 🝢 ——

MADE TO ORDER. Clockwise from upper left: Cranberry Waldorf Salad (p. 194); Ham with Currant Sauce, Rosemary Green Beans and Small Batch Popovers (p. 182); Orange-Glazed Pork Chops, Summer Squash Stir-Fry and Tortilla Fruit Pie (pp. 196 and 197); Chili for Two (p. 193); Fruity Cookie Tarts (p. 192).

Ham with Currant Sauce

(Pictured at far right and on page 180)

This tender ham slice cooks in no time...and the sweet and zippy glaze is so quick to make, with just two ingredients. —Sharon Shaw, Battle Creek, Michigan

> 1 bone-in fully cooked ham slice (about 1 pound)
> 1/4 cup water
> 1/3 cup currant jelly
> 1 teaspoon prepared horseradish

In a large skillet, bring ham and water to a boil. Reduce heat; cover and simmer until ham is heated through, turning once. Meanwhile, in a small microwave-safe bowl, combine jelly and horseradish. Cover and microwave on high for 2-3 minutes or until heated through, stirring occasionally. Serve over ham. **Yield:** 2 servings.

—————— ☕ ☕ ☕ ——————

Rosemary Green Beans

(Pictured at far right and on page 180)

Before my physician husband retired, he was rarely home for dinner, but now I do lots of cooking for the two of us. —Lucy Banks, Jackson, Mississippi

> 1 small onion, halved and thinly sliced
> 2 tablespoons butter *or* margarine, *divided*
> 2 tablespoons water
> 1/2 teaspoon minced fresh rosemary
> 1/4 teaspoon salt
> Dash coarsely ground pepper
> 2 cups frozen cut green beans

In a saucepan, saute onion in 1 tablespoon butter until tender. Stir in the water, rosemary, salt and pepper. Bring to a boil. Add beans and return to a boil. Reduce heat; cover and simmer for 6-10 minutes or until the beans are tender. Drain; top with the remaining butter. **Yield:** 2 servings.

—————— ☕ ☕ ☕ ——————

Small Batch Popovers

(Pictured at far right and on page 180)

These golden popovers are a great way to round out any meal. —Pauline Sniezek, Adams, Massachusetts

> 1/2 cup all-purpose flour
> 1/4 teaspoon salt
> 2 eggs
> 1/2 cup milk

In a bowl, combine flour and salt. Whisk together eggs and milk; stir into dry ingredients just until

blended. Pour into four greased and floured 8-oz. custard cups. Place on a baking sheet. Bake, uncovered, at 425° for 20 minutes or until puffed and edges are golden brown (do not open the oven door during baking). **Yield:** 4 popovers.

—————— ☕ ☕ ☕ ——————

Sunny Breakfast Special

Orange marmalade and pineapple lend a tangy twist to this hearty and flavorful bacon, egg and cheese English muffin. —Alberta Hanson Cushing, Wisconsin

> 1 tablespoon butter *or* margarine, softened
> 1 English muffin half
> 1 slice Canadian bacon
> 1 pineapple ring
> 1 teaspoon orange marmalade
> 1 egg, *separated*
> 1 tablespoon shredded cheddar cheese

Spread butter over muffin half; place on a baking sheet. Broil 4-6 in. from the heat for 1-2 minutes or until butter is bubbly. Top with bacon and pineapple; spoon marmalade into center of pineapple ring. Brush egg white over top and sides of muffin.

Sprinkle cheese on top. With a spoon, make a well in cheese; place egg yolk in well. Bake at 375° for 15 minutes or until egg is completely set and top is golden brown. **Yield:** 1 serving.

—————— ☕ ☕ ☕ ——————

Beef Patties with Gravy

This tasty entree makes a quick and hearty meal when served over mashed potatoes with a salad or veggie on the side. —Sharon Manus, Smyrna, Tennessee

> 1 egg
> 1/2 cup soft bread crumbs
> 1 tablespoon finely chopped onion
> 1/2 pound lean ground beef
> 1 can (10-3/4 ounces) condensed golden mushroom soup, undiluted
> 2/3 cup water
> 1/2 cup sliced fresh mushrooms
> Hot cooked noodles, rice *or* mashed potatoes

In a bowl, combine the egg, bread crumbs and onion. Crumble beef over mixture and mix well. Shape into two patties. In a skillet, cook patties until browned on both sides. In a bowl, combine the soup, water and mushrooms; pour over patties. Bring to a boil. Reduce heat; cover and simmer until meat is no longer pink. Serve over noodles, rice or potatoes. **Yield:** 2 servings.

Cashew Pear Melts

Pears, cashews and melted cheese top slices of cinnamon-raisin bread in this out-of-the-ordinary entree. These open-faced sandwiches make a yummy main course for breakfast or brunch. They're great for snacking, too. —Amy Renfroe, Key Largo, Florida

4 slices cinnamon-raisin *or* cinnamon-swirl bread

1 tablespoon butter *or* margarine, softened
1/4 cup chopped cashews
2 to 3 medium ripe pears, sliced
4 slices Colby *or* Monterey Jack cheese

Place bread on a baking sheet. Spread with butter; top with cashews, pears and cheese. Broil 4 in. from the heat for 1-2 minutes or until cheese is melted. **Yield:** 2 servings.

DINNER DUET. Delectable meal for two features Ham with Currant Sauce, Rosemary Green Beans and Small Batch Popovers (shown above).

TASTY TRIMMINGS like Batter-Fried Fish, Fruit 'n' Veggie Salad and Individual Peach Cobbler (shown above) will make the holiday season very merry.

Batter-Fried Fish

(Pictured above)

Whether I'm fixing cod fillets or my husband's catch of the day, this batter makes the fish fry up golden and crispy. Club soda gives it a different twist.
—Nancy Johnson, Connersville, Indiana

    1/2 **pound fresh *or* frozen cod fillets**
    2 **tablespoons all-purpose flour**
    2 to 3 **tablespoons cornstarch**
    1/4 **teaspoon *each* garlic powder,**
        onion powder, salt, cayenne pepper
        and paprika
    1/8 **teaspoon dried oregano**
    1/8 **teaspoon dried thyme**
    1/3 **cup club soda**
Oil for frying
    1/4 **cup orange marmalade**
    1 to 2 **tablespoons prepared horseradish**

Rinse fillets in cold water; pat dry. Coat with flour. In a shallow bowl, combine the cornstarch, seasonings and soda. In a heavy skillet, heat 1 in. of oil. Dip floured fillets into batter; fry over medium heat for 2-3 minutes on each side or until the fish flakes easily with a fork. Combine marmalade and horseradish; spoon over fish. **Yield:** 2 servings.

Fruit 'n' Veggie Salad

(Pictured at left)

This salad, which combines vegetables, fruit and a sweet-tart dressing, is a tasty change from the ordinary.
—*Jean Conway, Anaheim, California*

    2 tablespoons olive *or* vegetable oil
    1 tablespoon cider vinegar
    1 tablespoon honey
  1/4 teaspoon salt
  3/4 cup torn fresh spinach
  1/3 cup chopped apple
  1/4 cup broccoli florets
    2 tablespoons raisins
    2 dried apricots, chopped
    1 tablespoon sunflower kernels
    2 teaspoons sesame seeds, toasted
    1 teaspoon lemon juice

In a jar with a tight-fitting lid, combine the oil, vinegar, honey and salt; shake well. In a small bowl, combine the remaining ingredients. Drizzle with dressing and toss to coat. **Yield:** 1 serving.

Individual Peach Cobbler

(Pictured at left)

For a comforting old-fashioned treat, try this yummy peach cobbler. —*Doris Heath*
Franklin, North Carolina

1-1/2 teaspoons cornstarch
    1 tablespoon cold water
    1 can (8-1/2 ounces) sliced peaches, undrained
  1/2 cup biscuit/baking mix
    2 teaspoons sugar
    2 tablespoons milk
    1 tablespoon vegetable oil
Vanilla ice cream

In a small saucepan, combine cornstarch and water until smooth; stir in peaches. Bring to a boil; cook and stir for 1 minute or until thickened. Pour into two greased 8-oz. custard cups.

In a small bowl, combine biscuit mix and sugar; stir in milk and oil just until moistened. Drop by teaspoonfuls over hot peaches. Bake, uncovered, at 400° for 18-22 minutes or until topping is golden. Serve with ice cream. **Yield:** 2 servings.

Spaghetti Fish Supper

This colorful blend of fish, vegetables and pasta in a creamy sauce is so satisfying. I've also substituted cooked chicken for the fish, and it's just as good.
—*Charolette Westfall, Houston, Texas*

    4 green onions, chopped
    5 garlic cloves, minced
    2 tablespoons olive *or* vegetable oil
    1 can (14-1/2 ounces) chicken broth
    2 tablespoons dried parsley flakes
  1/2 teaspoon salt
  1/4 teaspoon pepper
  1/4 teaspoon ground cumin
    2 tablespoons cornstarch
  1/2 cup apple juice
  1/2 pound fresh *or* frozen orange roughy, haddock *or* red snapper fillets, thawed and cut into 1-inch pieces
    1 medium tomato, seeded and chopped
    1 cup chopped fresh broccoli florets
    8 ounces uncooked thin spaghetti
  1/4 cup sliced ripe olives

In a large skillet, saute onions and garlic in oil until tender. Stir in the broth, parsley, salt, pepper and cumin. Cover and simmer for 2 minutes. Combine cornstarch and apple juice until smooth; pour into the skillet. Cook and stir for 1-2 minutes or until thickened.

Stir in the fish, tomato and broccoli. Cover and cook for 2 minutes or until fish easily flakes with a fork. Meanwhile, cook spaghetti according to package directions; drain and toss with olives. Top with fish mixture. **Yield:** 2 servings.

Chicken Rice Hot Dish

My mother used to make this comforting main dish to serve to a group. When she became widowed, she converted the recipe to serve just herself.
—*Laurie Hobart, Wisconsin Rapids, Wisconsin*

  1/4 cup thinly sliced celery
    3 tablespoons chopped onion
    2 tablespoons butter *or* margarine
    1 cup chicken broth
    1 medium carrot, halved and thinly sliced
  1/3 cup uncooked long grain rice
  1/4 teaspoon salt
Dash pepper
  1/2 cup cubed cooked chicken
    1 tablespoon minced fresh parsley

In a small saucepan, saute celery and onion in butter. Add broth, carrot, rice, salt and pepper. Bring to a boil. Reduce heat; cover and simmer for 20 minutes. Stir in chicken and parsley. Cover and simmer 5-10 minutes longer or until rice and vegetables are tender. **Yield:** 1 serving.

Hearty Ham Omelet
(Pictured at far right)

My husband, Bob, and I operate a bed-and-breakfast, so omelets are our "friends". Omelets are sort of the "stew" of eggs—you can add almost any leftover vegetable or meat into the filling. This is one of our favorite combinations. —Charlotte Baillargeon
Hinsdale, Massachusetts

>   3 tablespoons butter *or* margarine, *divided*
>   1 cup diced fully cooked ham
>   1 cup diced cooked potato
>   1/4 cup shredded cheddar cheese
>   1 tablespoon milk
>   1/2 teaspoon prepared horseradish
>   1 bacon strip, cooked and crumbled
>   4 eggs
>   2 tablespoons water
>   1/4 teaspoon salt
> Dash pepper

In a 10-in. nonstick skillet, melt 2 tablespoons of butter over medium heat. Add the ham and potato; cook and stir until the potato is lightly browned. Stir in the cheese, milk, horseradish and bacon; cook until the cheese is melted. Remove from skillet and keep warm.

In the same skillet, melt remaining butter. In a bowl, beat the eggs, water, salt and pepper. Pour into skillet; cook over medium heat. As eggs set, lift the edges, letting uncooked portion flow underneath. When eggs are nearly set, spoon potato mixture over half of the omelet. Fold omelet over filling. Cover and cook for 1-2 minutes or until heated through. **Yield:** 2 servings.

Four-Fruit Compote
(Pictured at far right)

This different and refreshing combination of fruits is a welcome side dish my husband, Jim, and I enjoy with breakfast or lunch. The light dressing lets the goodness of the fruit come through. —Genise Krause
Sturgeon Bay, Wisconsin

> ✓ Uses less fat, sugar or salt. Includes Nutritional Analysis and Diabetic Exchanges.

>   1 can (8 ounces) unsweetened pineapple chunks
>   1 medium pink grapefruit, peeled and sectioned
>   1 medium red apple, cubed
>   1 tablespoon sugar
>   1 teaspoon cornstarch
>   1/8 teaspoon salt
>   1 tablespoon lime juice

Drain pineapple, reserving 1/4 cup juice. In a bowl, combine the pineapple, grapefruit and apple. In a saucepan, combine the sugar, cornstarch and salt. Gradually stir in lime juice and reserved pineapple juice until smooth. Bring to a boil; cook and stir for 1-2 minutes or until thickened. Pour over fruit and toss to coat. Serve immediately. **Yield:** 2 servings.

Nutritional Analysis: One serving (1 cup) equals 145 calories, trace fat (trace saturated fat), 0 cholesterol, 148 mg sodium, 37 g carbohydrate, 4 g fiber, 1 g protein. **Diabetic Exchange:** 2-1/2 fruit.

Applesauce Oat Muffins
(Pictured at right)

You can enjoy delicious muffins without having to make a dozen or more at a time. This recipe proves it. —Cassandra Corridon, Frederick, Maryland

> ✓ Uses less fat, sugar or salt. Includes Nutritional Analysis and Diabetic Exchanges.

>   1/2 cup all-purpose flour
>   1/4 cup quick-cooking oats
>   3 tablespoons brown sugar
>   1 teaspoon baking powder
>   1/4 teaspoon ground cinnamon
>   1/8 teaspoon salt
>   1 egg
>   1/4 cup milk
>   2 tablespoons unsweetened applesauce
>   1 tablespoon canola oil

In a bowl, combine the first six ingredients. In another bowl, combine the egg, milk, applesauce and oil. Stir into dry ingredients just until moistened. Fill four greased muffin cups two-thirds full. Bake at 400° for 12-15 minutes or until a toothpick comes out clean. Cool for 5 minutes before removing from pan to a wire rack. Serve warm. **Yield:** 4 muffins.

Nutritional Analysis: One muffin (prepared with fat-free milk) equals 173 calories, 5 g fat (1 g saturated fat), 53 mg cholesterol, 160 mg sodium, 27 g carbohydrate, 1 g fiber, 5 g protein. **Diabetic Exchanges:** 1-1/2 starch, 1 fat.

Solo Teriyaki Chicken

A simple marinade flavors the chicken nicely in this meal-in-one rice dish. I keep meals interesting for myself by cooking creatively. —Bill Hilbrich
St. Cloud, Minnesota

>   2 tablespoons plus 3/4 cup chicken broth, *divided*
>   1 tablespoon soy sauce

MORNING STARS. A Hearty Ham Omelet, Four-Fruit Compote and Applesauce Oat Muffins (shown above) make a terrific breakfast for two.

    1 garlic clove, minced
    1 teaspoon sugar
1/4 teaspoon ground ginger *or* 1 teaspoon minced fresh gingerroot
1/4 pound boneless skinless chicken breast, cubed
    1 teaspoon vegetable oil
1/3 cup uncooked long grain rice
    1 jar (4-1/2 ounces) sliced mushrooms, drained

In a resealable plastic bag, combine 2 tablespoons broth, soy sauce, garlic, sugar and ginger; add chicken. Seal bag and turn to coat; refrigerate for 30 minutes.

    Drain and discard marinade. In a small skillet, brown chicken cubes in oil. Stir in the rice, mushrooms and remaining broth. Bring to a boil. Reduce heat; cover and simmer for 12-17 minutes or until chicken juices run clear and the rice is tender. **Yield:** 1 serving.

Warm Chicken Spinach Salad

(Pictured below)

Since my husband, Bob, and I are empty nesters, I'm always looking for quick, healthy and eye-appealing dishes like this one for the two of us. —Shirley Glaab Hattiesburg, Mississippi

> 3 cups torn fresh spinach
> 1 can (11 ounces) mandarin oranges, drained
> 1/2 cup sliced fresh mushrooms
> 3 thin slices red onion, halved
> 1/2 pound boneless skinless chicken breasts, cut into strips
> 1/4 cup chopped walnuts

> 2 tablespoons olive *or* vegetable oil
> 2 teaspoons cornstarch
> 1/2 teaspoon ground ginger
> 1/4 cup orange juice
> 1/4 cup red wine vinegar *or* cider vinegar

On two salad plates, arrange spinach, oranges, mushrooms and onion; set aside. In a skillet, saute chicken and walnuts in oil until chicken is no longer pink.

In a small bowl, combine the cornstarch, ginger, orange juice and vinegar until smooth; stir into the chicken mixture. Bring to a boil; cook and stir for 2 minutes or until thickened and bubbly. Pour over salads and serve immediately. **Yield:** 2 servings.

DOUBLY DELICIOUS. Mouth-watering menu features Warm Chicken Spinach Salad, Cheddar Biscuit Cups and Soup for Two (shown above).

Cheddar Biscuit Cups
(Pictured at left)

It takes only four ingredients to stir up these tender cheddar biscuits. You can easily double the recipe if needed. —_Sara Dukes, Bartow, Georgia_

- 1 cup self-rising flour*
- 1/2 cup shredded cheddar cheese
- 1/2 cup milk
- 2 tablespoons mayonnaise

In a small bowl, combine the flour and cheese. Stir in milk and mayonnaise just until moistened. Fill five greased muffin cups two-thirds full. Fill empty muffin cups halfway with water. Bake at 425° for 17-20 minutes or until golden brown. **Yield:** 5 biscuits.

*Editor's Note: As a substitute for 1 cup of self-rising flour, place 1-1/2 teaspoons baking powder and 1/2 teaspoon salt in a measuring cup. Add all-purpose flour to measure 1 cup.

Soup for Two
(Pictured at left)

This colorful soup is loaded with old-fashioned goodness. The flavorful broth is chock-full of veggies, chicken and macaroni. —_Margery Bryan_
Royal City, Washington

✓ Uses less fat, sugar or salt. Includes Nutritional Analysis and Diabetic Exchanges.

- 1/2 cup chopped onion
- 1/2 cup chopped carrot
- 1 tablespoon butter _or_ stick margarine
- 1 can (14-1/2 ounces) chicken broth
- 2/3 cup cubed cooked chicken
- 1/2 cup cauliflowerets
- 1/2 cup canned kidney beans, rinsed and drained
- 1/4 cup uncooked elbow macaroni
- 1 cup torn fresh spinach
- 1/8 teaspoon pepper
- Seasoned salad croutons, optional

In a saucepan, saute onion and carrot in butter for 4 minutes. Stir in the broth, chicken, cauliflower, beans and macaroni. Bring to a boil. Reduce heat; cover and simmer for 15-20 minutes or until macaroni and vegetables are tender. Add spinach and pepper; cook and stir until spinach is wilted. Garnish with croutons if desired. **Yield:** 2 servings.

Nutritional Analysis: One 1-1/2-cup serving (calculated without croutons) equals 263 calories, 7 g fat (4 g saturated fat), 48 mg cholesterol, 888 mg sodium, 28 g carbohydrate, 5 g fiber, 22 g protein. **Diabetic Exchanges:** 2 lean meat, 1-1/2 starch, 1 vegetable.

Pork 'n' Potato Dinner

This comforting meal-in-one skillet dish is a delicious down-home dinner for two. —_Doris Heath_
Franklin, North Carolina

- 2 bone-in pork loin chops (1 inch thick)
- 1 tablespoon all-purpose flour
- 1 tablespoon vegetable oil
- 2 tablespoons plus 1-1/2 teaspoons grated Parmesan cheese, _divided_
- 1/8 teaspoon pepper
- 2 medium potatoes, thinly sliced
- 1 medium onion, thinly sliced
- 1 teaspoon beef bouillon granules
- 1/2 cup boiling water
- 1-1/2 teaspoons lemon juice

Coat pork chops with flour. In a skillet over medium-high heat, brown chops in oil on both sides. Combine 1 tablespoon Parmesan cheese and pepper; sprinkle over chops. Arrange potato and onion slices over chops. Sprinkle with 1 tablespoon Parmesan cheese.

Dissolve bouillon in boiling water; stir in lemon juice. Pour over chops. Sprinkle with the remaining Parmesan cheese. Cover and simmer for 18-22 minutes or until meat juices run clear. **Yield:** 2 servings.

Oatmeal Pancakes

This recipe yields a short stack of oat pancakes that's perfect for one or two. I measure out the dry ingredients for individual batches in resealable bags, then just combine with an egg, buttermilk and butter for a quick meal. —_Florence Groves_
Vancouver, Washington

- 3/4 cup quick-cooking oats
- 1/2 cup all-purpose flour
- 1/2 teaspoon baking soda
- 1/2 teaspoon sugar
- 1 egg
- 1 cup buttermilk
- 3 tablespoons butter _or_ margarine, melted

In a bowl, combine the oats, flour, baking soda and sugar. Combine the egg, buttermilk and butter; stir into the dry ingredients just until moistened. Pour batter by 1/3 cupfuls onto a greased hot griddle. Turn when bubbles form on top; cook until second side is golden brown. **Yield:** 7 pancakes.

Mushroom Strip Steaks

(Pictured at far right)

My husband and I enjoy the mouth-watering combination of beef, mushrooms, onions and cheese in this easy recipe. —Kay Riedel, Topeka, Kansas

> 2 boneless New York strip steaks (about 1/2 pound)*
> 1 to 2 tablespoons vegetable oil
> 1 can (10-1/2 ounces) condensed French onion soup, undiluted
> 1 jar (6 ounces) sliced mushrooms, drained
> 1/2 cup shredded mozzarella cheese

In a large skillet over medium-high heat, cook steaks in oil for 4-6 minutes on each side or until meat reaches desired doneness (for rare, a meat thermometer should read 140°; medium, 160°; well-done, 170°). Drain. Pour soup and mushrooms over steaks; sprinkle with cheese. Cover and cook for 2-4 minutes.

*Editor's Note: Steak may be known as strip steak, Kansas City steak, Ambassador steak or boneless Club steak in your region.

———— ☕ ☕ ☕ ————

Sesame Brussels Sprouts

(Pictured at far right)

I just love brussels sprouts. Prepared this way, they're nicely seasoned and get a bit of crunch from sesame seeds. —Melanie DuLac, Worcester, Massachusetts

☑ Uses less fat, sugar or salt. Includes Nutritional Analysis and Diabetic Exchanges.

> 1/2 pound fresh brussels sprouts, halved
> 1-1/4 cups water, *divided*
> 1 teaspoon chicken bouillon granules
> 1 teaspoon sugar
> 1 teaspoon cornstarch
> 4 teaspoons soy sauce
> 2 garlic cloves, minced
> 1 teaspoon sesame seeds, toasted

In a large saucepan, cook brussels sprouts in 1 cup water and bouillon for 6-8 minutes or until tender; drain and keep warm. In the same pan, combine the sugar, cornstarch, soy sauce, garlic and remaining water until blended. Bring to a boil over medium heat; cook and stir for 1 minute or until thickened. Add sprouts; toss to coat. Sprinkle with sesame seeds. **Yield:** 2 servings.

Nutritional Analysis: One 1/2-cup serving (prepared with reduced-sodium soy sauce) equals 88 calories, 1 g fat (trace saturated fat), trace cholesterol, 1,008 mg sodium, 16 g carbohydrate, 4 g fiber, 5 g protein. **Diabetic Exchange:** 3 vegetable.

Peanut Butter Cream Parfaits

(Pictured at right)

My husband and I think these cool creamy treats taste similar to a peanut butter pie, but they're so much easier to make for two. —Debbie Roberts
Lake City, Minnesota

> 1 carton (8 ounces) frozen whipped topping, thawed
> 1/2 cup peanut butter
> 18 milk chocolate kisses

In a bowl, stir half of the whipped topping into peanut butter. Stir in the remaining topping until blended. Set aside two chocolate kisses; coarsely chop the remaining chocolates.

Divide a third of the topping mixture between two parfait glasses; top each with a fourth of the chopped chocolate. Repeat layers. Top with remaining topping mixture and reserved kisses. Chill until serving. **Yield:** 2 servings.

———— ☕ ☕ ☕ ————

Little Lemon Meringue Pies

Since our sons went off to college, I'm back to cooking for just the two of us. This recipe is perfect for a couple. —Kathy Zielicke, Fond du Lac, Wisconsin

> 1/3 cup all-purpose flour
> 1/8 teaspoon salt
> 1 tablespoon shortening
> 1 tablespoon cold butter (no substitutes)
> 1 teaspoon cold water
> **FILLING:**
> 1/3 cup sugar
> 1 tablespoon cornstarch
> 1/8 teaspoon salt
> 1/2 cup cold water
> 1 egg yolk, beaten
> 2 tablespoons lemon juice
> 1 tablespoon butter
> **MERINGUE:**
> 1 egg white
> 1/8 teaspoon cream of tartar
> 2 tablespoons sugar

In a bowl, combine flour and salt; cut in shortening and butter until crumbly. Gradually add water, tossing with a fork until dough forms a ball. Divide in half. Roll each portion into a 5-in. circle. Transfer to two 10-oz. custard cups. Press dough 1-1/8 in. up sides of cups. Place on a baking sheet. Bake at 425° for 7-10 minutes or until golden brown.

In a saucepan, combine sugar, cornstarch and salt. Gradually stir in cold water until smooth. Cook and stir over medium heat until thickened and bubbly. Reduce heat; cook and stir 2 minutes more. Remove from the heat. Stir half of hot filling into egg yolk; return all to the pan. Bring to a gentle boil; cook and stir for 2 minutes. Remove from the heat; stir in lemon juice and butter. Pour into pastry shells.

In a small mixing bowl, beat egg white and cream of tartar on medium speed until soft peaks form. Gradually beat in the sugar, 1 tablespoon at a time, on high until stiff peaks form. Spread evenly over hot lemon filling, sealing edges to crust. Bake at 350° for 15-20 minutes or until the meringue is golden brown. Cool on a wire rack for 1 hour; refrigerate for at least 3 hours before serving. **Yield:** 2 servings.

SMALL-QUANTITY RECIPES like Mushroom Strip Steaks, Sesame Brussels Sprouts and Peanut Butter Cream Parfaits (shown below) satisfy hearty appetites.

1/2 cup shredded carrot
1 tablespoon finely chopped green pepper
1/4 cup mayonnaise
2 tablespoons milk
1 teaspoon snipped chives
1 teaspoon cider vinegar
1/4 teaspoon salt
Dash pepper
Lettuce leaves, optional

In a bowl, combine the cauliflower, celery, carrot and green pepper. In another bowl, combine the mayonnaise, milk, chives, vinegar, salt and pepper; mix well. Pour over the vegetables and toss to coat. Serve on top of lettuce leaves if desired. **Yield:** 2 servings.

Nutritional Analysis: One 3/4-cup serving (prepared with fat-free mayonnaise and fat-free milk) equals 56 calories, trace fat (trace saturated fat), trace cholesterol, 555 mg sodium, 14 g carbohydrate, 2 g fiber, 2 g protein. **Diabetic Exchange:** 2 vegetable.

Fruity Cookie Tarts

(Pictured above and on page 180)

Sliced strawberries, kiwi and whipped topping dress up a soft chocolate chip cookie in this easy recipe. A decorative drizzle of melted chocolate makes the delectable dessert fancy enough for a special dinner.
—Beverly Coyde, Gasport, New York

1/2 cup whipped topping
2 large soft chocolate chip cookies
1 kiwifruit, peeled and sliced
4 large strawberries, sliced
1/4 cup semisweet chocolate chips
1/2 teaspoon shortening

Spread whipped topping over cookies. Top with the kiwi and strawberries. In a microwave or heavy saucepan, melt chocolate chips and shortening; stir until smooth. Drizzle over fruit. Serve immediately. **Yield:** 2 servings.

Crunchy Vegetable Salad

A friend gave me the recipe for this colorful refreshing salad 30 years ago. It's wonderful alongside baked chicken. —*Gusty Crum, Dover, Ohio*

✓ Uses less fat, sugar or salt. Includes Nutritional Analysis and Diabetic Exchanges.

1 cup cauliflowerets
1/2 cup chopped celery

Beef Stir-Fry for One

With tender beef, vegetables and a hint of citrus, this mouth-watering stir-fry is a special meal just for me.
—*Joelle Silva, Fair Oaks, California*

1 teaspoon beef bouillon granules
1/4 cup boiling water
2 teaspoons cornstarch
1 teaspoon sugar
1/4 cup cold water
1 tablespoon cider vinegar
1/4 to 1/2 pound boneless beef sirloin steak, cut into 2-inch strips
1 to 2 tablespoons vegetable oil
2 cups frozen broccoli stir-fry vegetables, thawed
1 green onion, sliced
1 garlic clove, minced
1 teaspoon grated orange peel
Hot cooked rice

In a small bowl, dissolve bouillon in boiling water. In another bowl, combine cornstarch and sugar; gradually stir in cold water, vinegar and bouillon until smooth; set aside.

In a skillet, stir-fry beef in oil until no longer pink. Remove and set aside. Add vegetables, onion and garlic to skillet; stir-fry until crisp-tender. Stir bouillon mixture and add to pan. Bring to a boil; cook and stir for 1-2 minutes or until thickened. Return beef to pan; cook until vegetables are tender and beef is heated through. Stir in orange peel. Serve over rice. **Yield:** 1 serving.

Chive Mushroom Soup

I try to serve this rich savory soup at least once a month during our cold winters. It's quick to make and has wonderful fresh mushroom flavor.
—Laurie Suhrke, Plymouth, Wisconsin

- **1 cup finely chopped fresh mushrooms**
- **1/4 cup butter *or* margarine**
- **2 tablespoons all-purpose flour**
- **1/4 teaspoon salt**
- **1/8 teaspoon ground mustard**
- **1 cup chicken broth**
- **1 cup half-and-half cream**
- **2 tablespoons snipped chives**

In a saucepan, saute mushrooms in butter until tender. Stir in flour, salt and mustard until blended; gradually stir in broth. Bring to a boil; cook and stir for 2 minutes. Reduce heat; stir in the cream and chives. Cook 5 minutes longer or until heated through. **Yield:** 2 servings.

— ☕ ☕ ☕ —

Pork Chops with Rhubarb

A tart fruity sauce made from rhubarb makes these moist tender chops extra special.   —Bonnie Bufford Nicholson, Pennsylvania

- **1 tablespoon all-purpose flour**
- **Salt and pepper to taste**
- **2 bone-in pork loin chops (1/2 to 3/4 inch thick)**
- **2 tablespoons butter *or* margarine**
- **1/2 pound fresh *or* frozen rhubarb, chopped**
- **1 tablespoon honey**
- **1/8 teaspoon ground cinnamon**
- **1-1/2 teaspoons minced fresh parsley**

In a large resealable plastic bag, combine the flour, salt and pepper; add pork chops and shake to coat. In a skillet, cook the chops in butter until juices run clear. Remove and keep warm. Add the rhubarb, honey and cinnamon to the skillet; cook until rhubarb is tender. Serve over pork chops. Sprinkle with parsley. **Yield:** 2 servings.

— ☕ ☕ ☕ —

Chili for Two

(Pictured at right and on page 180)

This flavorful chili is still thick and hearty even though it makes a small batch. I serve it with a salad of grapefruit and avocado slices.   —Norma Grogg St. Louis, Missouri

- **1/4 pound ground beef**
- **1/4 cup chopped onion**

- **1 garlic clove, minced**
- **1 can (15-1/2 ounces) chili beans, undrained**
- **1 can (14-1/2 ounces) diced tomatoes, undrained**
- **1-1/2 teaspoons chili powder**
- **1/2 teaspoon ground cumin**

In a saucepan, cook beef, onion and garlic over medium heat until meat is no longer pink; drain. Stir in the remaining ingredients; bring to a boil. Reduce heat; cover and simmer for 10-15 minutes or until heated through. **Yield:** 2 servings.

— ☕ ☕ ☕ —

Apricot Cows

These creamy milk shakes have a fruity twist that's an appealing change from the more traditional chocolate or strawberry flavor. They're a real treat.
—Sharon Mensing, Greenfield, Iowa

- **1-1/2 cups apricot nectar, chilled**
- **1 cup vanilla ice cream**
- **1 tablespoon nonfat dry milk powder, optional**
- **1 tablespoon sugar**
- **Whipped topping, optional**

In a blender, combine apricot nectar, ice cream, milk powder if desired and sugar; cover and process until smooth. Stir if necessary. Pour into chilled glasses. Garnish with whipped topping if desired. Serve immediately. **Yield:** 2 servings.

nine! I'm up to the task, though, when dishes like this are the satisfying result.
—Virginia Dishman
Lansing, Michigan

   1 **bacon strip, diced**
   2 **tablespoons chopped onion**
   1 **tablespoon cider vinegar**
   1 **tablespoon water**
1-1/4 **teaspoons sugar**
  1/4 **teaspoon salt**
Dash pepper
   2 **cups shredded cabbage**
   1 **small tart apple, peeled and chopped**
  1/4 **cup sour cream**

In a skillet, cook bacon over medium heat until crisp. Remove to paper towel. In the drippings, saute onion until tender. Add the vinegar, water, sugar, salt and pepper; cook until bubbly. Stir in cabbage and apple; toss to coat. Cover and cook for 5-6 minutes or until cabbage is tender. Stir in sour cream; heat through (do not boil). Sprinkle with bacon. **Yield:** 1 serving.

Cranberry Waldorf Salad

(Pictured above and on page 180)

A small-quantity salad can still be special, as this recipe proves. I like the crisp apple and celery and chewy dried cranberries in a delightful dressing.
—DeLoris Nance, Auburn, Washington

✓ Uses less fat, sugar or salt. Includes Nutritional Analysis and Diabetic Exchanges.

   1 **medium apple, chopped**
   1 **celery rib, chopped**
  1/2 **cup dried cranberries**
  1/3 **cup mayonnaise**
   1 **tablespoon sugar**
   2 **teaspoons lemon juice**

In a serving bowl, combine the apple, celery and cranberries. In a small bowl, combine mayonnaise, sugar and lemon juice. Pour over apple mixture and toss gently to combine. **Yield:** 2 servings.
   Nutritional Analysis: One 1-cup serving (prepared with fat-free mayonnaise) equals 186 calories, trace fat (trace saturated fat), 0 cholesterol, 295 mg sodium, 48 g carbohydrate, 5 g fiber, trace protein.

Creamed Cabbage

This rich comforting cabbage dish has plenty of old-fashioned goodness. I admit, it has been a challenge to cook small quantities since I once fed a family of

Curried Lamb Chops

Treat yourself and someone special to a fancy dinner with these moist tender chops. The mild curry and apple flavors are wonderful with lamb.
—Imelda Cauley
Delaware, Ohio

   4 **bone-in loin lamb chops (about 3/4 pound)**
   1 **tablespoon vegetable oil**
  1/2 **cup chopped onion**
  1/2 **cup diced peeled tart apple**
  1/2 **teaspoon curry powder**
   4 **teaspoons all-purpose flour**
  1/2 **teaspoon salt**
  1/2 **teaspoon sugar**
  1/4 **teaspoon ground mustard**
1-1/3 **cups chicken broth**
   2 **tablespoons lemon juice**
Hot cooked rice

In a large skillet, brown lamb chops on both sides in oil. Remove and keep warm. In the same skillet, saute the onion, apple and curry until tender. Combine flour, salt, sugar and mustard; add to the pan. Gradually stir in broth and lemon juice until blended. Bring to a boil over medium heat; cook and stir for 2 minutes. Reduce heat.
   Return chops to the skillet; cover and simmer for 15 minutes, turning once, or until meat reaches desired doneness (for rare, a meat thermometer should read 140°; medium, 160°; well-done, 170°). Serve over rice. **Yield:** 2 servings.

Beef Paprika

My husband and I loved this savory dish when we first sampled it at a party. Of course, I had to have the recipe, which I downsized to serve just the two of us.
—*Nancy Nielsen, Orange, Connecticut*

      3/4 **pound beef stew meat, cut into 3/4-inch cubes**
        2 **teaspoons vegetable oil**
        1 **small onion, thinly sliced**
        1 **garlic clove, minced**
      3/4 **cup water,** *divided*
      1/4 **cup ketchup**
        1 **teaspoon brown sugar**
      3/4 **teaspoon paprika**
      3/4 **teaspoon Worcestershire sauce**
      1/2 **teaspoon salt**
      1/4 **teaspoon Dijon mustard**
Dash cayenne pepper
        1 **tablespoon all-purpose flour**
Hot cooked noodles

In a large saucepan, brown beef in oil on all sides. Add onion and garlic; cook until onion is tender. Add 1/2 cup water, ketchup, brown sugar, paprika, Worcestershire sauce, salt, mustard and cayenne; mix well. Bring to a boil. Reduce heat; cover and simmer for 1-1/2 to 1-3/4 hours or until the beef is tender.

Combine flour and remaining water until smooth; gradually stir into stew. Bring to a boil; cook and stir for 2 minutes or until thickened. Serve over noodles. **Yield:** 2 servings.

───── 🏆 🏆 🏆 ─────

Pork Chop Pear Skillet

My mother and grandmother taught me how to prepare easy meals that look and taste gourmet, like Mom's recipe for pork chops and pears. Seasoned with honey, ginger, lemon and pineapple juice, the yummy sauce adds delightful flavor to this distinctive dish.
—*Dawn Haggerty, Canyon Lake, California*

        2 **tablespoons pineapple juice**
        2 **tablespoons honey**
        2 **tablespoons water,** *divided*
    1-1/2 **teaspoons lemon juice**
Dash ground ginger
        1 **medium ripe pear, sliced**
        2 **bone-in pork loin chops (1/2 inch thick)**
        1 **tablespoon vegetable oil**
      1/8 **teaspoon salt**
Dash pepper
      3/4 **teaspoon cornstarch**

In a small bowl, combine the pineapple juice, honey, 1 tablespoon water, lemon juice and ginger. Stir

in pear slices; set aside. In a skillet over medium-high heat, brown pork chops in oil on both sides. Sprinkle with salt and pepper. Reduce heat. Pour pear mixture over chops. Bring to a boil. Reduce heat; cover and simmer for 3-4 minutes or until meat juices run clear.

Remove pork and pears with a slotted spoon and keep warm. Combine cornstarch and remaining water until smooth; stir into cooking juices. Bring to a boil; cook and stir for 1 minute or until thickened. Serve over pork and pears. **Yield:** 2 servings.

───── 🏆 🏆 🏆 ─────

Classic Stuffed Peppers

Classic stuffed peppers are pared down for two, and the result is a savory and satisfying dish that tastes so delicious, you'll want to double the recipe and serve it to guests. —*Donna Brockett, Kingfisher, Oklahoma*

✓ Uses less fat, sugar or salt. Includes Nutritional Analysis and Diabetic Exchanges.

        2 **medium green peppers**
        1 **egg, lightly beaten**
        1 **cup meatless spaghetti sauce,** *divided*
      1/4 **cup uncooked instant rice**
        1 **tablespoon finely chopped onion**
      1/4 **teaspoon salt**
      1/2 **teaspoon Worcestershire sauce**
Dash pepper
      1/2 **pound uncooked lean ground beef**

Cut tops off peppers and discard; remove seeds. In a large saucepan, cook peppers in boiling water for 5 minutes. Drain and rinse in cold water.

In a bowl, combine the egg, 1/4 cup of the spaghetti sauce, rice, onion, salt, Worcestershire sauce and pepper. Crumble beef over the mixture and mix well. Stuff into peppers. Place in an ungreased 1-1/2-qt. baking dish. Pour the remaining sauce over peppers. Cover and bake at 350° for 50-55 minutes or until a meat thermometer reads 160°. **Yield:** 2 servings.

Nutritional Analysis: One serving equals 375 calories, 15 g fat (5 g saturated fat), 146 mg cholesterol, 987 mg sodium, 29 g carbohydrate, 5 g fiber, 30 g protein. **Diabetic Exchanges:** 4 lean meat, 2 vegetable, 1 starch, 1/2 fat.

🥄 *Green Pepper Pointer*

To seed a green pepper, hold it tightly and slam the stem end down on the counter. This will loosen the seed core, allowing you to easily pull it out.

FINE FARE for a pair makes up this appetizing meal of Orange-Glazed Pork Chops, Summer Squash Stir-Fry and Tortilla Fruit Pie (shown above).

Orange-Glazed Pork Chops

(Pictured above and on page 180)

This recipe is not only a snap to prepare, it's delicious, too. A sweet orange glaze perks up these tender pork chops, and there's plenty of sauce to flavor the accompanying rice as well. —Nila Towler, Baird, Texas

  2 boneless pork loin chops (1/2 inch thick)
1/2 teaspoon salt
1/8 teaspoon pepper
  1 tablespoon vegetable oil
1/2 cup packed brown sugar
1/2 cup orange juice concentrate
Hot cooked rice

Sprinkle pork chops with salt and pepper. In a skillet over medium-high heat, brown chops in oil on both sides. Combine brown sugar and orange juice concentrate; pour over the chops. Bring to a boil. Reduce heat; cover and simmer for 7-9 minutes or until the meat juices run clear. Serve pork and sauce over rice. **Yield:** 2 servings.

Summer Squash Stir-Fry

(Pictured above and on page 180)

With an abundance of squash, green peppers, tomatoes and onion from our garden, this recipe is easy and economical. —Doris Stein, Ojai, California

  **1 small zucchini *or* yellow summer squash,
cut into 1/4-inch slices**

1 small green pepper, julienned
1 small onion, chopped
1 tablespoon butter *or* margarine
1 medium tomato, peeled and chopped
1/2 cup cubed fully cooked ham, optional
Salt and pepper to taste
1/2 cup shredded cheddar cheese, optional

In a skillet, saute the zucchini, green pepper and onion in butter until crisp-tender. Stir in the tomato and ham if desired; heat through. Sprinkle with salt and pepper. Remove from the heat. Top with cheese if desired; cover and let stand until cheese is melted. **Yield:** 2 servings.

— 🍴 🍴 🍴 —

Tortilla Fruit Pie

(Pictured at left and on page 180)

Here's a fun no-fuss way to fix dessert for one. Simply cook fresh peach slices with lemon juice, brown sugar and almond extract and bake inside a folded flour tortilla. —Ann Sobotka, Glendale, Arizona

3 teaspoons butter *or* margarine, *divided*
1 tablespoon brown sugar
2 teaspoons lemon juice
1/8 teaspoon almond extract
1 large ripe peach, peeled and sliced
1 flour tortilla (10 inches)
1 teaspoon sugar

In a small saucepan, melt 2 teaspoons butter. Stir in the brown sugar, lemon juice and extract. Add peach slices. Cook and stir over medium-low heat for 5 minutes.

Place tortilla on an ungreased baking sheet. Spoon peach mixture onto half of tortilla to within 1/2 in. of sides; fold tortilla over. Melt remaining butter; brush over the top. Sprinkle with sugar. Bake at 350° for 15-20 minutes or until golden brown. Cut in half. **Yield:** 1 serving.

— 🍴 🍴 🍴 —

Ham 'n' Cheese Biscuit Twists

I like to serve these tasty twists for lunch with split pea or vegetable soup and a fruit salad. The cheese-enhanced biscuits filled with homemade or deli ham salad also make great snacks. —Marie Kramer
Kirkwood, Missouri

2/3 cup all-purpose flour
3/4 teaspoon baking powder
1/8 teaspoon salt
4 teaspoons shortening
1/2 cup shredded cheddar cheese

1/3 cup milk
1/2 cup ham salad *or* 1 can (4-1/4 ounces) deviled ham spread

In a bowl, combine flour, baking powder and salt. Cut in shortening until the mixture resembles coarse crumbs. Stir in cheese. Stir in milk just until moistened. Turn onto a floured surface; knead 5-6 times. Roll into a 10-in. x 6-in. rectangle.

Spread ham salad over half of dough. Fold dough over to form a 5-in. x 6-in. rectangle; seal edges with water. Cut into six 1-in. strips. Twist strips and place on an ungreased baking sheet. Bake at 400° for 15-18 minutes or until golden brown. **Yield:** 2 servings.

— 🍴 🍴 🍴 —

Sausage-Topped Zucchini

I concocted this pleasing entree, which became my husband's favorite dish after just one bite. Cheese, spaghetti sauce and sausage are mounded on zucchini halves, giving the recipe its zesty Italian accent. —Alice Scollin, Saranac Lake, New York

1/2 pound bulk hot sausage
1 large onion, chopped
1/2 medium green pepper, chopped
1 garlic clove, minced
1 tablespoon olive *or* vegetable oil
1 tablespoon butter *or* margarine
1/4 cup grated Parmesan cheese
1 cup spaghetti sauce, *divided*
2 medium zucchini, cut in half lengthwise
1/4 pound sliced mozzarella cheese

In a skillet, cook sausage until no longer pink; drain. Remove sausage and set aside. In the same skillet, saute onion, green pepper and garlic in oil and butter until tender. Stir in sausage, Parmesan cheese and 1/2 cup of spaghetti sauce.

Place the zucchini halves cut side up in a greased 8-in. square baking dish. Spread with the sausage mixture. Cover and bake at 350° for 35-40 minutes or until the zucchini is tender. Top with cheese and the remaining spaghetti sauce. Bake, uncovered, for 5 minutes or until the cheese is melted. **Yield:** 2 servings.

Picking Zucchini

Choose firm zucchini with bright-colored skin free of spots and bruises. In general, the smaller the squash, the more tender it will be.

Store zucchini in a plastic bag in the refrigerator for no more than 5 days.

'My Mom's Best Meal'

Here, six daughters recall—and share the recipes for—the memorable meals made by their moms that they treasure the most.

— 🥄 🥄 🥄 —

STANDOUT SUPPERS. Clockwise from upper left: Traditional Easter Feast (p. 204), Down-Home Sunday Dinner (p. 208), Italian-Style Spread (p. 216) and Family-Pleasing Fare (p. 212).

Mom's family dinners were something special, but she always outdid herself during the holidays.

By Becky Brunette, Minneapolis, Minnesota

I TREASURE the memory of growing up and having a home-cooked meal every evening and enjoying Mom's extravagant feasts for the holidays.

My mother, Julie Brunette (above, of Green Bay, Wisconsin), is well-known as a wonderful cook and baker. Her talent has long been appreciated by more than just my dad, my brother, Nick, and me. She is a super hostess and shares dishes for many gatherings.

Mom often used to make a little extra for supper, just in case our friends happened to stop by. It's no surprise that they did so frequently, enjoying the good food and company. Mom always made them feel welcome. When I went away to college, her cooking was one of the things I missed the most.

Our Christmas dinners have always been a collection of our family's favorite recipes, including Rice-Stuffed Cornish Hens.

The golden hens are stuffed with a flavorful dressing made from scratch with wild rice, long grain rice, savory pork sausage, onions and celery, just like Mom learned it from her own mother. The Cornish hens are topped with a delicious and pretty apricot glaze.

Green beans are one of the most-requested veggies in our family, and Mom's recipe for Crunchy Green Beans makes them taste even better.

Christmas Wreath Salad is a festive and colorful gelatin side dish that looks as good as it tastes. The deep red color is so pretty sitting on a blanket of fresh greens.

To this day, all of us still make sure to save room for dessert when Mom is baking her yummy Pistachio Cake.

Since I live a distance away now, I can't just pop in for one of Mom's dinners. Recipes like these are truly a taste of home for me. Mom and I hope you enjoy them, too.

🍶 🍶 🍶

PICTURED AT LEFT: Rice-Stuffed Cornish Hens, Crunchy Green Beans, Christmas Wreath Salad and Pistachio Cake (recipes are on the next page).

tie drumsticks together. Bake, uncovered, at 350° for 45 minutes.

In a small saucepan, bring preserves and remaining water to a boil. Pour over hens. Bake 35-40 minutes longer, basting occasionally, until a meat thermometer reads 180° for hens and 160° for stuffing. Place baking dish of stuffing in the oven for the last 35-40 minutes of hens' baking time. **Yield:** 6 servings.

Crunchy Green Beans

Green beans taste terrific all by themselves, but my mom has managed to improve on Mother Nature! She adds mushrooms, celery and crisp slivered almonds to dress up the popular green vegetable.

  4 cups fresh *or* frozen green beans, cut
    into 2-inch pieces
1-1/2 cups diced celery
1-1/3 cups sliced fresh mushrooms
  3 tablespoons vegetable oil
  1 tablespoon cornstarch
  1 cup cold water
  1 tablespoon soy sauce
  1 teaspoon beef bouillon granules
1/2 cup slivered almonds

Place the beans in a large saucepan and cover with water. Bring to a boil; cook, uncovered, for 8-10 minutes or until crisp-tender.

Meanwhile, in a skillet, saute celery and mushrooms in oil until tender. Combine cornstarch, cold water and soy sauce until smooth; stir into celery

Rice-Stuffed Cornish Hens

My mom prepares this impressive-looking entree for the holidays and for other "company's coming" occasions. The savory rice stuffing goes wonderfully with the moist golden hens and sweet apricot glaze. She is often asked for the recipe.

5-1/2 cups water, *divided*
  2 teaspoons chicken bouillon granules
1-1/2 teaspoons salt
  3/4 cup uncooked wild rice
1-1/2 cups uncooked long grain rice
  1 pound bulk pork sausage
1-1/2 cups chopped celery
  3/4 cup chopped onion
  6 Cornish game hens (20 ounces *each*)
  1 jar (12 ounces) apricot preserves

In a large saucepan, bring 5 cups water, bouillon and salt to a boil. Add wild rice. Reduce heat; cover and simmer for 20 minutes. Add long grain rice; cover and simmer 25-30 minutes longer or until rice is tender and water is absorbed.

Meanwhile, in a large skillet, cook the sausage, celery and onion over medium heat until meat is no longer pink and vegetables are tender; drain. Stir in rice mixture. Spoon about 3/4 cup stuffing into each hen. Place remaining stuffing in a greased 2-qt. baking dish; cover and set aside. Place hens breast side up on a rack in a shallow baking pan;

mixture. Stir in bouillon. Bring to a boil over medium heat; cook and stir for 1 minute or until thickened. Drain beans and add to the celery mixture. Stir in almonds. **Yield:** 6 servings.

Christmas Wreath Salad

It's a jolly holiday when Mom makes this cool eye-catching salad. Pecans, pineapple and maraschino cherries are sweet surprises in every serving of this pretty side dish.

> 1 package (6 ounces) strawberry gelatin
> 1 cup boiling water
> 1 can (20 ounces) crushed pineapple
> 1 cup (8 ounces) plain yogurt
> 1 cup chopped pecans, optional
> 1/2 cup red maraschino cherries, halved
> **Lettuce leaves and additional cherries, optional**

In a bowl, dissolve gelatin in boiling water. Refrigerate until partially set, about 30 minutes. Drain pineapple, reserving juice; set pineapple aside. Add enough cold water to juice to measure 1-3/4 cups; stir into gelatin mixture. Whisk in yogurt until smooth. Fold in nuts if desired, cherries and reserved pineapple.

Pour into a 2-qt. ring mold that has been coated with nonstick cooking spray. Refrigerate until set. Unmold onto a lettuce-lined serving plate and garnish with additional cherries if desired. **Yield:** 6 servings.

Pistachio Cake

Mom is well-known for her holiday cookies, candies and cakes. This delicious dessert starts conveniently with a cake mix and instant pudding. You're sure to get requests for second helpings when you serve it.

> 1 package (18-1/4 ounces) white cake mix
> 1 package (3.4 ounces) instant pistachio pudding mix
> 1 cup lemon-lime soda
> 1 cup vegetable oil
> 3 eggs
> 1 cup chopped walnuts
> **FROSTING:**
> 1-1/2 cups cold milk
> 1 package (3.4 ounces) instant pistachio pudding mix
> 1 carton (8 ounces) frozen whipped topping, thawed
> 1/2 cup chopped pistachios, toasted
> **Whole red shell pistachios and fresh mint, optional**

In a mixing bowl, combine the first five ingredients. Beat on medium speed for 2 minutes; stir in walnuts. Pour into a greased 13-in. x 9-in. x 2-in. baking pan. Bake at 350° for 45-50 minutes or until a toothpick inserted near the center comes out clean. Cool on a wire rack.

For frosting, in a mixing bowl, beat milk and pudding mix on low speed for 2 minutes. Fold in the whipped topping. Spread over cake. Sprinkle with pistachios. Refrigerate for about 30 minutes before cutting. Garnish with whole pistachios and mint if desired. Refrigerate leftovers. **Yield:** 12-15 servings.

When we were growing up on the farm, Easter was a time for faith, family and Mom's tasty ham dinner.

By Lorrie Bailey, Pulaski, Iowa

EASTER was a memorable time when I was growing up on our family farm. After coming home from church in the morning, Mom (June Mullins, above) would serve the most terrific Easter dinner later in the afternoon.

Mom was always happy to share a warm smile and some good advice along with her wonderful cooking and baking. She especially loved to make bread and rolls and did so almost weekly to the delight of my dad, us four kids, our spouses and her six grandchildren.

For a special main dish on Easter Day, Mom fixed Pineapple Mustard Ham. Juicy ham slices get mouth-watering zip from the tangy glaze made with ground mustard, pineapple topping and horseradish.

To simplify the day, Mom rounded out the meal with items she could make ahead, like a creamy pota-to casserole, the world's best deviled eggs and Color-ful Vegetable Salad. That eye-catching combination of carrot, celery, tomatoes, broccoli and cauliflower is crisp and refreshing.

The mainstay of this holiday meal was her Hot Cross Buns. We all looked forward to them since Mom fixed these golden rolls only once a year. She used a recipe passed down from her own mother.

Mom's desserts were always spectacular. One of our favorites was Strawberry Satin Pie, made with the fresh-picked fruit of the season. This pie is as pretty as it is scrumptious.

Preparing delicious recipes like these was one of the many ways Mom showed her love for us on special oc-casions and every day of the year. We know she'd be thrilled to have you try them out on your family, too!

PICTURED AT LEFT: Pineapple Mustard Ham, Colorful Vegetable Salad, Hot Cross Buns and Strawberry Satin Pie (recipes are on the next page).

Pineapple Mustard Ham

Sweet and spicy ingredients combine in a fruity glaze to top this delightful ham, which was one of my mom's specialties. Our family enjoyed it many times for Easter. The horseradish and dry mustard in the glaze add delicious zip to the tender ham slices.

 1/2 spiral-sliced *or* semi-boneless fully cooked
     ham (8 to 10 pounds)
 1 jar (12 ounces) apple jelly
 1 jar (12 ounces) pineapple ice cream
     topping
 1 container (1-3/4 ounces) ground mustard
 2 tablespoons prepared horseradish
 1 tablespoon pepper

Place ham on a rack in a shallow roasting pan. Cover and bake at 325° for 1-3/4 hours. In a small bowl, combine the remaining ingredients until blended. Pour over the ham. Bake, uncovered, 30-45 minutes longer or until a meat thermometer reads 140°. **Yield:** 16-20 servings.

Colorful Vegetable Salad

Carrot, celery and tomatoes go so well with broccoli and cauliflower in this crisp refreshing salad with a light vinaigrette dressing. My mom used this popular salad to round out a variety of different meals.

 1 medium head cauliflower, broken into
     florets (8 cups)
 1 medium bunch broccoli, cut into florets
     (5 cups)
 3 large tomatoes, chopped

 1 medium onion, chopped
 2 celery ribs, chopped
 1 medium carrot, shredded
DRESSING:
 3/4 cup vegetable oil
 3 tablespoons lemon juice
 1 teaspoon salt
 1/2 teaspoon sugar
 1/2 teaspoon pepper

In a large salad bowl, combine the cauliflower, broccoli, tomatoes, onion, celery and carrot. In a jar with a tight-fitting lid, combine the dressing ingredients; shake well. Pour over vegetables and toss to coat. Serve immediately. **Yield:** 16-20 servings.

—— 🍷 🍷 🍷 ——

Hot Cross Buns

These golden buns, with a light seasoning from cinnamon and allspice, were a family Easter tradition. My mom made them only once a year using her mother's recipe. Icing crosses make a tasty topping and reflect the meaning of the holiday.

 2 packages (1/4 ounce *each*) active
     dry yeast
 1/4 cup warm water (110° to 115°)
 1 cup warm milk (110° to 115°)
 1/2 cup sugar
 1/4 cup shortening
 2 eggs
 2 teaspoons salt
 1 teaspoon ground cinnamon
 1/4 teaspoon ground allspice
4-1/2 to 5 cups all-purpose flour
 1 cup dried currants
 1 egg white, lightly beaten

ICING:
1-3/4 cups confectioners' sugar
1/2 teaspoon vanilla extract
4 to 6 teaspoons milk

In a mixing bowl, dissolve yeast in warm water. Add the milk, sugar, shortening, eggs, salt, cinnamon, allspice and 3 cups flour. Beat until smooth. Stir in currants and enough remaining flour to form a soft dough. Turn onto a floured surface; knead until smooth and elastic, about 6-8 minutes. Place in a greased bowl, turning once to grease top. Cover and let rise in a warm place until doubled, about 1 hour.

Punch dough down. Cover and let rest for 10 minutes. On a lightly floured surface, roll out to 1/2-in. thickness. Cut with a floured 2-1/2-in. biscuit cutter. Place 2 in. apart on lightly greased baking sheets. Cover and let rise until doubled, about 30 minutes.

Brush with egg white. Bake at 350° for 12-15 minutes or until golden brown. Remove from pans to wire racks to cool. For icing, combine sugar, vanilla and enough milk to achieve piping consistency. Pipe a cross on top of each bun. **Yield:** 2 dozen.

Strawberry Satin Pie

My mom loved to spoil us with tempting desserts like this pretty springtime treat. Toasted sliced almonds sprinkled over the bottom crust, a smooth-as-satin filling and a lovely strawberry glaze make this a memorable pie.

1 pastry shell (9 inches), baked
1/2 cup sliced almonds, toasted
1/2 cup sugar

3 tablespoons all-purpose flour
3 tablespoons cornstarch
1/2 teaspoon salt
2 cups milk
1 egg, lightly beaten
1 teaspoon vanilla extract
1/2 cup whipping cream, whipped
GLAZE:
3 cups fresh strawberries
1 cup water
1/3 cup sugar
2 tablespoons cornstarch
12 drops red food coloring, optional

Cover bottom of pie shell with almonds; set aside. In a saucepan, combine the sugar, flour, cornstarch and salt. Stir in milk until smooth. Bring to a boil; cook and stir for 2 minutes or until thickened. Remove from the heat. Stir a small amount of hot filling into egg. Return all to the pan, stirring constantly. Bring to a gentle boil; cook and stir 2 minutes longer. Remove from the heat. Stir in vanilla. Cool to room temperature. Whisk in whipped cream until blended. Pour into pie shell. Cover and refrigerate for at least 2 hours.

Crush 1 cup of strawberries; set remaining berries aside. In a saucepan, bring crushed berries and water to a boil; cook, uncovered, for 2 minutes. Strain through cheesecloth; discard fruit and set liquid aside to cool.

In another saucepan, combine sugar and cornstarch; gradually stir in berry liquid until blended. Bring to a boil; cook and stir for 2 minutes or until thickened. Stir in food coloring if desired. Cool for 20 minutes. Slice the reserved strawberries; arrange over chilled filling. Pour glaze evenly over berries. Refrigerate for at least 1 hour before serving. **Yield:** 6-8 servings.

Mom's Sunday dinners were especially satisfying when her mouth-watering chicken was on the menu.

By Cindy Kufeldt, Orlando, Florida

I RECALL many wonderful things about my mom's cooking as I was growing up. Mom (Nancy Kay Woodside, above, of Flagler Beach, Florida) often had from-scratch cookies and cakes with a glass of milk ready for my younger brother and me to snack on when we got home from school.

My parents frequently hosted guests for dinner and get-togethers…and my mom is known by many to be an excellent cook. Holidays were always a deliciously special time at our house, and the best menu of the week was typically Sunday dinner.

One of my mom's best Sunday meals begins with Marinated Baked Chicken. The chicken breasts are so tender and juicy, and they produce a wonderful aroma while baking in the oven.

Mushroom Oven Rice is homey and comforting, with lots of fresh mushrooms and celery stirred in. My brother and I rushed to the table when Mom was serving this side dish, which is also wonderful alongside ham.

Special enough for company, Broccoli Casserole is another satisfying side dish. The broccoli is baked with a rich and creamy sauce, then sprinkled with cheese-flavored cracker crumbs. One helping is never enough.

My mom has a great reputation for making delectable desserts. One of my favorites is easy-to-make Cherry Cheese Pie. A lovely combination of cream cheese and cherry pie filling, it's delicious served anytime of year.

I'm so thankful that my husband, Steve, and I and our two children, Seth and Abigail, live close enough to Mom to frequently enjoy her cooking. She and I are thrilled to share these recipes so you can make them for your own family, too.

PICTURED AT LEFT: Marinated Baked Chicken, Mushroom Oven Rice, Broccoli Casserole and Cherry Cheese Pie (recipes are on the next page).

Marinated Baked Chicken

This tender flavorful chicken is one of my mom's specialties. Soy sauce and bottled Italian dressing combine in a mouth-watering marinade that nicely complements the meat.

> 1/2 **cup Italian salad dressing**
> 1/2 **cup soy sauce**
>   6 **bone-in chicken breast halves**
> 1/8 **teaspoon onion salt**
> 1/8 **teaspoon garlic salt**
> **Kale and spiced apple rings, optional**

In a measuring cup, combine salad dressing and soy sauce. Pour 3/4 cup into a large resealable plastic bag; add chicken. Seal the bag and turn to coat; refrigerate for 4 hours or overnight, turning several times. Refrigerate remaining marinade for basting.

Drain chicken, discarding marinade. Place chicken, skin side up, on a rack in a roasting pan. Sprinkle with onion salt and garlic salt. Bake, uncovered, at 350° for 45-60 minutes or until juices run clear and a meat thermometer reads 170°, brushing occasionally with reserved marinade. Garnish platter with kale and apple rings if desired. **Yield:** 6 servings.

Mushroom Oven Rice

When I was growing up, we couldn't wait to get to the table when Mom was serving this delicious rice dish. With lots of fresh mushrooms and celery stirred in, it tastes so good you're sure to want seconds!

>   1 **cup uncooked long grain rice**
> 1/4 **cup butter *or* margarine**
> 1/2 **cup finely chopped celery**
> 1/2 **cup finely chopped onion**
>   1 **cup sliced fresh mushrooms**
>   1 **can (14-1/2 ounces) chicken broth**
> 1/3 **cup water**
>   1 **to 2 tablespoons soy sauce**
>   1 **tablespoon dried parsley flakes**

In a skillet, saute the rice in butter for 2 minutes or until golden brown. Add celery and onion; cook and stir for 2 minutes. Add mushrooms; cook and stir until the celery is tender. Transfer to a greased 1-1/2-qt. baking dish. Stir in the broth, water, soy sauce and parsley. Cover and bake at 350° for 45-50 minutes or until liquid is absorbed and rice is tender. **Yield:** 6 servings.

— 🍷 🍷 🍷 —

Broccoli Casserole

This colorful side dish is one my mom fixes often for Christmas dinner and other special occasions. The broccoli is baked with a rich creamy sauce...and cheese-flavored cracker crumbs are sprinkled over the top. Yum!

> **2 pounds fresh broccoli, cut into florets**
> **1 can (10-3/4 ounces) condensed cream of mushroom soup, undiluted**
> **1/2 cup mayonnaise**
> **1/2 cup shredded cheddar cheese**
> **1 tablespoon lemon juice**
> **1 cup crushed cheese-flavored snack crackers**

Place 1 in. of water and broccoli in a saucepan; bring to a boil. Reduce heat; cover and simmer for 5-8 minutes or just until crisp-tender. Drain and place in a greased 2-qt. baking dish. In a bowl, combine the soup, mayonnaise, cheese and lemon juice. Pour over broccoli. Sprinkle with crushed crackers. Bake, uncovered, at 350° for 25-30 minutes or until heated through. **Yield:** 6-8 servings.

Cherry Cheese Pie

My mom is known for her scrumptious desserts. This easy-to-make pie is one she has served often. It's one of my favorite desserts anytime of year. I love the combination of cream cheese and cherry pie filling.

> **3/4 cup all-purpose flour**
> **3 tablespoons sugar**
> **1/4 teaspoon salt**
> **1/4 cup butter *or* margarine, softened**

> **1 can (21 ounces) cherry pie filling**
> **1 package (8 ounces) cream cheese, softened**
> **1/3 cup sugar**
> **1 egg**
> **1 teaspoon vanilla extract**

In a bowl, combine the flour, sugar and salt. Add butter; stir until combined. Press onto the bottom and up the sides of a 9-in. pie plate. Bake at 350° for 10-12 minutes or until lightly browned. Pour pie filling into crust.

In a mixing bowl, beat cream cheese, sugar, egg and vanilla until smooth. Carefully spread around outside edges of pie, leaving a 3-in. circle of cherries exposed in the center. Bake for 30-35 minutes or until edges begin to brown. Cool on a wire rack. Refrigerate for several hours before serving. **Yield:** 8 servings.

Cooking Chicken

When you're cooking chicken parts, remember that dark meat takes longer to cook than white meat does because of its higher fat content.

Start the dark meat a few minutes before the white—assuming the parts are about the same size; smaller pieces of chicken will cook faster than larger ones. The white meat might be too dry if it is cooked as long as the dark.

Chicken parts should be cooked within 24 hours after being purchased.

Mom's time spent in the kitchen produced delicious results—family-pleasing dishes full of color and flavor.

By Cris O'Brien, Virginia Beach, Virginia

OVER THE YEARS, my mom has spent more time in her kitchen than any other room in the house.

When my two brothers and I were growing up, Mom (Louanne Davis, above, of Jackson, Michigan) made everything from scratch. And she canned the harvest from Dad's garden, so her meals were filled with fruits and vegetables. Because she didn't cater to picky eaters, we learned to enjoy a variety of foods.

In addition to feeding her family, Mom prepared meals for church dinners and, as a Girl Scout leader, taught many young girls how to bake. She went all out when relatives came to visit, lining the counter with yummy treats.

Mom's such an excellent cook that it's difficult to select one "best" meal, but there's a reason Favorite Pork Chops have that name. The tender chops are marinated for several hours, then baked and draped in a zippy red sauce. The whole family loves them.

For her comforting Au Gratin Potatoes, she coats thin potato slices with a rich creamy sauce.

My grandma taught Mom to make meals as colorful as possible. Mom's Bean Medley gets a rainbow of color from green pepper, tomato and four kinds of beans.

Chocolate Cake Roll was reserved for special occasions. No one was allowed to sample this delicious dessert until it was served, but it was definitely worth the wait!

Mom is in her 70s now and still cooks for my dad and herself. I enjoy preparing her recipes for my husband and two teenage sons. My sisters-in-law use Mom's recipes, too. I hope you'll find them just as appetizing as we do.

⸺ 🍵 🍵 🍵 ⸺

PICTURED AT LEFT: Favorite Pork Chops, Au Gratin Potatoes, Mom's Bean Medley and Chocolate Cake Roll (recipes are on the next page).

Favorite Pork Chops

My mom often served this dish when relatives were visiting. The night before, I'd watch her prepare the soy sauce marinade. As the pork chops baked the next day, the tantalizing aroma would fill the kitchen. It was always a hit!

       2 cups soy sauce
       1 cup water
   1/2 cup packed brown sugar
       1 tablespoon molasses
       6 bone-in pork loin chops (1-1/2 inches thick)
SAUCE:
   3/4 cup ketchup
   2/3 cup chili sauce
   1/4 cup packed brown sugar
       2 tablespoons water
1-1/2 teaspoons ground mustard

In a saucepan over medium heat, bring soy sauce, water, brown sugar and molasses to a boil. Remove from the heat; cool to room temperature. Pour into a large resealable plastic bag; add pork chops. Seal bag and refrigerate for 3-6 hours.

   Drain and discard marinade. Place pork chops in a greased 13-in. x 9-in. x 2-in. baking dish. Cover and bake at 350° for 30 minutes. Combine the sauce ingredients; pour over chops. Bake, uncovered, 30 minutes longer or until meat juices run clear. **Yield:** 6 servings.

Au Gratin Potatoes

These cheesy potatoes are always welcome at our dinner table, and they're so simple to make. A perfect complement to ham, this homey side dish also goes well with pork, chicken and other entrees.

       3 tablespoons butter *or* margarine
       3 tablespoons all-purpose flour
1-1/2 teaspoons salt
   1/8 teaspoon pepper
       2 cups milk
       1 cup (4 ounces) shredded cheddar cheese
       5 cups thinly sliced peeled potatoes (about 6 medium)
   1/2 cup chopped onion

In a large saucepan, melt butter over low heat. Stir in the flour, salt and pepper until smooth. Gradually add milk. Bring to a boil; cook and stir for 2 minutes or until thickened. Remove from the heat; stir in cheese until melted. Add potatoes and onion; stir well.

   Transfer to a greased 2-qt. baking dish. Cover and bake at 350° for 1 hour. Uncover; bake 30-40 minutes longer or until the potatoes are tender. **Yield:** 6-8 servings.

Mom's Bean Medley

Pinto, garbanzo, green and wax beans star in this snappy marinated salad. For a taste twist, Mom added tomatoes and mayonnaise to the colorful combination.

       1 can (15 ounces) pinto beans, rinsed and drained

1 can (15 ounces) garbanzo beans, rinsed
   and drained
1 can (8 ounces) cut green beans, drained
1 can (8 ounces) yellow wax beans, drained
1/2 cup thinly sliced green pepper
1/4 cup thinly sliced red onion
6 tablespoons vegetable oil
3 tablespoons cider vinegar
1 tablespoon sugar
1/4 teaspoon dried oregano
1/8 teaspoon garlic powder
3 tablespoons mayonnaise
1 medium tomato, chopped

In a large bowl, combine the beans, green pepper
and onion. In a jar with a tight-fitting lid, combine
the oil, vinegar, sugar, oregano and garlic powder; shake well. Pour over vegetables and toss to
coat. Cover and refrigerate for 8 hours or overnight.
Stir in mayonnaise. Add tomato; toss gently. **Yield:**
6-8 servings.

— 🍶 🍶 🍶 —

Chocolate Cake Roll

*This delectable dessert features sweet whipped cream
and moist chocolate cake rolled up and dusted with
powdered sugar. A family favorite, it winds up any special meal in festive fashion.*

6 eggs, *separated*
1 cup sugar, *divided*
1 teaspoon vanilla extract
1/4 cup all-purpose flour

1/4 cup baking cocoa
1/4 teaspoon salt
1/2 teaspoon cream of tartar
1-1/2 cups whipping cream
2 tablespoons confectioners' sugar
Additional confectioners' sugar

Place egg whites in a small mixing bowl; let stand
at room temperature for 30 minutes. In a large mixing bowl, beat egg yolks on high speed until light
and fluffy. Gradually add 1/2 cup sugar, beating until thick and lemon-colored. Stir in vanilla. Combine the flour, cocoa and salt; add to egg yolk
mixture until blended.

Beat egg whites on medium until foamy. Add
cream of tartar; beat until soft peaks form. Gradually add remaining sugar, 1 tablespoon at a time,
beating on high until stiff peaks form. Stir a fourth
of the egg white mixture into chocolate mixture.
Fold in remaining egg white mixture until no egg
white streaks remain.

Line a greased 15-in. x 10-in. x 1-in. baking
pan with parchment paper; grease the paper.
Spread batter evenly in pan. Bake at 350° for 12-
15 minutes or until cake springs back when lightly touched in center (do not overbake). Cool for 5
minutes; invert onto a kitchen towel dusted with
confectioners' sugar. Gently peel off parchment paper. Roll up cake in the towel jelly-roll style, starting with a short side. Cool completely on a wire
rack.

In a mixing bowl, beat cream and confectioners'
sugar until stiff peaks form; chill. Unroll cake;
spread with whipped cream to within 1/2 in. of
edges. Roll up again. Place seam side down on
serving platter; chill. Dust with additional confectioners' sugar before serving. **Yield:** 12 servings.

Her Italian mom's mouth-watering menus make fun-filled family dinners warm and memorable.

By Concetta Maranto Skenfield
Bakersfield, California

DINNERTIME holds some of my favorite childhood memories. With an Italian family, dinner was—and is—a big event. There's a lot of passing, laughing, sharing and talking…and much more food than can be consumed in one sitting!

Although my mom (Sarah Maranto, above) owned two quilt and needlework shops when my brother, Vincent, sister, Mary, and I were kids, we never had fast food for dinner. Dad would get home first and start the meal, then Mom would finish it when she arrived. On weekends, with more time to devote to cooking, she made wonderful meals.

Her Rice Balls with Meat Sauce was always my favorite. My parents emigrated from Sicily, so we took trips to Italy as a family. I had to have rice balls while we were there. When my mom made them at home, we knew we were in for a treat.

Mom's colorful Italian Zucchini Boats make a flavorful side dish. The aroma of the cheese, tomato and garlic cooking in the kitchen is enough to make your tummy growl.

She always had plenty of fresh zucchini, tomatoes and vegetables available, thanks to my dad. He grew produce and herbs in the backyard…and still gives me pots of parsley and basil.

Basil stars in Tomato Mozzarella Salad. We sometimes like to add capers to this simple melt-in-your-mouth side dish.

And there isn't a better way to end a big Italian meal than with refreshing Lemon Ice. It's cool and light… and a welcome snack on hot summer days.

Although my brother, sister and I are married now and have careers, we all live within a couple miles of Mom and Dad. We still get together on weekends and holidays to enjoy each other's company and Mom's memorable meals.

PICTURED AT LEFT: Rice Balls with Meat Sauce, Italian Zucchini Boats, Tomato Mozzarella Salad and Lemon Ice (recipes are on the next page).

Rice Balls with Meat Sauce

My mom's deep-fried rice balls, flavored with traditional Italian cheeses, make a hearty main dish. She serves them with her special spaghetti sauce—my favorite—featuring ground beef and artichoke hearts.

- 1 pound ground beef
- 1 small onion, finely chopped
- 3 garlic cloves, minced
- 2 cans (15 ounces *each*) tomato sauce
- 1 can (14 ounces) water-packed artichoke hearts, drained and chopped
- 1 cup frozen peas
- 1 jar (4-1/2 ounces) sliced mushrooms, drained
- 3 bay leaves
- 1 tablespoon sugar
- 2 teaspoons dried oregano
- 2 teaspoons dried basil
- 1/4 teaspoon pepper

CHEESE-STUFFED RICE BALLS:
- 3 eggs
- 2-1/2 cups cooked rice
- 1/3 cup butter *or* margarine, melted
- 2/3 cup grated Parmesan *or* Romano cheese
- 1/4 cup minced fresh parsley
- 1/2 teaspoon salt
- 1/4 teaspoon pepper

- 2 ounces mozzarella cheese, cut into 3/8-inch cubes
- 1 cup dry bread crumbs

Oil for deep-fat frying

In a large saucepan, cook beef, onion and garlic over medium heat until meat is no longer pink; drain. Stir in the next nine ingredients. Bring to a boil. Reduce heat; cover and simmer for 1 hour, stirring occasionally. In a bowl, lightly beat 2 eggs. Stir in the rice, butter, Parmesan cheese, parsley, salt and pepper. Cover and refrigerate for 20 minutes. Roll into 1-1/2-in. balls. Press a mozzarella cube into each; reshape balls.

In a small bowl, lightly beat remaining egg. Dip each ball into egg, then roll in bread crumbs. In a deep-fat fryer or electric skillet, heat oil to 375°. Fry rice balls until golden brown, about 4 minutes. Drain on paper towels. Discard bay leaf from meat sauce; serve with rice balls. **Yield:** 6-8 servings.

— 🍴 🍴 🍴 —

Italian Zucchini Boats

The tantalizing aroma of this savory side dish baking in the oven is sure to whet your appetite. Mom scoops the pulp out of zucchini halves and mixes it with tomato, Parmesan cheese, bread crumbs and parsley.

✓ Uses less fat, sugar or salt. Includes Nutritional Analysis and Diabetic Exchanges.

- 6 medium zucchini
- 2 cups dry bread crumbs

2 eggs, lightly beaten
1 large tomato, diced
1/3 cup grated Parmesan **or** Romano cheese
1/4 cup minced fresh parsley
2 garlic cloves, minced
1/2 cup chicken broth
1/2 teaspoon salt
1/8 teaspoon pepper
2 tablespoons butter **or** stick margarine,
   melted

Cut zucchini in half lengthwise. With a spoon, scoop out and reserve pulp, leaving a 3/8-in. shell. Cook shells in salted water for 2 minutes; remove and drain. Chop zucchini pulp; place in a bowl. Add the bread crumbs, eggs, tomato, Parmesan cheese, parsley and garlic. Stir in broth, salt and pepper. Stuff into zucchini shells.

Place in a greased 13-in. x 9-in. x 2-in. baking dish. Drizzle with butter. Bake, uncovered, at 350° for 20 minutes or until golden. **Yield:** 6 servings.

Nutritional Analysis: One serving (2 stuffed zucchini halves) equals 260 calories, 9 g fat (4 g saturated fat), 85 mg cholesterol, 741 mg sodium, 34 g carbohydrate, 4 g fiber, 11 g protein. **Diabetic Exchanges:** 2 starch, 1-1/2 fat, 1 vegetable.

─── ☕ ☕ ☕ ───

Tomato Mozzarella Salad

Instead of tossed salad, I serve these attractive tomato and mozzarella slices, drizzled with oil and sprin- kled with basil. They're especially tasty made with fresh tomatoes and basil from the garden.

3 large tomatoes, sliced
8 ounces mozzarella, sliced
1/4 cup olive *or* vegetable oil
1/4 teaspoon salt
1/8 teaspoon pepper
1/4 cup minced fresh basil

On a large serving platter, alternate tomatoes and mozzarella slices. In a jar with a tight-fitting lid, combine the oil, salt and pepper; shake well. Drizzle over tomatoes and mozzarella. Sprinkle with basil. **Yield:** 6-8 servings.

─── ☕ ☕ ☕ ───

Lemon Ice

Pucker up for this sweet-tart treat! The delicious lemon dessert is a perfectly refreshing way to end a summer meal...or any meal, for that matter.

2 cups sugar
1 cup water
2 cups lemon juice
1 tablespoon grated lemon peel

In a saucepan over low heat, cook and stir sugar and water until sugar is dissolved. Remove from the heat; stir in lemon juice. Pour into a freezer container. Freeze for 4 hours, stirring every 30 minutes, or until mixture becomes slushy. Sprinkle servings with lemon peel. **Yield:** 6 servings.

Mom deliciously combines old-world flavors with new, creating dishes that have become family favorites.

By Lisa Radelet, Boulder, Colorado

ENERGETIC is the word that best describes my mom (Theresa Handlos, above, of Menomonee Falls, Wisconsin).

When my sisters and I were growing up, Mom not only cooked nightly for us girls and our dad, but also for members of our extended family who frequently joined us at the dinner table.

Mom grew up in Austria near the Hungarian border and moved to the United States at age 13. Her cooking reflects traditional Austrian dishes, those of our dad's German heritage, plus American favorites she learned over the years.

One of Mom's most memorable meals starts with Old-World Pork Roast. Now that we girls and our families are spread across the country, we prepare this savory roast and dumplings for our own families, but we all agree that no one makes it quite like Mom.

Endive Salad with Potatoes is a unique salad, with slices of cooked red potatoes nestled among the greens and a deliciously tart dressing.

Mom never had a problem getting us kids to eat our vegetables when she served Colorful Veggie Bake. The first time she made this comforting casserole, it was an instant hit with our family.

One of her wonderful desserts that never fails to draw compliments is Cherry Cheese Torte. Pretty enough to serve to company, this impressive-looking treat is easy to make and tastes absolutely scrumptious.

In 1998, Mom gave all four of us girls subscriptions to *Taste of Home* and has continued to renew them ever since. We always enjoy discovering other families' favorite recipes and are so pleased to share our mom's best meal with you!

PICTURED AT LEFT: Old-World Pork Roast, Endive Salad with Potatoes, Colorful Veggie Bake and Cherry Cheese Torte (recipes are on the next page).

Meanwhile, combine the rolls and milk in a large bowl. Cover and refrigerate for 1 hour. Add 1 cup flour and eggs; mix well. Shape into 2-in. balls. In a soup kettle or Dutch oven, bring 3 qts. of water to a boil. Add dumplings. Boil, uncovered, for 15-20 minutes or until a thermometer reads 160°. Remove to a serving dish with a slotted spoon; keep warm.

Remove roast to a serving platter; keep warm. Strain pan drippings. Add enough broth to drippings to measure 1-3/4 cups. Pour into a small saucepan. Place remaining flour in a dish; stir in cold water until smooth. Stir into broth mixture. Bring to a boil; cook and stir for 2 minutes or until thickened. Serve with roast and dumplings. **Yield:** 8-10 servings (16 dumplings).

Old-World Pork Roast

No one makes this succulent pork roast and dumplings with gravy quite like my mom does. She learned how to prepare dishes like this when she was a young girl in Austria. For my sisters and me, this is truly a taste of home.

    1 teaspoon salt
  1/2 teaspoon garlic powder
  1/4 teaspoon pepper
    1 boneless rolled pork loin roast
      (about 3-1/2 pounds)
BREAD DUMPLINGS:
    8 day-old hard rolls, torn into small pieces
1-1/4 cups warm milk
    1 cup plus 3 tablespoons all-purpose flour,
      divided
    4 eggs, lightly beaten
    3 quarts water
    1 can (14-1/2 ounces) beef broth
    6 tablespoons cold water

Combine the salt, garlic powder and pepper; rub over roast. Place roast fat side up on a rack in a shallow roasting pan. Bake, uncovered, at 325° for 1-1/2 to 1-3/4 hours or until a meat thermometer reads 160°.

Endive Salad with Potatoes

Endive and cooked sliced red potatoes are the unusual combo Mom tossed together in this refreshing green salad. Her tart vinaigrette dressing brings out the best of both flavors.

    2 bunches curly endive, torn
      (about 8 cups)
    3 small red potatoes, cooked and sliced
  1/4 cup olive *or* vegetable oil
    3 tablespoons cider vinegar
    2 teaspoons sugar

1 teaspoon salt
1/8 teaspoon pepper

In a salad bowl, combine endive and potatoes. In a jar with a tight-fitting lid, combine the remaining ingredients; shake well. Drizzle over salad; toss to coat. Serve immediately. **Yield:** 8-10 servings.

— ▼ ▼ ▼ —

Colorful Veggie Bake

It's impossible to resist this cheesy casserole, which has a golden crumb topping sprinkled over colorful vegetables. A versatile side that goes with any meat, Mom has relied on this favorite to round out many family meals. For a fun taste twist, try varying the veggies.

2 packages (16 ounces *each*) frozen California-blend vegetables
8 ounces process cheese (Velveeta), cubed
6 tablespoons butter *or* margarine, *divided*
1/2 cup crushed butter-flavored crackers (about 13 crackers)

Prepare vegetables according to package directions; drain. Place half in an ungreased 11-in. x 7-in. x 2-in. baking dish. In a small saucepan, combine cheese and 4 tablespoons butter; cook and stir over low heat until melted. Pour half over vegetables. Repeat layers.

Melt remaining butter; toss with cracker crumbs. Sprinkle over the top. Bake, uncovered, at 325° for 20-25 minutes or until golden brown. **Yield:** 8-10 servings.

Cherry Cheese Torte

We always feel special when Mom brings out this delightful dessert, whether it's for a Sunday dinner or a holiday meal. You can't help but impress people when you set this lovely cheese torte in front of them.

2 packages (3 ounces *each*) ladyfingers
1 package (8 ounces) cream cheese, softened
1 cup plus 1 teaspoon sugar, *divided*
2 teaspoons vanilla extract, *divided*
2 teaspoons lemon juice
1 teaspoon grated lemon peel
2 cups whipping cream
1 can (21 ounces) cherry *or* blueberry pie filling

Place a layer of ladyfingers on the bottom and around the sides of an ungreased 9-in. springform pan. In a large mixing bowl, beat the cream cheese, 1 cup sugar and 1 teaspoon vanilla until smooth. Add lemon juice and peel; mix well.

In small mixing bowl, beat cream until it begins to thicken. Add remaining sugar and vanilla; beat until stiff peaks form. Fold into cream cheese mixture. Spread half over crust. Arrange remaining ladyfingers in a spoke pattern over top. Evenly spread with the remaining cream cheese mixture. Top with pie filling. Cover and refrigerate overnight. Remove sides of pan just before serving. **Yield:** 12 servings.

Editors' Meals

Taste of Home magazine is edited by 1,000 cooks across North America. On the following pages, you'll "meet" some of those cooks who share a family-favorite meal.

——— 🥄 🥄 🥄 ———

FAMILY APPROVED. Clockwise from upper left: Good for Gatherings (p. 226), Making Occasions Special (p. 230), Appeasing Hearty Appetites (p. 238) and Flavorful Patio Fare (p. 234).

Good for Gatherings

This young husband and father delights in putting dazzling dinners on the table for his family...and training an eager little assistant!

By Brad Moritz, Limerick, Pennsylvania

AS THE CHIEF COOK at our house, I really enjoy preparing meals for my family and guests. We love to entertain relatives and friends during the Christmas season and throughout the year.

My wife, Esther, and I have been married for 9 years and have a 2-year-old son, Adam. She and I have a rather unconventional arrangement regarding domestic duties. I am responsible for all food preparation and keeping the kitchen clean, while she handles upkeep on the rest of the house.

When it comes to cooking, I enjoy trying new recipes and learning to cook with unusual ingredients. I'm always up for a challenge. I do make cakes, pies and pastries, but I prefer to cook main dishes and absolutely love to grill outdoors. I am the only one in our neighborhood who grills 12 months of the year, despite rain or snow!

The recipe for Puff Pastry Chicken Bundles was inspired by a popular television cooking show. Wrapped in puff pastry that bakes to a golden brown, the tender chicken breasts are stuffed with spinach plus chive and onion cream cheese.

Sometimes I make the puff pastry from scratch, which is a labor of love. But I've found that frozen pastry sheets are a convenient shortcut when preparing this company-worthy entree.

After Esther—my official taste-tester—gave the dish her seal of approval, I served it to my family when they visited for a long weekend. They absolutely loved it!

Lessons in the Kitchen

My mother, Carol Moritz, took the time to teach me how to cook. Each of us kids was given a task like measuring or mixing, and we learned the basics.

PICTURED AT LEFT: Puff Pastry Chicken Bundles, Cheesy Mashed Potatoes, Vinaigrette for Mixed Greens and Raspberry Cheesecake Cups (recipes are on the next page).

Grandma Moritz was also a big influence in my love for cooking. I have fond childhood memories of helping my grandparents harvest and prepare vegetables from their garden.

As a child, I remember my Aunt Faye making Cheesy Mashed Potatoes for family gatherings. They were always one of my favorites. I've been fixing this creamy, flavorful casserole for years and have had numerous requests for the recipe.

Fresh salads are on our table year-round. When I had a hard time finding a dressing that I liked for mixed greens, I experimented with different ingredients until I came up with my own pleasantly tangy Vinaigrette for Mixed Greens.

I first tried the recipe for Raspberry Cheesecake Cups when we invited friends for a dinner party some years ago. Esther prompted me to prepare a treat that was both "beautiful and scrumptious".

When I presented the dessert to our guests, they commented that it was too pretty to eat! These cheesecake cups have become my wife's favorite dessert and make a wonderful finale for a holiday meal. It's worth the splurge for fresh raspberries.

Daddy's Little Helper

Lately, I've begun to teach Adam how much fun cooking can be. Although he's only 2, he is already adept at stirring cake batters, mixing meat loaf, removing husks from sweet corn and arranging vegetables on relish trays.

He loves to help Daddy cook. As soon as he sees me start to prepare a meal, he pushes his chair to the kitchen counter so he can assist.

Despite the extra time and patience it takes, I love having a little helper. It's a great way to spend quality time with my son.

We're active in our church and love to entertain friends from our congregation. It's fun to surprise guests with new dishes. Sounds of *"mmm"* and *"aah"* fill the room as folks taste my Puff Pastry Chicken Bundles and other specialties.

Besides giving you a "taste" of my festive meal, I hope this menu might be one you'll try for a holiday gathering. If your guests are like ours, they'll be quick with compliments for this appetizing and eye-appealing dinner!

Puff Pastry Chicken Bundles

Inside these golden puff pastry "packages", chicken breasts rolled with spinach, herbed cream cheese and walnuts are a savory surprise. I like to serve this elegant entree when we have guests or are celebrating a holiday or special occasion.

   8 boneless skinless chicken breast halves (about 6 ounces *each*)
   1 teaspoon salt
1/2 teaspoon pepper
 40 large spinach leaves
   2 cartons (8 ounces *each*) spreadable chive and onion cream cheese
1/2 cup chopped walnuts, toasted
   2 sheets frozen puff pastry, thawed
   1 egg
1/2 teaspoon cold water

Cut a lengthwise slit in each chicken breast to within 1/2 in. of the other side; open meat so it lies flat. Cover with plastic wrap; pound to flatten to 1/8-in. thickness. Remove plastic wrap. Sprinkle salt and pepper over chicken.

In a saucepan, bring 1 in. of water to a boil; add spinach. Cover and cook for 1-2 minutes or until wilted; drain. Place five spinach leaves on each chicken breast. Spoon 2 tablespoons of cream cheese down the center of each chicken breast; sprinkle with walnuts. Roll up chicken and tuck in the ends.

Unroll puff pastry; cut into eight portions. Roll each into an 8-in. x 7-in. rectangle. Combine egg and cold water; brush over edges of pastry. Place chicken at one short end; roll up tightly, tucking in ends. Place on a greased 15-in. x 10-in. x 1-in. baking sheet. Bake at 350° for 25-30 minutes or until golden brown. **Yield:** 8 servings.

Cheesy Mashed Potatoes

Everyone who has tasted these creamy, cheesy potatoes asks how to make them. Since this comforting casserole bakes at the same temperature as my chicken bundles, I get it started in the oven and pop in the entree a little later.

   6 large potatoes, peeled and quartered
   1 package (8 ounces) cream cheese, softened
   1 cup (4 ounces) shredded cheddar cheese
1/2 cup sour cream
1/3 cup chopped onion
   1 egg
   2 teaspoons salt
1/2 teaspoon pepper
Additional shredded cheddar cheese, optional

Place potatoes in a large saucepan; cover with water. Cover and bring to a boil. Cook for 20-25 minutes or until very tender; drain well.

In a mixing bowl, mash potatoes. Add cream cheese, cheddar cheese, sour cream, onion, egg, salt and pepper; beat until fluffy. Transfer to a greased 2-qt. baking dish. Cover and bake at 350° for 40-45 minutes or until heated through. Sprinkle with additional cheese if desired. **Yield:** 10 servings.

❦ ❦ ❦

Vinaigrette for Mixed Greens

This pleasantly tangy homemade vinaigrette dressing takes just minutes to make. I toss it with fresh greens and colorful red onion slices.

3/4 cup vegetable oil
1/4 cup red wine vinegar _or_ cider vinegar
2 tablespoons Dijon mustard
1 garlic clove, minced
Salt and pepper to taste
Mixed salad greens and sliced red onion

In a jar with a tight-fitting lid, combine the oil, vinegar, mustard, garlic, salt and pepper; shake well. In a salad bowl, combine greens and onion. Drizzle with dressing; toss to coat. **Yield:** 1 cup.

Raspberry Cheesecake Cups

I'm frequently told these festive individual desserts are too pretty to eat! Phyllo dough is easy to work with —don't be afraid to try it for these special treats. With the bright red raspberries, these creamy cheese cups make a fine finale for Christmas dinner.

8 sheets phyllo dough
1/4 cup butter (no substitutes), melted
1 egg
1 teaspoon lemon juice
1/2 teaspoon vanilla extract
1 package (8 ounces) cream cheese, cubed
1/2 cup small-curd cottage cheese
3 tablespoons sugar
RASPBERRY SAUCE:
3 packages (10 ounces _each_) frozen sweetened raspberries, thawed

1/4 cup sugar
1 tablespoon lemon juice
Fresh raspberries and mint

Unroll phyllo dough sheets; trim if necessary into 13-in. x 9-in. rectangles. While assembling, keep remaining dough covered with plastic wrap and a damp cloth. Brush one phyllo sheet with butter. Top with another sheet; brush with butter. Repeat with remaining phyllo and butter. Cut stack lengthwise into three pieces; cut widthwise into fourths. Lightly press each stack into a greased muffin cup.

In a blender, place the egg, lemon juice, vanilla, cheeses and sugar; cover and process until smooth. Spoon about 2 tablespoons into each phyllo cup. Bake at 350° for 12-15 minutes or until lightly browned. Carefully remove from pan to wire racks to cool. Cover and refrigerate.

For sauce, drain raspberries, reserving the juice in a small saucepan; set berries aside. Bring juice to a boil. Reduce heat; simmer, uncovered, for 15-20 minutes or until reduced to 3/4 cup. In a blender, puree reserved raspberries; press through a sieve to remove seeds. In a bowl, combine pureed raspberries, raspberry juice, sugar and lemon juice. Cover and refrigerate until chilled.

To serve, spoon raspberry sauce onto dessert plates; top each with a cheesecake cup. Garnish with fresh berries and mint. **Yield:** 12 servings.

Making Occasions Special

Family, friends and fellow parishioners know to expect an outstanding meal when this creative cook is in the kitchen.

By Mark Trinklein, Cedarburg, Wisconsin

GROWING UP in a frugal family, I was the oldest of five boys and learned early to pitch in on domestic chores. Mom, who worked outside the home, delegated tasks, and mine was cooking. She must have noticed my keen interest in it.

In those days, I mixed up sweet rolls because bakery rolls were too expensive. I made homemade pizza when it was still new to American kitchens. I used leftovers creatively to keep our dad happy by not throwing anything away.

When a meal turned out well and the family's response was "Make it again, Mark", I was thrilled.

Cooking for Crowds

To this day, I love to entertain and cook for family and friends and at my church. As minister of fellowship, I head up food preparation for gatherings that average 250 guests.

Be it a Friday night fish fry (a popular Wisconsin tradition), a wedding reception or a banquet, I still like to make "five loaves of bread and two small fish" go as far as possible.

This particular menu has proven especially popular for special occasions, regardless of the season.

An elegant entree, Stuffed Beef Tenderloin tastes great. I usually marinate the meat overnight, stuff the roast the morning of the party and refrigerate it until time to put it in the oven.

The savory stuffing blend is a "melting pot" of German and Italian tried-and-tested variations. Be sure to let the roast stand uncovered for 10 to 15 minutes before slicing. This resting period seals in the juices and makes for a prettier presentation.

I've learned many cooking tips and tricks by working as a caterer over the years. In college, I started my own small catering business to pay my tuition.

I kept it up for added income while my wife and I worked as teachers and raised our family. On weekends, the kids loved to stay up late to see if dad would bring home any good leftovers!

Great texture and eye-appealing color make Almond Wild Rice perfect with the tenderloin. It, too, can be made ahead; I've found it doesn't get sticky. If you ever make a rice dish that does, sprinkle on a few drops of olive oil and stir it in to glaze the grains.

Cheddar Potato Soup showcases excellent Wisconsin cheddar. The recipe evolved after I'd tasted a wonderful cheese soup at a restaurant. I left thinking, "I can make this!" and experimented until I came close to duplicating the flavor and consistency.

Rich and fairly thick, this soup is best made in a double boiler. If you don't have one, be careful not to let the cheese stick to the bottom of your kettle. For a nice change of pace, I sometimes add a little grated green pepper.

When entertaining friends or when my children visit, I usually make extra and give them soup to take home. Mike and Patti are both married now, and I have two adorable grandsons.

Any combination of seasonal fresh fruits is enhanced by Raspberry Vinaigrette. Time and again, people tell me how much they like its tangy flavor. The vinegar and lemon juice in the salad dressing also keep fruit like bananas, apples and pears from turning brown.

Moist, rich-tasting Mocha Bundt Cake was first served to me by a Swedish cook who told me his grandmother brought the recipe with her to the U.S.

All this cake needs is a dusting of confectioners' sugar. To dress it up, serve slices with whipped cream or ice cream topped with mocha sprinkles.

Welcomes Dinner Guests

Gatherings of family and friends have always been an important part of my life. "Company" often stopped in at my childhood home on Sunday afternoons—and always managed to stay for supper. Mom didn't mind.

If you fix my favorite meal, I hope you'll hear the same kind of compliments from your family and friends as I do.

PICTURED AT LEFT: Stuffed Beef Tenderloin, Almond Wild Rice, Cheddar Potato Soup, Fruit Salad with Raspberry Vinaigrette and Mocha Bundt Cake (recipes are on the next page).

Stuffed Beef Tenderloin

Slices of this easy special-occasion roast look so attractive. It's an entree I'm proud to serve guests.

    1 cup olive *or* vegetable oil
    2 tablespoons Worcestershire sauce
    1 teaspoon *each* dried oregano, basil
        and thyme
    1 teaspoon garlic salt
    1 teaspoon salt
  1/2 teaspoon pepper
    1 whole beef tenderloin (3 to 4 pounds),
        trimmed
STUFFING:
    2 cups sliced fresh mushrooms
  1/2 cup sliced green onions
    1 can (8 ounces) water chestnuts, drained
        and chopped
  1/2 cup butter *or* margarine
    2 cups seasoned bread crumbs
  3/4 cup egg substitute
  1/4 cup grated Parmesan cheese
  1/2 teaspoon dried oregano
  1/2 teaspoon dried rosemary, crushed
    1 teaspoon fennel seed
  1/2 teaspoon pepper

In a large resealable bag, combine the oil, Worcestershire sauce and seasonings. Make a lengthwise slit about three-fourths of the way through the tenderloin. Place in bag; seal and turn to coat. Refrigerate for 4 hours or overnight.

In a skillet, saute mushrooms, onions and water chestnuts in butter until onion is tender. Remove

from heat. Add remaining stuffing ingredients; mix well. Discard marinade. Open tenderloin; spoon stuffing on one side. Close and tie with kitchen string. Place in a greased shallow roasting pan.

Bake, uncovered, at 350° for 1-1/2 hours or until meat reaches desired doneness (for rare, a meat thermometer should read 140°; medium, 160°; well-done, 170°). Let stand 10-15 minutes before removing string and slicing. **Yield:** 12 servings.

— 🦃 🦃 🦃 —

Almond Wild Rice

I prepare this casserole the morning of the party, then refrigerate it in an ovenproof dish to heat later.

5-1/2 cups chicken broth, *divided*
    1 cup golden raisins
    6 tablespoons butter *or* margarine, *divided*
    1 cup uncooked wild rice
    1 cup uncooked brown rice
    1 cup sliced *or* slivered almonds
  1/2 cup minced fresh parsley
  1/4 teaspoon salt
  1/4 teaspoon pepper

In a small saucepan, bring 1/2 cup broth to a boil. Remove from the heat; add raisins and set aside (do not drain). In a large saucepan, bring 3 cups of broth and 2 tablespoons of butter to a boil. Add wild rice; cover and simmer for 55-60 minutes or until the rice is tender (drain if necessary).

Meanwhile, in another saucepan, combine the brown rice, 2 tablespoons butter and remaining broth. Bring to a boil. Reduce heat; cover and simmer for 35-40 minutes or until rice is tender (drain if necessary).

In a skillet, saute the almonds in remaining butter until lightly browned. In a serving bowl, combine the wild rice, brown rice, raisin mixture, almonds, parsley, salt and pepper. **Yield:** 10 servings.

Cheddar Potato Soup

This soup is also a great choice for lunch or supper when teamed with a salad and bread.

  1/3 cup chopped onion
  1/3 cup chopped celery
    2 tablespoons butter *or* margarine
    4 cups diced peeled potatoes
    3 cups chicken broth
    2 cups (8 ounces) shredded cheddar cheese
    2 cups milk
  1/4 teaspoon pepper
Dash paprika
Seasoned croutons and minced fresh parsley

In a large saucepan, saute onion and celery in butter until tender. Add potatoes and broth; bring to a boil. Reduce heat; cover and simmer for 10-15 minutes or until potatoes are tender.

Puree in small batches in a blender until smooth; return to the pan. Stir in the cheese, milk, pepper and paprika. Cook and stir over low heat until the cheese is melted. Garnish with croutons and parsley. **Yield:** 8 servings.

───── 🍴 🍴 🍴 ─────

Fruit Salad with Raspberry Vinaigrette

(Pictured on page 230)

This tangy vinaigrette is tasty served over any combination of fruit.

    1 package (10 ounces) frozen sweetened raspberries, thawed and drained
  1/3 cup seedless raspberry jam
    2 tablespoons cider vinegar
    2 tablespoons lemon juice
  1/2 cup olive *or* vegetable oil
  1/8 teaspoon salt
Dash pepper

Dash ground nutmeg
Assorted fresh fruit

In a blender, process raspberries until pureed. Strain to remove seeds. Return puree to the blender. Add the jam, vinegar and lemon juice; cover and process until smooth. Add the oil, salt, pepper and nutmeg; cover and process until blended. Serve with fruit. **Yield:** 1-1/4 cups.

───── 🍴 🍴 🍴 ─────

Mocha Bundt Cake

Bittersweet chocolate and coffee pair up to deliver this cake's distinctive taste.

1-1/2 cups butter (no substitutes)
   12 squares (1 ounce *each*) bittersweet chocolate
2-1/4 cups sugar
    3 eggs
    2 cups strong brewed coffee
    2 teaspoons rum extract
1-1/2 teaspoons vanilla extract
    3 cups all-purpose flour
1-1/2 teaspoons baking soda
  3/4 teaspoon salt
Confectioners' sugar
Whipped cream, optional

In a microwave, melt butter and chocolate; stir until smooth. Transfer to a large mixing bowl. Beat in sugar. Add eggs, one at a time, beating well after each addition. Beat in the coffee and extracts. Combine the flour, baking soda and salt; gradually add to the chocolate mixture.

Pour into a greased and floured 10-in. fluted tube pan. Bake at 325° for 55-65 minutes or until a toothpick inserted near the center comes out clean. Cool for 10 minutes before inverting onto a wire rack to cool completely.

Dust with confectioners' sugar. Serve with whipped cream if desired. **Yield:** 12-16 servings.

Flavorful Patio Fare

This enthusiastic Southern cook shares a casual flavorful menu for a spring or summer gathering on the patio.

By Pat Stevens, Granbury, Texas

ALL THAT'S MISSING from my favorite backyard barbecue menu is...your family or a group of your friends to enjoy it!

My husband, Richard, and I like to serve this savory warm-weather spread when we host parties on our poolside patio. Our grown son, David, and our extended families often request it for special celebrations.

Over the years, we've tried all kinds of pork roasts on the grill, buy many were too dry. After experimenting with several versions, we "invented" Grilled Pork Loin Roast. Cooked covered over indirect heat, the meat stays very moist.

The small town of Dublin, Texas, where Richard and I grew up, was a place that could have inspired Norman Rockwell. Community get-togethers involved delectable food made from scratch and always included that special ingredient—a pinch of love. So it was natural that I married my high school sweetheart.

Cooking Kicks Off

My own real interest in cooking developed in Philadelphia, where we lived for 6 years while Richard played offensive lineman for the Philadelphia Eagles.

Cooking and entertaining for the players and their wives was an important part of pro football. Team members came from all parts of the country, and we wives started cooking together. It was a wonderful opportunity to cultivate lifelong friends and to learn regional cooking.

Our love of Tex-Mex food inspired the Avocado Mandarin Tossed Salad. This colorful mixture complements the pork roast. It's a salad that also goes well with lots of Mexican main dishes.

After Richard's retirement from football, we moved

to Granbury, where he became a banker. I work as a writer and have had career/business and college preparation articles published.

I also write a cooking column—"Bon Appetit"—for my local newspaper, the *Hood County News*. In an early article, I shared my recipe for Buttery Bubble Bread, and readers still request that I rerun it. I think people are very surprised that this yummy pull-apart monkey bread is actually simple to make.

It was the first homemade bread I made for David when he was a toddler, more than 25 years ago. He lives in Florida now, so each homecoming dinner features comfort foods he requests by phone in advance.

Now that I have a bread machine, I mix the dough in the machine, take it out and let it finish rising the second time, then bake it conventionally.

For dessert, I like to serve Pecan Pralines. These traditional treats complement a variety of foods. Many praline recipes I've tried were complicated or unpredictable. This is one that I'm confident to share with even a beginner cook.

Pralines can be made ahead. But choose a nice sunny day, since high humidity can affect their texture. Be sure to let the mixture reach the soft-ball stage before stirring in the butter and vanilla.

Runs in the Family

To surprise my mom and mother-in-law, I wrote and published a cookbook of treasured family recipes. Both of them are fantastic cooks, and *Six Generations of Southern Cooking* preserves their great recipes along with some from other relatives.

Besides cooking, I like to work in my flower garden and swim. Richard and I now enjoy cooking together and experimenting with new recipes. We've even attended several cooking schools.

We enjoy hosting dinners for relatives and friends. To honor a recent milestone wedding anniversary, I gave Richard a surprise dinner party. The biggest challenge was keeping it a secret as I cooked a meal and desserts for 40.

I've enjoyed telling you a little about myself and my family and sharing the recipes for my always-popular patio meal. Like all the delicious dishes *Taste of Home* features, they are real favorites from real people.

Bon appetit!

PICTURED AT LEFT: Grilled Pork Loin Roast, Avocado Mandarin Tossed Salad, Buttery Bubble Bread and Pecan Pralines (recipes are on the next page).

Grilled Pork Loin Roast

A memorable main dish for any special meal, this moist, tender roast has a pleasant spicy flavor. It looks so pretty garnished with slices of apples and oranges and fresh herbs. Guests at our patio parties rave over it and request the recipe.

- 1/4 teaspoon pepper
- 1 boneless pork loin roast (4 to 5 pounds)
- 1/2 cup packed brown sugar
- 1 tablespoon cornstarch
- 1/4 teaspoon ground cinnamon
- 1/4 teaspoon ground cloves
- 1/8 teaspoon ground ginger
- 1/2 cup pineapple juice
- 1/2 cup sweet-and-sour sauce
- 1/4 cup Worcestershire sauce
- 3 tablespoons lemon juice

Apple and orange wedges, optional
Fresh sage and rose geranium leaves, optional

Rub pepper over top of roast. Grill, covered, over indirect medium heat for 2-1/2 to 3 hours or until a meat thermometer reads 160°. Let stand for 10 minutes before slicing.

Meanwhile, in a saucepan, combine the brown sugar, cornstarch, cinnamon, cloves and ginger. Stir in the pineapple juice, sweet-and-sour sauce, Worcestershire sauce and lemon juice until smooth. Bring to a boil; cook and stir for 2 minutes or until thickened. Serve with the pork roast. Garnish the serving platter with apple and orange

wedges, sage and rose geranium leaves if desired. **Yield:** 12-14 servings.

— 🝘 🝘 🝘 —

Avocado Mandarin Tossed Salad

Crunchy toasted pecans and slices of creamy avocado add to the variety of textures and tastes in this interesting mixture. The salad is a lovely complement to my pork roast.

- 1 can (11 ounces) mandarin oranges, drained
- 1/2 cup thinly sliced green onions
- 1/3 cup coarsely chopped pecans, toasted
- 1/8 teaspoon pepper
- 4 cups torn salad greens
- 1 medium ripe avocado, peeled and sliced
- 1/4 cup prepared Italian salad dressing

In a bowl, combine the oranges, onions, pecans and pepper; refrigerate for 30 minutes. Just before serving, place the greens in a salad bowl; top with orange mixture and avocado slices. Drizzle with dressing. **Yield:** 8 servings.

Avocado Advice

To remove an avocado pit, thrust the blade of a sharp knife into the pit, twist slightly, and the pit will come right out.

Buttery Bubble Bread

Homemade bread can be time-consuming, difficult and tricky to make. But this fun-to-eat "monkey bread", baked in a fluted tube pan, is easy and almost foolproof. If I'm serving it for breakfast, I add some cinnamon and drizzle it with icing.

- 1 package (1/4 ounce) active dry yeast
- 1 cup warm water (110° to 115°)
- 1/2 cup sugar
- 1/2 cup shortening
- 1 egg
- 1/2 teaspoon salt
- 4 to 4-1/2 cups all-purpose flour, *divided*
- 6 tablespoons butter *or* margarine, melted

In a large mixing bowl, dissolve yeast in warm water. Add the sugar, shortening, egg, salt and 1 cup of flour. Beat until smooth. Stir in enough remaining flour to form a soft dough. Turn onto a floured surface; knead until smooth and elastic, about 6-8 minutes. Place in a greased bowl, turning once to grease top. Cover and let rise in a warm place until doubled, about 1 hour.

Punch dough down. Turn onto a lightly floured surface; shape into 1-1/2-in. balls. Dip the balls in butter and arrange evenly in a greased 9-in. fluted tube pan. Drizzle with remaining butter. Cover and let rise in a warm place until doubled, about 45 minutes.

Bake at 350° for 30-35 minutes or until golden brown. Cool for 5 minutes before inverting onto a serving platter. Serve warm. **Yield:** 1 loaf.

Pecan Pralines

I concocted my own recipe for these delectable Southern sweets by adjusting several others I tried. My family thinks these pralines have the perfect texture and just the right taste. Packaged in colorful tins, they make great gifts.

- 1 cup sugar
- 1 cup packed brown sugar
- 1 cup milk
- 8 large marshmallows
- 2 cups coarsely chopped pecans
- 2 tablespoons butter (no substitutes)
- 1/2 teaspoon vanilla extract

Dash ground cinnamon

Lightly butter two baking sheets or line with waxed paper; set aside. In a saucepan, combine the sugars, milk and marshmallows. Cook and stir over low heat until marshmallows are completely melted. Cook over medium heat, stirring occasionally, until a candy thermometer reads 234°-240° (softball stage).

Without stirring or scraping, pour hot liquid into another saucepan. Add the pecans, butter, vanilla and cinnamon. Stir rapidly until mixture is thickened and creamy, about 3 minutes. Drop quickly by rounded tablespoonfuls onto prepared pans. Flatten slightly. Let stand until set. Store in an airtight container. **Yield:** about 2 dozen.

Editor's Note: We recommend that you test your candy thermometer before each use by bringing water to a boil; the thermometer should read 212°. Adjust your recipe temperature up or down based on your test.

Appeasing Hearty Appetites

Her hungry harvest crew looks forward to this ranch wife's hearty spread starring tender shredded beef on homemade hoagie buns.

By Betty Sitzman, Wray, Colorado

IN OUR small rural community, families often get together to help each other when we're working cattle. My husband, Bob, son Dan and I raise cattle, corn, alfalfa and pinto beans at our family partnership, Slash Diamond Farms.

Over the years, I've served many different dishes when neighbors have come to lend us a hand. But the recipes everyone seems to like best are the ones I've shared here.

A roaster filled with Mile High Shredded Beef is welcomed by the hungry crew when we gather and sort cattle. Usually we tailgate the meal from the pickup right at the corrals.

This tender, well-seasoned beef is also great for a potluck or picnic or to serve after a good game of cards.

The meat is even more satisfying served on my from-scratch Hoagie Buns. These buns may take a little effort, but they're well worth it.

Our children and grandchildren never tire of these hearty sandwiches. Our other son, David, lives in Fort Collins, Colorado with his wife, Phyllis, and sons.

Daughter Karen and husband Matt are in Grand Junction. Their daughters, Jennifer and McKenzie, visited us last summer and helped me make a big batch of salsa. It was fun peeling, slicing and grinding all the ingredients. They were proud to take some home.

Glorified Hash Browns—so tasty with the beef sandwiches—are easy to prepare. I got the recipe from a friend when we served on the fellowship dinner committee at our Methodist church.

Garden Goodness

Crispy cucumbers and fresh dill are the key ingredients in Grandma's Dill Pickles. We like our pickles a little zesty, so I've added garlic and chili peppers to the recipe my grandma passed down.

I can and freeze plenty of fruits and vegetables from our big garden. One year at the Yuma County Fair, I won best of show with my canned produce.

Through 4-H, our family has participated in many county fairs. Bob and I were also 4-H leaders for many years. As you might guess, cooking has always been my favorite 4-H project.

And, of course, ravenous ranch hands and hungry harvest crew members always have room for dessert! They love to see Coconut Cream Meringue Pie waiting for them. My mother-in-law taught me a basic cream pie recipe, and this is our favorite variation.

I've always loved to cook and prepared most of the meals for family since I was in my early teens. I used to ride my bike down a country road to our neighbors and watch their German grandmother cook and bake.

I still use many methods I learned from her. It was "mix it till it feels right" or "add a pinch of this or a handful of that."

Bob and I were married right after he was discharged from the army and celebrated our 45th anniversary in 2002. Originally, we farmed near Greeley, then moved to eastern Colorado to take advantage of the irrigation possibilities here.

We love the land and open spaces and consider it a privilege to work together on a day-to-day basis. I keep the books for our business, drive the truck and cook for us and our hired man daily and for our harvest crews.

A Tasteful Hobby

Cooking is one of my favorite hobbies, along with sewing and reading. I'm also a member of The Sage Hens, a club of about 10 women who do community projects. We often cook for farm sales and cater meals for special occasions in each other's families, such as a 50th anniversary or big birthday.

Our club name came about because the Wray area is known for its prairie chickens and their "booming grounds". There, the birds dance and emit a booming noise that can be heard for miles during their spring mating ritual.

I hope you enjoy my favorite down-home recipes. If you and your family have appetites as big as our harvest crew, you're sure to love them!

PICTURED AT LEFT: Mile High Shredded Beef on Hoagie Buns, Glorified Hash Browns, Grandma's Dill Pickles and Coconut Cream Meringue Pie (recipes are on the next page).

Mile High Shredded Beef

This tender beef has become a tasty tradition when I cook for our harvest crews each year.

      1 boneless beef chuck roast (3 pounds)
      1 can (14-1/2 ounces) beef broth
      1 medium onion, chopped
      1 celery rib, chopped
    3/4 cup ketchup
    1/4 cup packed brown sugar
      2 tablespoons white vinegar
      1 teaspoon salt
      1 teaspoon ground mustard
      1 teaspoon Worcestershire sauce
      1 garlic clove, minced
      1 bay leaf
    1/4 teaspoon garlic powder
    1/4 teaspoon paprika
      3 drops hot pepper sauce
     12 to 15 hoagie buns

Place the roast in a Dutch oven; add broth, onion and celery. Bring to a boil. Reduce heat; cover and simmer for 2-1/2 to 3 hours or until the meat is tender.

Remove roast and cool slightly; shred meat with two forks. Strain vegetables and set aside. Skim fat from cooking liquid and reserve 1-1/2 cups. Return the meat, vegetables and reserved cooking liquid to the pan.

Stir in the ketchup, brown sugar, vinegar, salt, mustard, Worcestershire sauce, garlic, bay leaf, garlic powder, paprika and hot pepper sauce. Bring to a boil. Reduce heat; cover and simmer for 30 minutes. Discard bay leaf. Serve beef on buns. **Yield:** 12-15 servings.

Glorified Hash Browns

You'll be surprised at how quick and easy it is to put together this dressed-up potato casserole!

      2 cans (10-3/4 ounces *each*) condensed
        cream of celery soup, undiluted
      2 cartons (8 ounces *each*) spreadable chive
        and onion cream cheese
      1 package (2 pounds) frozen cubed hash
        brown potatoes
      1 cup (4 ounces) shredded cheddar cheese

In a large microwave-safe bowl, combine the soup and cream cheese. Cover and cook on high for 3-4 minutes or until cream cheese is melted, stirring occasionally. Add the potatoes and stir until coated.

Spoon into a greased 13-in. x 9-in. x 2-in. baking dish. Bake, uncovered, at 350° for 35-40 minutes or until the potatoes are tender. Sprinkle with cheddar cheese. Bake 3-5 minutes longer or until cheese is melted. **Yield:** 10 servings.

Hoagie Buns

Fresh from the oven, these homemade buns provide a delicious and convenient way to serve my beef.

      2 packages (1/4 ounce *each*) active dry yeast
      3 cups warm water (110° to 115°), *divided*
      2 tablespoons sugar, *divided*
    1/4 cup vegetable oil
      1 tablespoon salt
      8 to 8-1/2 cups all-purpose flour

In a mixing bowl, dissolve yeast in 1/2 cup warm water. Add 1 tablespoon sugar; let stand for 5 minutes. Add the remaining warm water and sugar. Beat in oil, salt and 4 cups flour until smooth. Stir in enough remaining flour to form a soft dough. Turn onto a floured surface; knead until smooth and elastic, about 6-8 minutes. Place in a greased bowl, turning once to grease top. Cover and let rise in a warm place until doubled, about 45 minutes.

Punch dough down. Turn onto a lightly floured surface; divide into 18 pieces. Shape each into an oval. Place 2 in. apart on greased baking sheets. With a scissors, cut a 1/4-in.-deep slash across the top of each. Cover and let rise until doubled, about 20 minutes. Bake at 400° for 13-18 minutes or until golden brown. Remove from pans to wire racks to cool. **Yield:** 1-1/2 dozen.

Coconut Cream Meringue Pie

Friends line up for a creamy slice of this pie, topped with golden meringue and toasted coconut!

    2/3 cup sugar
    1/4 cup cornstarch
    1/4 teaspoon salt
      2 cups milk
      3 egg yolks, lightly beaten
      1 cup flaked coconut, finely chopped
      2 tablespoons butter *or* margarine
    1/2 teaspoon vanilla extract
MERINGUE:
      3 egg whites
    1/4 teaspoon cream of tartar
      6 tablespoons sugar
      1 pastry shell (9 inches), baked
    1/2 cup flaked coconut

Grandma's Dill Pickles

Treasured family recipes like this one become like old friends. The pickles are crisp and slightly salty.

     11 cups water
      5 cups white vinegar
      1 cup canning salt
     12 pounds pickling cucumbers, quartered *or* halved lengthwise
      9 dill heads
     18 garlic cloves
     18 small dried hot chili peppers

In a Dutch oven, bring water, vinegar and salt to a boil; boil for 10 minutes. Pack cucumbers into quart jars within 1/2 in. of top. Place one dill head, two garlic cloves and two peppers in each jar. Ladle boiling liquid over cucumbers, leaving 1/4-in. headspace. Adjust caps. Process for 10 minutes in a boiling-water bath. **Yield:** 9 quarts.

In a saucepan, combine the sugar, cornstarch and salt. Gradually stir in milk until smooth. Bring to a boil; cook and stir for 2 minutes or until thickened. Gradually stir 1 cup hot filling into egg yolks; return all to the pan, stirring constantly. Bring to a gentle boil; cook and stir for 2 minutes. Remove from the heat; stir in chopped coconut, butter and vanilla until butter is melted.

For meringue, in a mixing bowl, beat the egg whites on medium speed until foamy. Add cream of tartar; beat until soft peaks form. Gradually beat in sugar, 1 tablespoon at a time, on high until stiff peaks form.

Pour hot filling into crust. Spread with meringue, sealing edges to crust. Sprinkle with flaked coconut. Bake at 350° for 13-15 minutes or until golden brown. Cool on a wire rack for 1 hour; chill for 1-2 hours before serving. Refrigerate leftovers. **Yield:** 6-8 servings.

Friendship Flavors Foods

This savory summer dinner is flavored with friendship, thanks to the recipes others have shared with this cook.

By DiAnn Mallehan, Grand Rapids, Michigan

ONE OF my greatest joys is being surrounded by family, friends and good food.

My friends and I are always on the hunt for new and innovative recipes to share for our family meals and entertaining, and we have great fun on this quest.

In fact, two of the recipes for my favorite cookout featured here made their way to my kitchen from the files of good cooks I know.

My husband, Rob, daughter, Kahley, and son, Alec, give this summer spread their hearty stamp of approval. It's also a meal I can count on when company's coming.

A flavorful marinade makes the Grilled Sirloin Steak memorable. Rob raves about the appetizing aroma while it's cooking. One bite of this tender, tasty meat is the true test!

Cooking with Friends

The zesty marinade is one that my friend, Miriam Reyes, and I concocted. We've found that if you mix and refrigerate the ingredients a day ahead, the flavors become even more pronounced.

My best friend from college, Karen Inger, served Tomato Basil Linguine during a "girls' weekend" she hosted at her lake cottage. She's a fantastic cook, and I can always count on her to come up with something new and exciting.

Like Karen, I have found that whenever I serve this fresh-tasting dish, recipe requests are sure to follow. I love the distinctive flavor of Brie cheese—it really adds character to this special pasta. Camembert is a delicious alternative.

Swiss Cashew Tossed Salad has the perfect blend of crunch and sweetness. The Swiss cheese and nuts in this recipe accent the crisp lettuce. Speckled with poppy seeds, the attractive dressing is both sweet and tangy.

It's a side dish that fits nicely with many different menus. When I serve it to guests, which I do often, they comment about the interesting mix of salad ingredients and the dressing's attractive appearance and pleasing flavor.

I credit my neighbor, Linda Sargent, for the Walnut Apple Dessert. She's been making it for 33 years, and the recipe was passed down from her mom.

Always a crowd-pleaser, this timeless treat tastes something like apple pie but is conveniently made in a 13 x 9 baking dish. It is loaded with fruit, which makes the cake very moist.

My mom wasn't interested in cooking, but that didn't stop me! I can remember her admonishing me when I was 10 for making my cookies too big. She didn't realize I was making eclairs—not cookies—at the time!

While my earliest memories of cooking involve helping my great-grandmother in her kitchen, my love of cooking came from my wonderful grandmother, who was forever inviting family and friends over for delicious dinners after church.

Cafeteria Rendezvous

I met Rob during college. Immediately attracted to him, I knew he'd be the man I would marry. I borrowed a roommate's binoculars and tried to time my arrival at the cafeteria to coincide with his.

From December to May I did this—but to no avail. Since I had to run down four flights of stairs to get there, I arrived red-faced and out of breath each day—not exactly the best way to impress a guy!

Finally, the following April Fool's Day, I boldly told him that I'd like to get to know him. The direct approach worked! We celebrated our 20th wedding anniversary by returning to the same cafeteria.

Nowadays, we're busy with family activities, but cooking is one of my favorite creative outlets.

I hope that I've whetted your appetite to try our favorite steak dinner. I'm thrilled to have this opportunity to share some of the recipes I like best with *Taste of Home* cooks.

PICTURED AT LEFT: Grilled Sirloin Steak, Tomato Basil Linguine, Swiss Cashew Tossed Salad and Walnut Apple Dessert (recipes are on the next page).

Grilling IQ

Coat your grill rack with nonstick cooking spray before starting the fire, and then clean it shortly after you are through. Never spray the rack after the fire has started—it may cause a flare-up.

If the coals become too hot or flare up, spray them with water from a mister.

Remove food from the grill a minute or two before it's done—the residual heat will continue to cook it.

Tomato Basil Linguine

Hot pasta is tossed with a fresh-tasting sauce that includes tomatoes, basil and Brie cheese in this deliciously different dish. It's very pretty, too. Even when it cools off, this pasta tastes great.

>   1 pound Brie *or* Camembert cheese, rind removed and cut into small pieces
>   4 large tomatoes, coarsely chopped
>   1 cup chopped fresh basil
>   1/2 cup olive *or* vegetable oil
>   3 garlic cloves, minced
>   1/2 teaspoon salt
>   1/4 teaspoon white pepper
>   1-1/2 pounds uncooked linguine
> Shredded Parmesan cheese

In a large serving bowl, combine the Brie, tomatoes, basil, oil, garlic, salt and pepper. Let stand at

Grilled Sirloin Steak

Once you taste this delectable steak—a cookout favorite for my family—you'll think of it time and time again. The marinade gives it savory seasoning, plus it tenderizes the meat.

>   1 cup soy sauce
>   1/4 cup red wine vinegar *or* cider vinegar
>   1/4 cup olive *or* vegetable oil
>   4 garlic cloves, chopped
>   1 tablespoon pepper
>   1 tablespoon ground ginger *or* 1/4 cup minced fresh gingerroot
>   1 tablespoon honey
>   1 boneless beef sirloin steak (about 3 pounds and 2 inches thick)

In a large resealable plastic bag, combine the first seven ingredients; add beef. Seal bag and turn to coat; refrigerate for at least 3 hours or overnight.

Drain and discard the marinade. Grill steak, covered, over indirect medium heat for 1-1/2 to 2 hours, turning once, or until meat reaches desired doneness (for rare, a meat thermometer should read 140°; medium, 160°; well-done, 170°). **Yield:** 8 servings.

room temperature for up to 1-1/2 hours. Cook linguine according to package directions; drain. Toss with cheese mixture. Sprinkle with Parmesan cheese. Serve immediately. **Yield:** 10 servings.

Swiss Cashew Tossed Salad

Along with crunchy cashews and strips of Swiss cheese, a sweet-and-tangy poppy seed dressing makes this tossed salad something special. There are seldom any leftovers when I serve it!

    1/3 **cup white vinegar**
    3/4 **cup sugar**
      2 **teaspoons prepared mustard**
      1 **teaspoon grated onion**
Dash salt
      1 **cup vegetable oil**
      1 **teaspoon poppy seeds**
      1 **medium bunch romaine, torn**
      1 **cup salted cashew halves**
      4 **ounces Swiss cheese, julienned**

In a blender, combine the vinegar, sugar, mustard, onion and salt; cover and process until well blended. While processing, gradually add oil in a steady stream. Stir in poppy seeds. In a salad bowl, combine the romaine, cashews and Swiss cheese; serve with dressing. **Yield:** 8-10 servings.

Walnut Apple Dessert

The neighbor who shared this recipe with me predicted that I'd serve it often, just as she has for more than 30 years. It's easy to put together and is wonderfully fruity. I like to serve it with ice cream or a dollop of whipped cream.

      8 **cups sliced peeled tart apples (about 6 medium)**
2-1/4 **cups packed brown sugar,** _divided_
      2 **teaspoons ground cinnamon**
      1 **cup butter** _or_ **margarine, softened**
      2 **eggs**
      2 **cups all-purpose flour**
      1 **cup finely chopped walnuts,** _divided_
Vanilla ice cream, optional

Place apples in a greased 13-in. x 9-in. x 2-in. baking dish. Sprinkle with 1/4 cup brown sugar and cinnamon. In a mixing bowl, cream butter and remaining brown sugar. Add eggs. Stir in flour and 1/2 cup walnuts. Spread over apples. Sprinkle with remaining walnuts.

    Bake at 350° for 45-55 minutes or until the apples are tender. Serve warm with ice cream if desired. **Yield:** 12-16 servings.

Traditional Thanksgiving

A mixture of tasty tradition, garden goodness and lots of love make up this cook's Thanksgiving menu. Her family can't wait for the special day!

By Edna Hoffman, Hebron, Indiana

I TRULY BELIEVE I would rather cook than eat! For Thanksgiving, it's a joy to prepare a meal that everyone—from my husband, Martin, right down to our great-grandchildren—will enjoy.

I vary some of the side dishes each year because I love trying new recipes, but the recipes I shared here are mainstays at our holiday gathering.

Martin and I were married over 50 years ago. We were born and raised in neighboring communities and moved to the farm—where we still live—right after our honeymoon.

A few months after our wedding, we had 25 people over for our first Thanksgiving dinner. My sister helped me stuff and roast the turkey that year, but thereafter, I was on my own!

I prepare Stuffed Roast Turkey like my grandma used to, rubbing the skin with butter mixed with paprika. This gives it a rich color and keeps the turkey moist. The old-fashioned bread stuffing gets its distinctive taste from sage.

Flavored with pan drippings, the turkey gravy is so easy to stir up. Everyone loves it spooned over the tender turkey!

When I was young, we would go to my grandmother's for Thanksgiving dinner since my mom was ill. I lost her at an early age, and Grandma taught me to cook. I started helping with family meals when I was just 8 years old.

Fond Memories of Food

Mallow-Topped Sweet Potatoes is another recipe that includes a "secret ingredient" of fond memories for me. It was always on the menu for Thanksgiving dinner at Grandma's. As the casserole bakes, the marshmallows puff and create a golden-brown topping.

In Herbed Corn, frozen sweet corn from our garden tastes as fresh as the day we picked it. The recipe is the result of my experimenting with combinations of different herbs to dress up a vegetable my family has always enjoyed.

One of our daughters and our daughter-in-law have large herb gardens, and I have a small one. So I have plenty of taste-tempting varieties to try.

Some of the grandchildren—we have 15, plus four great-grandkids—call this dish "Grandpa and Grandma's Indiana Corn" and request it when they come to visit. Our other daughter lives in China with her family. They'll be coming home for a visit and already have their order in for this corn!

One of our sons farms with us—we raise corn and soybeans on about 1,500 acres. The other one is the pastor at our church, where I do a lot of volunteer work.

I encourage our grandchildren to help out in the kitchen, to set the table and make things pretty for a meal. Several of our granddaughters are taking a great interest in cooking and have their own subscriptions to *Taste of Home*!

Taste Twist

It wouldn't be Thanksgiving without pumpkin pie, but mine puts a twist on the traditional. The festive filling of Walnut-Date Pumpkin Pie is a bit different and has earned the Hoffman family stamp of approval.

I never tire of trying out new recipes and different methods of cooking. Martin jokes that he hasn't had the same meal twice since we've been married!

Besides cooking for the family, I like to bake and take goodies to friends in need. We also invite guests to our home for theme dinners about once a month.

My collection of cookbooks is large. I enjoy reading and studying them—and my *Taste of Home* issues—like novels. When we travel, my souvenir is always a cookbook. I've brought them home from Holland, where some of my family came from, and from Germany and Austria, too.

I look forward to a busy, happy time in the kitchen this Thanksgiving. I'm sure many of you feel the same way. And if you decide to try one or more of my recipes for your celebration, I'd be delighted!

PICTURED AT LEFT: Stuffed Roast Turkey, Mallow-Topped Sweet Potatoes, Herbed Corn and Walnut-Date Pumpkin Pie (recipes are on the next page).

Stuffed Roast Turkey

For our Thanksgiving dinner, this moist golden-brown stuffed turkey is a treasured tradition. My grandmother always served her bird this way...and now my children, grandchildren and great-grandchildren enjoy turkey with us in the same savory way!

- 1 turkey (14 to 16 pounds)
- 6 cups water
- 3/4 cup egg substitute
- 2 pounds day-old white bread, cubed and toasted
- 2 medium onions, chopped
- 2 celery ribs, chopped
- 1 tablespoon poultry seasoning
- 1 teaspoon salt
- 1 teaspoon rubbed sage
- 1/4 teaspoon pepper
- 6 tablespoons butter *or* margarine, melted
- 1/2 to 1 teaspoon paprika

GRAVY:
- 2 teaspoons chicken bouillon granules
- 2 cups boiling water
- 5 tablespoons all-purpose flour

Remove giblets from turkey; discard liver if desired. In a saucepan, bring water, giblets and neck to a boil. Reduce heat; cover and simmer for 1 hour or until tender. Remove giblets with a slotted spoon; dice. Set aside 3 cups cooking liquid.

In a large bowl, combine egg substitute, bread cubes, onions, celery, giblets, poultry seasoning, salt, sage and pepper. Add reserved cooking liquid; mix well. Just before baking, loosely stuff turkey with about 8 cups stuffing. Place remaining stuffing in a greased 2-qt. baking dish; refrigerate until ready to bake. Skewer turkey openings; tie drumsticks together. Place on a rack in a roasting pan. Brush with butter; sprinkle with paprika.

Bake, uncovered, at 325° for 4-1/2 to 5-1/2 hours or until a meat thermometer reads 180° for turkey and 165° for stuffing, basting every 30 minutes (cover loosely with foil if turkey browns too quickly). Bake additional stuffing for 35-40 minutes or until heated through.

For gravy, dissolve bouillon in water. In a saucepan, combine flour and 1/4 cup pan drippings; whisk until smooth. Gradually add bouillon mixture. Bring to a boil; cook and stir for 2 minutes or until thickened. Serve with turkey and stuffing. **Yield:** 14-16 servings (2 cups gravy).

Mallow-Topped Sweet Potatoes

My grandmother taught me how to fix this sweet potato casserole that she always served at Thanksgiving. The puffy marshmallow topping gives the dish a festive look, and spices enhance the sweet potato flavor.

- 6 cups mashed sweet potatoes (about 5 large)
- 1 cup milk
- 6 tablespoons butter *or* margarine, softened
- 1/2 cup packed brown sugar
- 1 egg
- 1-1/2 teaspoons ground cinnamon
- 1-1/2 teaspoons vanilla extract
- 3/4 teaspoon ground allspice
- 1/2 teaspoon salt

1/4 teaspoon ground nutmeg
18 large marshmallows

In a large mixing bowl, combine the sweet potatoes, milk, butter, brown sugar, egg, cinnamon, vanilla, allspice, salt and nutmeg; beat until smooth. Transfer to a greased shallow 13-in. x 9-in. x 2-in. baking dish.

Bake, uncovered, at 325° for 40-45 minutes or until heated through. Top with marshmallows. Bake 5-10 minutes longer or until marshmallows just begin to puff and brown. **Yield:** 10-12 servings.

——— 🝙 🝙 🝙 ———

Herbed Corn

A pleasant blend of herbs dresses up this buttery, fresh-flavored corn dish that's part of "all the trimmings" for our Thanksgiving meal. I also serve it frequently throughout the year and always take a bowl along to carry-in dinners.

  12 cups frozen corn
   1 cup water
  1/2 cup butter *or* margarine, cubed
   2 tablespoons minced fresh parsley
   2 teaspoons salt
   1 teaspoon dill weed
  1/2 teaspoon garlic powder
  1/2 teaspoon Italian seasoning
  1/4 teaspoon dried thyme

In a large saucepan, bring corn and water to a boil. Reduce heat; cover and simmer for 4-6 minutes or until corn is tender. Drain; stir in the remaining ingredients. **Yield:** 10-12 servings.

Walnut-Date Pumpkin Pie

I'm forever looking for a little something extra to enhance a favorite recipe. In this case, crunchy walnuts and chewy dates take traditional pumpkin pie to a new level.

   1 cup all-purpose flour
  1/2 cup cold butter *or* margarine
   1 cup packed light brown sugar, *divided*
   2 eggs
   1 teaspoon ground cinnamon
  1/4 teaspoon ground cloves
   1 cup cooked *or* canned pumpkin
   1 cup evaporated milk
  1/2 cup finely chopped dates
  1/3 cup chopped walnuts, toasted
Whipped cream and toasted walnut halves, optional

In a food processor, combine the flour, butter and 1/3 cup brown sugar. Cover and pulse until mixture resembles coarse crumbs. Press onto the bottom and up the sides of a 9-in. pie plate. Bake at 350° for 5 minutes; cool on a wire rack.

In a mixing bowl, beat the eggs, cinnamon, cloves and remaining brown sugar. Beat in the pumpkin and milk. Stir in the dates and walnuts. Pour into crust. Cover edges loosely with foil.

Bake at 350° for 55-60 minutes or until a knife inserted near the center comes out clean. Cool for 2 hours on a wire rack. Refrigerate until serving. Garnish with whipped cream and walnut halves if desired. Refrigerate leftovers. **Yield:** 6-8 servings.

Meals in Minutes

A hot home-cooked meal is just minutes away with this host of rapid recipes that can be ready in less than half an hour.

——— 🍵 🍵 🍵 ———

FOOD THAT'S FAST. Clockwise from upper left:
Italian-Style Supper (p. 266), Flavorful Stir-Fry Is
Simple Way to Serve Supper (p. 254), Company
Will Fall for Special Chicken Dinner (p. 262) and
Fishing for Fast Fare? Look No Further! (p. 256).

Made-in-a-Hurry Meal Ideal for Hectic Holiday

IF the hustle and bustle of the holiday season keeps your time in the kitchen to a minimum, a satisfying quick meal may be just the gift to give yourself and your family.

The fast menu here is made up of favorite recipes shared by three great cooks and combined in our Test Kitchen. You can have it all ready to serve in a mere 30 minutes!

Peppered Rib Eye Steaks are an easy yet elegant-looking entree suggested by Julee Wallberg of Carson City, Nevada. "These steaks grill up nice and juicy with a pleasant peppery zip," Julee says. "We enjoy them all year-round."

Colorful Rice Medley gets its start with convenient instant rice. "Steak sauce gives this rice dish a different flavor twist," notes Terri Griffin of Salisbury, Maryland, who shares the recipe for the tasty side dish. "Carrot, red onion and parsley add a nice touch of color."

No-Bake Fudgy Oat Cookies are sweet treats suggested by Elizabeth Hunter of Prosperity, South Carolina. "These fuss-free cookies have stood the test of time," reports Elizabeth. "I got the recipe from my mother-in-law back in 1949...and my grown daughter asked me to share it with her so she could make them for Christmas!"

— ☕ ☕ ☕ —

Peppered Rib Eye Steaks

2 tablespoons vegetable oil
1/2 teaspoon paprika
1/2 teaspoon pepper
1/4 teaspoon *each* salt, garlic powder and lemon-pepper seasoning
1/8 teaspoon *each* dried oregano, crushed red pepper flakes, ground cumin and cayenne pepper
4 boneless rib eye steaks (about 2-1/2 pounds)

In a bowl, combine the oil and seasonings; brush over steaks. Broil or grill over medium-hot heat for 7 minutes on each side or until meat reaches desired doneness (for rare, a meat thermometer should read 140°; medium, 160°; well-done, 170°). Baste occasionally with seasoning mixture. **Yield:** 4 servings.

Colorful Rice Medley

✓ Uses less fat, sugar or salt. Includes Nutritional Analysis and Diabetic Exchanges.

2 cups water
2 cups uncooked instant rice
1/3 cup shredded carrot
1/4 cup finely chopped red onion
1-1/2 teaspoons steak sauce
1 teaspoon butter *or* stick margarine
1/2 to 1-1/2 teaspoons salt
1/2 teaspoon pepper
1 teaspoon minced fresh parsley

In a saucepan, bring water to a boil. Remove from the heat; add rice. Cover and let stand for 3 minutes. Stir in the remaining ingredients. Cover and let stand for 5 minutes. **Yield:** 4 servings.

Nutritional Analysis: One 1-cup serving (prepared with 1/2 teaspoon salt) equals 139 calories, 1 g fat (1 g saturated fat), 3 mg cholesterol, 339 mg sodium, 29 g carbohydrate, 1 g fiber, 3 g protein. **Diabetic Exchange:** 2 starch.

— ☕ ☕ ☕ —

No-Bake Fudgy Oat Cookies

2-1/4 cups quick-cooking oats
1 cup flaked coconut
1/2 cup milk
1/4 cup butter *or* margarine
2 cups sugar
1/2 cup baking cocoa
1 teaspoon vanilla extract

Combine the oats and coconut; set aside. In a saucepan, combine milk and butter. Stir in sugar and cocoa; bring to a boil. Add oat mixture, stirring constantly; cook for 1 minute. Remove from heat; stir in vanilla. Drop by rounded tablespoonfuls 1 in. apart onto waxed paper. **Yield:** about 3 dozen.

Speedy Staple

Instant rice has been fully or partially cooked, then dehydrated; it only takes a few minutes to cook.

Flavorful Stir-Fry Is Simple Way to Serve Supper

SPEED is sometimes the key ingredient in what you whip up for supper—especially on days when you feel you only have seconds to spare.

The complete-meal menu here combines family favorites from three time-conscious cooks. Thirty minutes is all you need to set all three dishes on the dinner table!

Pork with Three Peppers is a hearty main dish you can prepare in a jiffy. "I like to cut the meat and vegetables ahead of time," says Sheri La Fleche of New Bedford, Massachusetts. "Then this entree goes from the skillet to the table in no time."

Creamy French Dressing makes an excellent salad topper that is thick and well seasoned. "I fix this easy and economical dressing often," relates Ruth Ann Stelfox of Raymond, Alberta. "It goes great over a variety of salad greens."

It's a snap to make Pear Parfaits since they're comprised of only four ingredients. "My husband and I regularly enjoy this handy dessert," notes Heather Kobe of Vancouver, Washington.

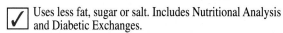

Pork with Three Peppers

✓ Uses less fat, sugar or salt. Includes Nutritional Analysis and Diabetic Exchanges.

- **1 pound pork tenderloin, cut into 1/4-inch strips**
- **2 medium onions, sliced and separated into rings**
- **1 garlic clove, minced**
- **1 tablespoon canola oil**
- **1 can (14-1/2 ounces) beef broth**
- **1 *each* medium sweet red, yellow and green pepper, julienned**
- **1/4 cup tomato paste**
- **1/4 cup salsa**
- **1 to 2 teaspoons chili powder**
- **1/2 teaspoon salt**
- **3 tablespoons all-purpose flour**
- **1/4 cup cold water**
Hot cooked rice

In a large skillet, stir-fry the pork, onions and garlic in oil for 3 minutes. Stir in the broth, peppers, tomato paste, salsa, chili powder and salt. Bring to a boil. Reduce heat; cover and simmer for 10-12 minutes or until pork is no longer pink, stirring occasionally.

Combine flour and water until smooth; gradually add to pan. Bring to a boil; cook and stir for 2 minutes or until thickened. Serve over rice. **Yield:** 4 servings.

Nutritional Analysis: One serving (calculated without rice) equals 274 calories, 8 g fat (2 g saturated fat), 74 mg cholesterol, 896 mg sodium, 23 g carbohydrate, 4 g fiber, 29 g protein. **Diabetic Exchanges:** 3 lean meat, 1 starch, 1 vegetable.

Creamy French Dressing

- **1/2 cup mayonnaise *or* salad dressing**
- **1/2 cup ketchup**
- **1/4 cup white vinegar**
- **1/2 cup sugar**
- **1 small onion, cut into wedges**
- **1/2 teaspoon salt**
- **1/4 teaspoon pepper**
- **1 cup vegetable oil**
Salad greens, tomato wedges and cucumber slices *or* vegetables of your choice

In a blender, place the mayonnaise, ketchup, vinegar, sugar, onion, salt and pepper; cover and process until smooth. While processing, gradually add the oil in a steady stream until blended. Serve over salad. Refrigerate any leftover dressing. **Yield:** 2-1/2 cups.

Pear Parfaits

- **1-1/2 cups vanilla yogurt**
- **1/4 cup confectioners' sugar**
- **2 cans (15-1/4 ounces *each*) sliced pears, well drained**
- **1-1/4 cups finely crushed cinnamon graham crackers (about 18 squares)**

In a bowl, combine yogurt and sugar. Place three to four pear slices each in four parfait glasses; top each with 2 tablespoons cracker crumbs and 3 tablespoons yogurt mixture. Repeat layers. Sprinkle with remaining crumbs. Refrigerate until serving. **Yield:** 4 servings.

Fishing for Fast Fare? Look No Further!

YOUR FAMILY will fall hook, line and sinker for this fresh and flavorful dinner, which you can put before them in no time flat.

It's a complete meal made up of three fast-to-fix dishes from fellow hurried cooks that can be ready to serve in just half an hour!

"Chow Mein Tuna Salad is a delicious variation on standard tuna salad," notes Marilyn Coomer of Louisville, Kentucky. "Served over a bed of crunchy chow mein noodles, this creamy tuna salad makes a quick yet memorable supper."

From Hagerstown, Maryland, Priscilla Weaver recommends her sweet French-style Pantry Salad Dressing. Says Priscilla, "I like this recipe because it's fast to fix, tastes fresh and calls for ingredients I usually have on my pantry shelf."

"Crisp Cheese Breadsticks are a delicious way to use up day-old bread," shares Elizabeth Tonn of Waukesha, Wisconsin. "They are great served alongside soup or salad. And guests at my card game parties love them as appetizers."

— 🍴 🍴 🍴 —

Chow Mein Tuna Salad

3 cans (12 ounces *each*) tuna, drained and flaked
1-1/2 cups mayonnaise
1-1/2 cups chopped cashews
3/4 cup finely chopped green onions
3 jars (2 ounces *each*) diced pimientos, drained and finely chopped
3 tablespoons finely chopped green pepper
3 tablespoons sour cream
1 tablespoon cider vinegar
3/4 teaspoon salt
3 cups chow mein noodles

In a large bowl, combine the first nine ingredients. Serve over chow mein noodles. **Yield:** 6 servings.

— 🍴 🍴 🍴 —

Pantry Salad Dressing

1 cup sugar
1 cup ketchup
3/4 cup white vinegar
3/4 cup vegetable oil
1/2 small onion, cut into wedges
1/2 teaspoon salt
1/2 teaspoon garlic salt
1/4 teaspoon pepper
Torn salad greens

In a blender, combine the first eight ingredients; cover and process until the sugar is dissolved. Serve over salad greens. Refrigerate any leftover dressing. **Yield:** 3 cups.

— 🍴 🍴 🍴 —

Crisp Cheese Breadsticks

1 jar (5 ounces) sharp American cheese spread
1/2 cup butter *or* margarine, softened
1 egg white
1 teaspoon Italian seasoning
1/4 teaspoon garlic powder
1 unsliced loaf (1 pound) day-old white *or* wheat bread

In a small mixing bowl, combine the cheese spread, butter, egg white, Italian seasoning and garlic powder; beat until fluffy and blended.

Remove crust from bread. Cut loaf in half widthwise. Cut each half horizontally into thirds; cut each portion lengthwise into fourths. (Strips will measure about 4 in. x 1 in. x 1 in.) Spread cheese mixture over all sides of strips; place 2 in. apart on a greased baking sheet. Bake at 350° for 12-15 minutes or until lightly browned. **Yield:** 2 dozen.

Tuna Tidbits

Canned tuna is pre-cooked and can be water- or oil-packed. It comes in three grades, the best being solid or fancy (large pieces), followed by chunk (smaller pieces) and flaked (bits and pieces).

In 1997, canned tuna was the most popular fish sold in the United States. In fact, the average American consumes about 4 pounds of canned tuna annually.

Warm-Weather Supper Keeps Your Kitchen Cool

COME SUMMERTIME, when "the living is easy", making supper for your hungry family should also be a breeze.

Thanks to three time-minded cooks, you can have this fuss-free fare ready in under 30 minutes!

Halibut Steaks are moist and flavorful when they're topped with a soy sauce mixture and lemon, wrapped in foil and grilled. Says Donna Goutermont of Jackson, Wyoming, "Each year we travel to Alaska to visit friends and catch our limit of halibut. We especially enjoy it prepared this way."

Seasoned with herbs and butter, Grilled Cherry Tomatoes make a colorful and tasty side dish. "Just tuck the foil packet beside any meat you happen to be grilling," suggests Lucy Meyring of Walden, Colorado.

Scrumptious No-Bake Cereal Bars combine peanut butter, chocolate and butterscotch flavors. "These quick treats are popular with both young and old," notes Hennie Scholten of Edgerton, Minnesota.

— 🛒 🛒 🛒 —

Halibut Steaks

    1/2 cup soy sauce
    1/4 cup packed brown sugar
      2 garlic cloves, minced
    1/8 teaspoon pepper
Dash hot pepper sauce
Pinch dried oregano
Pinch dried basil
      4 halibut steaks (6 ounces *each*)
    1/2 cup chopped onion
      4 lemon slices
      4 teaspoons butter *or* margarine

In a small bowl, combine the first seven ingredients. Place each halibut steak on a double thickness of heavy-duty foil (about 18 in. x 12 in.); top with soy sauce mixture, onion, lemon and butter. Fold foil around fish and seal tightly. Grill, covered, over medium heat for 10-14 minutes or until fish flakes easily with a fork. **Yield:** 4 servings.

— 🛒 🛒 🛒 —

Grilled Cherry Tomatoes

    2 pints cherry tomatoes, halved
    2 garlic cloves, minced

    1/2 teaspoon dried oregano
      3 tablespoons butter *or* margarine

Place the cherry tomato halves on a double thickness of heavy-duty foil (about 24 in. x 12 in.). In a skillet, saute the garlic and oregano in butter for 2 minutes. Pour over the tomatoes. Fold foil around tomatoes and seal tightly. Grill, covered, over medium heat for 8-10 minutes or until the tomatoes are heated through, turning once. **Yield:** 4-6 servings.

— 🛒 🛒 🛒 —

No-Bake Cereal Bars

      6 cups Special K
1-1/2 cups peanut butter
      1 cup corn syrup
      1 cup sugar
      1 cup semisweet chocolate chips
      1 cup butterscotch chips

Place cereal in a large heatproof bowl; set aside. In a saucepan, combine the peanut butter, corn syrup and sugar. Cook over medium heat until sugar is dissolved, stirring occasionally. Pour over cereal and stir until well coated.

Spread into a greased 13-in. x 9-in. x 2-in. pan. In a microwave or heavy saucepan, melt chocolate and butterscotch chips; stir until smooth. Spread over bars. Cool completely before cutting. **Yield:** 1-1/2 dozen.

Tomato Savvy

Cherry tomatoes can range in size from smaller than 1 inch in diameter to almost 2 inches. Typically, they are perfectly round with smooth, thin skins that can be red or yellow. They are sweeter than other varieties.

Tomatoes get their pigment from lycopene, a valuable nutritive substance related to beta-carotene, that helps reduce the risk of certain cancers. Cooked tomatoes are higher in lycopene than fresh tomatoes because the substance is concentrated by cooking.

Summer Calls for Quick-and-Easy Cuisine

A DAY of fun in the sun can quickly build appetites. Feed your family fast with this satisfying spread that is light, tasty and timely.

The made-in-a-flash recipes come from three great cooks and have been combined by our Test Kitchen. You can take them to the table in just 30 minutes!

Orange marmalade gives a citrus twist to moist Grilled Turkey Burgers, suggested by Patty Kile of Greentown, Pennsylvania. "Ground turkey offers a nice change from the usual hamburger patty," she says.

"Vegetable Cheese Tortellini is so good, even kids eat it up and get nutritious vegetables in the process," relates Jennifer Marriott from Batavia, New York.

Perlene Hoekema's no-fuss Banana Cream Pie is full of old-fashioned flavor. The Lynden, Washington cook stirs up this pie in no time using instant vanilla pudding and a ready-made crust.

— 🏆 🏆 🏆 —

Grilled Turkey Burgers

✓ Uses less fat, sugar or salt. Includes Nutritional Analysis and Diabetic Exchanges.

- 1 egg, lightly beaten
- 2/3 cup dry bread crumbs
- 1/4 cup finely chopped green pepper
- 2 green onions, finely chopped
- 2 tablespoons milk
- 1/2 teaspoon salt
- 1/8 teaspoon pepper
- 1 pound ground turkey
- 2 tablespoons orange marmalade
- 5 hamburger buns, split
- 5 slices Swiss cheese (1/2 ounce *each*)
- 5 onion slices
- 5 tomato slices
- 1/2 cup shredded lettuce

In a bowl, combine the first seven ingredients. Crumble turkey over mixture and mix well. Shape into five 1/2-in.- thick patties.

Coat grill rack with nonstick cooking spray before starting the grill. Grill the patties, uncovered, over medium heat for 8-10 minutes; turn and brush with the marmalade. Grill 8-10 minutes longer or until a meat thermometer reads 170°.

Grill buns cut side down for 2-4 minutes or until lightly browned. Serve burgers on buns with cheese, onion, tomato and lettuce. **Yield:** 5 servings.

Nutritional Analysis: One burger (prepared with fat-free milk, lean ground turkey and reduced-fat Swiss cheese) equals 415 calories, 15 g fat (5 g saturated fat), 124 mg cholesterol, 743 mg sodium, 41 g carbohydrate, 2 g fiber, 27 g protein. **Diabetic Exchanges:** 3 lean meat, 2-1/2 starch, 1 vegetable, 1 fat.

— 🏆 🏆 🏆 —

Vegetable Cheese Tortellini

- 8 cups water
- 1 package (16 ounces) frozen California-blend vegetables, thawed
- 1 package (9 ounces) refrigerated cheese tortellini
- 1/2 cup sharp cheddar *or* Swiss cheese spread
- 2 tablespoons milk
- 1/4 teaspoon pepper

In a large saucepan, bring water to a boil. Stir in vegetables and tortellini. Return to a boil; cook for 2-3 minutes or until tortellini is tender.

Meanwhile, in a small saucepan, combine cheese spread, milk and pepper. Cook over low heat until heated through. Drain tortellini mixture and toss with cheese sauce. **Yield:** 4 servings.

— 🏆 🏆 🏆 —

Banana Cream Pie

- 1 cup cold milk
- 1 package (3.4 ounces) instant vanilla pudding mix
- 1/2 teaspoon vanilla extract
- 1 carton (12 ounces) frozen whipped topping, thawed, *divided*
- 1 graham cracker crust (9 inches)
- 2 medium firm bananas, sliced

Additional banana slices

In a mixing bowl, beat the milk and pudding mix on low speed for 2 minutes; beat in vanilla. Fold in 3 cups whipped topping. Pour 1-1/3 cups of the pudding mixture into pie crust. Layer with banana slices and remaining pudding mixture. Top with remaining whipped topping. Garnish with additional banana slices. **Yield:** 8 servings.

Company Will Fall for Special Chicken Dinner

IMPRESS GUESTS—while keeping kitchen time to a minimum—with this special yet simple-to-make chicken dinner.

Ready to set before company in just half an hour, the complete menu here combines recipes from three busy cooks, who like to serve the time-saving dishes at their own gatherings.

Swiss Mushroom Chicken is easy to prepare but looks and tastes special enough for company and special-occasion suppers. "Everyone enjoys the golden chicken breasts topped with ham, melted Swiss cheese and fresh mushrooms," says Jan Baxter of Humarock, Massachusetts.

Fork-tender and flavorful Parsley Potatoes make an easy yet elegant accompaniment to any main entree. The recipe comes from Suzanne Cleveland of Lyons, Georgia.

Broccoli with Mustard Sauce is a delightfully tasty and simple side dish suggested by Marie Hoyer from Lewistown, Montana. "The creamy mustard sauce is also a nice complement to cauliflower," she notes.

—— 🥄 🥄 🥄 ——

Swiss Mushroom Chicken

4 boneless skinless chicken breast halves
  (about 1-1/4 pounds)
1 egg, lightly beaten
1 cup crushed butter-flavored crackers
  (about 25 crackers)
3/4 teaspoon salt
1/2 pound fresh mushrooms, sliced
2 tablespoons butter _or_ margarine, _divided_
4 slices ham _or_ salami
4 slices Swiss cheese

Flatten chicken to 1/4-in. thickness. Place egg in a shallow bowl. Combine cracker crumbs and salt in another shallow bowl. Dip chicken in egg, then in crumbs; set aside.

In a large ovenproof skillet, saute mushrooms in 1 tablespoon butter until tender; remove and set aside. In the same skillet, melt remaining butter. Add chicken; cook over medium heat for 3-4 minutes on each side or until juices run clear. Top each chicken breast half with a ham slice, mushrooms and a cheese slice. Broil 4 in. from the heat for 1-2 minutes or until cheese is melted. **Yield:** 4 servings.

Parsley Potatoes

✓ Uses less fat, sugar or salt. Includes Nutritional Analysis and Diabetic Exchanges.

1-1/2 pounds small red potatoes
1 medium onion, chopped
1 garlic clove, minced
1 tablespoon canola oil
1-1/2 cups chicken broth
1 cup minced fresh parsley, _divided_
1/2 teaspoon salt, optional
1/2 teaspoon pepper

Cut a strip of peel from around the middle of each potato if desired; set potatoes aside. In a large skillet, saute onion and garlic in oil until tender. Stir in broth and 3/4 cup parsley; bring to a boil. Add the potatoes.

Reduce heat; cover and simmer for 20 minutes or until the potatoes are tender. Sprinkle with salt if desired, pepper and remaining parsley. **Yield:** 4 servings.

Nutritional Analysis: One 1-cup serving (prepared without salt) equals 116 calories, 5 g fat (1 g saturated fat), 2 mg cholesterol, 393 mg sodium, 15 g carbohydrate, 6 g fiber, 4 g protein. **Diabetic Exchanges:** 1 starch, 1 fat.

—— 🥄 🥄 🥄 ——

Broccoli with Mustard Sauce

4 cups fresh _or_ frozen broccoli florets
1/2 cup water
1/2 teaspoon salt, _divided_
1 tablespoon butter _or_ margarine
1 tablespoon all-purpose flour
1/2 cup plus 2 tablespoons milk
1-1/2 teaspoons prepared mustard
1/4 teaspoon dill weed

In a large saucepan, bring the broccoli, water and 1/4 teaspoon salt to a boil. Reduce heat; cover and simmer for 5-8 minutes or until broccoli is crisp-tender. Drain and keep warm.

In a small saucepan, melt butter. Stir in flour until smooth. Gradually stir in milk. Bring to a boil; cook and stir for 2 minutes or until thickened. Stir in the mustard, dill and remaining salt. Drizzle over broccoli. **Yield:** 4 servings.

New Year's Breakfast

SPENDING the night celebrating the arrival of a new year can build big appetites. So wake up tired taste buds with a hearty breakfast. A cup of Cinnamon Mocha Coffee will perk you right up as will Strawberry-Topped Waffles, crisp bacon and broiled Maple-Glazed Fruit Rings. Our Test Kitchen dreamed up these eye-opening dishes.

Cinnamon Mocha Coffee

Most store-bought flavored coffees are quite expensive. So here's a special early morning beverage you can make at home. The aroma of cinnamon and cocoa makes this coffee hard to resist.

- 1/3 **cup ground coffee (not instant coffee granules)**
- 3/4 **teaspoon ground cinnamon**
- 1 **cup milk**
- 2 **to 3 tablespoons sugar**
- 2 **tablespoons baking cocoa**
- 1 **teaspoon vanilla extract**
- 4 **cinnamon sticks, optional**

Whipped cream, optional

In a coffeemaker basket, combine the coffee and ground cinnamon. Prepare 4 cups brewed coffee according to manufacturer's directions.

Meanwhile, combine the milk, sugar, cocoa and vanilla in a saucepan. Cook over medium-low heat for 5-7 minutes or until small bubbles appear on the sides of the pan, stirring occasionally (do not boil). Pour hot milk mixture into four coffee cups, then add cinnamon-flavored coffee. Garnish with cinnamon sticks and whipped cream if desired. **Yield:** 4 servings.

Strawberry-Topped Waffles

This warm fruity sauce takes only minutes to make. It's a nice way to present frozen waffles or even pancakes and French toast. If you don't have cranberry juice, orange juice can be used.

- 1 **package (16 ounces) frozen unsweetened whole strawberries**

- 1/2 **cup cranberry juice, *divided***
- 2 **tablespoons honey**
- 2 **tablespoons cornstarch**
- 8 **frozen waffles**

In a saucepan, combine the strawberries, 1/4 cup cranberry juice and honey. Cook over low heat for 10 minutes, stirring occasionally. In a small bowl, combine cornstarch and remaining cranberry juice until smooth; stir into strawberry mixture. Bring to a boil; cook and stir for 2 minutes or until thickened. Toast waffles according to package

directions; top with warm strawberry sauce. **Yield:** 4 servings.

—— ☕ ☕ ☕ ——

Maple-Glazed Fruit Rings

This recipe pleasantly proves that fruit doesn't just taste great cold. The pineapple and oranges topped with a sweet glaze will warm you up on winter mornings. Or use the glaze to top vanilla ice cream or pound cake slices and serve as a dessert.

2 cans (8 ounces *each*) pineapple slices, drained
1 medium navel orange, peeled and sliced
1/4 cup maple syrup
2 tablespoons orange marmalade
1/4 teaspoon vanilla extract

Place pineapple and orange slices on a broiler pan. Combine the maple syrup, marmalade and vanilla; brush over fruit. Broil 4 in. from the heat for 4-5 minutes or until sauce is bubbly. Serve warm. **Yield:** 4 servings.

Italian-Style Supper

IS YOUR FAMILY tired of ho-hum hamburgers? With Italian sausage and spaghetti sauce, Pizza Patties will become a newfound favorite. Italian Pasta and Peas is a snappy dish sure to please. After one bite of Chocolate Marshmallow Squares, your family will be asking for "S'more"! Try out these tasty recipes from our Test Kitchen tonight.

Pizza Patties

To cut preparation at mealtime, mix and shape these patties the night before and refrigerate. If you like lots of sauce, you may want to serve extra spaghetti sauce on the side for dipping.

> 1 **pound bulk Italian sausage**
> 1/3 **cup finely chopped green pepper**
> 1 **small onion, finely chopped**
> 1/4 **cup grated Parmesan cheese**
> 1 **cup spaghetti sauce**
> 4 **sandwich buns, split**
> 1/2 **cup shredded mozzarella cheese**

In a bowl, combine the sausage, green pepper, onion and Parmesan cheese. Shape into four patties. In a skillet, cook patties over medium heat for 15 minutes or until meat is no longer pink, turning occasionally; drain.

Add the spaghetti sauce; cover and simmer for 7 minutes. On the bottom of each bun, place a sausage patty and some sauce. Sprinkle with mozzarella cheese; replace tops. **Yield:** 4 servings.

Italian Pasta and Peas

If your family doesn't care for peas, substitute frozen green beans or broccoli. By stirring in cubed cooked chicken or ham, this becomes a mouth-watering main dish with little effort.

> 1-1/2 **cups water**
> 1/2 **cup milk**
> 1 **tablespoon butter *or* margarine**
> 1 **package (4.1 ounces) quick-cooking bow tie pasta and Parmesan/Romano sauce mix***
> 1 **cup frozen peas**
> 1 **can (4 ounces) mushroom stems and pieces, drained**

> 1/2 **teaspoon dried oregano**

In a saucepan, bring water, milk and butter to a boil; stir in pasta and sauce mix. Cook over medium heat for 8 minutes, stirring occasionally. Stir in peas, mushrooms and oregano; cook 3-4 minutes longer or until pasta is tender. Remove from heat. Sauce will thicken upon standing. **Yield:** 4 servings.

*Editor's Note: This recipe was tested with Lipton's Bow Tie Pasta in a Creamy Parmesan and Romano Cheese Sauce Mix.

Chocolate Marshmallow Squares

You don't need to gather the family around the camp-fire to capture the kid-pleasing taste of S'mores. Every-one will have fun helping out by covering the graham crackers with marshmallows, chocolate chips and ice cream topping.

8 whole graham crackers (about 5 inches x 2-1/2 inches)
1 cup miniature marshmallows
1/2 cup semisweet chocolate chips
2 tablespoons caramel *or* butterscotch ice cream topping

Place whole graham crackers 1 in. apart on a baking sheet. Top each cracker with marshmallows and chocolate chips. Drizzle with ice cream topping. Bake at 350° for 5-7 minutes or until the marshmallows are puffed and the chips are slightly melted. Cool for 2-3 minutes before serving. **Yield:** 4 servings.

Down-Home Dinner

ARE YOU CRAVING country-style cooking but don't want to spend hours in the kitchen? Our Test Kitchen created this meal with you in mind. Savory Beef and Noodles, along with Herb-Roasted Vegetables, is a speedy variation of beef Stroganoff that's long on flavor. Pop the Mini Apricot Turnovers in the oven for a "homemade" dessert in minutes.

— ☕ ☕ ☕ —

Savory Beef and Noodles

No one will be able to resist a hearty entree like this... it's true comfort food at its finest. The recipe only calls for 1/2 cup gravy. Refrigerate the remainder and serve it with mashed potatoes or leftover roast beef at another meal.

- **1 pound ground beef**
- **1 can (10-1/2 ounces) condensed French onion soup, undiluted**
- **1/2 cup beef gravy**
- **1 can (4 ounces) mushroom stems and pieces, drained**
- **1 tablespoon all-purpose flour**
- **1 tablespoon water**

Hot cooked noodles
Minced fresh parsley, optional

In a large skillet, cook beef over medium heat until no longer pink; drain. Stir in the soup, gravy and mushrooms. Bring to a boil. Reduce heat; cover and simmer for 5 minutes.

In a small bowl, combine flour and water until smooth; stir into beef mixture. Bring to a boil; cook and stir for 2 minutes or until thickened. Serve over hot cooked noodles. Garnish with fresh parsley if desired. **Yield:** 4 servings.

— ☕ ☕ ☕ —

Herb-Roasted Vegetables

Frozen vegetables can often be a bit bland by themselves. But tossing them with a little olive oil and some seasonings and then baking them brings out their wonderful flavor.

- **1 package (24 ounces) frozen California-blend vegetables**
- **3 to 4 tablespoons olive *or* vegetable oil**

- **3/4 teaspoon garlic salt**
- **3/4 teaspoon dried oregano**
- **1/2 teaspoon sugar**
- **1/2 teaspoon dried thyme**
- **1/4 teaspoon pepper**

Place vegetables in a single layer in an ungreased 15-in. x 10-in. x 1-in. baking pan. Combine the remaining ingredients; drizzle over vegetables and toss to coat. Bake, uncovered, at 425° for 20-23 minutes or until tender, stirring occasionally. **Yield:** 4 servings.

Mini Apricot Turnovers

Turnovers don't have to be time-consuming when you use prepared pie pastry and fruit preserves. These oven-fresh goodies are just right for breakfast, lunch and dinner as well as late-night snacks. Feel free to experiment with other fruit preserve flavors.

1 package (15 ounces) refrigerated pie pastry
1 jar (12 ounces) apricot *or* peach preserves
2 tablespoons milk

1 tablespoon sugar
1/4 teaspoon ground cinnamon

Cut each pastry into four wedges. Place a rounded tablespoonful of preserves in the center of each. Moisten edges with water. Fold pastry over filling; press edges with fork to seal.

Place turnovers on an ungreased baking sheet. Cut a small slit in the top of each. Brush with milk. Combine sugar and cinnamon; sprinkle over turnovers. Bake at 425° for 16-18 minutes or until golden brown. Serve warm. **Yield:** 8 turnovers.

Terrific Taste Twists

A FEW TWISTS on the traditional can make any meal extraordinary. Tangy Tossed Salad tastes great alongside Ham 'n' Broccoli Pizza, which features a cheesy ranch dressing instead of the usual tomato base. Spiced Cookie Strips give ordinary sugar cookies a new look and flavor. These three fresh ideas come from our Test Kitchen.

— 🝙 🝙 🝙 —

Tangy Tossed Salad

This colorful salad features a delicious vinaigrette dressing made with stock pantry items. When you don't have much time, use prepackaged salad greens.

- 6 tablespoons vegetable oil
- 2 tablespoons white wine vinegar *or* cider vinegar
- 1 tablespoon minced chives *or* fresh parsley
- 2 teaspoons sugar
- 1/2 teaspoon salt
- 1/4 teaspoon pepper
- 4 cups torn salad greens
- 1/2 cup chopped fresh tomatoes

In a jar with a tight-fitting lid, combine the first six ingredients; shake well. In a salad bowl, combine greens and tomatoes. Just before serving, add dressing and toss to coat. **Yield:** 4 servings.

— 🝙 🝙 🝙 —

Ham 'n' Broccoli Pizza

Even finicky eaters will eagerly eat their broccoli when it's part of this unique pizza. Family and friends will be pleasantly surprised by the cheesy ranch-flavored sauce.

- 1/4 cup process cheese spread
- 3 tablespoons prepared ranch salad dressing
- 1 tablespoon prepared mustard
- 1/4 teaspoon pepper
- 1 prebaked Italian bread shell crust
- 1 cup cubed fully cooked ham
- 1-1/2 cups broccoli florets
- 1/2 cup finely chopped onion
- 3/4 cup shredded Swiss cheese
- 2 tablespoons grated Parmesan cheese

In a bowl, combine the cheese spread, salad dressing, mustard and pepper. Place the crust on an

ungreased 12-in. pizza pan; spread with cheese mixture. Top with the ham, broccoli and onion. Sprinkle with Swiss and Parmesan cheeses. Bake at 425° for 12-14 minutes or until cheese is melted. **Yield:** 4 servings.

— 🝙 🝙 🝙 —

Spiced Cookie Strips

Convenient refrigerated sugar cookie dough and a few spices from your cupboard are all you need to bake a

batch of these yummy cookie strips. Your family will want to gobble them up right out of the oven. They're that good!

1 **tube (18 ounces) refrigerated sugar cookie dough**
2 **tablespoons all-purpose flour**
2 **tablespoons butter *or* margarine, melted**
1/2 **teaspoon ground nutmeg**
1/4 **teaspoon ground cinnamon**
1/4 **teaspoon ground cloves**

Remove cookie dough from package and coat with flour. Shake excess flour onto work surface. Roll out dough on floured surface into a 12-in. x 8-in. rectangle. Using a pizza cutter or sharp knife, cut rectangle in half lengthwise. Cut widthwise into 1-in. strips. Carefully transfer strips to two ungreased baking sheets.

Combine butter and spices; brush over strips. Bake at 425° for 10-12 minutes or until edges are golden brown. Cool for 2 minutes before removing from pans to wire racks. **Yield:** 2 dozen.

Signs of Spring

CELEBRATE the return of warm weather by firing up the grill for Quick Barbecued Chicken. The homemade sauce has a slightly smoky flavor that's finger-lickin' good. Paprika Potatoes 'n' Beans is a nutritious side dish. For a fruity finale, why not try Blueberry Graham Dessert? Compliments will crop up when you serve these dishes from our Test Kitchen.

Quick Barbecued Chicken

Cooking outdoors is a great way to make dinner when time is tight. To prevent the sauce from burning while grilling, only brush it on during the last few minutes.

- 1 **cup ketchup**
- 1/4 **cup packed brown sugar**
- 2 **tablespoons red wine vinegar *or* cider vinegar**
- 2 **teaspoons soy sauce**
- 1 **tablespoon dried minced onion**
- 1/4 **teaspoon celery seed**
- 1/2 **teaspoon salt, *divided***
- 1/4 **teaspoon crushed red pepper flakes, optional**

Dash liquid smoke, optional

- 4 **boneless skinless chicken breast halves (about 1-1/4 pounds)**
- 1 **tablespoon vegetable oil**

In a saucepan, combine the ketchup, brown sugar, vinegar, soy sauce, onion, celery seed, 1/4 teaspoon salt, pepper flakes and liquid smoke if desired. Cook and stir over low heat for 10 minutes.

Meanwhile, rub chicken with oil and sprinkle with remaining salt. Grill, covered, over medium heat for 3 minutes on each side. Set aside 1/2 cup barbecue sauce for serving. Brush half of the remaining sauce over chicken. Grill 4-6 minutes longer or until chicken juices run clear, turning and basting occasionally with sauce. Serve with reserved sauce. **Yield:** 4 servings.

Paprika Potatoes 'n' Beans

Red potato skins are very thin and tender, so cooks often leave them on not only for the color but for the extra vitamins.

- 1/2 **pounds medium red potatoes, cut into 3/4-inch pieces**
- 2 **cups frozen cut green beans**
- 3 **tablespoons butter *or* margarine, melted**
- 1/2 **teaspoon salt *or* garlic salt**
- 1/4 **teaspoon pepper**
- 1/4 **teaspoon paprika**

Place potatoes in a saucepan; cover with water. Bring to a boil. Reduce heat; cover and cook for 8 minutes. Add beans; cover and cook 3-5 minutes longer or until potatoes and beans are tender. Drain. Combine the butter, salt, pepper and paprika; drizzle over potatoes and gently stir to coat. **Yield:** 4 servings.

Graduates®

Save $1.00

when you buy any two
Graduates® Fruit Strips™

841799

Gerber

Consumer: May not be reproduced for store redemption. You pay any sales tax. Void if transferred to any person, firm or group prior to store redemption. You pay any sales tax. **Retailer:** Gerber will reimburse you for the value of this coupon plus 8 cents for handling if you and the customer have complied with the terms of this coupon and upon proof of sufficient stock to cover coupons redeemed. Send coupons to Gerber Products Company, NCH, P.O. Box 880517, El Paso, TX 88588-0517. (Cash value 1/20th of a cent.)

©2007 Gerber Products Company

5 150000 59133 0   (8100) 0 84179

Save $1.00 on Graduates® Fruit Strips™

- Delicious organic fruit bars made with 99% real fruit

Blueberry Graham Dessert

When you're running short on time but are longing for cheesecake, try this fruity dessert. Ricotta and cream cheeses give every bite the flavor of cheesecake but without the fuss.

3/4 cup graham cracker crumbs (about 12 squares)
1/4 cup chopped walnuts
2 tablespoons sugar
1/4 teaspoon ground cinnamon
2 tablespoons butter *or* margarine, melted
1 package (3 ounces) cream cheese, softened
1/3 cup confectioners' sugar
1/2 cup ricotta cheese
2 teaspoons lemon juice
4 cups fresh blueberries
Whipped cream, optional

In a bowl, combine the cracker crumbs, walnuts, sugar and cinnamon. Stir in butter; set aside. In a mixing bowl, beat cream cheese and confectioners' sugar until smooth. Beat in ricotta cheese and lemon juice.

Place 1/2 cup blueberries each in four dessert dishes. Top with cream cheese mixture, crumbs and remaining blueberries. Garnish with whipped cream if desired. Refrigerate until serving. **Yield:** 4 servings.

Skillet Sensations

ARE steamy summer days keeping you out of the kitchen? Instead of turning on the oven, switch on the stovetop and reach for some skillets to make Ginger Beef Stir-Fry and Zesty Sugar Snap Peas. Then keep your cool with Easy Boston Cream Cake. Our Test Kitchen came up with this sizzling supper with summer in mind.

— 🏳 🏳 🏳 —

Ginger Beef Stir-Fry

This savory stir-fry showcases tender slices of beef, while colorful carrots add a nice crunch. For devoted meat-and-potatoes fans, replace the cooked rice with mashed potatoes.

> 3 tablespoons cornstarch, *divided*
> 2 tablespoons water
> 1/4 teaspoon salt
> 1-1/2 pounds boneless beef sirloin steak, thinly sliced into 3-inch strips
> 2 tablespoons vegetable oil, *divided*
> 3/4 cup thinly sliced carrots
> 3/4 cup beef broth
> 2 tablespoons soy sauce
> 2 teaspoons grated orange peel
> 1 teaspoon ground ginger

Hot cooked rice

In a large bowl, combine 2 tablespoons cornstarch, water and salt until smooth. Add beef; toss to coat. In a large skillet, stir-fry beef in batches in 1 tablespoon oil until meat reaches desired doneness; remove and keep warm. Stir-fry carrots in remaining oil for 5-6 minutes. Place remaining cornstarch in a bowl; stir in broth until smooth. Add the soy sauce, orange peel and ginger. Return beef to skillet; stir in broth mixture. Bring to a boil. Cook and stir for 2 minutes or until thickened. Serve over rice. **Yield:** 4 servings.

— 🏳 🏳 🏳 —

Zesty Sugar Snap Peas

Lemon-pepper and garlic make these crisp-tender sugar snap peas flavorful and a nice accompaniment to a variety of entrees. You'll come to rely on this six-ingredient recipe.

> 1 pound fresh *or* frozen sugar snap peas
> 1/2 cup water
> 1 tablespoon butter *or* margarine
> 1 garlic clove, minced
> 3/4 teaspoon lemon-pepper seasoning
> 1/4 teaspoon salt

In a skillet, bring peas and water to a boil. Reduce heat. Cover and cook for 6-7 minutes or until tender; drain. Add the remaining ingredients. Cook and stir for 2-3 minutes or until well-coated. **Yield:** 4 servings.

Easy Boston Cream Cake

Why make a Boston cream pie from scratch when this cake version is so simple? Preparing the pudding with half-and-half cream instead of milk gives this dessert an added richness that's hard to beat.

1-1/2 cups cold half-and-half cream
   1 package (3.4 ounces) instant vanilla pudding mix
   1 loaf (10-3/4 ounces) frozen pound cake, thawed
  3/4 cup confectioners' sugar
   2 tablespoons baking cocoa
   4 to 5 teaspoons hot water

In a bowl, whisk together cream and pudding mix; let stand for 5 minutes. Split cake into three horizontal layers. Place bottom layer on a serving plate; top with half of the pudding. Repeat layers. Top with third cake layer. In a small bowl, combine the confectioners' sugar, cocoa and enough water to reach a spreading consistency. Spread over top of cake, letting glaze drizzle down sides. **Yield:** 4-6 servings.

Meals on a Budget

On a budget? You won't break the bank with these mouthwatering meals that only taste like a million bucks!

🛒 🛒 🛒

MONEY-SAVING MEALS. Clockwise from upper left: Aunt May's Lasagna, Garlic Tomato Bruschetta and Walnut Romaine Salad (p. 284); Country Roasted Chicken, Dot's Corn Muffins and Creamed Carrots (p. 282); Slow-Cooked Mac 'n' Cheese, Sunflower Broccoli and Peanut Butter Chocolate Cake (p. 280); Pineapple Ham Loaf, Broccoli Cream Soup and Buttermilk Rolls (p. 288).

Feed Your Family for $1.62 a Plate!

CAN YOU EAT WELL around the holidays without breaking the family grocery budget? You bet.

This down-home dinner is tasty, filling, colorful and economical. The recipes come from three terrific cooks, two who live on opposite coasts and one from just about in the middle.

Our Test Kitchen estimates the cost at just $1.62 per setting, which will come in handy when you're trying to save money to go Christmas shopping. In fact, this menu will be appreciated any time of year—it's that good.

Swiss Pot Roast is suggested by Darlene Markel of Salem, Oregon. "My family loves the taste of this tender roast," says Darlene. "I love the fact that it's so easy to prepare—it even makes its own gravy. The house smells wonderful when this hearty main dish is cooking, so I'm apt to hear the question, 'How long until dinner?'"

Cucumbers in Cream is a five-ingredient salad that goes together quick as a wink. The refreshing recipe comes from Dolores Hayes of Fort Plain, New York, who notes, "This salad is a great way to use locally produced cream."

And just to show that even a budget-conscious meal can have a festive finale, Katherine Kuhlemeier of Pearl City, Illinois shares her recipe for Homemade Eggnog Pie. "It's rich and scrumptious," she promises.

Swiss Pot Roast

- 1 boneless beef chuck roast (3 pounds)
- 1 tablespoon vegetable oil
- 8 medium potatoes, peeled and quartered
- 8 medium carrots, cut into chunks
- 1 medium onion, sliced
- 3 tablespoons all-purpose flour
- 1 cup water
- 1 can (8 ounces) tomato sauce
- 1 teaspoon beef bouillon granules
- 1/2 teaspoon salt
- 1/2 teaspoon pepper

In a Dutch oven, brown the roast on all sides in oil; drain. Add the potatoes, carrots and onion. In a bowl, combine the flour, water, tomato sauce, beef bouillon granules, salt and pepper; mix until smooth. Pour over the roast and vegetables. Cover and bake at 325° for about 2-1/2 to 3 hours or until the meat and vegetables are tender. **Yield:** 8 servings.

Cucumbers in Cream

- 1/4 cup white vinegar
- 1 cup whipping cream
- 5 medium cucumbers, sliced
- 1/4 teaspoon salt
- 1/8 teaspoon pepper

In a large bowl, gradually whisk the vinegar into the cream. Gently stir in the cucumbers, salt and pepper. Serve immediately or refrigerate for a short time. Serve with a slotted spoon. **Yield:** 8 servings.

— 🍵 🍵 🍵 —

Homemade Eggnog Pie

1-1/8 teaspoons unflavored gelatin
1/4 cup cold water
3/4 cup sugar
2 tablespoons cornstarch
2/3 cup milk
3 egg yolks, lightly beaten
1 teaspoon vanilla extract
1-1/2 cups whipping cream, whipped
1 pastry shell (9 inches), baked
1/8 teaspoon ground nutmeg

In a small bowl, soften gelatin in cold water; set aside. In a saucepan, combine sugar and cornstarch. Gradually stir in milk until smooth. Bring to a boil; cook and stir for 2 minutes or until thickened. Remove from the heat. Stir a small amount of hot mixture into egg yolks. Return all to the pan; bring to a gentle boil, stirring constantly.

Remove from the heat; stir in gelatin and vanilla. Cool to room temperature, stirring occasionally. Fold in whipped cream. Pour into pie shell. Sprinkle with nutmeg. Refrigerate until set, about 2 hours. **Yield:** 8 servings.

Feed Your Family for 99¢ a Plate!

NOT ONLY is this comforting meal full of kid-appeal, it's approved by budget-minded cooks, too!

Three such cooks suggested the fun yet frugal recipes found here. Our Test Kitchen staff then combined them into one family-pleasing meal you can serve for just 99¢ per person!

Slow-Cooked Mac 'n' Cheese is a classic casserole kids of all ages will fall for. "It's a rich and cheesy meatless main dish," notes Bernice Glascoe of Roxboro, North Carolina. "I've never met anyone who didn't ask for second helpings of the cheesy dish."

Sunflower Broccoli has great flavor and a nice crunch. The easy recipe is from Jean Artus of Aurora, Colorado. Even kids who don't normally care for broccoli will gobble it up.

Since chocolate and peanut butter are two of her granddaughters' favorite flavors, Elaine Medeiros of Wamego, Kansas frequently fixes Peanut Butter Chocolate Cake as a finale to her meals. "It's moist and scrumptious," describes Elaine.

Slow-Cooked Mac 'n' Cheese

      1 package (16 ounces) elbow macaroni
  -1/2 cup stick margarine, melted
      2 eggs, beaten
      1 can (12 ounces) evaporated milk
      1 can (10-3/4 ounces) condensed cheddar cheese soup, undiluted
      1 cup milk
      4 cups (16 ounces) shredded cheddar cheese, *divided*
  1/8 teaspoon paprika

Cook macaroni according to package directions; drain. Place in a 5-qt. slow cooker; add margarine. In a bowl, combine the eggs, evaporated milk, soup, milk and 3 cups cheese. Pour over macaroni mixture; stir to combine. Cover and cook on low for 4 hours.

Sprinkle with the remaining cheese. Cook 15 minutes longer or until cheese is melted. Sprinkle with paprika. **Yield:** 10 servings.

Sunflower Broccoli

☑ Uses less fat, sugar or salt. Includes Nutritional Analysis and Diabetic Exchanges.

      2 garlic cloves, minced
      3 tablespoons canola oil
  2-1/2 pounds fresh broccoli, cut into florets (about 10 cups)
    1/4 cup chicken broth
    1/2 teaspoon dried oregano
    1/2 teaspoon salt
    1/8 teaspoon pepper
      2 tablespoons sunflower kernels

In a large skillet, saute garlic in oil for 1 minute. Add broccoli; cook and stir for 3 minutes. Add the broth, oregano, salt and pepper; cover and cook until broccoli is crisp-tender, about 4 minutes. Sprinkle with sunflower kernels. **Yield:** 10 servings.

Nutritional Analysis: One serving (3/4 cup) equals 80 calories, 6 g fat (trace saturated fat), 0

cholesterol, 174 mg sodium, 7 g carbohydrate, 3 g fiber, 4 g protein. **Diabetic Exchanges:** 1 vegetable, 1 fat.

—— 🍷 🍷 🍷 ——

Peanut Butter Chocolate Cake

2-1/4 cups all-purpose flour
1-1/2 cups sugar
   1/3 cup baking cocoa
1-1/2 teaspoons baking soda
   1/2 teaspoon salt
1-1/2 cups water
   1/2 cup vegetable oil
4-1/2 teaspoons white vinegar
1-1/2 teaspoons vanilla extract
PEANUT BUTTER BATTER:
    4 ounces cream cheese, softened
   1/4 cup creamy peanut butter

1/3 cup plus 1 tablespoon sugar, *divided*
   1 egg
1/8 teaspoon salt
1/2 cup semisweet chocolate chips
1/2 cup chopped pecans

In a large bowl, combine the flour, sugar, cocoa, baking soda and salt. Stir in water, oil, vinegar and vanilla; mix well. Pour into a greased 13-in. x 9-in. x 2-in. baking pan.

In a mixing bowl, beat cream cheese, peanut butter, 1/3 cup sugar, egg and salt until smooth. Stir in chocolate chips. Drop by tablespoonfuls over cake batter; cut through batter with a knife to swirl the peanut butter mixture. Sprinkle with pecans and remaining sugar.

Bake at 350° for 30-35 minutes or until a toothpick inserted near the center comes out clean. Cool on a wire rack before cutting. Refrigerate leftovers. **Yield:** 24 servings.

Feed Your Family for $1.64 a Plate!

DISHING OUT hearty helpings of down-home foods to your family doesn't mean you also have to dish out hoards of money.

Three frugal cooks prove it with this delicious fare perfect for a Sunday dinner. Our Test Kitchen estimates the total cost at just $1.64 per setting.

"Country Roasted Chicken gets wonderful flavor from the celery, onion and parsley tucked inside," says Judy Page of Edenville, Michigan. "This is my family's favorite way to eat poultry. When my daughter was away at school, she even called home to ask me for the recipe so she could make it herself."

Dot's Corn Muffins are from Dorothy Smith, an El Dorado, Arkansas cook. "Moist and golden, these muffins are quick to make and go well with almost any meal," she says. "They're especially good with a hot bowl of soup."

"Creamed Carrots are always popular at my table," declares Eva Bailey of Olive Hill, Kentucky. "The rich sauce coats the carrots nicely and really perks up their flavor."

— 🛒 🛒 🛒 —

Country Roasted Chicken

- 1 broiler/fryer chicken (3 pounds)
- 1/2 teaspoon dried thyme
- 2 teaspoons salt, *divided*
- 1 large onion, cut into eighths
- 2 celery ribs with leaves, cut into 4-inch pieces
- 4 fresh parsley sprigs
- 8 small red potatoes
- 1/4 cup chicken broth
- 1/4 cup minced fresh parsley

Sprinkle inside of chicken with thyme and 1 teaspoon salt. Stuff with onion, celery and parsley sprigs. Place in a greased Dutch oven. Cover and bake at 375° for 30 minutes. Sprinkle remaining salt over chicken. Add potatoes and broth to pan. Cover and bake 25 minutes longer.

Increase oven temperature to 400°. Bake, uncovered, for 10-15 minutes or until potatoes are tender and a meat thermometer inserted in the chicken thighs reads 180°. Sprinkle with minced parsley. **Yield:** 4 servings.

— 🛒 🛒 🛒 —

Dot's Corn Muffins

- 1/2 cup all-purpose flour
- 1/2 cup cornmeal
- 3 tablespoons sugar
- 1/2 teaspoon baking soda
- 1/2 teaspoon salt
- 1 egg
- 1 cup (8 ounces) sour cream

In a bowl, combine the flour, cornmeal, sugar, baking soda and salt. In another bowl, beat egg and sour cream; stir into dry ingredients just until moistened. Fill greased muffin cups two-thirds full. Bake at 400° for 15-18 minutes or until a toothpick in-

serted near the middle comes out clean. Cool for 5 minutes before removing from pan to a wire rack. **Yield:** 8 muffins.

— 🛒 🛒 🛒 —

Creamed Carrots

- **1 pound carrots, sliced**
- **1 tablespoon butter *or* margarine**
- **1 tablespoon all-purpose flour**
- **2 tablespoons finely chopped onion**
- **2 teaspoons chopped fresh basil**
- **1/2 teaspoon seasoned salt**
- **1/8 teaspoon pepper**
- **1 cup evaporated milk**

In a large saucepan, bring 1 in. of water and carrots to a boil. Reduce heat; cover and simmer for 7-9 minutes or until crisp-tender. Meanwhile, in another saucepan, melt butter. Stir in flour, onion,

basil, seasoned salt and pepper until blended. Gradually stir in milk. Bring to a boil; cook and stir for 2 minutes or until thickened. Drain carrots; place in a serving bowl. Add sauce and stir to coat. **Yield:** 4 servings.

Keeping Carrots

Carrots were originally red, purple or black until the early 17th century, when the orange variety was developed in Holland.

Remove the green leafy tops from the carrots before they are stored. Otherwise, the tops will draw moisture from the carrots, cause them to become bitter and reduce their storage life. Carrots should be stored in sealed plastic bags in the refrigerator.

Feed Your Family for $1.30 a Plate!

DOES GOING OUT for Italian food feel like you've spent enough money to visit that country in person? Then feast your eyes on this mouth-watering meal and travel no further than your kitchen.

Three home cooks share the good-as-a-restaurant dishes, which add up to a mere $1.30 per plate!

Tomatoes, ground beef and mozzarella cheese flavor Aunt May's Lasagna. "Some people don't like ricotta cheese, traditionally found in lasagna. This is a nice alternative," says Angie Estes of Elko, Nevada.

Garlic Tomato Bruschetta from Jean Franzoni of Rutland, Vermont makes a crispy complement to any Italian entree. "I started with my grandmother's recipe and just added fresh tomatoes," she explains.

"Walnut Romaine Salad offers plenty of crunch," notes Harriet Stichter of Milford, Indiana, "and a zippy vinegar and oil dressing."

— 🛒 🛒 🛒 —

Aunt May's Lasagna

- **1 pound ground beef**
- **1 large onion, chopped**
- **2 garlic cloves, minced**
- **1 can (28 ounces) stewed tomatoes**
- **2 cans (6 ounces *each*) tomato paste**
- **1 teaspoon dried basil**
- **1/2 teaspoon dried oregano**
- **1/4 teaspoon pepper**
- **1 bay leaf**
- **9 lasagna noodles**
- **1 can (6 ounces) pitted ripe olives, drained and coarsely chopped**
- **2 cups (8 ounces) shredded mozzarella cheese**
- **1/2 cup grated Parmesan cheese**

In a large saucepan, cook beef, onion and garlic over medium heat until meat is no longer pink; drain. Stir in the tomatoes, tomato paste, basil, oregano, pepper and bay leaf. Bring to a boil. Reduce heat; cover and simmer for 40-50 minutes or until thickened. Meanwhile, cook noodles according to package directions; drain. Discard bay leaf from meat sauce. Stir in olives.

Spread a fourth of the sauce in a greased 13-in. x 9-in. x 2-in. baking dish. Top with three noodles and a third of the mozzarella and Parmesan cheeses. Repeat layers. Top with the remaining noodles, sauce mozzarella and Parmesan cheeses. Bake, uncovered, at 350° for 35-40 minutes or until bubbly. Let stand for 15 minutes before cutting. **Yield:** 12 servings.

— 🛒 🛒 🛒 —

Garlic Tomato Bruschetta

✓ Uses less fat, sugar or salt. Includes Nutritional Analysis and Diabetic Exchanges.

- **1/4 cup olive *or* canola oil**
- **3 tablespoons chopped fresh basil**
- **3 to 4 garlic cloves, minced**

1/2 teaspoon salt
1/4 teaspoon pepper
4 medium tomatoes, diced
2 tablespoons grated Parmesan cheese
1 loaf (1 pound) unsliced French bread

In a bowl, combine oil, basil, garlic, salt and pepper. Add tomatoes and toss gently. Sprinkle with cheese. Refrigerate for at least 1 hour. Bring to room temperature before serving. Cut bread into 24 slices; toast under broiler until lightly browned. Top with tomato mixture. Serve immediately. **Yield:** 12 servings.

Nutritional Analysis: One serving (2 pieces) equals 156 calories, 6 g fat (1 g saturated fat), 1 mg cholesterol, 347 mg sodium, 22 g carbohydrate, 1 g fiber, 4 g protein. **Diabetic Exchanges:** 1 starch, 1 vegetable, 1 fat.

Walnut Romaine Salad

1 small bunch romaine, torn
1 small zucchini, chopped
1 cup seasoned salad croutons
1/4 cup chopped walnuts
6 tablespoons olive *or* vegetable oil
2 tablespoons red wine vinegar *or* cider vinegar
2 tablespoons Dijon mustard
2 tablespoons honey
1 garlic clove, minced
Dash pepper

In a large bowl, toss the romaine, zucchini, croutons and walnuts. In a small bowl, whisk the oil, vinegar, mustard, honey, garlic and pepper until smooth. Serve with the salad. Refrigerate any leftover dressing. **Yield:** 12 servings.

Feed Your Family for $1.72 a Plate!

YOU CAN save on your grocery bill without scrimping on flavor when feeding your family…this nicely seasoned Mexican meal proves it!

Our Test Kitchen home economists have combined the three recipes here into a delicious and satisfying meal you can put on the table for just $1.72 per person.

The hearty Turkey Enchiladas are generously stuffed with cubed turkey, cheese and chilies in a mild creamy sauce. "My daughter made this dish for us, and it was excellent," raves Leona Therou of Overland Park, Kansas.

Sweet Pepper Salad, from Lu Ann Kessi of Eddyville, Oregon, is crisp and colorful with a tangy dressing.

Light and spongy Chiffon Cake makes a fitting finale to any meal. Arlene Murphy of Beverly Hills, Florida shares the delicious recipe.

— 🥄 🥄 🥄 —

Turkey Enchiladas

- 1 **medium onion, chopped**
- 1/3 **cup chopped green pepper**
- 2 **tablespoons vegetable oil**
- 2 **cups cubed cooked turkey**
- 1 **cup (4 ounces) shredded Colby-Monterey Jack cheese, *divided***
- 1 **can (4 ounces) chopped green chilies**
- 1 **cup (8 ounces) sour cream**
- 1 **can (10-3/4 ounces) condensed cream of chicken soup, undiluted**
- 1/4 **teaspoon ground coriander**
- 1/8 **teaspoon ground cumin**
- 6 **flour tortillas (8 inches), warmed**

In a large skillet, saute onion and green pepper in oil until tender; remove from the heat. Stir in the turkey, 1/2 cup of cheese and chilies; set aside. In a saucepan, combine the sour cream, soup, coriander and cumin. Cook and stir over low heat until warm; stir 1/2 cup into the turkey mixture.

Spoon about 1/3 cup turkey filling down the center of each tortilla; roll up tightly. Place seam side down in a greased 13-in. x 9-in. x 2-in. baking dish. Spoon remaining soup mixture down center

of tortillas. Sprinkle with remaining cheese. Bake, uncovered, at 350° for 20-25 minutes or until heated through. **Yield:** 6 servings.

— 🥄 🥄 🥄 —

Sweet Pepper Salad

- 3 **medium green peppers, thinly sliced**
- 1 **medium sweet red pepper, thinly sliced**
- 1 **medium red onion, thinly sliced**
- 1 **teaspoon grated lemon peel**
- 1/2 **cup red wine vinegar**
- 4-1/2 **teaspoons vegetable oil**
- 1 **tablespoon minced fresh basil**
- 1 **tablespoon sugar**
- 1/4 **teaspoon salt**
- 1/8 **teaspoon pepper**

In a salad bowl, combine the peppers, onion and lemon peel. Combine vinegar and oil; pour over vegetables and toss to coat. Cover and refrigerate overnight. Just before serving, add the basil, sugar, salt and pepper; mix well. **Yield:** 6 servings.

———— 🍴 🍴 🍴 ————

Chiffon Cake

6 eggs, *separated*
1/2 teaspoon salt
1-1/2 cups sugar, *divided*
1/2 cup warm water
1-1/2 cups all-purpose flour, *divided*
1 teaspoon vanilla extract
1/2 teaspoon cream of tartar
1/2 cup chocolate ice cream topping

In a mixing bowl, beat the egg yolks and salt for 2 minutes. Gradually beat in 1 cup sugar; beat 2 minutes longer. Gradually add the water; beat about 2-1/2 minutes longer or until frothy. Beat in 3/4 cup flour. Beat in vanilla extract and all of the remaining flour.

In another mixing bowl, beat the egg whites until foamy. Add cream of tartar; beat until soft peaks form. Gradually beat in remaining sugar, 1 tablespoon at a time, on high until stiff peaks form. Fold into egg yolk mixture.

Transfer to an ungreased 10-in. tube pan. Bake at 325° for 55-60 minutes or until top springs back when lightly touched and cracks feel dry. Immediately invert pan onto a wire rack; cool completely. Run a knife around sides of pan to remove cake. Slice; drizzle with ice cream topping. **Yield:** 12 servings.

Feed Your Family for $1.51 a Plate!

COME FALL, country cooks head to the kitchen to prepare hearty down-home fare for their families.

You can be frugal and still prepare a full-flavored dinner—three budget-conscious cooks prove it with this trio of home-style recipes. Our Test Kitchen estimates the total cost for this meal at just $1.51 per serving!

Pineapple Ham Loaf is a satisfying and inexpensive main dish. "This loaf is nice enough for the holidays, but we have it often for everyday meals, too, since it's so easy to prepare and easy on the pocketbook," shares Linda Manley of Morgantown, West Virginia.

Broccoli Cream Soup has a wonderful fresh flavor. "I've never had a better broccoli soup," says Beth Hart of Walworth, New York.

And you don't have to break the bank to enjoy a batch of golden rolls. Buttermilk Rolls, from Bernice Morris of Marshfield, Missouri, are a real treat.

— ▼ ▼ ▼ —

Pineapple Ham Loaf

  2 eggs
  1 cup milk
  1 cup crushed saltines (about 30 crackers)
  1/2 teaspoon salt
  1/8 teaspoon pepper
1-1/2 pounds ground fully cooked ham
  1/2 pound ground pork
  1/4 cup packed brown sugar
  2 tablespoons cider vinegar
  1 teaspoon ground mustard
  1 can (8 ounces) sliced pineapple, drained

In a large bowl, combine the first five ingredients. Crumble ham and pork over mixture; mix well. Combine the brown sugar, vinegar and mustard; pour into an ungreased 9-in. x 5-in. x 3-in. loaf pan. Arrange three pineapple slices in pan (refrigerate remaining pineapple for another use). Pat meat mixture into pan.

Cover and bake at 325° for 1-1/2 hours. Uncover; bake 30 minutes longer or until meat a thermometer reads 160°. Let stand for 15 minutes. Invert onto a serving platter. **Yield:** 8 servings.

Broccoli Cream Soup

  9 cups fresh broccoli florets
  4 cups chicken broth
  1 medium onion, chopped
  8 tablespoons butter *or* margarine, *divided*
  1 bay leaf
  3/4 teaspoon *each* salt and white pepper
  1/4 teaspoon *each* onion salt and garlic salt
Pinch *each* dried basil, thyme and rubbed sage
Dash hot pepper sauce
  7 tablespoons all-purpose flour
  2 cups milk
  1 cup buttermilk
  1/2 cup whipping cream

In a large saucepan, bring broccoli and broth to a boil. Reduce heat; simmer for 5 minutes. In a small skillet, saute onion in 2 tablespoons butter until

tender; add to broccoli mixture. Stir in the bay leaf and remaining seasonings. Simmer, uncovered, for 5 minutes.

In a small saucepan, melt the remaining butter. Stir in flour until smooth. Gradually add milk. Bring to a boil; cook and stir for 2 minutes or until thickened. Stir into broccoli mixture; add buttermilk and cream. Heat through (do not boil). Discard bay leaf. **Yield:** 8 servings (about 2 quarts).

Buttermilk Rolls

1 package (1/4 ounce) active dry yeast
1/4 cup warm water (110° to 115°)
1-1/2 cups warm buttermilk (110° to 115°)*
1/2 cup vegetable oil
3 tablespoons sugar
1 teaspoon salt
1/2 teaspoon baking soda
4-1/2 cups all-purpose flour

In a mixing bowl, dissolve yeast in water. Beat in the buttermilk, oil, sugar, salt, baking soda and 2 cups flour until smooth. Stir in enough remaining flour to form a soft dough. Turn onto a floured surface; knead until smooth and elastic, about 6-8 minutes. Place in a greased bowl, turning once to grease top. Cover and let rise in a warm place until doubled, about 1-1/2 hours.

Punch dough down. Divide into 18 pieces; roll into balls. Place on greased baking sheets. Cover and let rise until doubled, about 30 minutes. Bake at 400° for 15-20 minutes or until golden brown. Cool on wire racks. **Yield:** 1-1/2 dozen.

***Editor's Note:** Warmed buttermilk will appeared curdled.

Getting in the Theme of Things

Add a festive feel to any get-together with these theme-related menus featuring fabulous recipes and fun decorating ideas.

GET THE PARTY STARTED. Clockwise from upper left: Festive Foods Fit for the Fourth (p. 298), Golfers' Party Is Right on Par (p. 296), Brunch—It's Snow Trouble at All! (p. 292) and "Welcome to the World" Dinner (p. 294).

Brunch—It's Snow Trouble at All!

By Shelly Rynearson, Dousman, Wisconsin

AS A KICKOFF to the Christmas season, my parents, my brother and his family come to our house for a theme brunch. One year's theme was snowmen and snowflakes.

My layered Potato Ham Omelet Pie can be prepared the day before, then baked the morning of the party.

Chocolate chips and pecans add a flavorful crunch to Banana Split Bread. Since finding this recipe a decade ago, I seldom make plain banana bread.

Cute as can be, Minty Snowmen have nice fresh flavor. They are easy to shape…and it's so simple to add colorful hats and earmuffs.

I also served spicy Gingerbread Snowflakes with hot spiced cider, and everyone said the party had gotten them into the holiday spirit.

Potato Ham Omelet Pie

  1 package (17-1/4 ounces) frozen puff pastry, thawed
1/4 cup butter *or* margarine
  3 cups sliced peeled red potatoes
  1 cup thinly sliced onion
1/4 teaspoon salt
1/4 teaspoon pepper

OMELETS:
  6 eggs
1/4 cup minced fresh parsley
  2 tablespoons water
Dash *each* salt and pepper
  2 tablespoons butter *or* margarine, *divided*

FILLING:
  2 cups (8 ounces) shredded cheddar cheese, *divided*

1-1/2 cups cubed fully cooked ham
1 egg, lightly beaten
1 tablespoon water

On a floured surface, roll each puff pastry sheet into a 12-in. square. Place one square in a 10-in. quiche dish; set dish and remaining pastry aside.

In a skillet, melt butter. Add potatoes, onion, salt and pepper; cover and cook for 10-12 minutes or until potatoes are tender and golden brown, stirring occasionally. Set aside.

Beat eggs, parsley, water, salt and pepper. In a 10-in. skillet, melt 1 tablespoon butter; add half of the egg mixture. Cook over medium heat. As eggs set, lift edges, letting uncooked portion flow underneath. Continue cooking until set. Slide omelet onto a baking sheet. Repeat with remaining butter and egg mixture to make a second omelet.

Sprinkle 1 cup cheese over prepared pastry. Top with one omelet and half of the potato mixture. Layer with ham and the remaining potato mixture, cheese, omelet and puff pastry. Trim pastry to fit dish; seal and flute edges.

In a small bowl, combine beaten egg and water; brush over pastry. Bake at 375° for 30-35 minutes or until golden brown. Let stand for 10 minutes before serving. **Yield:** 8 servings.

Banana Split Bread

1/2 cup butter *or* margarine, softened
1 cup sugar
1 egg
1 cup mashed ripe bananas (about 2 large)
3 tablespoons milk
2 cups all-purpose flour
1 teaspoon baking powder
1/2 teaspoon baking soda
1 cup (6 ounces) semisweet chocolate chips
1/2 cup chopped pecans

In a mixing bowl, cream butter and sugar. Beat in egg. In a small bowl, combine bananas and milk. Combine the flour, baking powder and baking soda; add to creamed mixture alternately with banana mixture. Fold in chocolate chips and pecans.

Pour into a greased 9-in. x 5-in. x 3-in. loaf pan. Bake at 350° for 60-70 minutes or until a toothpick inserted near the center comes out clean. Cool for 10 minutes before removing from pan to a wire rack. **Yield:** 1 loaf.

Minty Snowmen

1 tablespoon butter (no substitutes), softened
1 tablespoon light corn syrup

1/2 teaspoon mint extract
1/8 teaspoon salt
1 cup confectioners' sugar
1 drop *each* blue, yellow and red food coloring
Colored sprinkles and cake decorator candies

In a bowl, combine butter, corn syrup, extract and salt, mixing with a wooden spoon until blended. Gradually stir in confectioners' sugar. Knead by hand for 1-2 minutes or until mixture becomes pliable.

To 1 tablespoon of dough, add blue food coloring; knead until blended. Add yellow food coloring to another tablespoon of dough and knead. Add red food coloring to another tablespoon of dough and knead. Leave remaining dough white.

Roll white dough into a log; remove one-fourth of the log and set aside. For the snowmen's bodies, divide the remaining log into 8 pieces and roll into balls. For the snowmen's heads, divide the reserved dough into 8 pieces and roll into balls. Stack 1 smaller ball on top of each larger ball. Use the colored dough to form hats, scarves and earmuffs as desired. Used colored sprinkles and candies to make eyes, noses and buttons. **Yield:** 8 snowmen.

Gingerbread Snowflakes

1 cup butter (no substitutes), softened
1 cup sugar
1 cup molasses
1/2 cup water, *divided*
5 cups all-purpose flour
2-1/2 teaspoons ground ginger
1-1/2 teaspoons baking soda
1-1/2 teaspoons ground cinnamon
1/2 teaspoon ground allspice
1/4 teaspoon salt
3-3/4 cups (1 pound) confectioners' sugar
1-1/2 teaspoons light corn syrup
1/2 teaspoon vanilla extract

In a mixing bowl, cream butter and sugar. Beat in molasses and 1/4 cup water. Combine the flour, ginger, baking soda, cinnamon, allspice and salt; gradually add to creamed mixture. Cover and refrigerate for 1 hour or until easy to handle.

On a lightly floured surface, roll out dough to 1/4-in. thickness. Cut with 2-1/2-in. cookie cutters dipped in flour. Place 2 in. apart on ungreased baking sheets. Bake at 350° for 10-12 minutes or until edges are firm. Remove to wire racks to cool.

In a mixing bowl, combine confectioners' sugar, corn syrup, vanilla and remaining water until smooth. Transfer to a plastic bag. Cut a small hole in one corner; pipe frosting onto cookies. **Yield:** about 5 dozen.

'Welcome to the World' Dinner

By Ame Andrews, Little Rock, Arkansas

WHEN FRIENDS of mine had a new baby, I came up with a "Welcome to the World" dinner to deliver when they came home from the hospital.

From personal experience, I knew how difficult it can be in those first few weeks to care for a new baby and the rest of the family. I didn't have time to make many home-cooked meals, and I appreciated it when someone stopped by with a tasty dish.

For my friend's theme menu, I combined several favorite recipes that were easily portable and came up with clever names for them.

Special Delivery Chicken is a simple but delicious casserole that can be made ahead and refrigerated or frozen. With a buttery crumb topping, this main dish is comforting and popular with all ages. I was quite sure my friend's toddler would love it, because mine does.

The casserole was accompanied by two vegetable dishes. Bringing Home Baby Carrots are cooked with honey and apple juice. The baby carrots fit my theme nicely and are so sweet and tender, just like a newborn.

For Green Bean Bundles of Joy, I used fresh green beans and tied them with bacon strips to make the "bundles". They take on a pleasantly tart taste when baked in Italian dressing.

And finally, I made 2 a.m. Feeding Snack Bars for dessert or a late-night snack when Mom or Dad gets up with the baby. The decadent triple-chocolate brownies with a candy-bar topping are great with a glass of milk anytime.

The proud parents were delighted with their special dinner—and putting it together was fun for me.

Special Delivery Chicken

This favorite chicken casserole took on a new name when I delivered it to my friends as part of their "Welcome to the World" dinner. Baked in a creamy sauce, it is a comforting main dish popular with all ages.

> 2 cups (16 ounces) sour cream
> 1 can (10-3/4 ounces) condensed cream of chicken soup, undiluted
> 2 teaspoons poppy seeds
> 2-1/2 cups cubed cooked chicken
> 1-3/4 cups butter-flavored cracker crumbs (about 36 crackers)
> 1/2 cup butter *or* margarine, melted

In a bowl, combine the sour cream, soup and poppy seeds. Stir in chicken. Pour into a greased 11-in. x 7-in. x 2-in. baking dish. Combine the cracker crumbs and butter; sprinkle over top. Bake, uncovered, at 350° for 25-30 minutes or until heated through. **Yield:** 4 servings.

——— 🥄 🥄 🥄 ———

Bringing Home Baby Carrots

Carrots cooked in apple juice and honey are a tasty, sweet accompaniment to the chicken casserole. Of course, I used baby carrots in this recipe for my theme menu. The word does double duty in the title for this dish.

> ✓ Uses less fat, sugar or salt. Includes Nutritional Analysis and Diabetic Exchanges.

> 1 package (16 ounces) fresh baby carrots
> 1 cup apple juice
> 3/4 cup water
> 1/3 cup honey

In a large saucepan, combine the carrots, apple juice, water and honey. Bring to a boil. Reduce heat; cover and simmer for 10-14 minutes or until the carrots are tender. Serve carrots with a slotted spoon. **Yield:** 4 servings.

Nutritional Analysis: One serving (1/2 cup) equals 157 calories, 1 g fat (trace saturated fat), 0 cholesterol, 43 mg sodium, 40 g carbohydrate, 2 g fiber, 1 g protein. **Diabetic Exchanges:** 1 starch, 1 vegetable, 1 fruit.

——— 🥄 🥄 🥄 ———

Green Bean Bundles of Joy

To make green beans fit the new baby theme dinner, I baked them in little bundles, secured with strips of bacon. A few minutes under the broiler makes the bacon crispy. This dish gets its tang from Italian dressing, which the beans are baked in.

> 6 cups water
> 1/2 pound fresh green beans, trimmed
> 4 to 6 bacon strips
> 3/4 cup Italian salad dressing

In a saucepan, bring water to a boil. Add beans; cover and cook for 3 minutes. Drain and set aside. Cut bacon in half lengthwise; place on a microwave-safe plate. Microwave on high for 2-1/2 to 3 minutes or until edges curl. Place four or five beans on each bacon strip; wrap bacon around beans and tie in a knot.

Place the green bean bundles in an 8-in. square baking dish. Drizzle with the salad dressing. Bake, uncovered, at 350° for 10-15 minutes or until the beans are crisp-tender. Broil 4 in. from the heat for 2-3 minutes or until the bacon is crisp. **Yield:** 4-6 servings.

——— 🥄 🥄 🥄 ———

2 a.m. Feeding Snack Bars

I assured my friend that she didn't have to wait to try one of these scrumptious brownies until she got up in the middle of the night to feed the baby! But the chocolaty treats are a perfect pick-me-up (anytime) for new parents short on sleep and energy.

> 1-1/3 cups all-purpose flour
> 1-1/4 cups sugar
> 1/2 cup baking cocoa
> 1 teaspoon baking powder
> 1/2 teaspoon salt
> 4 eggs, beaten
> 3/4 cup butter *or* margarine, melted
> 1/2 cup *each* milk chocolate chips, semisweet chocolate chips and vanilla *or* white chips
> 3 Snickers candy bars (2.07 ounces *each*), cut into 1/4-inch pieces

In a bowl, combine the flour, sugar, cocoa, baking powder and salt. Combine the eggs and butter; add to the dry ingredients and mix well. Stir in the chips.

Transfer to a greased 13-in. x 9-in. x 2-in. baking pan. Bake at 350° for 25-30 minutes or until a toothpick inserted near the center comes out clean. Immediately sprinkle with candy bar pieces. Cool on a wire rack. Cut into bars. **Yield:** 2 dozen.

🥄 Bean Basics

When broken open, fresh green beans should have a crisp snap. Beans are available year-round, but are best from May through August.

Golfers' Party Is Right on Par

By Sue Ann O'Buck, Sinking Spring, Pennsylvania

A GOLF GETAWAY my husband, Nick, had planned inspired us to host a theme dinner that scored well with our guests.

Nick and a friend had recruited two other guys for a golf trip to South Carolina. A couple weeks before they left, we hosted a casual dinner for the foursome and their wives so everybody could get to know each other.

Wanting to link our menu to the golf course, I used lingo golfers would pick up on. I had such fun naming the foods!

My tried-and-true chicken cacciatore—a standby from my recipe file—became Clubhouse Chicken for this gathering. And in honor of today's most popular golfer, Tiger Woods, we sipped on glasses of Tiger Tea. It's a very refreshing citrus iced tea that's easy to make using frozen juice concentrate.

On-the-Green Cake qualified for lots of compliments. You don't have to be a skilled player to have a little fun frosting this deliciously moist and fruity dessert.

For table decorations, I gathered golf accents I've collected over the years. I am an avid golfer, too! Decorative birdhouses called Hacker's Hideaway and Pro Shop formed the centerpiece. Colorful golf tees were scattered on the table, and a golf ball weighted down the bright napkin on each plate.

It was such a fun way to celebrate the game we love that we've decided to make our golf dinner an annual event. It's a party that could easily be adapted for your own golf group.

When guests ask where you got the idea, tell them a little "birdie" told you!

Clubhouse Chicken

Golfers can work up a healthy appetite during a round! So in planning the menu for a golf theme party my husband and I hosted, I served this tasty and hearty skillet meal. This easy-to-fix main dish is a tried-and-true favorite from my recipe file.

 Uses less fat, sugar or salt. Includes Nutritional Analysis and Diabetic Exchanges.

     8 boneless skinless chicken breast halves
       (2 pounds)
     2 tablespoons canola oil
     1 can (28 ounces) stewed tomatoes, cut up
 1-1/2 cups sliced fresh mushrooms
     1 large green pepper, julienned
     1 medium onion, chopped
   1/2 cup water
     3 teaspoons Italian seasoning
   1/4 teaspoon pepper
     3 tablespoons all-purpose flour
   1/4 cup cold water
Hot cooked rice

In a large skillet, brown chicken on both sides in oil. Stir in the tomatoes, mushrooms, green pepper, onion, water, Italian seasoning and pepper. Bring to a boil. Reduce heat; cover and simmer for 10-15 minutes or until chicken juices run clear.

Remove chicken and keep warm. Combine the flour and cold water until smooth; stir into tomato mixture. Bring to a boil; cook and stir for 2 minutes or until thickened. Serve chicken and sauce over rice. **Yield:** 8 servings.

Nutritional Analysis: One chicken breast with 1/2 cup sauce (calculated without rice) equals 210 calories, 5 g fat (1 g saturated fat), 66 mg cholesterol, 254 mg sodium, 13 g carbohydrate, 2 g fiber, 28 g protein. **Diabetic Exchanges:** 4 very lean meat, 1 vegetable, 1/2 starch.

—— 🏌 🏌 🏌 ——

Tiger Tea

"Tee time" was deliciously refreshing when we poured this thirst-quenching iced tea at our golf party. I enjoyed coming up with the recipe titles for our theme foods. Even non-golfers know this bright beverage is named for famous young pro Tiger Woods.

     3 quarts water, *divided*
     6 individual tea bags
   3/4 cup lemonade concentrate
   3/4 cup orange juice concentrate
     1 cup sugar

In a large kettle, bring 1 quart water to a boil. Remove from the heat; add tea bags. Steep for 5 minutes. Discard tea bags. Stir in the lemonade and

orange juice concentrates, sugar and remaining water. Serve over ice. **Yield:** about 3 quarts.

—— 🏌 🏌 🏌 ——

On-the-Green Cake

There's nothing rough about making this yummy cake. Guests at our golf dinner never suspected that it started with a convenient boxed mix. They were delighted with the golf green motif, the cake's fruity flavor and the fluffy icing.

     1 package (18-1/4 ounces) yellow cake mix
     1 can (11 ounces) mandarin oranges
     1 can (20 ounces) crushed pineapple
     1 carton (8 ounces) frozen whipped
       topping, thawed
     1 package (3.4 ounces) instant vanilla
       pudding mix
     3 to 6 drops green food coloring
     1 wooden skewer (about 6 inches)
     1 Chuckles candy
     1 miniature white marshmallow

Prepare cake batter according to package directions. Drain oranges, reserving 2 tablespoons juice; set juice aside. Stir oranges into the batter. Pour into a greased 13-in. x 9-in. x 2-in. baking dish. Bake at 350° for 30-35 minutes or until a toothpick inserted near the center comes out clean. Cool on a wire rack.

Using a toothpick, poke holes into the cake about an inch apart. Drain pineapple, reserving 2 tablespoons juice; set pineapple aside. Combine the reserved orange and pineapple juices; pour over cake. Refrigerate until chilled.

In a bowl, combine whipped topping and pudding mix. Remove 1 cup to a small bowl; add food coloring. Pipe onto cake in a kidney bean shape to form a putting green. Fold pineapple into the remaining whipped topping mixture; spread over unfrosted portion of cake.

Insert wooden skewer into putting green for the pin. Cut candy into a triangle; attach to top of skewer for flag. Cut marshmallow in half and roll into a ball; place on green. Refrigerate until serving. **Yield:** 12-15 servings.

🥄 *Iced Tea Tip*

Serve iced tea over ice cubes made from tea, not water. This will ensure the drink won't become watered down, especially on warm summer days when the drink is most popular.

Festive Foods Fit for the Fourth

By Laurie Neverman, Green Bay, Wisconsin

MY SISTER, Lois Jacobsen (on right), and I got into the spirit of things last July with an Independence Day party that was red, white and blue right down to the menu!

Flavorful barbecued Yankee-Doodle Sirloin Roast was a tasty alternative to hamburgers and hot dogs.

A touch of Italian flavor perks up my Patriotic Pasta, which has red cherry tomatoes, white pasta and cauliflower, plus dressing made with blue cheese.

Eye-catching Red, White 'n' Blue Salad really brightened up the table, while Liberty Sauerkraut Salad was both tangy and refreshing.

Luscious Stars and Stripes Torte was the impressive finale to our festive Fourth of July meal.

Yankee-Doodle Sirloin Roast

(Also pictured on front cover)

1/2 cup beef broth
1/2 cup teriyaki *or* soy sauce
1/4 cup vegetable oil
  2 tablespoons brown sugar
  2 tablespoons finely chopped onion
  3 garlic cloves, minced
  1 teaspoon Worcestershire sauce
1/2 teaspoon hot pepper sauce
  1 boneless beef sirloin tip roast (about 4 pounds)

In a large resealable plastic bag, combine the first eight ingredients; add roast. Seal bag and turn to coat; refrigerate overnight.

Discard marinade. Grill roast, covered, over indirect medium heat for 2 to 2-1/2 hours or until meat reaches desired doneness (for rare, a meat thermometer should read 140°; medium, 160°; well-done, 170°). Let stand for 10-15 minutes before slicing. **Yield:** 12-14 servings.

— 🛒 🛒 🛒 —

Patriotic Pasta

1/4 cup mayonnaise
1/4 cup sour cream
1/4 cup crumbled blue cheese
1-1/2 teaspoons milk
1/2 teaspoon salt
1/2 teaspoon white vinegar
1/4 teaspoon garlic powder
1/4 teaspoon pepper
1/2 teaspoon honey mustard
1/8 teaspoon cayenne pepper
SALAD:
2-1/2 cups uncooked medium tube pasta
1 garlic clove, minced
3/4 teaspoon minced fresh basil
2 tablespoons olive *or* vegetable oil
1-1/2 cups cauliflowerets
1 cup cherry tomatoes, halved
3 green onions, chopped
1/4 cup chopped sweet red pepper
4 ounces mozzarella cheese, cut into 1-inch strips
2 tablespoons grated Parmesan cheese

In a small bowl, combine the first 10 ingredients; set aside. Cook pasta according to package directions; rinse in cold water and drain. Place in a large bowl. In a skillet, saute garlic and basil in oil until garlic is tender. Pour over pasta. Add the vegetables, cheeses and dressing; toss to coat. Refrigerate until serving. **Yield:** 12-14 servings.

— 🛒 🛒 🛒 —

Red, White 'n' Blue Salad

1 package (3 ounces) berry blue gelatin
2 cups boiling water, *divided*
2-1/2 cups cold water, *divided*
1 cup fresh blueberries
1 envelope unflavored gelatin
1 cup whipping cream
6 tablespoons sugar
2 cups (16 ounces) sour cream
1 teaspoon vanilla extract
1 package (3 ounces) raspberry gelatin
1 cup fresh raspberries
Whipped topping and additional berries

In a bowl, dissolve berry blue gelatin in 1 cup boiling water; stir in 1 cup cold water. Add blueberries.

Pour into a 3-qt. serving bowl. Refrigerate until firm, about 1 hour.

Meanwhile, in a saucepan, sprinkle unflavored gelatin over 1/2 cup cold water; let stand for 1 minute. Add the cream and sugar; cook and stir over low heat until gelatin and sugar are completely dissolved. Cool to room temperature. Whisk in sour cream and vanilla. Spoon over the blue layer. Refrigerate until firm.

In a bowl, dissolve raspberry gelatin in remaining hot water; stir in remaining cold water. Add raspberries. Spoon over cream layer. Chill until set. Garnish with whipped topping and additional berries. **Yield:** 14-16 servings.

— 🛒 🛒 🛒 —

Liberty Sauerkraut Salad

1 can (14 ounces) sauerkraut, rinsed and drained
1 medium green pepper, diced
1 cup diced celery
1 medium onion, diced
3/4 to 1 cup sugar
1/2 cup cider vinegar
1 jar (2 ounces) diced pimientos, drained

In a 1-qt. serving bowl, combine all of the ingredients. Cover and refrigerate overnight. Serve with a slotted spoon. **Yield:** 8 servings.

— 🛒 🛒 🛒 —

Stars and Stripes Torte

1 package (18-1/4 ounces) white cake mix
1-1/2 cups cold milk
1 package (3.3 ounces) instant white chocolate pudding mix
1/2 teaspoon almond extract
1 cup whipping cream, whipped
1-2/3 cups raspberry pie filling
1-2/3 cups blueberry pie filling
Fresh blueberries and raspberries

Prepare and bake cake according to package directions, using two greased 9-in. round baking pans. Cool for 10 minutes before removing from pans to wire racks to cool completely.

In a small mixing bowl, beat milk and pudding mix on low speed for 2 minutes. Beat in extract. Refrigerate for 10 minutes. Fold in whipped cream.

Split each cake into two horizontal layers. Place bottom layer on a cake plate; spread with raspberry filling. Top with second cake layer; spread with 1-2/3 cups pudding mixture. Top with third cake layer; spread with blueberry filling. Top with remaining cake layer and pudding mixture. Garnish with blueberries and raspberries. **Yield:** 10-14 servings.

A Honey of a Party Idea

By Sheila Bradshaw, Columbus, Ohio

A BEE TEA I hosted for my co-workers was all the buzz around the office.

My guests were greeted at the door by the Queen Bee—me, wearing a yellow shirt and black antennae on my head! Printed menus featuring a bee that I designed on my computer listed the fare.

Honey-Citrus Iced Tea was perfect for my party. It can be made ahead, except for its sparkle. That comes from ginger ale added just before you serve this refreshing fruity blend.

My Honeybee Ham Salad Sandwich is simple to put together, but it's a real eye-catcher. I used a round loaf of bread and a roll to create the bee's body, wings and head.

I frosted the sandwich with cream cheese tinted yellow and used black olives to make the stripes.

My guests thought the Beehive Cake was so clever! I displayed the cake on the table, alongside a cute honeybee garden sign that I secured in a yellow and white flowerpot.

Hosting theme parties is my favorite pastime, inspired by my mom, who loved to have fun with food. She taught me that the extra effort in planning a theme can elevate a nice gathering into a memorable event.

My Bee Tea proved her right again. It was a sweet success!

Honey-Citrus Iced Tea

A frozen orange or lemon slice in the glass looks pretty and keeps this punch nice and cold. Appropriately for my bee theme, the blend is sweetened with honey.

✓ Uses less fat, sugar or salt. Includes Nutritional Analysis and Diabetic Exchanges.

    4 individual tea bags
    2 cups boiling water
    3 medium navel oranges
    2 medium lemons
    2 cups orange juice
1/4 cup lemon juice
    3 tablespoons honey
    1 liter ginger ale, chilled

Place tea bags in a teapot; add boiling water. Cover and steep for 3 minutes; discard tea bags. Pour tea into a pitcher. Peel and section two oranges and one lemon; add to tea. Stir in the orange juice, lemon juice and honey. Cover and refrigerate for 6 hours or overnight. Cut remaining orange and lemon into slices; freeze.

Just before serving, strain and discard fruit from tea. Stir in ginger ale. Serve with frozen fruit slices. **Yield:** 8 servings.

Nutritional Analysis: One serving (1 cup) equals 124 calories, trace fat (trace saturated fat), 0 cholesterol, 11 mg sodium, 32 g carbohydrate, 1 g fiber, 1 g protein. **Diabetic Exchange:** 2 fruit.

— 🍵 🍵 🍵 —

Honeybee Ham Salad Sandwich

The crowd was abuzz at the sight of this striped sandwich at my Bee Tea theme luncheon. For a large crowd, make a "swarm" of bees and offer several choices.

1/2 pound ground fully cooked ham
1/4 cup mayonnaise
    2 hard-cooked eggs, chopped
1/4 cup chopped pecans
1/4 cup crushed pineapple, drained
    2 tablespoons honey
    1 round loaf (1 pound) Italian bread
    1 round Italian roll (6 inches)
    2 packages (one 8 ounces, one 3 ounces) cream cheese, softened
    1 tablespoon whipping cream
    8 to 10 drops yellow food coloring
1/4 cup butter *or* margarine, softened
    1 can (6 ounces) pitted large ripe olives, drained
    1 pimiento strip
    1 celery rib, cut into thirds

In a bowl, combine the first six ingredients until blended. Slice the loaf and roll in half horizontally. Cut a third off one end of the loaf; slice the smaller portion in half.

In a mixing bowl, beat cream cheese, cream and food coloring until light and fluffy. Spread over top of all bread sections and roll. Spread butter over inside of bread sections and roll; fill with ham salad.

To assemble, place large loaf piece on a serving platter or covered board for bee's body. Place roll next to body for head. For wings, position two small loaf pieces, rounded edges facing each other, above body.

Set aside 12 whole olives. Slice remaining olives in half lengthwise; make stripes on body with halved olives. Cut 11 olives into slices. Position one slice on head for eye; decorate wings with remaining slices. Add pimiento for mouth. Place last whole olive on one piece of celery; insert into top of head for antenna. Insert remaining celery into ham salad for legs. **Yield:** 10-12 servings.

— 🍵 🍵 🍵 —

Beehive Cake

Guests at my Bee Tea thought this cake was so cute! Honey adds character to the spice cake's flavor.

    1 package (18-1/4 ounces) spice cake mix
1-1/4 cups water
    3 eggs
1/2 cup honey
1/3 cup vegetable oil
    1 can (16 ounces) vanilla frosting
    9 to 10 drops yellow food coloring
    1 chocolate wafer (2-1/2 inches)

In a large mixing bowl, beat cake mix, water, eggs, honey and oil on low speed for 2 minutes. Grease and flour a 6-oz. and a 10-oz. custard cup and a 1-1/2-qt. round baking dish. Pour 1/3 cup batter into the 6-oz. cup, 1 cup batter into the 10-oz. cup and remaining batter into the baking dish.

Bake the small cake at 350° for 30-35 minutes, the medium cake for 40-45 minutes and the large cake for 55-60 minutes or until a toothpick inserted near the center comes out clean. Cool for 15 minutes before removing from dishes to wire racks to cool completely.

In a mixing bowl, beat frosting and food coloring. Place large cake on a serving plate; spread with frosting. Top with medium cake; frost. Add small cake; frost top and sides of entire cake. Using a wooden spoon and beginning at bottom of cake, make circles in frosting around cake to form the beehive. Position chocolate wafer at the base for the entrance. **Yield:** 10-12 servings.

'50s Party Menu Stirs Memories

By Judy Nix, Toccoa, Georgia

SINCE my sister, Dot Davis, and I grew up in the 1950s, I decided to surprise her with a Fabulous '50s Party on her birthday. I planned the menu to reflect the decade and was inspired by its music when thinking up names for the foods.

Elvis Presley's hit *You Ain't Nothing But a Hound Dog* seemed to fit the hearty chili dogs I served. Bebop Baked Beans were a popular accompaniment to the hot dogs. I used hickory smoke-flavored barbecue sauce to give the beans a spicy tang.

Crisp, colorful coleslaw was named after the famous '50s crooner Nat King Cole. Its dressing has a pleasant kick, thanks to a little chili powder.

There really is cola in the refreshing Cherry Coke Salad! It adds to the bright, sparkling taste.

Instead of birthday cake, I served a lemon pie our mom used to make that Dot always loved. The song *Sugartime* by the McGuire Sisters came to mind as a tag for this sweet treat.

For a centerpiece, I set out a bowl filled with old-time candies. Candles were fitted with pink poodle skirts I made from felt.

I cut "record" place mats from black poster board. Mini strawberry soda favors were made with tiny plastic cups painted pink, topped with cotton balls (ice cream) and red beads (cherries). A Coca-Cola glass completed each setting.

It was worth the effort just to see my sister's face when she walked in—and stepped back into her teens! Everyone loved the '50s food…the reminiscing was nonstop…and, as the newspaper social columns used to end back then, "A good time was had by all!"

You Ain't Nothin' But a Hound Dogs

Like Elvis' tune, these chili dogs were a big hit at my sister's Fabulous '50s Party!

- 1/2 pound ground beef
- 2 tablespoons chopped onion
- 3/4 cup ketchup
- 1/4 cup water
- 1-1/2 teaspoons Worcestershire sauce
- 3/4 teaspoon chili powder
- 1/4 teaspoon pepper
- 1/8 teaspoon cayenne pepper
- 8 hot dogs, cooked
- 8 hot dog buns, split

In a large saucepan, cook beef and onion over medium heat until meat is no longer pink; drain. Stir in the ketchup, water, Worcestershire sauce, chili powder, pepper and cayenne. Bring to a boil. Reduce heat; simmer, uncovered, for 5 minutes or until mixture reaches desired thickness. Place hot dogs in buns; top each with about 2 tablespoons beef mixture. **Yield:** 8 servings.

Bebop Baked Beans

Timeless baked beans are still favorites at picnics and casual gatherings, just like they were back in the '50s.

- 3 bacon strips, diced
- 1/2 cup chopped green pepper
- 2 cans (15 ounces *each*) pork and beans
- 1/3 cup hickory smoke barbecue sauce
- 1/3 cup packed brown sugar
- 2 teaspoons prepared mustard

In a skillet, cook bacon over medium heat until crisp; remove to paper towels. Drain, reserving 1 tablespoon drippings. Saute green pepper in drippings until tender. Drain one can of beans. In a bowl, combine both cans of beans, barbecue sauce, brown sugar, mustard and green pepper.

Transfer to a greased 1-qt. baking dish. Bake, uncovered, at 350° for 35-40 minutes or until bubbly and heated through. Sprinkle with bacon. **Yield:** 6 servings.

Nat King Cole Slaw

Dill pickles add tang to this crispy coleslaw, named in honor of the famous '50s singer.

- 4 cups shredded cabbage
- 1 medium onion, chopped
- 1 medium green pepper, chopped
- 1 jar (2 ounces) diced pimientos, drained
- 2 tablespoons vegetable oil
- 2 tablespoons white wine vinegar *or* cider vinegar
- 1/2 teaspoon salt
- 1/2 teaspoon chili powder
- 1/4 to 1/2 teaspoon pepper

In a salad bowl, combine the cabbage, onion, green pepper and pimientos. In another bowl, combine the remaining ingredients. Pour over cabbage mixture; toss to coat. Cover and refrigerate for at least 2 hours. **Yield:** 6-8 servings.

Cherry Coke Salad

This sparkling salad was as popular at my sister's party as the cherry-flavored cola was back in the 1950s.

- 1 can (20 ounces) crushed pineapple
- 1/2 cup water
- 2 packages (3 ounces *each*) cherry gelatin
- 1 can (21 ounces) cherry pie filling
- 3/4 cup cola

Drain pineapple, reserving juice; set pineapple aside. In a saucepan or microwave, bring pineapple juice and water to a boil. Add gelatin; stir until dissolved. Stir in pie filling and cola. Pour into a serving bowl. Refrigerate until slightly thickened. Fold in reserved pineapple. Refrigerate until firm. **Yield:** 10-12 servings.

Sugartime Lemon Pie

When we were growing up, my sister preferred this creamy sweet-tart treat that our mom made over any kind of cake.

- 1-1/4 cups graham cracker crumbs (about 20 squares)
- 2 tablespoons sugar
- 1/3 cup butter (no substitutes), melted

FILLING:
- 2 cans (14 ounces *each*) sweetened condensed milk
- 1/2 cup lemon juice
- 1 teaspoon grated lemon peel
- 2 to 3 drops yellow food coloring, optional

In a bowl, combine cracker crumbs, sugar and butter; press onto the bottom and up the sides of an ungreased 9-in. pie plate. Refrigerate for 30 minutes.

For filling, in a bowl, whisk milk and lemon juice until smooth. Add lemon peel and food coloring if desired. Pour into crust. Refrigerate for 3-4 hours. Garnish with whipped topping. **Yield:** 6-8 servings.

Substitutions & Equivalents

Equivalent Measures

3 teaspoons	=	1 tablespoon	16 tablespoons	=	1 cup
4 tablespoons	=	1/4 cup	2 cups	=	1 pint
5-1/3 tablespoons	=	1/3 cup	4 cups	=	1 quart
8 tablespoons	=	1/2 cup	4 quarts	=	1 gallon

Food Equivalents

Grains

Macaroni	1 cup (3-1/2 ounces) uncooked	=	2-1/2 cups cooked
Noodles, Medium	3 cups (4 ounces) uncooked	=	4 cups cooked
Popcorn	1/3 to 1/2 cup unpopped	=	8 cups popped
Rice, Long Grain	1 cup uncooked	=	3 cups cooked
Rice, Quick-Cooking	1 cup uncooked	=	2 cups cooked
Spaghetti	8 ounces uncooked	=	4 cups cooked

Crumbs

Bread	1 slice	=	3/4 cup soft crumbs, 1/4 cup fine dry crumbs
Graham Crackers	7 squares	=	1/2 cup finely crushed
Buttery Round Crackers	12 crackers	=	1/2 cup finely crushed
Saltine Crackers	14 crackers	=	1/2 cup finely crushed

Fruits

Bananas	1 medium	=	1/3 cup mashed
Lemons	1 medium	=	3 tablespoons juice, 2 teaspoons grated peel
Limes	1 medium	=	2 tablespoons juice, 1-1/2 teaspoons grated peel
Oranges	1 medium	=	1/4 to 1/3 cup juice, 4 teaspoons grated peel

Vegetables

Cabbage	1 head	=	5 cups shredded	Green Pepper	1 large	=	1 cup chopped
Carrots	1 pound	=	3 cups shredded	Mushrooms	1/2 pound	=	3 cups sliced
Celery	1 rib	=	1/2 cup chopped	Onions	1 medium	=	1/2 cup chopped
Corn	1 ear fresh	=	2/3 cup kernels	Potatoes	3 medium	=	2 cups cubed

Nuts

Almonds	1 pound	=	3 cups chopped	Pecan Halves	1 pound	=	4-1/2 cups chopped
Ground Nuts	3-3/4 ounces	=	1 cup	Walnuts	1 pound	=	3-3/4 cups chopped

Easy Substitutions

When you need...		*Use...*
Baking Powder	1 teaspoon	1/2 teaspoon cream of tartar + 1/4 teaspoon baking soda
Buttermilk	1 cup	1 tablespoon lemon juice *or* vinegar + enough milk to measure 1 cup (let stand 5 minutes before using)
Cornstarch	1 tablespoon	2 tablespoons all-purpose flour
Honey	1 cup	1-1/4 cups sugar + 1/4 cup water
Half-and-Half Cream	1 cup	1 tablespoon melted butter + enough whole milk to measure 1 cup
Onion	1 small, chopped (1/3 cup)	1 teaspoon onion powder *or* 1 tablespoon dried minced onion
Tomato Juice	1 cup	1/2 cup tomato sauce + 1/2 cup water
Tomato Sauce	2 cups	3/4 cup tomato paste + 1 cup water
Unsweetened Chocolate	1 square (1 ounce)	3 tablespoons baking cocoa + 1 tablespoon shortening *or* oil
Whole Milk	1 cup	1/2 cup evaporated milk + 1/2 cup water

Cooking Terms

HERE'S a quick reference for some of the cooking terms used in *Taste of Home* recipes:

Baste—To moisten food with melted butter, pan drippings, marinades or other liquid to add more flavor and juiciness.

Beat—A rapid movement to combine ingredients using a fork, spoon, wire whisk or electric mixer.

Blend—To combine ingredients until *just* mixed.

Boil—To heat liquids until bubbles form that cannot be "stirred down". In the case of water, the temperature will reach 212°.

Bone—To remove all meat from the bone before cooking.

Cream—To beat ingredients together to a smooth consistency, usually in the case of butter and sugar for baking.

Dash—A small amount of seasoning, less than 1/8 teaspoon. If using a shaker, a dash would comprise a quick flip of the container.

Dredge—To coat foods with flour or other dry ingredients. Most often done with pot roasts and stew meat before browning.

Fold—To incorporate several ingredients by careful and gentle turning with a spatula. Used generally with beaten egg whites or whipped cream when mixing into the rest of the ingredients to keep the batter light.

Julienne—To cut foods into long thin strips much like matchsticks. Used most often for salads and stir-fry dishes.

Mince—To cut into very fine pieces. Used often for garlic or fresh herbs.

Parboil—To cook partially, usually used in the case of chicken, sausages and vegetables.

Partially set—Describes the consistency of gelatin after it has been chilled for a small amount of time. Mixture should resemble the consistency of egg whites.

Puree—To process foods to a smooth mixture. Can be prepared in an electric blender, food processor, food mill or sieve.

Saute—To fry quickly in a small amount of fat, stirring almost constantly. Most often done with onions, mushrooms and other chopped vegetables.

Score—To cut slits partway through the outer surface of foods. Often used with ham or flank steak.

Stir-Fry—To cook meats and/or vegetables with a constant stirring motion in a small amount of oil in a wok or skillet over high heat.

Guide to Cooking with Popular Herbs

HERB	APPETIZERS SALADS	BREADS/EGGS SAUCES/CHEESE	VEGETABLES PASTA	MEAT POULTRY	FISH SHELLFISH
BASIL	Green, Potato & Tomato Salads, Salad Dressings, Stewed Fruit	Breads, Fondue & Egg Dishes, Dips, Marinades, Sauces	Mushrooms, Tomatoes, Squash, Pasta, Bland Vegetables	Broiled, Roast Meat & Poultry Pies, Stews, Stuffing	Baked, Broiled & Poached Fish, Shellfish
BAY LEAF	Seafood Cocktail, Seafood Salad, Tomato Aspic, Stewed Fruit	Egg Dishes, Gravies, Marinades, Sauces	Dried Bean Dishes, Beets, Carrots, Onions, Potatoes, Rice, Squash	Corned Beef, Tongue Meat & Poultry Stews	Poached Fish, Shellfish, Fish Stews
CHIVES	Mixed Vegetable, Green, Potato & Tomato Salads, Salad Dressings	Egg & Cheese Dishes, Cream Cheese, Cottage Cheese, Gravies, Sauces	Hot Vegetables, Potatoes	Broiled Poultry, Poultry & Meat Pies, Stews, Casseroles	Baked Fish, Fish Casseroles, Fish Stews, Shellfish
DILL	Seafood Cocktail, Green, Potato & Tomato Salads, Salad Dressings	Breads, Egg & Cheese Dishes, Cream Cheese, Fish & Meat Sauces	Beans, Beets, Cabbage, Carrots, Cauliflower, Peas, Squash, Tomatoes	Beef, Veal Roasts, Lamb, Steaks, Chops, Stews, Roast & Creamed Poultry	Baked, Broiled, Poached & Stuffed Fish, Shellfish
GARLIC	All Salads, Salad Dressings	Fondue, Poultry Sauces, Fish & Meat Marinades	Beans, Eggplant, Potatoes, Rice, Tomatoes	Roast Meats, Meat & Poultry Pies, Hamburgers, Casseroles, Stews	Broiled Fish, Shellfish, Fish Stews, Casseroles
MARJORAM	Seafood Cocktail, Green, Poultry & Seafood Salads	Breads, Cheese Spreads, Egg & Cheese Dishes, Gravies, Sauces	Carrots, Eggplant, Peas, Onions, Potatoes, Dried Bean Dishes, Spinach	Roast Meats & Poultry, Meat & Poultry Pies, Stews & Casseroles	Baked, Broiled & Stuffed Fish, Shellfish
MUSTARD	Fresh Green Salads, Prepared Meat, Macaroni & Potato Salads, Salad Dressings	Biscuits, Egg & Cheese Dishes, Sauces	Baked Beans, Cabbage, Eggplant, Squash, Dried Beans, Mushrooms, Pasta	Chops, Steaks, Ham, Pork, Poultry, Cold Meats	Shellfish
OREGANO	Green, Poultry & Seafood Salads	Breads, Egg & Cheese Dishes, Meat, Poultry & Vegetable Sauces	Artichokes, Cabbage, Eggplant, Squash, Dried Beans, Mushrooms, Pasta	Broiled, Roast Meats, Meat & Poultry Pies, Stews, Casseroles	Baked, Broiled & Poached Fish, Shellfish
PARSLEY	Green, Potato, Seafood & Vegetable Salads	Biscuits, Breads, Egg & Cheese Dishes, Gravies, Sauces	Asparagus, Beets, Eggplant, Squash, Dried Beans, Mushrooms, Pasta	Meat Loaf, Meat & Poultry Pies, Stews & Casseroles, Stuffing	Fish Stews, Stuffed Fish
ROSEMARY	Fruit Cocktail, Fruit & Green Salads	Biscuits, Egg Dishes, Herb Butter, Cream Cheese, Marinades, Sauces	Beans, Broccoli, Peas, Cauliflower, Mushrooms, Baked Potatoes, Parsnips	Roast Meat, Poultry & Meat Pies, Stews & Casseroles, Stuffing	Stuffed Fish, Shellfish
SAGE		Breads, Fondue, Egg & Cheese Dishes, Spreads, Gravies, Sauces	Beans, Beets, Onions, Peas, Spinach, Squash, Tomatoes	Roast Meat, Poultry, Meat Loaf, Stews, Stuffing	Baked, Poached & Stuffed Fish
TARRAGON	Seafood Cocktail, Avocado Salads, Salad Dressings	Cheese Spreads, Marinades, Sauces, Egg Dishes	Asparagus, Beans, Beets, Carrots, Mushrooms, Peas, Squash, Spinach	Steaks, Poultry, Roast Meats, Casseroles & Stews	Baked, Broiled & Poached Fish, Shellfish
THYME	Seafood Cocktail, Green, Poultry, Seafood & Vegetable Salads	Biscuits, Breads, Egg & Cheese Dishes, Sauces, Spreads	Beets, Carrots, Mushrooms, Onions, Peas, Eggplant, Spinach, Potatoes	Roast Meat, Poultry & Meat Loaf, Meat & Poultry Pies, Stews & Casseroles	Baked, Broiled & Stuffed Fish, Shellfish, Fish Stews

General Recipe Index

This handy index lists every recipe by food category, major ingredient and/or cooking method, so you can easily locate recipes to suit your needs.

✓ Recipe includes Nutritional Analysis and Diabetic Exchanges

✓ Recipe includes Nutritional Analysis and Diabetic Exchanges

✓ Recipe includes Nutritional Analysis and Diabetic Exchanges

✓ Recipe includes Nutritional Analysis and Diabetic Exchanges

✓ Recipe includes Nutritional Analysis and Diabetic Exchanges

✓ *Recipe includes Nutritional Analysis and Diabetic Exchanges*

✓ Recipe includes Nutritional Analysis and Diabetic Exchanges

✓ Recipe includes Nutritional Analysis and Diabetic Exchanges

✓ Recipe includes Nutritional Analysis and Diabetic Exchanges

✓ Recipe includes Nutritional Analysis and Diabetic Exchanges

Alphabetical Recipe Index

This handy index lists every recipe in alphabetical order
so you can easily find your favorite recipes.

✓ Recipe includes Nutritional Analysis and Diabetic Exchanges

✓ Recipe includes Nutritional Analysis and Diabetic Exchanges

✓ Recipe includes Nutritional Analysis and Diabetic Exchanges

✓ *Recipe includes Nutritional Analysis and Diabetic Exchanges*